D1234782

The Improbable
First Century of
Cosmopolitan Magazine

JAMES LANDERS

The Improbable
First Century of
Cosmopolitan Magazine

University of Missouri Press
Columbia and London

Copyright © 2010 by
The Curators of the University of Missouri
University of Missouri Press, Columbia, Missouri 65201
Printed and bound in the United States of America
All rights reserved
5 4 3 2 1   14 13 12 11 10

Library of Congress Cataloging-in-Publication Data

Landers, James, 1947–
  The improbable first century of Cosmopolitan magazine / James Landers.
      p. cm.
  Includes bibliographical references and index.
  ISBN 978-0-8262-1906-0 (cloth : alk. paper)
  1. Cosmopolitan (New York, N.Y. : 1952) 2. Cosmopolitan. 3. American periodicals—History—
19th century. 4. American periodicals—History—20th century. I. Title.
  PN4900.C68L36 2010
  051—dc22
                              2010024173

♾™ This paper meets the requirements of the
American National Standard for Permanence of Paper
for Printed Library Materials, Z39.48, 1984.

Design and composition: Jennifer Cropp
Printing and binding: Thomson-Shore, Inc.
Typefaces: Minion and Bordeaux

Contents

Preface

By all rights, *Cosmopolitan* should not have survived its first hundred years.

Born in March 1886, it nearly died during summer 1888 when it suspended publishing for two months. A publisher of a religious magazine revived it, then sold it to a wealthy adventurer-entrepreneur from Colorado who saved it. It was dying again by summer 1905. William Randolph Hearst rescued it. Hearst Corporation executives were ready to kill it early in 1965, but they took a chance on an editor who promised a dramatic transformation. Helen Gurley Brown kept her promise.

Cosmopolitan survived because it transformed itself: from a family literary magazine to a general magazine filled with articles on national and international topics and fiction; then to a sensationalist magazine that emphasized exposé articles and political commentary from 1905 to 1912; then to a quality fiction magazine that published the most popular and highly paid authors, and enlivened their stories with fine illustrations from the most popular and highly paid artists of the 1920s; and, finally, to a magazine for younger women, either married or single, who liked its mix of articles on careers, celebrities, relationships, sex, and various topics the traditional women's periodicals had not presented in such a lively and occasionally risqué style.

From a floundering publication at its start to its centenary stature as the centerpiece of the Hearst publishing empire, *Cosmopolitan* was alternately mediocre, admirable and respectable, sensational, literary, mediocre again, and sensational again.

It might seem obvious that a magazine, or any business, must be dynamic to survive. Yet many dynamic magazines that competed with *Cosmopolitan* during its first hundred years failed—some because they changed editorial format too quickly and alienated loyal readers while not attracting new readers; some because they blended old and new formats, thereby losing a specific editorial identity and purpose; some because they chose a new format in a category already occupied by dominant magazines. Consider this list of magazines, each one a competitor of *Cosmopolitan* at different times during its first hundred years and each one a casualty of intense competition for readers and advertisers: *American, Century, Collier's, Liberty, Forum, Mademoiselle, McCall's, McClure's, Munsey's, Outlook, Scribner's.* Also consider these other famous failures, victims of economic or social trends: *Life, Look, Pictorial Review, Saturday Evening Post, Woman's Home Companion.* All tried to survive, but either their readers stopped reading them or—more often the case—advertisers stopped buying pages because other publications had better demographics (age, gender, income) or another choice was more economical and efficient.

The importance of advertising revenue to the survival of *Cosmopolitan,* or any magazine, cannot be overemphasized. Many of the magazines previously listed among the dead were quite popular with readers, but disappeared anyway. *Life* distributed five million copies a week until its demise, *Pictorial Review* distributed three million copies, and *Collier's* nearly as many. Advertising revenue has been a matter of life or death to most magazines since the 1890s.

Editorial dynamics enabled *Cosmopolitan* to publish, and eventually prosper, for more than a century. In an industry known for spectacular failures, for startups that disappeared quickly, and for legendary titles that suffered slow, sad deaths, *Cosmopolitan* demonstrated remarkable agility to find a niche in the magazine marketplace. Its readership demographics from the 1890s until the mid-1930s were exceptional, composed of affluent men and women who lived in classy city neighborhoods and upscale suburbs. *Cosmopolitan's* slide into mediocrity from the 1950s to the mid-1960s reflected its lackluster demographics. The revival of *Cosmopolitan* under the leadership of Helen Gurley Brown generated a unique demographic consisting mostly of twenty-something to thirty-something women who were employed and earning good money—exactly the readers that advertisers wished to reach.

Dynamic personalities determined the fate of *Cosmopolitan,* too: Paul Schlicht, its founder and a person whose ambition exceeded his ability; John Brisben Walker, an energetic and impulsive idealist whose restive mind fostered editorial excellence; William Randolph Hearst, an intelligent and irresponsible publisher whose editorial vendettas and crusades did damage and also brought reform; Ray Long, a brilliant and vain editor whose literary judgment attracted a million-plus faithful readers; Helen Gurley Brown, an ambitious and savvy achiever whose sense of what younger women wanted in a magazine proved incredibly perceptive.

Gurley Brown certainly became the most well-known *Cosmopolitan* editor. To many readers of the magazine, she was *Cosmopolitan.* Her monthly column near the front was a conversation with them about writers and photographers whose work appeared in that month's issue, about the celebrities she had seen or met recently, about her jetting off to Europe and Japan with husband, Da-

vid Brown, or traveling to Hollywood for a weekend of parties and movie pre-
mieres. Gurley Brown lived a glamorous life, and she shared her great luck with
millions of women who dreamed of such a life. Gurley Brown created an editorial format to appeal to women whose lives were similar to hers before she
had become fabulously successful—"girls" who fended for themselves, worked
dreary jobs, searched for the right man, and wanted to enjoy life while they
were young. A recent biography by Jennifer Scanlon, *Bad Girls Go Everywhere:
The Life of Helen Gurley Brown,* examines the editor's personal experiences
from childhood to late life, her various careers, her contributions to feminism,
and the reaction of feminists to her *Cosmopolitan* philosophy.

This book is a history of *Cosmopolitan* and the influence on it by several
individuals. The author makes no claims concerning *Cosmopolitan*'s specific
cultural or social impact during its first century. It would be impossible to determine anyway. *Cosmopolitan* existed from the Gilded Age to the 1980s within
a society that offered multiple sources of information to its readership. The
magazine's debut placed it among a media universe of books, magazines, and
newspapers. Then came the movies, then radio, then television. Readers of *Cosmopolitan* throughout this hundred-year span presumably obtained information from other media sources, and the influence of any single source cannot
be ascertained. What can be determined about *Cosmopolitan* from its creation to its centenary was its distinctiveness at certain specific intervals, which
brought it an eminence and a popularity that lasted from several years to several decades.

The magazine initially attracted a sizable readership late in the nineteenth
century because it was an affordable, quality general magazine that gave readers of a nascent middle-class society informative articles on serious topics and
fine fiction from the best authors of the era; meanwhile, the few other contemporary magazines of similar editorial excellence were expensive and written for a genteel readership. *Cosmopolitan* suddenly became a sensationalistic
muckraker early in the twentieth century whose dramatic articles documented
corrupt relationships between United States senators and powerful financiers,
industrialists, and owners of railroads, while another exposé series on hazardous and unhealthy conditions for child laborers pressured Congress to enact
reform legislation. The magazine subsequently achieved prominence as a fiction showcase displaying the work of notable short-story writers and novelists,
and ultimately attained iconic status during its ninth decade when its pages
carried brazen articles on topics not seen in other women's magazines.

These editorial transformations took *Cosmopolitan* to the top tier of magazines. Hundreds of thousands of people subscribed to it or bought it at newsstands from the 1890s to World War I. Millions of people were subscribers
or single-copy buyers from the 1920s through the 1940s. The mid-1960s saw

a resurgence, with circulation again surpassing a million copies and steadily increasing to three million copies by its centennial. Obviously, it had value to many people.

This book began as an idea for a biography of John Brisben Walker. His was such an interesting life and his personality so fascinating that he seemed the perfect subject. Walker had transformed a nondescript magazine into a popular, successful publication that presented articles on important topics of the 1890s: labor strife, the power of industrialist robber barons, reform of curriculums at colleges and universities, America's global role, and the possibility of war with European nations. Unfortunately, Walker left no paper trail that could be discovered despite inquiries to various local historical societies in California, Colorado, and New York.

When my plan to write a biography of Walker reached a dead end, a conversation with my wife led to this book. My interest in *Cosmopolitan* had originated while a middle-age graduate student at the University of Wisconsin in Madison. A research paper examining the editorial content of quality general magazines at the time of the Spanish-American War in 1898 introduced me to the amazing history of *Cosmopolitan*. It was regarded as one of the top magazines for its serious articles and superb fiction. As a man who had never read the modern-day *Cosmopolitan* and who had only heard about its obsession with sex, my reaction to learning about this other *Cosmopolitan* was pure astonishment. My conversation with Carrie persuaded me to tell the story of *Cosmopolitan*.

The decision to focus on the magazine's first hundred years was based on the conclusion that the editorial format developed by Gurley Brown during the mid-1960s had not changed since then. Although more explicit at the end of the first decade of the twenty-first century than at its centennial edition in March 1986, *Cosmopolitan* continued to follow the basic formula concocted fifty years previously.

This book required much research. Valuable assistance was provided by Michele Morgan, a professional researcher, whose conscientious effort and professionalism yielded numerous documents from the William Randolph Hearst Papers at University of California–Berkeley. Morgan enthusiastically reviewed many cartons filled with papers and identified the small percentage that were actually noteworthy. Linda Templer Alexander found pertinent court documents in Rochester, New York, and on her own initiative located newspaper articles from the 1880s regarding people involved with the creation of *Cosmopolitan* in that city. Marlene Bergren, a genealogist with Foothills Genealogical Society in Colorado, assisted with research on John Brisben Walker. Elizabeth Sadewhite, the local history librarian for Irvington, New York, verified basic information about the Cosmopolitan Building, added useful details about its present use, and found a wonderful photograph of the majestic edifice from the early 1900s.

Writing was the fun part, although organizing the vast amount of material—including hundreds of articles, columns, and stories photocopied after examination of approximately 1,040 issues of *Cosmopolitan* from March 1886 to March 1986—required many, many hours. An entire downstairs closet at home was emptied to store crates of research material of all sorts.

My wife, Carrie, spent dozens of hours reading the manuscript. She found grammatical errors, typos, awkwardly written sentences, misplaced paragraphs, and all the things a good editor finds.

Whoever reads this book will do so at a time when print media are endangered by economic, social, and technological factors. The Web has diverted ad revenue and the public's attention from books, magazines, and newspapers. Some younger adults still devote time to reading words and viewing images on the printed page, but many receive most of their information and an ever-increasing amount of entertainment from handheld digital devices.

Magazines won't disappear. Some will survive in print and on the Web, but most survivors will be electronic publications only—no expenses for paper, ink, postage, but with the capability to archive material electronically and make it easily accessible to almost everyone.

Magazines were important. One pleasurable memory of my twentieth-century childhood was stopping at the mailbox on the way home from school, taking a copy of *Time* or *Life* or *Saturday Evening Post* or *Popular Science* into the house and flipping through the pages, seeing a picture and looking at it, turning to the cover story and reading some of it, then skimming pages until the end. The magazine would be there on the coffee table or somewhere in the house, waiting to be picked up and looked at later, and would be there until the next copy arrived in the mail. Magazines helped me learn about the world beyond my small-town home.

The Improbable
First Century of
Cosmopolitan Magazine

1

Creation

May 1888, Rochester, New York

At noon on a Tuesday late in the month, twenty-eight men met for a hastily scheduled conference at the downtown Powers Hotel. They sat at tables in an ornate reception room adorned with candlesticks and chandeliers for festive occasions, but these local businessmen had convened to learn the extent of their financial loss from the sudden bankruptcy of Schlicht & Field Company. A manufacturer and international distributor of office equipment based in Rochester, Schlicht & Field somehow owed banks and creditors $301,400 it could not pay.[1]

Reaction among the businessmen to details about the reasons for the bankruptcy varied from astonishment to anxiety to outrage. Many men in the room owned stock in Schlicht & Field, their certificates now worthless—and because the men had pledged their company stock as surety for tens of thousands of dollars in bank loans they were liable personally for much of the debt. Several men at the meeting held promissory notes from the company, their value now zero. Some creditors attended, too, their bills for services and supplies now worth pennies on the dollar. Seven bankers also were in the room, their role to tally company assets consisting of warehouse inventory and ownership of numerous patents for various desk drawer and desktop devices essential to filing and recordkeeping for nineteenth-century businesses. Everyone knew the assets would not cover much of the debt.[2]

How had this happened? The only man with an answer was absent. Paul Schlicht, at age twenty-nine the president of the company, had refused to attend. His absence dismayed some at the conference; they "thought it strange," while others there might "draw their own inferences" why Schlicht had stayed away, according to a newspaper article published the same day. So, instead of an explanation from Schlicht, whose deception and mismanagement had bankrupted the company, a bookkeeper from the nearby corporate office told stockholders, creditors, and bankers what had happened. His blunt explanation was that a subsidiary venture of Schlicht & Field—a monthly magazine, *The Cosmopolitan*—had bled the company dry. "The magazine had been a failure," the newspaper reported. "It had lost $130,000."

Not only had the magazine failed, taking with it the direct expenditure of a sizable sum, but Schlicht had given away thousands of items from the company's inventory to induce people to subscribe. Then he had stopped paying providers of services and supplies to Schlicht & Field because *Cosmopolitan* needed the money to survive. However, the most stunning revelation at the May conference was that Schlicht & Field had not owned *Cosmopolitan* for months. A secret transaction by Schlicht in late January had transferred ownership of the magazine—without any payment to the Rochester company—to a new publisher located in Manhattan, and Schlicht had become one of the partners.

Since the debut of *Cosmopolitan* two years earlier as a literary magazine for the family, Schlicht & Field had supported its creation and publication of twenty-five issues. The disastrous venture began with $95,000 borrowed from banks. Stockholders authorized the bank loans for the magazine upon review of a plan submitted by Schlicht, who anointed himself publisher. According to the plan presented to stockholders, revenue from subscribers and advertisers eventually would enable *Cosmopolitan* to operate independently. The banks accepted surety notes signed by stockholders, the majority of them proprietors of Rochester businesses.[3]

All of them soon would learn that magazine publishing was more unpredictable than selling office supplies. Schlicht encountered the harsh reality of the intensely competitive magazine marketplace of the Gilded Age. *Cosmopolitan's* startup proved costlier than predicted. Door-to-door canvassing for potential subscribers in cities from New England through the Midwest was expensive to organize and coordinate, fees to illustrators and writers exceeded budget, and occasional color for frontispieces inflated the original printing estimate. Despite a substantial amount of capital for its creation, *Cosmopolitan* required more money just months after its appearance. Schlicht persuaded several company stockholders to provide an additional sum in return for promissory notes. This supplemental investment of $67,000 did not last long either.[4]

Schlicht & Field was in a bind. Revenue derived from its core business of manufacturing and selling clipboards, desk-drawer organizers, desktop file boxes, file dividers, file holders, paper hole-punchers, and typewriters to office customers across the nation simultaneously financed the company's operations and the magazine's persistent deficit. Bills for services and supplies went unpaid.[5]

The first indication to stockholders of a crisis surfaced near the end of 1887. Schlicht asked them for another $50,000 to help *Cosmopolitan*. He assured them the magazine was popular, and that subscriptions and advertisements were increasing each month. Schlicht told stockholders that *Cosmopolitan* distributed 35,000 copies to subscribers and vendors, compared with an initial distribution of 20,000 copies. Stockholders at the bankruptcy conference in May remembered Schlicht then telling them "all that was needed was a little time and money." They agreed to sign another batch of surety notes to secure the additional money from banks.[6]

Why these presumably sensible Rochester businessmen, including Edward Bausch and Carl Lomb of Bausch and Lomb Optical Company, continued to underwrite *Cosmopolitan* cannot be determined from the historical record. Perhaps it was Schlicht's persuasive personality, or perhaps it was the unique status conferred by association with a new national magazine, one known for its quality fiction, poetry, and illustrations. Or maybe it was the prospect of a lucrative return on their investment.

Cosmopolitan survived on cash siphoned from Schlicht & Field for two more months. Schlicht then enticed several investors in New York City, including Ulysses S. Grant Jr., the late president's son, to assume responsibility for the magazine's finances from that point onward, leaving Schlicht & Field responsible for prior debts. Some confusion ensued at the bankruptcy conference in May concerning ownership of *Cosmopolitan* because stockholders were unaware of the ownership transfer and could not understand how Schlicht arranged it. Incorporation documents for the new ownership entity filed January 1888 in Albany did not list any prior connection to the Rochester company.[7]

Although the January transaction had relieved further financial burden on Schlicht & Field, it was too late. The company remained responsible for payments to a printer, paper producer, and ink supplier for *Cosmopolitan*'s final issue under its ownership prior to the secret transfer by Schlicht. Also, the lengthy subsidy for *Cosmopolitan* caused Schlicht & Field to default on its own bank loans and promissory notes. "The magazine was losing money faster than it could possibly be made by the business," participants heard at the bankruptcy conference. "The entire business had been managed with the most reckless extravagance."[8]

One extravagant item revealed to stockholders, bankers, and creditors at the conference demonstrated questionable judgment by Schlicht about expenses necessary for *Cosmopolitan,* despite its dire situation. "Considerable amusement was caused by the statement of one of the creditors that over $1,000 was spent in the way of flowers and presents on Sarah Bernhard[t] with the hope of getting her to write an article for the magazine," the newspaper reported.[9]

Miss Bernhardt, a famous stage actress whose name the newspaper misspelled, never wrote for *Cosmopolitan* while Schlicht was publisher. Her byline ultimately appeared in the March 1896 issue, at which time *Cosmopolitan* was among the best and most popular magazines in the nation.

Magazine "Mania"

The appearance of *Cosmopolitan,* its creation by a person without any publishing experience, and its financing by businessmen unfamiliar with magazines exemplified the "mania" described by historian Frank Luther Mott in the third volume of his five-volume classic, *A History of American Magazines.* Mott documented the appearance of several hundred new monthly magazines during the first half of the 1880s. One hundred and fifty titles appeared during 1886, the year *Cosmopolitan* rolled off the presses. This surge preceded the Magazine Revolution of the mid-1890s, a period when circulation (total subscriptions and vendor sales) of top-tier monthly magazines tripled, quadrupled, or grew by multiples of ten and twelve for a fortunate few, attaining popularity and prosperity inconceivable to publishers a decade earlier.[10]

The final twenty years of the nineteenth century were media heaven for many new national magazines. No other national media diverted public attention or advertiser dollars from magazines. Movies had yet to become popular, and radio as a commercial enterprise and provider of free entertainment was years away. A veritable explosion in magazine popularity occurred because a dynamic American economy propelled dramatic cultural and social changes. People who wanted, and could afford, entertainment and information other than from newspapers bought monthly magazines, which differed considerably from newspapers in terms of quality and variety.

Factors fueling new magazines included higher literacy rates, a nascent middle class, migration of millions of people to cities from rural areas, development of national brand-name products, cheap postage, rapid distribution by railroads, and better printing technology. The resultant synergy produced affordable quality publications at one end of the spectrum and cheap trashy publications at the other end. *Cosmopolitan* was an affordable quality magazine.

An obvious prerequisite for the magazine market was a literate populace. By the 1880s, the United States had a self-reported literacy rate of 90 percent, which placed it among the top three in the world, the others being Scotland and Sweden. American public schools were not responsible for achieving this high literacy rate. Twelve states of the nation's thirty-eight states had enacted compulsory education legislation prior to the 1880s and eight more mandated it during the decade. Mandatory classroom time ranged from a mere dozen weeks to six school years. Newspapers get much credit for contributing to national literacy because almost every community in the nation had a weekly or a daily, and reading was a spectator sport of sorts for a citizenry amused by and fascinated with politics.

During the mid-1880s, enrollment in public schools nationwide was an average 63 percent of school-age residents, or five of every eight eligible people (the mandatory maximum age for compulsory education varied from sixteen to twenty-one). Actual classroom attendance on a regular basis was 38 percent, or three of every eight school-age residents. Enrollment and attendance were highest in California, Connecticut, Delaware, Illinois, Indiana, Massachusetts, Michigan, New Hampshire, New York, Ohio, and Rhode Island; lowest enrollment and attendance were in Alabama, Georgia, Louisiana, Mississippi, and the Carolinas. These education patterns explained the concentration of magazine circulations in northeastern states and the Midwest until the 1920s.

The percentage of school-age residents who completed their education was quite low. On average, only one of every twenty-two students, or slightly more than 4 percent, received a high school diploma during the 1880s. Still, however brief their time in the classroom, millions of Americans learned basic reading and writing skills. Their teachers introduced them to the concept of literature—prose and poetry that expressed timeless ideals and ideas. Reading also increased awareness. Scholars of literacy have determined that "knowledge about faraway events and ideas was introduced through newspapers and magazines."[11]

Literacy alone did not expand readership for monthly magazines of the era. A person's income mattered. The growth of magazines published in the United States near the end of the nineteenth century correlated with the rise in the number of Americans who ascended to the middle class, a category defined by income and social standards. Most of the nouveau middle class lacked familiarity with forms of behavior, etiquette, fashion, and moral values deemed proper by arbiters of polite society. Magazines served to introduce middle-class men and women to these customs.[12]

The middle class emerged as an economic force during the Gilded Age, often defined as an era from the late 1870s to early 1890s. Industrial enterprises—factories, foundries, manufacturers, railroads—hired thousands upon thousands of administrators, engineers, managers, and supervisors. These men coordinated systems of delivery or production, devised mechanical improvements, kept the books, monitored inventory, and ruled the workplace. Their weekly on-the-job time was fifty-eight hours, similar to the men whose physical labor accomplished the tasks, but the men in the white-collar shirts had special status and took home bigger paychecks. Nicer furniture, prettier dinnerware, classier home décor, and other visible improvements were evidence of social status. Middle-class families enthusiastically imitated upper-class households by hiring maids and cooks, buying fine furniture, and wearing fashionable clothes.[13]

Aspirations for self-improvement accompanied materialistic acquisitions. Men and women joined Chautauqua forums in hundreds of communities that met weekly to discuss lessons on literature, science, religion, and the power of the human mind. Magazines purposely catered to this self-improvement impulse with quality fiction and informative articles about architecture, biology, chemistry, Christianity and evolution, geography, medical research, and world cultures.[14]

Industrialization had made class distinction a fixture of the American work-place. The term *blue collar* had originated to describe laborers in factories and foundries who customarily wore denim shirts at work; the designation *white collar* applied to managers, supervisors, bookkeepers, draftsmen, and others who wore a shirt with a detachable, washable white cloth on a cardboard strip. A white-collar job meant entry to the middle class. Industrial workplaces em-ployed 190,000 white-collar workers when the Gilded Age ended compared with 80,000 when it began.[15]

Beyond the gates of industrial America, a legion of proprietors of cartage companies, insurance agencies, and retail stores earned a middle-class income, as did many contractors, grocers, and wholesalers. Their presence strength-ened democracy. Community involvement and political awareness among this "multitude of little proprietorships continued to be socially important," an economist remarked. The number of owner-operator businesses grew 90 percent to a total of 780,000 during the Gilded Age and the number of accoun-tants, architects, engineers, and lawyers doubled to 89,000. Owner-operators, professionals, and industrial middle-class occupations constituted 5 percent of the nation's workforce in 1890.[16]

A typical middle-class household income was $1,400 to $2,200 a year during the late 1800s, equal to weekly pay of $27 to $42. Practically all middle-class households could afford monthly magazines, which generally cost $2.50 to $4 a year, and within a few years the Magazine Revolution era would reduce yearly subscription prices by half for many publications. (For comparison, the $2.50 subscription would be the equivalent of $62.50 in 2010 dollars, while the $4 subscription would be $92.)

Magazines were a luxury item for working-class households, however. Un-skilled laborers earned weekly pay of $8 to $9.50 and skilled laborers made $13 to $18 weekly. Because most working-class families spent their income on food and rent, with some money to spare for an occasional visit to an amusement park or music hall or corner tavern, the purchase of a magazine was expensive. Research by the Massachusetts Bureau of Labor Statistics determined that a typical working-class family allocated twelve cents a week for reading mate-rial; thus, a worker might pull two pennies from a pocket for a newspaper, but would hesitate to subscribe to a magazine priced at more than a day's wage or available from a vendor for twenty-five cents.[17]

Middle-class families ate better, dressed better, and lived in better apart-ments or houses than their working-class counterparts, yet they also had mon-ey for discretionary purchases, quite possibly a magazine subscription. Unlike newspapers, which middle-class adults regarded as a necessity for information about community events and political topics, most monthly magazines available prior to the Magazine Revolution entertained and edified readers rather than informed them about contemporary events.

Despite its affluence, the nouveau middle class was budget conscious. It preferred newer monthly magazines priced at $2.50 a year over older titles such as *Atlantic Monthly* and *Harper's* at $4 a year. An annual subscription to *Cosmopolitan* cost $2.50 initially. Schlicht, despite his extravagant style, chose to promote *Cosmopolitan* to the middle class rather than compete against literary magazines favored by affluent Americans.[18]

Magazines could reach the middle class more efficiently during the 1880s because industrialization and ancillary economic development had spurred the growth of cities. This clustering of the population reduced delivery time from printer to subscriber, simplified the effort to sell subscriptions door-to-door, and provided access to networks of vendors with newsstands and shelf-space in bookstores. Magazine readership was concentrated in older cities of the East, newer cities of the Midwest, and a patchwork of cities along the rail lines to the West Coast through the first decade of the twentieth century.

Throughout the Gilded Age and into the early 1900s, American cities spread outward from a core to encompass dozens of square miles and transform formerly rural towns into suburban communities. The number of cities with more than 100,000 residents increased from 14 to 49 and the number with 10,000 to 100,000 residents rose from 211 to 547. The first national census of the twentieth century reported that 46 percent of Americans resided in urban areas.[19]

An urban economy offered a year-round income to those whose services were essential, including craftsmen, contractors, and owner-operators of businesses necessary to city life. Evolution of commerce altered consumer behavior. City dwellers shopped in a department store, not a corner retail emporium. They purchased clothes, shoes, dishes, household wares, stoves, and ice boxes manufactured by national corporations. At the grocer, they bought food processed and packed in boxes, cans, and jars by national producers, rather than bulk food items sold in barrels, crates, and sacks. Merchandise available for consumers displayed an imprint or label identifying its maker, a brand name. New brand names competed for the attention of consumers at an accelerated pace during the nineteenth century's final decades. The array of new items generated by national enterprises was evidence that mass production of consumer goods was changing the American marketplace.[20]

Magazines played a useful role establishing brand-name identity among consumers. Advertisements placed by national manufacturers and producers filled dozens of pages in popular magazines every month. Among the ads were Baker's Breakfast Cocoa, Colgate Dental Powder, Eastman Kodak cameras, Elgin National Watch Company, Gold Dust Washing Powder, Gold Medal

Flour, H. J. Heinz Company (horseradish, pickles, ketchup), Lord and Taylor, Monarch Bicycles, Pillsbury Flour, Pond's Extract (healing cream), Procter and Gamble (Ivory soap), Quaker Oats, Remington typewriters, Richman Brothers (clothes), Singer Sewing Machines, Wabash Line (passenger trains), and Yale Locks.[21]

Advertisers recognized the efficiency that magazines offered, circulating to consumers everywhere. A scholar documented "the increase in manufacturers' national advertising of branded products, especially in magazines" beginning late in the nineteenth century, and its acceleration early in the twentieth century. Advertisements for national brands touted their advantages over local products. The sales pitch, which varied according to merchandise, promoted either durability, fashion, quality assurance, reliability, or sanitary packaging and processing. Advertisements implied that local goods lacked such standards.[22]

Advertisers believed that married women were primary consumers. Because a majority of them stopped working outside the home upon becoming mothers, women were perceived as household managers who shopped for the entire family—food, clothing, soap, dishware, sundry items.

Advertising revenue spawned a new business model for magazines. The old model applied to pricey literary magazines established long before the Gilded Age; these periodicals for the upper class relied on subscription revenue. Their $4 annual subscriptions covered fees to writers and illustrators, mailing, printing, and staff salaries. The few pages of advertisements segregated to the back sections of quality literary magazines, consisting mostly of quarter- and half-page ads by book publishers and piano manufacturers and high-end apparel makers, raised profits somewhat for the literary magazines. Image mattered, however. Publishers and editors of pricey literary magazines disdained overt commercialism. Newer, affordable monthly magazines founded during the mania era depended on advertising revenue. A $2.50 annual subscription did not cover all expenses, much less allow a profit. Publishers of affordable magazines actively solicited advertisers.

Within several years, an unprecedented amount of advertising revenue permitted some popular monthly magazines to reduce annual subscription prices to $1. At that price, magazines became even more affordable and attracted hordes of new subscribers, which then boosted advertising rates formulated on total readership. A larger circulation among middle-class households also lured other national brands to place advertisements. The 1890s marked an economic turning point when most magazines received at least half their revenue from advertisements. Forever after, magazine publishers were addicted to ads.[23]

A combination of advertising pages plus sixty-four to ninety-six pages of essays, fiction, poetry, and reviews added weight to popular magazines. Weight determined the cost of mailing a magazine to a subscriber, which rarely was a concern to publishers prior to the 1880s. The majority of literary magazines weighed a pound or less per copy; at three cents per pound for postage delivery anywhere in the nation, the annual mailing expense for a copy of a monthly magazine usually was under forty cents, which a $4 yearly subscription amply covered.

Fortunately for publishers, Congress played benefactor to publishers of newspapers and magazines. For political and social reasons, including a genuine belief among lawmakers that inexpensive newspapers and magazines benefited citizens and democracy, Congress passed legislation in 1879 to establish four classes of mail, each with a specific postage rate. Intense lobbying by publishers of newspapers and magazines rewarded those publications with second-class postage at two cents per pound. A 160-page magazine printed on paper typical for periodicals of the era weighed one pound. Postage was a bargain.

Then it got better. Congress, again responding to lobbying by publishers while proclaiming its belief in a public benefit, lowered second-class postage to a penny per pound in 1885. Magazines fat on advertisements and thin on fiction or nonfiction editorial material rode the rails across the country at minimal cost. Congressional largesse passed along the real expense of delivery to all Americans, magazine readers and nonreaders alike. Years later, a special government commission computed the actual expense of handling and delivering second-class mail at nearly six cents a pound—a nickel more than publishers paid a postmaster. Much of the cost to the U.S. Post Office was directly linked to distance because a magazine copy traveled an average 1,049 miles for delivery to a subscriber.

Whether the public benefit outweighed private gain was debatable. A publisher of a 160-page magazine consisting, for example, of 120 pages of ads could thank taxpayers for a gift of approximately $500 for each 10,000 copies mailed every month. Cheap postage encouraged profit-seekers to publish magazines. The volume of new titles overwhelmed the postal system. Congress grudgingly reformed postal rates in 1917 to somewhat lessen the subsidy. At that time, the federal government sensibly set a dual-rate structure calculated on the proportional weight of pages for advertisements and pages for editorial material; afterward, using distance as a rate variable, advertising pages paid two to six times the postal rate set for editorial pages.[24]

Cheap postage coupled with rapid distribution by railroads also worked to the advantage of magazines. A nationwide network of railroads connecting all major cities and most larger towns virtually guaranteed timely delivery. Publishers scheduled monthly promotional blurbs in local newspapers and colorful posters pasted on outdoor walls near vendors to coincide with magazine delivery the last week of each month. Promotion by ads and posters was crucial whenever a magazine ran an excerpt from a forthcoming novel or rushed into print a story serendipitously purchased from an unknown author who just recently had become a hot commodity.[25]

The final factor fueling magazine growth late in the nineteenth century was remarkable progress in printing technology. Mechanical and technical developments made possible high-speed printing on quality paper with superb clarity of black-and-white photographs and color illustrations. Magazines had a better feel, better look, and better value.

Hoe and Company manufactured a rotary press during the mid-1880s that printed about 95,000 pages an hour. Press setup and actual press run of the $80,000 machine took about twenty hours for twenty thousand copies of an eighty-page magazine, comparable to *Cosmopolitan* at its start. The monstrous press printed, cut, folded, and sorted eight-page leafs of paper fed from a 750-pound roll. Pages wet with ink were let to dry for up to four hours, then collated with other eight-page leafs, and hauled by cart to a workstation for stapling.[26]

An expensive rotary press was not a worthwhile investment for most magazine publishers, considering that an entire press run could be accomplished in a day or two or at most a week. Instead, a publisher contracted with a local commercial printer for typesetting, preparation of printing plates, and a press run. In cities host to numerous publishers, a local firm with Hoe presses often had contracts to print several titles every month.

At some point a magazine publisher with an extremely popular single title or a sizable aggregate circulation for two or more titles might purchase a printing press to reduce cost and to control the production schedule. Owning one also meant hiring trained pressmen and a maintenance crew, because the Hoe rotary press was a mechanical nightmare; a press unit consisted of fifteen thousand movable parts.[27]

Not every magazine publisher cared about quality, either editorial or print. Publishers who cared about print quality spent extra money for superior paper. The reason most magazines looked better than newspapers was coated paper, which had a glossy tone. Newspapers were printed on paper made from wood pulp, called newsprint. Basic pulp paper was porous, and ink seeped through, creating a splotchy finish, which blurred illustrations and text. This was acceptable to a newspaper buyer whose copy cost two or three cents. It was not acceptable for a magazine copy priced at twenty to thirty-five cents. Coated paper was clean compared to gritty newsprint. The coating process brushed fine clay powder onto pulp paper treated with a thin layer of adhesive. The result was paper that sealed ink to its surface rather than absorbing it like a sponge. Ink applied to coated paper needed to dry prior to collation so it would not smear, but patience paid off because the clarity of illustrations, photographs, and text was superb. Paper mills sold coated paper for $87 per ton on average during the Gilded Age compared to $38 per ton for basic pulp.

Newer magazines enthusiastically displayed photographs from the 1890s onward, upon perfection of the halftone process. Photographs were modern, realistic, and inexpensive to reproduce. Older magazines, their editors and publishers self-appointed guardians of genteel culture, stayed with woodcut illustrations for aesthetic reasons, preferring art to realism. Readers liked photographs, however, and competition for subscribers eventually compelled all editors and publishers to accompany text with black-and-white photographs. At one-tenth the cost of preparing woodcuts for publication, photographs appealed to publishers of newer magazines who were less fussy about artistic concerns. (Color photography came along by the 1920s.)

Photographers had taken pictures of people and places since the 1840s, but no inexpensive and reliable method existed to reproduce photographic images in magazines or newspapers for thirty years. To reproduce a photographic image in print, artists for newspapers and magazines engraved the image on a wooden block or etched it on a copper plate. The next step created relief lines by treatment with acid. The printed image was a line drawing. Experimentation by Frederic Ives during the 1870s culminated in a technological breakthrough necessary to publish photographs. Ives, a youthful lab technician at Cornell University, devised a cross-line screen through which a photo of a photographic negative was taken. The horizontal and vertical lines of the screen separated an image into dots, varying in tone from black to gray to white. This halftone process finally enabled publications to print photographs. A halftone published in a magazine was much sharper than one in a newspaper, its clarity attributable to coated paper.[28]

Although color photographs could not be published until color film was invented, magazines could print color illustrations of paintings and portraits from woodcut engravings. The process was complex and expensive. A quality reproduction required four separate woodcut engravings, one for each color of ink: black, cyan, magenta, yellow. The clarity of the illustration depended on absolutely perfect registration, or positioning, for application of each color. Because of expense, color illustration usually was restricted to the frontispiece only. Competition among magazines to attract readers sometimes would compel publishers to add color illustrations to other pages.

Gilded Age media entrepreneurs benefited from important economic, social, and technological developments. A monthly magazine promised potential personal, professional, and financial rewards. Paul Schlicht seized the opportunity.

Creating *Cosmopolitan*

Cosmopolitan made an inauspicious debut in March 1886. Its premiere issue arrived late to subscribers and vendors. A note from the publisher on the inside front cover of the April issue offered no apology or explanation: "While we had great hopes that our patrons would find that the unavoidable delay in the first issue of The Cosmopolitan had redounded to their interests, we were quite unprepared for the words of generous praise that they have showered upon it."[29]

The publisher's note written by Paul Schlicht displayed his predilection for accentuating the positive. Born in Canada in June 1859 and a resident of Rochester since 1875, Schlicht had advanced from clerk-bookkeeper for an insurance company at age sixteen to junior partner at age twenty-three for a small manufacturer of office supplies, then to chief executive at age twenty-six for the manufacturer and international distributor of office equipment. Schlicht & Field was a corporate entity financed by several Rochester businessmen who each had bought a hundred or more shares of stock at $100 apiece in 1885. The company operated a central office in Rochester and branch offices in New York City, Chicago, Toronto, and Germany; it employed a hundred sales representatives and clerks.[30]

Schlicht also was an inventor. He held patents on devices useful for business paperwork, including a drawer-file holder, file organizer, and desktop file index. He was fluent and literate in French and German, the latter language probably learned from his father, a naturalized American citizen. Schlicht enjoyed fiction and poetry from both nations, an interest that would result in his translations of literature for *Cosmopolitan*.[31]

Evidently an industrious and intelligent man, Schlicht started *Cosmopolitan* within weeks of beginning his leadership of Schlicht & Field. From a modern perspective it might seem unusual that an executive for an office equipment manufacturer and distributor would want to publish a magazine, but the media environment during the late nineteenth century closely resembled the dot-com frenzy of the World Wide Web during the early twenty-first century. Separated by a dozen decades, magazine publishers of the Gilded Age and online entrepreneurs of the millennium shared a belief in the potential of new media. Some were rational and practical people, others dreamers, and some were simply schemers. Most from each media generation would fail miserably. A select few would succeed fabulously.

Schlicht observed a vast universe of magazines at the midpoint of the Gilded Age, stratified by category: commercial (business), family, fashion, financial, fraternal, household, literary, matrimonial, religious, trade, women's. A category mattered because the annual publication directories consulted by advertising agencies and manufacturer representatives for placement of advertisements allowed a magazine publisher to choose only one designation. Accordingly, Schlicht might describe *Cosmopolitan* as a "family literary" magazine to potential readers, but *N. W. Ayer and Son's Annual* would list it either as family or literary, not both. Three categories—literary, women's, fashion—were the most popular among the general public, and each category had its top-tier magazines. The directory listed *Cosmopolitan* in the literary category, where it would remain for several decades.[32]

Media historians, however, have rightly separated some literary magazines to a category not seen in *N. W. Ayer and Son's Annual* or other directories of the day—general interest. This retroactive classification was necessary because the original literary category was too inclusive and too dependent on a publisher's self-designation. These historians examined many literary magazines to ascertain preponderant editorial content and apparent editorial intent; on that basis, a magazine retained its original classification or was reclassified. Literary magazines that allocated decidedly more space to nonfiction articles and essays on contemporary topics than to fiction, poetry, and reviews were considered general interest.

Many magazines drifted into the general category over time, particularly from the late 1880s into the early 1900s, because dramatic domestic and international occurrences warranted immediate attention, thereby reducing pages normally given to fiction, poetry, and reviews.

The residual literary category encompassed magazines that published popular literature for ordinary people and magazines that provided cerebral literature for genteel readers. Other than fiction, poetry, and reviews, many literary magazines also offered a small selection of nonfiction articles, biographies of notable historical persons, and essays on contemporary subjects.[33]

Historians have identified the era's top tier of literary magazines as *Atlantic Monthly, Century,* and *Harper's New Monthly Magazine.* Editors of these magazines took seriously their role as guardians of culture, an arrogance that doomed their publications. These demonstrably intelligent men "resisted the popularization of editorial content, and in so doing, they removed themselves ever further from the mainstream of American life," a historian declared. Editors and publishers of newer magazines catered to the middle class.[34]

Widely regarded as best in the literary category, *Atlantic Monthly* was an elitist magazine whose editors would allow only prose and poetry they personally judged superior to grace its pages. Book reviews and commentary on contemporary authors filled the back pages of every issue. *Atlantic Monthly* editors commissioned essays from intellectuals, scholars, and statesmen concerning American, British, and continental European life and literature. The magazine was an adjunct of Houghton Mifflin, a book publisher, and would run the occasional excerpt from a forthcoming novel to be released by its corporate parent. Priced at $4 a year or thirty-five cents a copy at a vendor, *Atlantic Monthly* distributed 13,000 copies monthly thirty years after its founding in 1857 in Boston.[35]

Century, created in 1881 as successor to *Scribner's Monthly,* and *Harper's,* founded in 1850, cost the same as *Atlantic Monthly,* but both magazines offered lively, quality fiction and book reviews, mixed with essays about germane political and social topics. This less stuffy format rewarded them with larger circulations. With offices in New York City, both magazines solicited the work of esteemed authors and poets, although *Harper's* preferred British names to American and editors would find any excuse to allocate space for another essay on Milton, Shakespeare, or Thackeray. *Harper's*, a subsidiary of Harper and Brothers book publishers, had attained 170,000 circulation by the mid-1880s and stayed there for years.

Circulations for *Century* and *Harper's* were exceptionally large for pricey magazines. Each had experienced a recent surge in readership responding to publication of biographies about Civil War commanders and political leaders that marked the twentieth anniversary of the war's end. Richard Watson Gilder, the editor of *Century* from its start and into the twentieth century, opened its pages to American authors of merit and promise. *Century* peaked at 220,000 copies to subscribers and vendors in 1887; it would attempt belatedly and unsuccessfully to compete against newer magazines during the 1890s by bolstering its nonfiction component, which placed it in the general magazine category later. Gilder disdained photographs, insisting that *Century* retain its numerous superb woodcut illustrations for their artistic merit.[36]

General magazines emphasized articles and essays, although all contained literary material, too. The oldest general magazine was *North American Review,* issued from Boston in 1815; it had a monthly circulation of 17,000 copies by the mid-1880s. Much more popular and much less reputable was *Frank Leslie's Popular Monthly,* since 1876 a magazine prone to focus on stage actors and actresses, celebrities, illustrations of scantily clad women posed on pedestals against a pseudo-classical backdrop, and infrequent serious articles; a circulation of 105,000 copies resulted, at an annual price of $2.50 or twenty-five cents a copy at a vendor. *Forum,* a noteworthy magazine that emerged in March 1886, the same month as *Cosmopolitan,* devoted its pages to serious presentations of political and social topics; it attracted two thousand subscribers initially and would rise to 30,000 subscriptions ten years later.[37]

Women's magazines featured fiction and poetry deemed suitable for ladies, but the preponderance of material pertained to family and household topics. The astounding success of *Ladies' Home Journal* from its inception in December 1883 to early 1886 probably dissuaded Schlicht from entering a new magazine in the women's category. Cyrus Curtis, publisher, and Louisa Knapp Curtis, his wife and editor, built *Ladies' Home Journal* from a monthly supplement for a larger weekly publication to an independent magazine. In only twenty-eight months, the Curtis partnership escalated readership from 25,000 subscribers and vendor copies to 270,000 total circulation, the largest in the nation. Although designated a magazine, *Ladies' Home Journal* was printed on newsprint, not coated paper, for several years and cost fifty cents for a yearly subscription, a dime at vendors.[38]

Fashion publications provided abundant descriptions and illustrations of apparel and guides to sewing patterns. Butterick Company, one of the nation's leading pattern makers, published 165,000 copies monthly of *Delineator* to augment its pattern sales. Gilded Age fashion magazines were not known for thoughtful articles or essays, nor were they stylistic trendsetters until Condé Nast transformed *Vogue* during the 1910s.[39]

An option available to Schlicht was to publish a mail-order journal, the dominant magazine category of the era. Publishers by the hundreds eagerly took advantage of the penny-per-pound postage rate to distribute magazines priced at fifty cents a year that were mere catalogs laden with advertisements accompanied by puffery. Articles extolled the virtues of the products being advertised or simply reprinted text from promotional brochures issued by manufacturers. Readers would submit orders for products sold cash-on-delivery. Publishers added to their subscription revenue by selling lists of their subscribers to other mail-order publications for two cents per hundred names. Mail-order journals flourished until reform of postal rates in 1917.[40]

Schlicht aspired to bring inspirational and moral literature to readers. He decided to focus his new magazine on a niche within the literary category, a family publication. "It will contain articles by competent American and foreign writers that will interest every member of the family," he announced. "There will be a department devoted exclusively to the interests of the household, and also one devoted to the entertainment of the younger members of the family." The editorial format consisted of how-to columns on household chores, stories for children, mainstream fiction and poetry, and nonfiction articles. Whether the magazine's title was chosen after selecting a category or vice versa cannot be ascertained, but *Cosmopolitan* was an appropriate choice for a literary periodical.[41]

The decision to create a family literary magazine could have been affected by location. Rochester, in western New York, was not a literary center like Boston, New York City, and Philadelphia. Neither was Rochester an important economic, political, or social center, which was a handicap for a general magazine. A women's magazine might have been feasible, but that category already was dominated by familiar titles.

It required a few months to prepare to publish *Cosmopolitan*. Schlicht hired an editor, who began soliciting manuscripts from authors and poets, illustrators, and writers. Schlicht also hired department managers. A circulation manager dispatched subscription canvassers to peddle the magazine door-to-door in hundreds of communities from the New England region through the Midwest. An advertising manager contacted ad agencies with national clients and businesses with national products or services. Later, a production manager would supervise preparation for printing the magazine.

Cosmopolitan needed to establish its name in the marketplace just like a new brand of cereal or soap. Schlicht coordinated a promotional campaign to make people aware a new magazine was coming. Promotional efforts for magazines of the era involved newspaper advertisements, which listed authors and articles in an upcoming issue, and color posters pasted on storefront windows and walls, each poster listing authors and articles against a background of brightly colored illustrations and caricatures. Newspaper advertisements and posters were a continuous budget item, necessary prior to publication of each magazine issue to alert the public about upcoming features. Posters required paying a printer for a sufficient number of color copies to display in key cities and payment of fees to owners of buildings for permission to paste the paper sheets on exterior walls and windows. *Ladies' Home Journal* spent $20,000 on promotion one year during its rapid rise to dominance in the women's magazine category.[42]

Door-to-door canvassing for subscriptions was the traditional technique to build readership initially; its other useful function was to publicize the title. During a magazine's introductory phase, teams of salesmen rode from town to town aboard wagons, knocked on doors all day and into the night to speak with residents or leave flyers on the doorstep if no one responded. Salesmen received a commission amounting to one-fourth the annual subscription price; subscribers paid cash and signed a receipt or later mailed a money order to the publisher. Selling ten or a dozen *Cosmopolitan* subscriptions daily during an introductory campaign that might last a few weeks resulted in a good wage for an agent when multiplied by a commission of sixty cents each. (Publishers kept the entire sum for subscription renewals.)[43]

The best method for sustainable, stable circulation was the presence of a network of community subscription agents. After the door-to-door canvass crews had departed, local agents went to work. *Cosmopolitan* actively recruited men and women to sell subscriptions to neighbors. "We offer so generous a percentage to agents that they find no difficulty making a large salary," *Cosmopolitan* vowed. "They can canvass among their neighbors, and if they are sufficiently persistent and persuasive, they can induce nine out of every ten families to subscribe." Subscription agents also coordinated the organization of neighborhood magazine clubs, which met each month to discuss stories, poems, and articles. An agent offered a free subscription to each organizer of a club if at least four additional households subscribed. Community subscription agents typically received a commission of fifty cents for a *Cosmopolitan* order.[44]

Schlicht's last essential task prior to the debut of *Cosmopolitan* was to arrange distribution to vendors. One national distributor controlled the market to thousands of vendors, and it set a high price for getting magazines from printers to newsstands in cities and towns.[45]

Cosmopolitan, Debut and Demise

The most memorable feature of *Cosmopolitan*'s first issue in March 1886 was its design. The cover template, an L-shape illustration that framed a table of contents, presented artful, evocative imagery and a statement of *Cosmopolitan*'s philosophy: the Statue of Liberty towering over New York harbor, ships at anchor with sails furled, and the piers of lower Manhattan; the table of contents listed every item inside; the motto across the top declared, "The World Is My Country and All Mankind Are My Countrymen." Compared to the simplistic cover designs of many contemporaneous magazines emblazoned with a title and a small symbolic caricature to convey a sense of the magazine's purpose— a chic woman, or a quill pen, or an elegant house—the *Cosmopolitan* cover was exceptionally ornate. The template lasted until Schlicht commissioned Stanford White, the famous architect, to create a new look in 1887.

The magazine was standard size for the era at seven by ten inches, or slightly smaller than a sheet of printer paper today. The page size did not change for thirty years.

The table of contents for March 1886 listed these items: six fiction stories, four poems, six nonfiction articles, a Little Ones section, a Household section, and four full-page illustrations. *Cosmopolitan* presented sixty-four pages of editorial material: twenty-two fiction pages, twenty-three nonfiction pages, six pages for Little Ones, four pages for Household, four stand-alone illustration pages, three pages for a musical score, and two cumulative pages for poems.[46]

The publisher's note on the inside front cover stated, "The Cosmopolitan will be a first-class magazine." It definitely made an effort, although it hardly seemed a family magazine. The premiere issue led with an eight-page story by Hjalmar Hjorth Boyesen, an author with a reputation for stark depictions. Next, informative articles about the British prime minister and British oppression of the Irish were impressive. Fourteen quarter-page or smaller illustrations accompanied stories, poems, and articles. The frontispiece was a full-page portrait of William Ewart Gladstone, prime minister of Britain, and the facing page started the premier fiction piece, "The Story Of A Blue Vein" by Boyesen. To have an illustration unrelated to the text opposite was common practice for magazines then; its sole purpose was to offer a strong visual entry to the magazine.[47]

Schlicht assigned prime placement to Boyesen, a Columbia University literature professor firmly aligned with the literary realism genre. This seemed to conflict with the idea of a family literary magazine. Realism battled romanticism

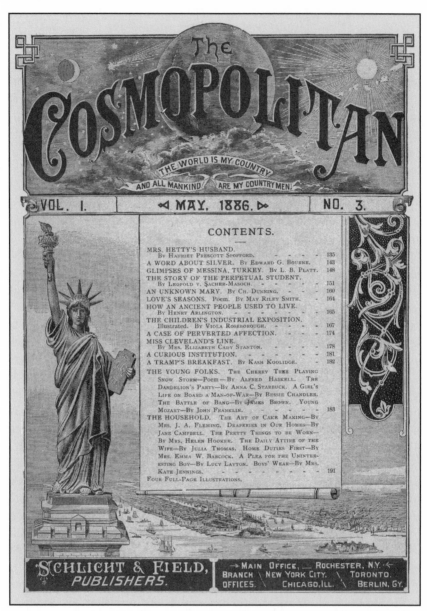

Cosmopolitan presented an unusual design upon its debut in 1886. An ornate nameplate and a functional L-shape illustration framed a useful listing of the magazine's contents. *Cosmopolitan,* May 1886. Source: Michener Library, University of Northern Colorado.

for space in the pages of American magazines throughout the Gilded Age and into the twentieth century. Editors risked alienating readers if they tipped the scale overmuch to either genre. "The Story Of A Blue Vein" by Boyesen was about a daughter and foster son orphaned by a drunkard father. Boyesen crafted an emotional tale of abusive parents, despair, youthful determination, and the triumph of friendship. Its upbeat conclusion certainly affirmed fundamental values, but whether parents might have wished to share this stark story with children was questionable.

Cosmopolitan alternated fiction and nonfiction throughout the first issue. A five-page article about oppressive British governance of Ireland, "A People Governed To Death," followed the lengthy fiction opener. The writer was *Cosmopolitan* editor Frank P. Smith, who also wrote the Gladstone profile that began deeper in the magazine.

Surprisingly, Schlicht found time away from his publisher's tasks to contribute an article, and possibly a second. His three-page article titled "The Manner Of Electing The President" interspersed declarations of opinion with factual statements, a subjectivity acceptable for nonfiction writing then. Schlicht argued for a constitutional amendment to eliminate the electoral college, which he called an "unnatural" remnant of bygone days. "Citizens do not vote as citizens of the United States, but as New Yorkers, as Virginians, as Texans," Schlicht wrote. "We are a united nation, not a mere assemblage of independent states whose interests clash in the choice of a president." Schlicht referred to the 1884 election won by Grover Cleveland, a Democrat, over James Blaine, a Republican, by less than 1 percent out of ten million votes cast, but by a much wider margin in the electoral college. Blaine could easily have won the popular vote, but lost the electoral. Schlicht contended, "Not until the time comes when the people shall vote directly for president can a man say that the constitution confers upon him the full dignity of national citizenship."[48]

It was possible Schlicht also wrote a descriptive account of Saint Paul's Cathedral, a London landmark. Of all the stories and articles in *Cosmopolitan*'s premiere issue, it was the only one lacking a byline; instead, credit went to "A Rambler." Such modesty was uncharacteristic of Schlicht, but he surely had visited London on business trips for Schlicht & Field's predecessor company, which also had branch offices in Germany. Schlicht did credit himself for a translation of a French poem, "My Normandy," alongside a full page of illustrations. Another possibility was that *Cosmopolitan* simply stole the cathedral article from a British publication. International copyright law was nonexistent until 1891, and American newspapers and magazines freely took material from elsewhere to fill pages at no cost. The first issue of *Cosmopolitan,* for example, carried two translations—one an anonymous story from French and the other

This frontispiece from the first issue of *Cosmopolitan,* March 1886, typified the illustrations placed on the first page of each month's issue until the early 1900s. Illustrations were horizontally placed, which meant a reader turned the magazine to view it properly. Some illustrations were color. Occasional frontispieces presented portrait illustrations of statesmen and literary legends. Source: Morgan Library, Colorado State University.

A "Young Folks" section replaced "Little Ones" soon after *Cosmopolitan*'s debut in March 1886. The purpose remained the same, however: to offer short stories and poems for children. The section was discontinued by autumn 1887. Source: Morgan Library, Colorado State University.

The "Household" section provided advice about cleaning garments, washing windows, and preparing meals. Women readers also learned about the latest fashions among the upper class and received instructions on dinner party etiquette. "Household" disappeared from the magazine by summer 1887. Source: Morgan Library, Colorado State University.

an anonymous article from German. The absence of bylines was an indication the material was pirated.[49]

The first issue was predominantly international. Readers perused a profile of Gladstone, information about Ireland and Saint Paul's Cathedral, translations of French and German stories and poems, and a seasonal piece titled "Easter In Russia," a descriptive three-page explanation of Orthodox rites. The writer of the latter piece also informed readers about how persons celebrated Easter: "The people generally attend mass, but after that even the most devout have no conscientious scruples against taking frequent and liberal potions of 'votky,' a strong, intoxicating drink, and by nightfall many of them are not able to distinguish between the sun and the moon."[50]

The Little Ones section featured a story told from the perspective of a sea gull, also a tribute to a dog named Rover, and a poem about a child's sleigh ride. Relevant illustrations of a gull, dog, and sleigh enlivened the section. Starting with the second issue, Young Folks became the section name.

Household was the weakest part of the first issue. A series of short how-to advisory articles crammed with instructions to accomplish the most mundane chores filled the section: fashion ("Red dresses remain popular for misses and young ladies" and "yellow will again be the fashionable color for brightening hats and bonnets"); housecleaning ("Many excellent housekeepers are strangely ignorant of the best method of sweeping . . . if they do know, they neglect to impart the knowledge to their servants"); starching and ironing ("to starch or iron properly requires much practice and care. . . . The things needed are boiling water, good white starch—Duryea's satin gloss, a teacup, spoon, and a piece of pure white castile soap"). The section, despite its dullness, was acknowledgment that women readers must be courted.[51]

Excepting the long story by Boyesen and article by editor Smith, the length of most *Cosmopolitan* items was three pages of text. Schlicht sought to make brevity a selling point. His introductory note to readers guaranteed that fiction and nonfiction items "will all be short and bright, never long and tedious, as is usually the case."[52]

Whatever criticism Schlicht would receive later from irate stockholders and creditors for extravagance, his expenditures for the debut were prudent. Payments to authors and writers of star status generally ranged from $50 to $200 for a story or article. Only one author in the debut issue, Boyesen, rated a star's fee. Smith, the editor, wrote two articles and Schlicht definitely wrote one. Little-known authors and writers, who supplied text for quality magazines at the prevailing rate of $5 per page, filled eighteen pages. Six pages presumably came free of cost from foreign publications. Engravings of woodcut and line-drawing illustrations occupied the equivalent of six pages at a probable sum of $1,200.[53]

Despite Schlicht's brevity pledge, *Cosmopolitan* soon allowed lengthier stories and articles written by people who were paid handsome sums. Subsequent issues of *Cosmopolitan* offered stories and articles from well-known authors and writers: Charles Abbott, a naturalist; Edward Gaylord Bourne, a political historian; Julian Hawthorne, son of novelist Nathaniel Hawthorne and popular in his own right; Louisa Chandler Moulton, a poet and author often seen in *Atlantic Monthly, Century,* and *Harper's;* the Reverend R. Heber Newton, a controversial Episcopal priest accused of heresy for his advocacy of Social Gospel doctrine and lectures on evolution; Harriet Prescott Spofford, a storyteller whose fiction appeared in many quality magazines, including *Atlantic Monthly;* and Elizabeth Cady Stanton, a women's suffragist leader and social activist. This roster of star contributors demonstrated that *Cosmopolitan* strived for quality.

Each monthly issue began with a premier fiction piece of seven to eight pages and a premier article of six pages. Whenever the magazine presented more than a single story or an article written by a literary star, the table of contents listed fewer items. Some issues contained only fourteen or fifteen editorial pieces while others had eighteen or nineteen. Woodcut images and line drawings usually equaled six pages. Based on known costs for illustrations, fees paid to ordinary contributors and the range of fees to star contributors, *Cosmopolitan* spent at least $1,800 on editorial material each month during its extended startup phase.[54]

Other expenditures added appreciably to the magazine's monthly cash disbursements. Schlicht told investors and potential advertisers that *Cosmopolitan* published 25,000 copies each month its first year, which incurred these costs for the standard sixty-four-page issue: $1,800 for editorial material; $1,900 for typesetting, electroplating of printing plates, and printing itself; $450 for coated paper; $200 for mailing to subscribers and placing copies with vendors. Investors belatedly learned at the bankruptcy meeting in May 1888 that the magazine had only eight thousand paid subscribers.[55]

The sum of probable editorial, production, and distribution items was at least $4,350 for each issue, resulting in a single-copy cost of seventeen cents for 25,000 magazines. On top of that amount were unknown payroll expenses—including the publisher, editor, advertising manager, business manager, distribution manager, production manager, and several clerks to process subscriptions and various paperwork. Schlicht, as publisher, might have received a modest salary to supplement his executive's pay, but the editor and other magazine managers probably earned middle-class salaries of at least $120 a month. It would be reasonable to assume that the operational budget of *Cosmopolitan* was at least $5,000 each month. This would not have included clerical salaries or essential promotional costs, primarily advertisements in newspapers and the printing and display of posters.[56]

The substantial investment to prepare and print *Cosmopolitan* every month made circulation growth imperative. Schlicht intended to have ten thousand subscription agents in communities across the nation. A full-page promotional ad inside the magazine blared a message to recruit community agents, especially women. "The subscription price is so low and the premium so attractive that little effort is required to obtain subscribers," an announcement assured readers.[57]

The "premium" was a gift to each new subscriber. Ever the salesman, Schlicht boasted to *Cosmopolitan* readers that the "value of the articles, the beauty of the illustrations and letter press, and the fine quality of the paper, have excited universal admiration." Schlicht's experience selling office supplies prompted him to send a gift upon receipt of a subscription order. *Cosmopolitan* gave a free desktop file index useful for letters and bills, worth $2.25 retail. Such subscription premiums were standard magazine practice during an introductory campaign, although *Cosmopolitan* deviated from the norm by extending its premium into summer 1887, sixteen months after its debut. *Cosmopolitan* should have reimbursed Schlicht & Field for the wholesale value of each desktop index, an unknown amount. However, discussion at the bankruptcy meeting in May 1888 indicated that the company was not reimbursed.[58]

Commissions to canvassers, subscription agents, free subscriptions to club organizers, and the tacit obligation to debit the expense of premiums to subscribers meant *Cosmopolitan* possibly retained only a dollar from each subscription order of $2.50. Equivalent to approximately eight cents a copy, this sum was half the actual cost of publishing and distribution. A subscription renewal brought prorated revenue of twenty-one cents a copy each month, but renewals would not begin until *Cosmopolitan*'s second year.

Newsstand sales by vendors did not provide much financial relief either. *Cosmopolitan* placed 10 percent of its total press run with vendors. The magazine sold for twenty-one cents apiece at vendors, but the publisher received only eleven cents. Because only one national distributor controlled placement to most vendors, it levied a monopolistic fee of four cents to place each *Cosmopolitan* for sale and then collected another penny on consignment. A vendor pocketed five cents for a sale. Of course, each unsold copy meant no revenue. This was a serious problem if a high percentage of copies did not sell any month. The standard percentage of single-copy sales for magazines of the era was 50 percent; for *Cosmopolitan,* this would have meant 1,250 copies sold and 1,250 copies unsold—meaning approximately $60 revenue compared to a cost of $525.[59]

With revenue from subscriptions and vendor sales insufficient to pay for basic expenses, revenue from advertisers was crucial to *Cosmopolitan*. Early in 1887, Schlicht instructed ad sales representatives to tell prospective advertisers that *Cosmopolitan* had a circulation of 25,000 copies, although the publisher did not submit any circulation statement to *N. W. Ayer and Son's Annual,* a national directory of publications. Most publishers sent unverified circulation statements to *Ayer,* while a select few submitted so-called sworn statements, which verified the number of magazines mailed by the U.S. Post Office. The refusal by Schlicht to submit any circulation statement was certain to raise suspicions among already skeptical ad buyers. Magazine publishers routinely exaggerated circulation numbers and ad buyers routinely cut those numbers by half. (Certified, audited circulations were not standard until 1914.) Advertisers did not rush to buy space in the new magazine.[60]

Cosmopolitan carried an average twenty-six pages of advertisements monthly the first year, conforming to the custom of segregating ads from the editorial material by clustering them at the front and back.[61] Each page supposedly was worth $60 at rate price. But magazines, then and now, sold ad space at a discount, or off-rate, to advertisers who signed long-term contracts and to first-time advertisers whose presence on a page might persuade others to advertise. Also, each ad page incurred a production and printing cost. The actual revenue per ad page to *Cosmopolitan* probably was $38. Twenty-six pages generated at best $990 each month.[62]

With total probable monthly revenue during the first year of approximately $1,100 from subscriptions, vendor sales, and advertising, the magazine's minimum operational monthly deficit was perhaps $3,900—again excluding expenditures for clerical staff and promotional efforts. Schlicht was depleting startup capital rapidly. Stringent budget management was essential, perhaps attainable by printing substantially fewer copies for door-to-door subscription agents or scaling back promotional expenses. Schlicht was not one to economize.

Instead, he chose to increase costs. *Cosmopolitan* moved from Rochester to Manhattan in May 1887. The magazine rented an office suite at 29 Park Row, amid the towers of the city's newspapers—*New York Tribune,* a legacy of Horace Greeley; *New York Herald,* owned by James Gordon Bennett Jr., son of its founder; *New York World,* purchased in 1884 by Joseph Pulitzer of St. Louis; and other dailies, of which one was the *New York Times,* a floundering mediocrity at the time. The new offices in lower Manhattan, near city hall and the Brooklyn Bridge, placed *Cosmopolitan* in the nation's publishing capital. One-fifth of all American magazines operated from there, double the proportion from Boston and triple that of Chicago. The magazine had easier access to advertising agencies, which advised clients about placement in magazines. Decisions to place advertisements tended to be based on personal relationships with editors and publishers, perceptions of quality, and presumptions about the readership a magazine attracted. It was guesswork and salesmanship; demographic analysis and market research would not be part of the craft for decades.[63]

An ad in the *New York Times* announced the magazine's arrival, "The first number of The Cosmopolitan issued from its New-York office is now on the news stands." The ad also proclaimed E. P. Roe as a contributor. Roe's presence in *Cosmopolitan* signified a major step in a new direction. Roe was an immensely popular author whose books had sold hundreds of thousands of copies; sales of six novels had surpassed 50,000 copies each. *Cosmopolitan* had signed well-known authors and writers since its inception, but now it had landed someone reputed to earn "the largest income of any American author." Roe was more than a star; he was a literary legend whose minimum fee was $300.[64]

A final flourish during summer 1887 was a striking new cover design. Schlicht commissioned Stanford White, the flamboyant architect who would design the first Madison Square Garden and Washington Memorial Arch, to give the cover a modernistic look. White previously had designed a new cover for his friend Richard Watson Gilder at *Century* and one for the new *Scribner's,* launched earlier in 1887. White's designs for *Century, Cosmopolitan,* and *Scribner's* differed from the usual magazine covers: a dynamic, dominant typeface, not a faux script; figurative, representational imagery, not literal symbolic images; and no table of contents, because most readers received the magazine at home and therefore would see what it contained upon turning to a list on an inside page. The cover template by White also was economical; the sole cover element that would require changing each issue was the date. White charged $500 to design a magazine cover.[65] Starting with the July 1887 issue, *Cosmopolitan* displayed a modernistic magazine cover: a globe crisscrossed by lines of latitude and longitude, within a starburst of radiating lines, and the magazine title at the center.

Schlicht had escalated overhead costs at a critical moment. To attain some stature within the magazine universe and among advertisers, Schlicht had spent scarce money on prestige items: a Park Row address, assuredly quite expensive compared to the Schlicht & Field office in Rochester; a star author, Roe, in the table of contents; a modernistic cover template by White. These decisions intended to create an illusion that *Cosmopolitan* was succeeding. Perhaps the publisher also began wooing Miss Bernhardt with bouquets of flowers and gifts at this time.

Other actions by Schlicht reflected the desperate reality of the magazine. His refusal to list *Cosmopolitan*'s circulation in the *Ayer* directory signaled a serious problem with subscriptions and single-copy sales. The magazine probably had only a few thousand subscribers, a likelihood substantiated several weeks after the move to Manhattan when *Cosmopolitan* abandoned its original format—further evidence that subscription renewals were weak. *Cosmopolitan* would have stayed the same if renewals were strong. Instead, the magazine dropped the Household section altogether and Young Folks dwindled to two items, then disappeared that autumn. The most obvious distress signal was a price reduction to $2 for an annual subscription, a fifty-cent markdown, and to twenty cents for a copy at vendors, a penny cut.

Schlicht had increased operational and editorial costs, yet had decreased revenue. Although subscription renewals eliminated commissions to agents, the $2 a subscriber sent to continue the magazine amounted to seventeen cents a copy for *Cosmopolitan*. Meanwhile, the per-copy cost had inched upward past that amount because of its higher editorial and overhead costs. *Cosmopolitan* could survive only by immediate circulation growth, which would enable it to raise the ad rate, and additional advertising revenue. It was a gamble.

It might have paid off if *Cosmopolitan* was the most affordable quality general magazine on the market. It wasn't. *Scribner's* had appeared in January 1887, priced at $3 a year and twenty-five cents a copy at vendors. *Scribner's* sold for a nickel more at vendors and was a dollar pricier for a subscription than *Cosmopolitan,* but it was a fine magazine—and arguably the reason why Schlicht had reduced his magazine's subscription price to seem a better bargain. The new competitor was a subsidiary of Charles Scribner's Sons, a prominent book publisher and familiar name to Americans. Name recognition had a tremendous advantage in the marketplace. It also didn't hurt that *Scribner's* began with $500,000 startup capital, an incredible sum for the era.[66]

Scribner's was the successor to *Scribner's Monthly,* an esteemed literary magazine that had disappeared in 1881 when the book publisher relinquished the title to focus on books; the original magazine became *Century.* The *Century* spin-off deal stipulated that Charles Scribner's Sons could not reenter the magazine marketplace for five years. In year six, *Scribner's* resurrected the format of its namesake. It published excerpts from forthcoming Charles Scribner's Sons novels, ran serials authored by stars and legends affiliated with the book publishers, offered nonfiction articles, and otherwise took advantage of its powerhouse connections to find talent. *Scribner's* had raised the ante.

Cosmopolitan was out of money by year's end. Schlicht received the emergency infusion from stockholders after lying to them about circulation and advertising. His assurance to them of 35,000 copies sent to readers or canvassers each month omitted any reference to actual subscriptions and single-copy sales—and if the 35,000 figure actually was true and not simply another boast by Schlicht, the additional 10,000 copies would have boosted the monthly deficit by at least $400 for printing and distribution.

Cosmopolitan, similar to many magazines of the era, simply kept mailing the magazine to people who had not renewed their subscriptions. Schlicht hoped the artificially inflated circulation number would persuade advertisers to buy space. On the matter of advertising, Schlicht told stockholders *Cosmopolitan* soon would bill $5,000 an issue. This was fantasy. To bill that sum, the magazine needed eighty-four pages of ads; it carried forty-four pages.[67]

Schlicht, of course, knew the real story. He began promoting *Cosmopolitan* to potential investors. The sale of *Cosmopolitan* presumably should have reimbursed Schlicht & Field stockholders for some of their lost money. Schlicht, though, could not find any takers, apparently because of the shaky circulation numbers and barely acceptable advertising revenue. Just a month after the stockholders had shown faith in him, Schlicht funneled other money from the Rochester company to *Cosmopolitan,* apparently to keep the magazine alive until it could be disposed of.[68]

At last, late in January 1888, Schlicht transferred ownership to investors from New York City. The new ownership incorporated a separate entity, The Cosmopolitan Magazine Company. Schlicht had found three men from Manhattan willing to risk money on the magazine, but unwilling to buy it outright from Schlicht & Field or to assume its debts. The incorporation documents filed with a state agency in Albany listed Ulysses S. Grant Jr., son of the former president and Civil War commander, and two others; Schlicht also was on the list. Grant was a lawyer reviving his law career after an investment scandal in which he was an innocent dupe whose famous name had lent luster to a thieving partnership. Schlicht somehow remained *Cosmopolitan* publisher. The man was persuasive.[69]

The incorporation documents stipulated a maximum of three thousand shares could be sold at a par value of $50 apiece. This did not mean the new owners put up $150,000 for *Cosmopolitan,* but was a nominal value should any investor wish to sell shares to another person. The Cosmopolitan Magazine Company started with a clean financial slate.

NOT SERIOUSLY INJURED.

THE COSMOPOLITAN MAGAZINE WILL
CONTINUE PUBLICATION.

A Rochester dispatch printed yesterday
stated that the Schlicht & Field Company, dealing in office supplies and labor-saving devices,
had suspended business, and that since
Paul S. Schlicht, who is the head of the
firm, is also President of the company which is
publishing the *Cosmopolitan Magazine* of this
city, the magazine might possibly suffer. At the
office of the *Cosmopolitan* yesterday a
TIMES reporter was told that the failure would not seriously injure that
publication. It was started two years
ago by the Schlicht & Field Company, but last
February the proprietors formed themselves
into a stock company and removed the offices
to this city. When the reorganization took
place Mr. Schlicht was elected President. The
managers of the magazine said also that the
suspension of the company had only caused
them slight inconvenience, and that preparations for the publication of the June number
were going on as usual.

Confusion about whether a Rochester, New York, company continued
to own *Cosmopolitan* caused erroneous reporting in May 1888 about
the magazine's bankruptcy and its continuation. *New York Times,* May
24, 1888, page 1.

NO FURTHER ASSISTANCE.

ROCHESTER, N. Y., May 24.—Ex-City Attorney John N. Beckley, who is the attorney for
the Schlicht & Field Company, which has up to
two months ago published the *Cosmopolitan
Magazine,* was shown a clipping from THE NEW-
YORK TIMES to-day stating that the magazine
company would not be affected materially by the
embarrassment of the Schlicht & Field Company, and he stated that the New-York *Cosmopolitan* Company's stock was practically all held
by the members of the Schlicht & Field Company and by that company in its corporate
capacity, and that the company and its members would certainly not furnish further assistance to the *Cosmopolitan* Company or attempt
to further publish that periodical.

The day after the *New York Times* reported the death of *Cosmopolitan*
a follow-up article correctly noted that the magazine belonged to new
owners and would continue. *New York Times,* May 25, 1888, page 2.

The new owners let Schlicht continue his extravagant ways. *Cosmopolitan* began publishing a full-page color illustration in the middle of the magazine, not at the beginning. It was unusual because it was expensive. Rather than being printed and then folded for placement at the front of the magazine, the inside color page had to be inserted and then folded. Schlicht declared in a promotional statement that *Cosmopolitan* "has been a success from the start, as indeed its popular literature, filling a field distinctly on its own perhaps midway between the daily papers and the more antiquated magazine, entitles it to."[70]

Although the magazine's financial condition was precarious by the summer of 1887, the publisher commissioned Stanford White, a prominent architect, to design a new cover template for *Cosmopolitan*. That summer, too, the magazine abandoned its original format as a family literary magazine. *Cosmopolitan*, August 1887; source: Memorial Library, University of Wisconsin–Madison; courtesy of Daniel Friedrich.

Cosmopolitan published its March, April, May, and June issues under new ownership. Articles demonstrated a focus on women: a profile of Louisa May Alcott; an eight-page article, "A Congress Of Famous Women," with a full-page photograph of leaders at the International Conference of Women and seven quarter-page woodcuts that included Susan B. Anthony, Elizabeth Cady Stanton, and Clara Barton; and "The Ladies Of The American Court," primarily about first lady Frances Folsom Cleveland.[71]

Other articles, "The Superstitions Of The Negro" and "The Chinese In New York," both of which oozed racist stereotypes, presented information about subcultures mysterious to white middle-class readers. The racism inherent to white Americans manifested itself in *Cosmopolitan,* a product of its time. The significance of articles perpetuating racist stereotypes was not publication itself, rather it was the failure of editors and writers to attempt to truly inform readers about nonwhite culture and society. Editors and writers saw America through a white veil.

"The Superstitions Of The Negro" writer strung together four pages of anecdotes and examples of folk beliefs derived from a conversation with one elderly black woman, whom the writer acknowledged was bizarre. "She was such a queer specimen of humanity," the article stated, "and ideas and fancies from her weird world of ignorance flew so rapidly to her tongue, that one was enticed into desire to hear more of her jargon." The writer repeated her words, in an approximation of dialect, to describe a representation of death: "En dat shadder en darkness hit comes drappin' down on yer, creepin' up on yer; hit gits hol 'er yo' feet . . . yer gone—case yer breaf hit's yer soul!" Superstitions arose from segregation, according to the writer, "Among those of the race that live far from white people, their teaching and their influence, there is a barbarous belief that, whereas God is indeed Creator of the dominant white race, they, poor blacks, are the handiwork of Satan." After listing a series of folk tales that foretold imminent death, the article explained the effects of superstitions: "The larger amount . . . bear upon little daily events which their ignorant minds translate into signs and wonders."[72]

At no point did the article incorporate conversations from other blacks living in the woman's community, people whose comments might have provided perspective to the role superstitions played in everyday life. Certainly, ethnic whites had superstitions, too, but folk tales often were mere curiosities or objects of humor, not meaningful tenets of life.

"The Chinese In New York" at least contained perspective on anti-Asian attitudes and policies. The article referred to a California statute excluding Chinese from residency and to a recent federal law barring immigration from China. The writer proceeded to analyze the factors that had made Chinese synonymous with laundry. "There are probably a little over two thousand such

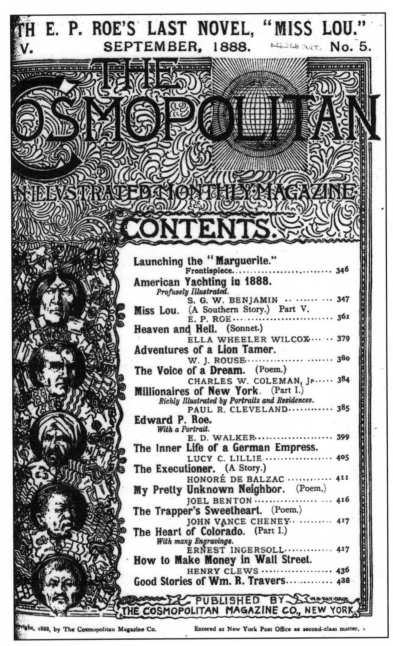

Cosmopolitan ceased publishing for two months during the summer of 1888, was sold to another publisher, and resumed in September. Its editorial format emphasized nonfiction articles, including a section devoted to commentary on recent national and international news. *Cosmopolitan*, September 1888; source: New York Public Library.

laundries in the city of New York alone, some eight hundred or nine hundred in Brooklyn, and about one hundred and fifty in Jersey City (mosquito land, as Chinamen call it)," the writer noted. "They become laundrymen here simply because there is no other occupation by which they can make money as surely and quickly. The prejudice against the race has much to do with it."[73]

Mott Street and nearby blocks in lower Manhattan had become known as Chinatown by the 1890s, the article mentioned. Despite their segregation from other immigrant groups, the Chinese seemed to lack racial unity. "There is nothing of the clan habit among Chinamen," the writer stated. "Indeed, had they any such civilized peculiarities, their own country would not now be ruled by a foreign race." Street thugs preyed on Chinese victims because of indifference. "One Chinaman will stand and see another mobbed without using the least effort to save him," the article reported. There followed a lengthy section on opium usage.[74]

Chinese operated laundries, lived in a separate neighborhood, and some smoked opium. Facts, for sure, but an article focused on a community several blocks from *Cosmopolitan*'s office suite should have presented a more complete portrait. If the purpose of the magazine was to inform and edify, it had an opportunity to offer readers insight to cultures and societies visible to whites yet unknown to them, to do more than perpetuate stereotypes. It would be many decades before the magazine offered such context and perspective.

Schlicht devoted his efforts to the magazine's appearance. He again ran a color frontispiece. *Cosmopolitan* also contracted with Roe for an eight-part serial, "Miss Lou." In an attempt to boost single-copy sales and pique the curiosity of the public, ads for *Cosmopolitan* in various newspapers touted the color frontispiece, a woodcut of a fierce dervish. But this either was false advertising or a last-minute budgetary decision had eliminated color because the frontispiece instead was a sharp black-and-white photograph of a Turk mystic titled "Howling Dervish."[75]

The promotional campaign for the June 1888 issue included an unusual element, too—an odd article in the *New York Times* headlined "An Interesting Interview." The alleged news piece consisted of a five-line first paragraph stating that *Cosmopolitan* was "one of the brightest and most readable of the magazines." It continued with a lengthy second paragraph composed entirely of an extended quote from Schlicht, twenty-seven lines in all: "I conceived the idea of colored illustrations while in Europe. At the time I gave some attention to literature and art matters, although, to tell the truth, I was so nearly dead from malaria that at times I could scarcely hold up my head." Upon his return to the United States, Schlicht met with a friend who "saw my wretched condition, and declared that he had something he was certain would positively cure it." The elixir? Schlicht testified, "I was entirely cured of malaria in its worst form, wholly by the use of Duffy's Pure Malt Whisky—no quinine, no drugs."[76]

This obviously was not a news article, despite the headline. It was a form of chicanery called a reading notice, a publishing ploy to trick people into reading an ad disguised as news. Newspaper publishers were fond of reading notices because advertisers gladly paid a higher rate than for a display ad, on the assumption that news was more credible. (Congress required newspapers and magazines to label such material as advertisements in 1912 when it passed a postal rate reform law.) Whether the cash for the personal endorsement of Duffy's Pure Malt Whisky went to Schlicht or to the ailing *Cosmopolitan* was not recorded. Schlicht's behavior to date suggested he probably kept the money.[77]

Schlicht would have needed cash. He was unemployed. *Cosmopolitan* was finished. The same week the Duffy's Pure Malt Whisky notice ran in the *New York Times* the June issue of *Cosmopolitan* rolled through a printing press. It was apparently its last.[78]

Revival

At the meeting of Schlicht & Field stockholders and creditors in Rochester late in May 1888, one man recommended the company retain ownership of *Cosmopolitan*. The magazine "might be made a paying enterprise," the man advised. "It would be a mistake to throw up such a valuable asset." The speaker, and others there, did not comprehend that Schlicht & Field was not the owner anymore. Unfortunately for stockholders and creditors, the sleight-of-hand ownership transfer arranged by Schlicht had not reimbursed the company for any money directly spent on *Cosmopolitan*, including the premiums given to subscribers. Stockholders lost everything, but bankers and creditors recovered $80,000 of the $301,400 total loss by taking possession of Schlicht & Field's warehouse inventory and selling patent licenses for several items.[79] Fortunately for the future of *Cosmopolitan*, however, the magazine was a separate corporate entity and was not entangled by the web of lawsuits filed against Schlicht the next several months by stockholders nor was it encumbered by the eventual settlement with creditors.

The investors who controlled the magazine from late January to June 1888 had published only four issues when they quit. They had learned how few actual subscriptions and renewals existed and how few advertisers actually bought pages. The Cosmopolitan Magazine Company was shunted to another owner, Joseph Hallock, publisher of *Christianity at Work* and a shrewd buyer of magazines in distress, in midsummer 1888. No purchase price, if any, was revealed.[80]

After a two-month hiatus, *Cosmopolitan* published a September 1888 issue. The modernistic cover template by Stanford White was gone. The new cover design presented facial representations symbolizing the inhabitants of the continents and included a table of contents.

Hallock had bought a magazine with eight thousand subscribers. He slashed the press run to 15,000 copies, which eliminated delinquent subscribers but maintained distribution of complimentary copies to subscription agents for solicitation of new readers. Also eliminated was the monthly color frontispiece. Hallock retained the editor, who promptly replaced most woodcuts with photographs and divided the pages evenly between nonfiction and fiction. Roe's serial "Miss Lou" picked up where it had left off in June. (Roe had died in the interim.) A back-of-the-book section, Live Questions, occupied six pages with commentary on contemporary topics. Hallock increased editorial material to ninety-six pages, but continued the $2 annual subscription price.[81]

The public responded. Distribution increased to 16,000 copies for the December issue. Advertisements filled sixty-four pages. *Cosmopolitan* had a chance to survive, although the increase of 1,000 copies hardly inspired confidence. Hallock had a reputation for killing magazines if the potential for profitability required too much investment. The magazine industry was merciless. Half of all new magazines died within four years of their founding.[82]

Then a wealthy adventurer and entrepreneur from Colorado contacted Hallock to ask about buying the magazine. John Brisben Walker had learned of *Cosmopolitan*'s problems the preceding summer. Walker had decided he should buy it, but the magazine was sold to Hallock by the time Walker obtained money from selling a lengthy stretch of riverfront property in downtown Denver and a vast tract of valuable farmland just north of the city. Walker could have waited in Denver for another opportunity to publish a national magazine. In those days, same as now, magazines were in distress all the time. But Walker did not want just any magazine. *Cosmopolitan* was a quality magazine, and it could be a tremendous success if the right man ran it. Hallock had shown moderate success. Walker believed he could do better.[83]

Walker, age forty-one, arrived in New York City in early December to negotiate with Hallock. Walker's personal wealth would enable him to buy the magazine, pay the fees commanded by literary stars and legends, afford plentiful illustrations and photographs, and absorb losses for two to three years without worry. Aside from money, Walker had some experience as a newspaper reporter, editor, and publisher. His insider's knowledge of publishing and his own business savvy gave him the confidence to risk his own fortune, not the fortune of others.

Negotiations didn't take long. The purchase price never was disclosed. The magazine was so inconsequential that its ownership transfer was noted only by *Publisher's Weekly,* a trade journal, with a two-sentence item. *Cosmopolitan* belonged to Walker in mid-December 1888.[84]

2

Salvation

"A Flying Trip Around The World"

Elizabeth Bisland awoke in the bedroom of her apartment to the usual sound of her maid bringing a tray on which breakfast, newspapers, and mail were tidily arranged. Bisland opened the mail, "read the papers leisurely, made a calm and uneventful toilet," and readied herself for work. At ten-thirty, she received "a hurried and mysterious request . . . that I would come as soon as possible to the office of the Cosmopolitan Magazine—of which I am one of the editors."[1]

Seven hours later, Bisland, age twenty-eight, was riding a train west from New York City. She would not return to the comfort of her residence and her daily routine for seventy-six days, the time it took her to travel around the world.

This most eventful journey of her life began November 14, 1889, a Thursday. An impulsive decision by *Cosmopolitan* editor John Brisben Walker sent his associate editor around the world in a direction opposite that of Nellie Bly of the *New York World,* who had begun her own global trip the same day. Bly, age twenty-five, was a reporter for the immensely successful newspaper owned by Joseph Pulitzer and hoped to return to the *World*'s newsroom on Park Row in under eighty days, the fictional span concocted by Jules Verne in a popular novel from the 1870s. This grand stunt was to boost circulation for the *World,* already the largest in the city and therefore the nation.[2]

Bisland was book editor of *Cosmopolitan,* hardly a "stunt journalist" like Bly whose reportorial work involved undercover assignments that produced sensational exposés. Bisland, therefore, was less than enthused when Walker excitedly told her his scheme. "On my arrival the editor and owner of the magazine asked if I would leave New York that evening for San Francisco and go around the world in some absurdly inadequate space of time," Bisland remembered. "My appetite at eleven in the morning for even the most excruciatingly funny jokes may be said to actually not exist, and this one, I remember, bored me more than most."[3]

Walker thrived on competition. The prospect of *Cosmopolitan* against the *New York World!* Had the newspaper sent a man on this stunt, Walker might have gone himself rather than dispatch a junior editor. But it had to be a woman.

Still, the idea was foolish. *Cosmopolitan* was a monthly magazine, the *World* a daily newspaper. Bisland was traveling west and would cross the Pacific Ocean to Japan, leaving her without access to the telegraph for transmitting information back to the United States. Weeks would pass before delivery of any handwritten articles transported by steamship, then railroad. *Cosmopolitan* might not print a word from her until its February issue.

Meanwhile, Bly would have access to the transoceanic telegraph cable from England and connections in Europe, although her articles would lag behind her actual travel. Crossing into Arabia and Persia, then sailing to India, Bly would be lost to the *World* for many days and eventually weeks during the final phase of her trip to Japan and across the Pacific. If all went well, either Bly or Bisland would return to New York City by late January; if Bisland beat Bly, Walker could hold March's press run a few days to benefit *Cosmopolitan.*

Cosmopolitan first told its readers about the Bisland versus Bly race in its January 1890 issue, six weeks into the event. The article referred only to the start of the race and Bisland's novice status as a traveler. "She has never before been abroad," Walker wrote. "It is, of course, understood that no important results are likely to be attained from such a trip, nor anything of scientific value demonstrated; but, under the sprightly pen of Miss Bisland, the incidents of the journey are likely to prove of a thoroughly entertaining character."[4]

Walker neglected to let readers know he wanted publicity most of all. He had owned *Cosmopolitan* for nearly a year by mid-November 1889. The magazine had grown impressively, adding thousands of new subscribers and some new advertisers. *Cosmopolitan* also had continued to lose money—$50,000 since Walker purchased it. Walker, though, instinctively reacted to the news about Bly's quest and seized the opportunity to get free ink in newspapers around the country, despite the expense of $1,500 attached to the ploy. What newspaper editor could resist conveying such drama to readers?[5]

Most could, and did. An initial flurry of newspaper articles focused on Bly. Subsequent to her departure and until her final rush east by train from California, Bly's travel elicited scant attention. Bisland barely received any notice at all. Editors at other newspapers were not about to give Pulitzer space for his latest stunt, and Walker's opportunism was too blatant to merit mention. The *New York Times* society editor deigned to report Bisland's journey ten days after departure, granting a mere paragraph in a column on page 11: "Society people are much interested in the westward trip around the world of Miss Elizabeth Bisland, who started last week to surpass the famous record of 'Phileas' Fogg. Miss Bisland, who is a New-Orleans girl of excellent social position, and who is exceedingly pretty, has won for herself a wide circle of friends for her plucky work in supporting herself since she came to New-York three years ago." Nary a reference to *Cosmopolitan*.[6]

Ten weeks passed, then a six-paragraph piece in the *New York Times* reported Bisland had sailed from England for New York. "The treatment of this lone and unprotected lady on board by passengers, officers, and crew was all that heart could desire," the newspaper stated, alluding to Bisland's extended ocean travel. Again, nothing about *Cosmopolitan*.[7]

Bisland and Bly endured bouts of intense seasickness, tropical heat, and continual discomfort. Of course, Bisland lost the race around the world. Bly completed her trip January 25, 1890—seventy-two days. Bisland arrived January 29. Bly, real name Elizabeth Cochrane, became a national celebrity and made a small fortune on a lecture tour and from a book. Bisland wrote a fine series of articles for *Cosmopolitan*, "A Flying Trip Around The World," that appeared in monthly issues from April through October 1890. The articles basically were travelogues: anecdotes about other travelers and experiences aboard ship; colorful descriptions of people in Hong Kong, Singapore, Egypt, and elsewhere; and vivid tales of storms at sea.[8]

Bisland gladly returned to her office desk to review books and write an occasional article until she quit *Cosmopolitan* the next year to marry.

Walker's Way

John Brisben Walker created a modern, affordable quality magazine. The editor-publisher emphasized timely articles and commentary in *Cosmopolitan* throughout his tenure from January 1889 to June 1905. Many articles were journalistic, meaning that the writers described conditions or events they had observed and for which they sometimes had interviewed participants or other pertinent people. *Cosmopolitan* charted new editorial territory for magazines. "He has introduced the newspaper ideas of timeliness and dignified sensationalism into periodical literature," *Journalist* magazine declared of Walker in April 1892. (Sensationalism was not in any sense pejorative. It meant *Cosmopolitan*'s editor-publisher presented informative articles rather than reflective essays, which *Atlantic Monthly* and *Century* preferred at the time.)[9]

Walker placed *Cosmopolitan* up against the likes of popular, prestigious, pricier *Century, Harper's,* and *Scribner's.* He could have avoided taking on the giants and stepped down a level to battle with *Leslie's,* and soon *Munsey's,* by providing a similar format of entertainment articles, useful travelogues, profiles of famous persons, and information on mundane current topics. Walker's pride and intellect ordained a different path. A national magazine was a lectern. *Cosmopolitan* would submit to its readers provocative ideas from thinkers across the ideological spectrum concerning the nation's social structure, its economic system, the obligations of wealthy Americans to everyone else, and the global role of the United States.

The decision to risk his personal fortune on *Cosmopolitan* was sudden, and Walker sold most of his Colorado property quickly to buy the magazine. "Impulsive" aptly described John Brisben Walker. Other descriptions fit, too: energetic, insubordinate, obstinate, adventurer, entrepreneur, Republican congressional candidate, Democratic-Populist activist, Catholic, Social Gospel advocate, progressive, pragmatist, futurist, moralist, naturalist, optimist.

Optimism was a religion unto itself for Walker. Never destitute, he had gotten rich once and lost it all at age twenty-seven. Now another personal fortune worth $620,000 was at stake. (The amount would equal almost $15 million in today's money.) His wife, six sons, and daughter would not starve if the money vanished, but financial failure had humiliated many families in nineteenth-century America.[10]

Walker was ever a practical man. *Cosmopolitan* would not be pretentious or too serious; to build readership, it would entertain and devote pages to mundane topics, too. But the magazine also would dare to propose solutions to contemporary problems: industrial violence, workplace hazards, racial relationships, public education, urban squalor. Walker was neither a conservative nor a liberal in the modern sense; he was a progressive. Walker envisioned an orderly, practical, and rational society. And because of Walker's insatiable curiosity about how things worked, the magazine would explain to its readers scientific and technological developments.

The *Cosmopolitan* for January 1889 was the first of 198 issues to proclaim at the bottom of the cover, "Edited By John Brisben Walker." A full-page promotional ad on the inside front cover listed an annual subscription price of $2.40 and promised color illustrations every month, plus more photographs. The forty-cent price increase meant Walker risked losing thousands of $2 subscribers who might not renew if they did not perceive his transformation of the magazine as an improvement. The initial response was strong, however, and *Cosmopolitan* raised its price at vendors to twenty-five cents in autumn 1889, while simultaneously pushing the subscription price to $3. The pricing strategy demonstrated the new editor-publisher's absolute faith that his magazine would appeal to middle-class readers.

One immediately tangible reward for readers was additional items to read. Walker boosted editorial material to a consistent 128 pages throughout his first three years, and an occasional 136 to 144 pages for issues packed with front- and back-section ads in December and January for Christmas. The enlarged magazine greatly inflated the printing budget, but higher revenue from subscriptions and single-copy sales would offset it. Of course, additional pages also required a bigger budget for articles, stories, and illustrations, but editorial material comprised a fixed cost and actually would lower the overall expense for each magazine copy for every 10,000 boost to the press run. It was a tremendous gamble. If canvassers did not continually sell enough subscriptions to build circulation month after month and if subscription renewals lessened, the gap between revenue and expenditures would widen.[11]

According to an introductory promotional ad from the new editor-publisher, *Cosmopolitan* "under its new administration" would focus "special attention to bright and timely subjects." Walker dropped the back-of-the book Live Questions in February and replaced it with Social Problems, a three- to four-page commentary on contemporary events written by Edward Everett Hale. The promotional ad stated that Hale's commentary would "agitate every earnest mind." The selection of Hale, a revered leader of the Unitarian Church and an esteemed intellectual, signaled Walker's intention to make *Cosmopolitan* a forum for serious discourse.[12]

During the first year, Walker would add Murat Halstead to write Review Of Current Events, a four-page section summarizing, and commenting on, international and national events. Halstead, a longtime newspaper editor in Cincinnati and Brooklyn, was an early advocate of popular election of United States senators.

The *Cosmopolitan* agenda immediately emphasized three items: humane treatment for working-class men and women, including better workplace conditions and the right to negotiate with employers; amelioration of racial relationships; and women's status in contemporary America. The first item was a bold choice for Walker because the American middle class generally did not sympathize with the working class, regarding it as vulgar and violent; on this item, *Cosmopolitan* advocated a safe and sanitary work environment, reasonable hours of work, and equitable pay for workers to ensure a democratic, stable society. The second agenda item pertained to the notion of racial hierarchy, which was accepted by many upper- and middle-class whites who generally disparaged blacks and Asians; on this item, *Cosmopolitan* rejected blatant racist policies, but favored a degree of racial separatism, not segregation. The final agenda item pertained to effects of industrialization and urbanization on families and women, which necessitated a different perspective on women's roles and rights; on this, *Cosmopolitan* was ambivalent.[13]

The rapid rise of industrial America had created unprecedented tension and hostility between employees and employers. Long hours, low pay, and hazardous conditions ignited protests and strikes. American workers, whether laborers or office employees, spent an average of fifty-eight hours on the job each week at the start of the 1890s. *Cosmopolitan* endorsed an eight-hour workday, six days a week. "To begin work at half past eight, to take an hour at dinner, to be free after half past five—that seems a reasonable day's work," an editor's column by Walker suggested. "If all men gave that many hours to useful production, the markets of this country would be supplied far beyond the capacity of consumption." At forty-eight hours a week, the schedule would reduce by ten hours the typical person's labor for a workweek that varied from five to six days, with Saturday sometimes a half-day schedule.[14]

(A few years later when *Cosmopolitan* was printed on its own presses Walker set an eight-hour workday for everyone: the men who operated presses and typesetters, the women who ran folders and binders, editors, secretaries, clerks, bookkeepers, and himself.)[15]

Halstead, too, urged an eight-hour workday in a Current Events column describing parades and speeches by labor activists on May Day in Chicago and cities in Europe. Halstead complimented labor activists for trying to persuade the public to support the cause of workingmen by staging May 1 events. "All civilized countries [have] expressed their conviction that the time had come when eight hours should constitute a day's work," his column stated. Mainstream newspapers and magazines of the era rarely were sympathetic to labor activists.[16]

Elizabeth Bisland, the intrepid traveler, journeyed into social commentary occasionally as book editor. Her review in June 1889 of a report by the Bureau of Labor Statistics noted the twelve-hour workday a Brooklyn mother and two daughters endured to sew coats and trousers. Their effort paid a total wage for the three of $16 a week. Bisland described a lace clipper whose wife and four children depended on his paycheck of $11.50 weekly. "A large portion of humanity spend their lives in unremitting toil to procure food to enable them to continue that toil, and the number who are obliged to exist upon an insufficient quantity is much larger than it should be," Bisland wrote.

Bisland acknowledged that industrial efficiency had created employment, lowered costs for clothing and food, provided regular income, and enabled women to work outside the home. Her proposal to help working-class families did not involve better pay. Bisland believed "co-operative housekeeping" was the solution. The establishment of dining halls to buy food in bulk, hire cooks and kitchen assistants to prepare common meals, and employ nutritionists to plan healthful diets was necessary. "[It] would be an admirable substitute for the hasty bread-and-tea meals prepared by tired working-women," Bisland stated.[17]

Walker contributed a lengthy article on the need for each tenement community to have a public bathhouse, cooperative kitchen, and common laundry. *Cosmopolitan* had asked architects to submit plans, offering $200 for the best design in each category; architectural blueprints accompanied the article. Walker explained that users of each facility were to pay nominal fees of pennies per visit to cover all costs after construction. To build these beneficial and essential facilities would be the duty of the nation's wealthy. "There are not a few fortunes in the country which might bear the cost of such an undertaking without appreciable inconvenience," Walker wrote.[18]

Hale urged employers to put all employees on weekly salary rather than hourly wage. The cyclical nature of construction work and of some factories and foundries caused periodic layoffs that made it impossible for families to support themselves at times. Hale thought a regular salary was feasible year-round because it would be based on a year's worth of hours, thereby accounting for workweeks of sixty hours during busy periods and workweeks of a few hours to none during slow periods. "The workingman who begins to receive a salary instead of receiving wages is, from that moment, in a new position," Hale asserted. "That is to say, a man who is paid by the year a perfectly regular stipend is better off than the man who is paid the same amount irregularly as the year goes by." Hale believed a salary imparted dignity, too: "Let 'labor' stand for the drudgery, which it denoted originally, and make the word 'work' stand for the triumph of mind over matter."[19]

Cosmopolitan informed readers about hazardous and unhealthy conditions for employees. Approximately 2,400 railroad employees died on the job each year during the 1890s. The death toll was unknown in steel, textiles, and other manufacturing sectors, but was probably in the thousands each year. For every death on the job, several workers were maimed or permanently disabled. Halstead angrily reacted to the collapse of a poorly built factory in Manhattan that had killed seventy men and women. "Civilization is a failure if there is not somewhere responsibility for a crime so distressing and so hideous," he wrote. "That structure was a death trap, and all who had responsibility for it were criminal." Halstead blamed corrupt municipal inspectors who took bribes from owners of unsafe workplaces. His column also reminded readers about endemic corruption in municipal government nationwide.[20]

An article commissioned by Walker for the magazine explained hazards associated with occupations for women. Teenage girls at soap processors wrapped each cake in paper immediately upon the cake's removal from a vat. "The caustic soda used in the manufacture first turns [the girls'] nails yellow, then eats away the ends of their fingers," the writer reported. Women who earned money making artificial flowers in their tenement apartments suffered long-term illnesses from arsenic in dye. The women developed "sores on the face and hands, swelling of the limbs, finally nausea and convulsions." Seamstresses worked from 5 a.m. to 7 p.m. five days a week for $6, less if they did not complete a dozen coats each day. Other women sewed dresses in their two-room hovels. "Here, amid filth and vermin inconceivable, they are made into robes of the latest style, returned to the factory to be draped, and then may be seen behind the plate-glass windows of up-town stores," the writer noted. The article ended with a plea, "Will you give up your bargain counter for the sake of your suffering, starving sisters?"[21]

Younger women who had completed school could avoid the horrid conditions in the tenements. Although only 6 percent of youths graduated high school at the end of the nineteenth century, girls outnumbered boys by two to one. Girls learned clerical and typing skills, which allowed them entry to office work. A *Cosmopolitan* article detailed the life of women clerks: sorting, filing, typing, collating; tedious work for nine hours a day, not including a half-hour lunch break. The pay was miserable, ranging from $4 to $6 a week, but it did not involve arsenic or corrosive chemicals. This sum afforded certain independence. "Marriage is good enough, of course, but it is regarded rather as a possible chance or accident than as a necessary means to an end," the writer concluded.[22]

The background to the magazine's attention to workplace conditions and treatment of the working class was an eruption of labor violence. Coal miners, railroad engineers and firemen, factory laborers, and foundry stokers had gone on strike numerous times since the mid-1880s. The governors of several states—including Illinois, Massachusetts, Nebraska, New Jersey, Ohio, and Pennsylvania—had deployed militia at the behest of owners to rout strikers and escort strikebreakers to resume work. At their peak, strikes involved one of every fourteen workers in the United States and disrupted the national economy. Other quality magazines, notably *Century,* deplored the violence while expressing anxiety about working-class unrest. *Century* hoped workers would be reasonable, and it endorsed deploying troops to suppress strikers. The magazine represented the interests of its affluent readers.[23]

Cosmopolitan expressed markedly different ideas. It defended workers who agitated for better pay and shorter hours. *Cosmopolitan* also condemned industrialists who used violence to suppress strikes. The worst year for violence was 1892, and the most dramatic episode was at Homestead, Pennsylvania. A dispute over severe wage reductions for laborers at steel plants owned by Andrew Carnegie led to a walkout. Managers hired Pinkerton Agency enforcers to secure the streets and plant entrances so strikebreakers could proceed. Laborers erected barricades and loaded their rifles and shotguns. A shootout killed sixteen men. The strike lasted from early July through November. The laborers lost. Their wages were cut 25 percent and their workday increased to twelve hours.

In *Cosmopolitan* of September 1892, an incensed Walker penned a six-page indictment of government collusion with industrialists. "In the strife for wealth the law-making power was found to be a useful auxiliary," Walker stated. "Judges were bought, senatorships were sold in the interests of railways and the great corporations." Homestead was the latest, most sinister example of government collusion. "Within the last ten years we find wealth—not contented with the advantages which the laws, confessedly in its favor, give it—hiring private armies to give force to edicts allotting to the laborer a lesser share of the product."[24]

Walker labeled Carnegie and other industrialists "rich Romans . . . surrounding themselves by hired bands of fighting bullies." Walker advised laborers to protect their interests against "our modern rich man [and] his gladiators." He proposed a radical strategy. Laborers should fight back. "There is nothing to prevent a body of American citizens from organizing themselves as a militia organization with proper arms and equipments," Walker suggested. "It might possibly be well for their interests to have a few thousands of their own men enrolled in this same militia."

What an astonishing idea—a militia of workers, each armed with a weapon. This radical proposal came not from a labor anarchist or militant, but from the editor-publisher of a magazine for the American middle class, which historians have identified as steadfastly unsympathetic to the working class. Perhaps written in a moment of anger upon learning of the Homestead tragedy, Walker risked alienating many subscribers. Or, possibly, Walker might have expressed their own outrage.[25]

Americans knew full well the economic power held by robber barons. The progressive movement would become a political force within several years, and already apparent were the concerns that middle-class adults felt about labor violence and their resentment toward the authoritarian arrogance of the industrialists. (In 1882, William H. Vanderbilt, the railroad magnate, had responded to a reporter's question about possible public reaction to elimination of a train route: "The public be damned!")

Walker's article warned about dire consequences if government continued to ally with industrialists against workers. Revolution was possible, he believed: "Any stray spark may produce disastrous results. The crucial hour of the Republic will have arrived." The *Cosmopolitan* editor-publisher, himself a wealthy man, advocated a peaceful solution to forestall the formation of laborer militias. "The well-known expedient of income tax" would curtail the "modern Romans" and their mercenary gladiators; if government taxed income at an incremental rate, the robber barons could not evade their obligation to finance a remedy for the ills they had inflicted upon society.[26]

Another curative was governmental ownership of basic services. "Take out of the control of private individuals the power to amass great fortunes at the expense of the public, through the management of functions like railway, express and telegraph, which are purely of a public character," Walker advocated. This extraordinary proposal to seize railroads owned by the Goulds, Harrimans, Stanfords, and Vanderbilts had no chance, but it was another startling idea—and perhaps was sensible to middle-class Americans, who were becoming aware they paid higher prices than necessary because of collusion among private cartels.

A final recommendation by Walker echoed a policy planned by former president Grover Cleveland to require federal arbitration of labor disputes for railroads and state arbitration for other industry. Congress had not acted on the policy. "Let it be a recognized principle that when men employ many laborers their business ceases to be purely a private affair, but concerns the state," Walker argued. "Disputes between proprietor and workmen must be submitted, not to the brute force of so many Pinkerton mercenaries, but to arbitration."[27]

The reaction by Walker to deaths at Homestead escalated strident rhetoric he had first voiced in March 1891. Asked to speak to faculty, priests, and students at Catholic University in Washington, D.C., Walker delivered an impassioned argument for church involvement in social reform. His oratory received a standing ovation, and copies of "The Church and Poverty" speech were circulated among Catholic educators. Perhaps encouraged by the ovation and subsequent congratulatory letters, Walker boldly adopted for *Cosmopolitan* the motto, "From Every Man According To His Ability: To Every One According To His Needs"; the motto appeared on every cover from June 1892 to June 1905. The motto was revised slightly in 1899 to state, "From Every Man According To His Ability: To Every Man According To His Needs." This closely resembled the credo of dialectical materialism attributed to Karl Marx, but the motto expressed on *Cosmopolitan*'s cover apparently came from Louis Blanc, a French socialist. Its placement on the cover by Walker expressed the Social Gospel ideology he embraced—that wealthy citizens should not be obsessed by materialism, but must be charitable to ensure everyone the basic necessities of life.[28]

The editor-publisher was keenly aware that articles written by him and others in *Cosmopolitan* and his speeches might antagonize subscribers. Walker explained his philosophy to *Cosmopolitan* readers. "The editor sometimes publishes an article or a series of articles, which he very well knows will lose him the kindly feeling of many subscribers and result in some pecuniary loss," Walker acknowledged. "But he must, nevertheless, follow the dictates of his best judgment." Ultimately, the editor-publisher trusted Americans to appreciate and tolerate candor. "The average citizen of the United States likes sincere utterance, even if it does not correspond with his own ideas," Walker wrote.[29]

On the next agenda item, racial relationships, *Cosmopolitan* dealt candidly with the gulf that separated blacks and whites. "It haunts the White House, and the Capitol from the corridors to the dome," Halstead, the columnist, wrote in April 1890. Months afterward, following incidents of racial violence north and south, Halstead reiterated the primacy of dealing with racial attitudes: "We may be sure, above all, the race question will vex us for centuries."[30]

The end of Reconstruction in 1877 had removed Republican administrators from southern states. Whites regained control of local and state governments. Intimidation and murder of blacks diminished their participation in the political system. Lynching became common. During the 1880s, an average of 80 black men were lynched each year; during the early 1890s, the average was 110. Violence against blacks was not considered a crime in southern states, and intimidation dissuaded blacks from seeking political office and from voting. To further exclude blacks from electoral participation, Mississippi legislators approved a literacy test and a subjectively graded general knowledge exam for voters, effectively barring most blacks from the polls. Other southern states would do the same.

Mississippi's law dismayed Halstead because it "makes a plaything of the venerated Constitution itself." The *Cosmopolitan* columnist refused to debate whether a state's right to determine suffrage for its citizens trumped the federal Constitution's Fifteenth Amendment guarantee of suffrage for male citizens regardless of "race, color, or previous condition of servitude." Halstead instead cleverly recommended immediate reapportionment of each state's representation in Congress based on the percentage of its citizenry denied suffrage. "[This] would cost the Southern States forty members of Congress and electoral votes, and these would be restored as the colored citizens were finally in fact enfranchised," he explained. "The States that would, for the sake of discriminating against the blacks, cut down their apportionment, could do it." Rather than isolate blacks, Halstead appealed to idealism: "It was time to try the statesmanship of kindness, and strengthen the foundations of the republic by the broad acceptance of the doctrine of inherent rights of men, irrespective of race."[31]

Another column supported the idea of racial separation. Some newspapers and public speakers had advocated a separate state for blacks. "There was an interest in the proposed Black State," Halstead wrote, "and it was considered the Indian Territory could be made serviceable in opening an opportunity for the blacks, who would get along comfortably with the Indians, and enjoy the exercise of political functions." Congress had discussed a plan to encourage voluntary emigration of blacks from southern states to the Indian Territory, which would become Oklahoma in 1907. Incentives for black emigration included land grants and federal suffrage. Halstead predicted the result of a separate black state, "The appearance of a new star in the Union, faithful entirely to the history and traditions of the nation."[32]

Hale, the other eminent thinker for *Cosmopolitan,* also believed relocation of blacks from southern states was a remedy to the sharecropper system that had evolved after the Civil War. "We pretend to have given the colored people freedom," Hale wrote. "We have not given them freedom until they may select their place of work and their employer. The simplest way to bring this about is to arrange organized emigration so that a few of them may relieve the congestion, and may establish themselves on soil yet unbroken."[33]

Less lofty words in *Cosmopolitan* about the "race question" represented ideas permeating white society. Henry Watterson, editor of the *Louisville Courier-Journal* and reputedly a racial moderate, contributed a six-page article lecturing northerners on their misguided perceptions of southern blacks. "There is as little likeness between the negro field-hand of Mississippi and the colored domestic of Massachusetts as there is between the Boston dude and the New York bruiser," Watterson wrote. "The blacks of the Gulf States form a dense mass of ignorance and squalor; at rest, kindly, indolent and passive; under excitement, fierce, blind and cruel. Under present conditions, they can only be politically arrayed to bad ends."

Denial of suffrage on the basis of literacy, knowledge, or property ownership was justifiable, according to Watterson. "It is a question of the existence of responsible government and civilized society on the one hand; ruin, anarchy and chaos on the other," he argued. "There is no help for it except through the good offices of time and repose." Watterson reminded readers that he had personally "labored unceasingly for the education and elevation of blacks of the South" and was regarded as "something of a crank on the benevolent and sentimental side of the question." Northerners must recognize the peculiar regional perspective. "The benevolent side of it is the Southern side of it," Watterson concluded.[34]

Another question confronting the American public as the nineteenth century gave way to the twentieth was the status of women. *Cosmopolitan* was not a women's magazine, but its readership included middle-class women who presumably were interested in and affected by contemporary controversies concerning education, economic rights, and responsibilities of their gender. The magazine, which had denounced loss of suffrage for southern blacks, paid no heed to national and state campaigns for women's suffrage. By the 1890s, twenty-two states allowed women to vote, although a patchwork of restrictions denied full suffrage for local and state ballots in most of those. *Cosmopolitan* instead concentrated its articles on career opportunities, household management, and reverence for motherhood.

Opportunities awaited women in a variety of careers, according to *Cosmopolitan* articles: at the lower end—domestic service (cooks, household servants, maids) and shop girls (retail clerks); in the middle—bookkeepers, office clerks, and teachers; at the higher end—laboratory assistants, the professions (lawyers, physicians), and scientists. The magazine did not advise women to strive for the top. Its middle-class readership perhaps knew of a rare woman who practiced law or medicine, but such a choice was not realistic. *Cosmopolitan* treated the lower-end jobs as undesirable for its women readers. Most articles pertained to attainable, satisfactory occupations squarely in the middle of the career spectrum.[35]

A cautionary article, "What Society Offers Mary Grew," took its title from a *Cosmopolitan* fiction piece published early in 1893. The story told the sad fate of a young working-class woman whose lack of education and skills consigned her to cycles of unemployment when factory jobs were scarce and interludes of domestic service for irresponsible, selfish upper-class wives. The message of the story was that working-class women were always at the mercy of others because they had nothing to enhance their prospects. The article warned middle-class women that their young daughters faced the same fate should they not complete school or acquire a useful skill.

An uneducated, unskilled young woman had no future. "There was no prospect whatever that her pay would be increased," the writer explained. "Any number of girls were ready to take her place at the same figure, girls living at home, and requiring a salary only for dress and pocket money." Prostitution or life as a mistress awaited girls who quit dead-end jobs only to learn no respectable work was available. It was an "an old story, often repeated, that the insufficient pay of shop girls drove them often into lives of shame." Domestic service entailed "long hours and night and Sunday duties in the solitude of the distinctly menial position." Maids and servant girls held jobs "deemed a barrier to social advancement and desirable marriage."[36]

Cosmopolitan noted that clerks earned wages comparable to shop girls, but pay raises and promotion to supervisory positions were possible for dependable, smart women. "Women Clerks In New York" mentioned an office supervisor who made $40 a week. What's more, clerks retained their femininity. "There is nothing in clerical training that detracts from the finest womanly qualities, and men have outgrown their admiration for feminine helplessness and have come to look upon independence as something worth having," the writer commented. Women should attend business school to learn clerical, secretarial, or general office skills. Care must be taken, though, before accepting a job offer. The writer provided a for-instance: "Many clerks complain of the enormous amount of work they are compelled to perform in law offices, to say nothing of the dry and uninteresting character of the labor itself."[37]

Teachers eked out a living, making an average $320 a year during the 1890s. Two-thirds of the nation's 380,000 elementary and secondary schoolteachers were women. Low pay and political patronage produced a lamentable situation in most classrooms where incompetent, unqualified men and women taught children. Educational reform, including teacher certification, advanced at glacial speed for decades. *Cosmopolitan* featured articles on teachers' colleges.[38]

"No movement in modern times is so full of promise for the betterment of our city populations," stated an article extolling a teachers' college in New York

City. Students learned techniques for science lab, strategies for grammar and math lessons, and methods for controlling inattentive or disruptive youngsters. Admission to the two-year program was competitive. "A high standard for entrance is maintained," the article noted.[39]

A teachers' college in Philadelphia for women required students to complete coursework in biology, botany, chemistry, and zoology for secondary-school certification. A *Cosmopolitan* article described scientific education as one component of a multifaceted program: "First, the laboratories where student teachers gain first-hand knowledge . . . second, the school for the professional training of teachers in the history and theory of education, and finally, the school for observation and practice." Classroom lectures included lantern-slide presentations for visual material.[40]

Cosmopolitan and other middle-class magazines of the era exposed women readers to opportunities they otherwise might not have considered. Education of women was itself a fairly recent development in the United States. Educating women to teach science led to the next level, educating women to be scientists. Women worked in college research labs and assisted astronomers.[41]

Coeducation was the norm at many campuses of public institutions. *Cosmopolitan* informed its middle-class readership about the life of co-eds at a large public university. A lengthy, nicely descriptive article on women students at the University of Michigan, written by a co-ed and accompanied by photographs, including one with three women students in academic gowns, affirmed that enrollment of women was routine at the Ann Arbor campus. "No one ever looks upon the girls now with curiosity, as they did in the early days," the writer declared. "No one ever discusses their rights in the University, for long ago they were firmly established."

Students appreciated the campus atmosphere. "There is nothing which pleases a student more than to meet on the walk a professor who can call him by name, with a pleasant word of greeting," the writer noted. The university president "never forgets to give us all a nod and pleasant recognition whenever he may meet us."[42]

Publication of the article indicated that Walker considered college education for women attainable among the magazine's readers. By the 1890s, one of every nine high school graduates attended college or university, a very small pool of students considering the few who earned a high school diploma. Money was not a serious problem for the middle class. Tuition, fees, room and board, and associated expenses for a year at most private or public colleges and universities varied from $140 to $180. Although amounting to 10 percent or more of a middle-class family's annual income, it was comparable to today's cost ratio. Relevance was more germane. Very few occupations required a college degree.[43]

The magazine portrayed successful women in academe. "Women As College Presidents" described the administrative and academic responsibilities of the presidents of Barnard, Mount Holyoke, and Radcliffe. "The duty of the modern college president is to do things, not to teach others to do," the article asserted. "To create harmony, therefore, and avoid conflict is one of the first uses for the college president's applied higher education." Each of the women presidents was personable and approachable, contrary to the "cold and aloof" professorial style that "never won for the president of a college one moment's genuine respect."[44]

Not all women and certainly not most men welcomed a change in women's status. An overwhelming majority of state referenda to expand women's suffrage were rejected during the nineteenth century's final decades. Male voters preferred the status quo. *Cosmopolitan* presented both sides of the gender argument: the traditional point of view from a notable professor whose rationale spanned two articles, and the progressive viewpoint from a notable poet-thinker. The series of articles carried the main title, "For Maids And Mothers."[45]

Harry Thurston Peck, an intellectual, scholar, and essayist known for critiques of society, argued for the status quo in "The Overtaught Woman." Peck sarcastically referred to the common caricature of male opponents of women's suffrage and economic independence as portraying "Man the Tyrant grinding his hobnailed shoes into the tender neck of innocent womanhood." This description favored by activists at public lectures invariably caused "the women who were gathered to listen . . . to feel themselves writhing horribly in a bondage of unspeakable atrocity."

Peck did not oppose the entry of women to all careers. "Every one recognizes that it is entirely reasonable to give them the means of fitting themselves for primary and secondary teaching," he granted. "Though perhaps even the wisdom of this might be seriously questioned." Other employment that required higher education or managerial skills was not suitable for women, Peck argued, because of their gender's impatience, inattentiveness, and sensitivity to criticism. "When woman enters the field of specialization, she brings with her all the intensity, the overwrought enthusiasm and the mental myopia of her sex," he wrote. "These truths are formulaic. They are axioms. They underlie the whole great question that is raised to-day regarding woman's evolution as a social and economic factor in our life."[46]

A second article from Peck, "The Woman Of To-Day And Of To-Morrow," blamed activists for dismissing the benefits to women from traditional dependence on men. "Man in these days seems to be very largely ignored by the fluent women who have set before themselves the simple task of revolutionizing human society by means of several courses of popular lectures, a book or two of essays, and a volume of vehement verse," Peck asserted. Men did hard physical labor, men managed businesses and industries, men understood the natural world. "These considerations make it obvious why man should set his face like flint against this new crusade for woman's economic independence," Peck concluded.[47]

Charlotte Perkins Stetson, a proponent of gender equality, wrote a rebuttal commissioned by Walker. Stetson, known for incisive essays about society's imperative need to let women choose whatever careers their qualifications warranted, had written an influential book, *Women and Economics.* She told *Cosmopolitan* readers, "Woman's position in a progressive civilization is a changing one, and shows a wider range, a greater freedom, a fuller power, as civilization advances."

Stetson perceived women as instinctive reformers who would improve workplace conditions and foster humane policies in business and industry. Men resisted reform because it threatened their authority. "It was essential at the beginning of our racial progress that man, the fighter, be the most active factor in the crude social processes of the time," Stetson explained. "The dominant need of this age is a better ordering of our industrial processes, and it is this necessity which calls for wider activity of woman." Women sought opportunity. "It is not a question of personal rebellion on the part of women," Stetson wrote. "Each woman should earn her living by the interchange of some form of productive labor with the labor of others; that she should be in direct economic relation with society—a producer as well as a consumer."[48]

Walker instigated the interchange between Peck and Stetson, who remarried and whom scholars now refer to as Charlotte Perkins Gilman. A *Cosmopolitan* trademark was the presentation of divergent viewpoints in successive editions. Walker and his associate editors, usually five men (Bisland was an exception), convened each Saturday afternoon to discuss topics for the magazine. *Cosmopolitan* articles were commissioned from experts, public figures, and scholars at least two months prior to publication.[49]

Walker may have expressed radical opinions about some topics, but he was a traditionalist on the American family. *Cosmopolitan* recognized the importance of family care and household management. Occasional articles informed women about the advisability of planning a budget and scheduling tasks. Middle-class women, if they had held jobs when their education was done, usually became full-time homemakers upon marriage; only one of every seven married women worked outside the home. The magazine believed some women were not ready for the responsibility of homemaker. Walker himself wrote "Motherhood As A Profession" to praise homemakers and to recommend formal schooling. "There will be training and preparation for the one who is to assume the care of children," he predicted. "There will be careful study into all the physiological and psychological facts connected with motherhood. In other words, motherhood will come to be looked upon as truly a profession."[50]

A series provided specific budgets for food, clothing, household items, reading material, and travel. Each of the four articles was written by a woman who had responded to prize offers of $150 to $200 from *Cosmopolitan* upon publication. The magazine sought model budgets for three separate annual income categories—$800 minimum, $1,600 to $2,500, and $4,000—to guide a five-person family: husband, wife, three children. The fact that the lowest category approximated the top income for a working-class household indicated the magazine's readership profile was solidly middle class.

The first article advised husbands to confer with wives about budgeting: "A woman whose husband does not take her into his confidence financially, but doles out five- or ten-dollar bills when she teases him for them, is worse than hampered. She is degraded." Also important was agreeing on what to pay the household help. "It is the worst sort of mistake to economize on a servant's wage," the article warned, and recommended payment of $12 to $15 a month. The writer told wives not to let husbands indulge themselves if money was tight: "A man unable to provide more than one thousand six hundred dollars a year with which to support [a family] ought not to permit himself any such luxuries as tobacco and liquors."[51]

Another article in the series suggested that wives insist their husbands buy life insurance. "The amount of money that is appropriated from the yearly income for insurance depends somewhat upon the temperament of the man," the article stated. "Some men will carry five thousand dollars, but most are contented with one or two thousand dollars."[52]

The last article listed items a household must have: one refrigerator for meat and vegetables; an ice chest for butter, milk, and cream; and a pantry for storage of bulk food in bags and barrels, such as cheese, chocolate, coffee, oatmeal, olives, and rice. A full page of meal menus offered nutritious fare. (Sample meal for maximum nutrition: roast lamb, spinach, potatoes, milk.)[53]

While it was not a women's magazine, *Cosmopolitan* regularly attended to topics of special interest to them. Articles about careers, education, and family life informed all its readers about relevant contemporary topics. Some articles advocated progressive treatment of women—education, workplace safety, economic opportunity. Other articles upheld the rigid gender code of conduct and roles that dominated. In that regard, *Cosmopolitan* differed from *Ladies' Home Journal,* which rejected any changes in women's status. Edward Bok, the editor of *Ladies' Home Journal,* invoked religion and moral duty to endorse steadfast adherence to traditional roles for women as wives, mothers, and homemakers.[54]

Walker's impetuous decision to send a young woman associate editor on a race around the world against a young woman reporter was more symbolic than

intended. Nellie Bly and Elizabeth Bisland were not models of genteel womanhood. They were young, educated, successful career women, and they were perfectly capable of accomplishing an arduous task that would have challenged a
man. Significantly, too, their employers understood their value to their respective
publications.

Cosmopolitan's middle-class subscribers appreciated the candid, helpful, perceptive, and occasionally provocative articles. Subscription renewals were high
and new subscriptions poured in, undoubtedly ascribed to word-of-mouth
praise by readers to neighbors, co-workers, and family. Walker maintained a
consistently intense circulation campaign, which further boosted circulation.
On the fourth anniversary of editor-publisher Walker's name on its cover, *Cosmopolitan* for January 1893 distributed 150,000 copies—a sevenfold increase.
Cosmopolitan had attained the top tier of quality magazines, ranking third in
size behind *Century* (190,000) and *Harper's* (175,000), and ahead of *Scribner's*
(133,000).[55]

Fortune, Misfortune, Recovery

The life of John Brisben Walker was not a Horatio Alger rags-to-riches fable.
Rather, his life was a recurring tale of cashmere-to-denim. He was born in a
country manor house fifteen miles south of Pittsburgh, Pennsylvania, in September 1847. His father owned a sizable tract of land near the Monongahela
River and had prospered selling lumber and building cargo boats. The Walkers
were socially prominent and politically connected. "His father was a rich man
and not without influence," a magazine profile later stated. Brisben Walker attended Gonzaga Classical School in Washington, D.C., and was a student for
one year at Georgetown College, a Jesuit campus there. (It is now Georgetown
University.) His father was a former army major, and the son became a cadet in
1865 at the U.S. Military Academy in West Point, New York.[56]

Biographic information supplied by Walker to various sources later in life,
including newspapers and annual publications similar to *Who's Who*, stated he
"resigned" from the academy. True enough, although his resignation was invol-
untary. Walker did not follow the rules.

His first infraction occurred March 1866, his freshman or plebe year. Walker apparently had tired of his three-hour evening stint as a sentinel outside
cadet barracks and went inside prior to replacement by another sentinel, who
notified superiors. A court-martial file recorded a "deserting post" judgment
against Walker and a ten-week suspension from the academy. He restarted his
freshman year the next summer, completed it, and was halfway through his second year when he stretched a seven-day New Year's holiday leave to seventeen
days. Walker again faced court-martial and was guilty of absent-without-leave,

a serious offense for a future army officer. A procedural error voided the conviction, however. A subsequent War Department review stipulated that Walker's military dossier must contain an "admonition that an officer cannot be relied upon for efficient service who allows himself to be persuaded that absence, without leave, from his post is an excusable offense." Walker resigned from the army in June 1868 to go to China.[57]

From this point forward, Walker's formal biography mixed fact and exaggeration, if not outright fiction. He accompanied a State Department diplomat, J. Ross Browne, to China. Browne had served during the Polk presidency as an assistant to U.S. Secretary of the Treasury Robert J. Walker, a distant kin, and was on his way to Peking shortly after cadet Walker reentered civilian life. Walker told interviewers years later that he served with the Chinese army as an officer, advising local commanders on reorganization of infantry units. Browne and Walker returned to the United States in summer 1870. No mention of young Walker's military service in China appeared in *Foreign Relations of the United States* correspondence for 1868 through 1870, although Browne communicated regularly with the State Department.[58]

Walker settled in Charleston, West Virginia. He married, bought land on the western edge of the city, perhaps with financial assistance from his family, and began to make his first fortune. Using basic engineering skills learned at the military academy, Walker supervised clearing of residential sites and grading of streets for development. He reinvested profits to buy more land and used the property as collateral for bank loans to acquire large tracts near the city. In less than three years Walker had accumulated two thousand acres. He also started a small foundry to process ore.

Prosperous and prominent at age twenty-five, Walker received the Republican nomination for U.S. House of Representatives in November 1872; he was defeated. Two years later, the aftermath of a nationwide financial "panic" rippled through financial, manufacturing, and real estate sectors. Walker, heavily in debt, forfeited property valued at $500,000 and the foundry closed.

Walker studied the effects of the 1873 economic depression. He formulated a plan to establish a national bank clearinghouse that would track loan activity and also note the volume of industrial and retail transactions to provide a statistical basis for measuring the economy. Walker wrote a series of articles explaining all this. He evidently could write well. The *Cincinnati Commercial* published his series in 1875. Murat Halstead, then editor of the Cincinnati newspaper, recommended Walker to the *Pittsburgh Telegraph*, which needed an editor.

A brief career in newspapers ensued, although its duration and details are sketchy. A self-written entry by Walker published by a national biographical encyclopedia in 1899 referred only to "three years" as editor of the *Washington*

Chronicle after the Pittsburgh job. Other publications, including the *Rowell Directory* for 1887, cited his employment as editor of *Nation* magazine and editor of a weekly national edition of *Inter-Ocean,* a Chicago newspaper affiliated with Republicans. Walker never clarified facts concerning his newspaper days.

Walker quit newspapers in 1879 to become an aide to Browne, the former diplomat, who was director of a land survey and assessment of mineral resources in the Rocky Mountain region for the U.S. Department of the Interior. Several months into the survey Walker began buying sizable parcels of land near Denver, Colorado. He never explained where he got the money. Considering that he was bankrupt five years earlier and that newspapers paid editors a generous but not substantial salary, Walker probably had family assistance initially.

Alfalfa became the source of Walker's second fortune. Water was a scarce commodity on the semi-arid plateau east of the Rocky Mountains. Irrigation systems dependent on reservoirs were a necessity in some areas. Applying his engineering skills, Walker supervised construction of a hillside irrigation system consisting of a private reservoir, a feeder canal, sluice gates, ditches, and drainpipes. The system relied on gravity and a deep-plowing technique favored by local farmers to aid absorption of scarce rainfall into soil: first, a measured volume of reservoir water flowed through the canal; then, gates opened to divert the flow to a network of ditches lined with drainpipes; then, water trickled from the drainpipes down to the alfalfa fields, where it seeped into soil loosened by deep plowing. Walker quickly expanded his tract to 1,600 acres, named it Berkeley Farm, hired a field crew to work the fields, and harvested three thousand tons of alfalfa annually.

Walker described the wondrous qualities of alfalfa in a May 1890 issue of *Cosmopolitan:* "The alfalfa plant, which sends down its roots fifteen or twenty feet, was well adapted to this soil. Three crops from the same soil from the latter part of May until the end of November—a clover admirably adapted for fattening cattle—meant in itself a vast source of wealth."[59]

Revenue from bountiful harvests allowed Walker to diversify. He purchased dozens of acres of bottomland along the South Platte River adjacent to downtown Denver. Riverfront acreage was cheap because the South Platte periodically overflowed from mountain snowmelt and heavy rain. Walker, though, again used basic engineering knowledge for land reclamation. He bought ash and other residue from furnaces and foundries in Denver, mixed the substances with pulverized rock and soil for landfill, and constructed a mile-long berm on the southern riverbank to shield his property from floods.[60]

At six feet tall, when the average height for a male was five feet-six, and with an athletic physique, Walker was a man people noticed. "He would not have lacked for backers in any prize ring," a journalist remarked. His courage impressed others, too. An incident in Denver became well known. Reclamation of bottom-land was hazardous to workers and the horses that hauled wagons piled with ash, earth, and crushed rock; the landfill itself was unstable until a section of berm had topped off, allowing the density and weight of the manmade barrier to hold back the river. But a flash flood one day washed away freshly dumped landfill, and swept a horse into the muck. Several workers stood on the riverbank watching the horse thrash and slowly sink deeper. Walker heard the horse's frightful whinny and ran to the scene. He told the men to get the horse out; they refused because the floodwater had not fully receded and the muck was too dangerous. Walker grabbed a wood plank and then another, laid them end-to-end atop the muck until he could reach the horse; he grabbed its bridle and pulled the horse inches at a time toward the riverbank. Finally, with Walker pulling it, the horse gained a foothold on the riverbank and emerged from the muck. Walker then turned to the workers and fired them.[61]

Walker finished the reclamation and platted 550 new city lots by 1888. Some lots he sold to individuals, but most he sold for a railroad yard, which lay north of Union Station depot. Years later, newspapers and other publications reported Walker received a million dollars for the lots, a sum he volunteered to interviewers. An examination of property deeds for 1888–1889 filed for Arapahoe County determined that Walker sold the lots for $290,000.[62]

Denver was a boom-or-bust city the latter half of the nineteenth century. Settlers, miners, and speculators had flocked to Denver during the 1859 gold rush to nearby mountains; several years later, the city lost half its population when miners and speculators moved on. The city boomed again during the 1880s because of silver mines. The federal government minted silver coins freely to satisfy demands from farmers and rural communities for currency, a monetary policy derided by eastern bankers and gentry who preferred gold-backed dollars.

The boom years of the 1880s dramatically increased land value, and Walker sold Berkeley Farm to real estate developers from Kansas City and St. Louis. Walker subsequently told interviewers the sale of Berkeley Farm brought $362,000. Property deeds filed for Arapahoe County indicated a lower amount—$330,000 for property sold from early 1887 to late 1888. It is possible Walker sold farm equipment and property improvements, such as roads and bridges, separately.[63]

A devout Catholic, Walker excluded from the sale of Berkeley Farm a fifty-acre parcel as a gift to Sacred Heart College for a campus. (The college became Regis University, which continues to occupy the site.)[64]

At age forty-one, Walker was wealthy again—and fortunate. Whatever the actual amount of money he received for all his property, Walker could not have timed his exit better. Congress stopped coinage of silver in 1893, and Denver went bust again.

The reason John Brisben Walker risked his second fortune on a national magazine rather than another kind of business cannot be determined. Plenty of opportunity for a venture in any endeavor existed in the United States at the close of the Gilded Age. Except for a brief stint with newspapers, Walker had spent his adult life as a real estate developer, innovative farmer, and land speculator. But if the excitement, notion of influence, and variety of responsibilities associated with a newspaper editor's job had captivated him somehow, Walker had enough money to buy or start a newspaper in any major city. Instead, he chose a national magazine. Walker made *Cosmopolitan* a pioneer in magazine journalism.

Literary Legends

Listening that day in March 1891 to the impassioned speech by John Brisben Walker at Catholic University was William Dean Howells. "The Church and Poverty" speaker exhorted priests and laity to help the poor by training them for skilled jobs and by beseeching affluent Americans to allocate a portion of their wealth to replace tenement squalor with livable, sanitary cooperative settlements. Howells stood and applauded with the entire audience.

Then he wrote a letter to Walker to express his admiration. Walker was flattered. Howells was an eminent author, book reviewer, editor, and advocate of literary realism. His recent novels, *The Rise of Silas Lapham* and *A Hazard of New Fortune,* had won acclaim and popularity. Previously, Howells at age thirty-three was chosen editor of *Atlantic Monthly,* a job that lasted for a decade; he then edited *Harper's* for several years. Now age fifty-four, Howells spent his time on the lecture tour and writing.

More letters followed. Near the end of 1891, Walker asked Howells to be *Cosmopolitan* literary editor, in effect coeditor with "absolute control in literature." Howells accepted. The job paid $15,000 a year. The editors of *Century* and *Harper's* each earned $10,000.[65]

The February 1892 frontispiece of *Cosmopolitan* displayed an oval photograph of Howells. The frontispiece always featured the most outstanding illustration in the magazine; for Walker to place the photo of Howells there signified his fame and stature. The caption read: "On March the first, Mr. Howells will take editorial control of the Cosmopolitan Magazine conjointly with the present editor." *Cosmopolitan* had its own literary legend.[66]

Generous salary aside, hiring Howells marked quite a departure for *Cosmopolitan*'s editorial format. Fiction was not the magazine's strength. From the earliest months, Walker had decided on a monthly format of eight to ten articles with numerous photographs, two or three stories, three poems, four full-page illustrations, and three sections of three to four pages each—Current Events, Social Problems, and In The Library, which was discontinued in 1891.

An adventurer and entrepreneur, John Brisben Walker sold a prosperous alfalfa farm in Colorado and numerous riverfront lots in Denver to buy *Cosmopolitan* late in 1888. Walker, an intelligent and energetic editor-publisher, transformed *Cosmopolitan*'s editorial format to focus on timely national and international events, developments in science and technology, and commentary on strife at factories and foundries, racial relationships, and America's global role. *Cosmopolitan,* January 1893; source: Morgan Library, Colorado State University.

(Opposite, top) Elizabeth Bisland, book editor of *Cosmopolitan,* was sent on an impromptu around-the-world journey by John Brisben Walker, who hoped she would complete the travel by boat, train, and wagon before Nellie Bly did. Bly, a reporter for Joseph Pulitzer's *New York World,* had begun her journey several hours prior to Bisland, who had no idea what Walker had planned. *Cosmopolitan,* January 1890; source: Morgan Library, Colorado State University.

(Bottom right) Mutual admiration and respect persuaded William Dean Howells to accept the invitation of John Brisben Walker to become "co-editor" of *Cosmopolitan* during early 1892. The arrangement lasted two months. *Cosmopolitan,* February 1892; source: Morgan Library, Colorado State University.

WM. DEAN HOWELLS.   (*By kind permission of Mr. G. C. Cox.*)

On March the first, Mr. Howells will take editorial control of the Cosmopolitan Magazine conjointly with the present editor.

Other sections regarding science, art, and literature would come and go. *Cosmopolitan* gave its readers a standard 128 pages of editorial material and usually allocated 32 pages for fiction and poetry. Walker stopped publishing stories altogether in six issues from late 1889 through early 1890, instead featuring a novella of forty to forty-four pages in each issue. That tactic ended soon enough, and a return to the two- or three-story quota subsequently prevailed.

Walker enjoyed literature. He belonged to the Shakespeare Society of New York and the Aldine Club, a literary organization that funded public exhibitions of art and readings by authors. However, he preferred reality to fiction in his magazine.[67]

Cosmopolitan for several years during the 1890s ran a monthly column on developments in science and technology. Walker believed in the promise of scientific progress. Source: Morgan Library, Colorado State University.

H. G. Wells's perennially popular science fiction novel *War of the Worlds* first appeared in the United States in *Cosmopolitan* as a serial during 1897. Source: Morgan Library, Colorado State University.

Although willing to risk offending *Cosmopolitan* readers with articles on controversial topics, John Brisben Walker decided *The Awakening* by Count Leo Tolstoy was too risqué and stopped its serialization during summer 1899. Tolstoy, left, is with Maxim Gorky, another author whose work appeared in *Cosmopolitan*. John Brisben Walker notified *Cosmopolitan* readers that Tolstoy's novel would not continue because of "undesirable" text. Photograph from *Cosmopolitan*, January 1903; source: Morgan Library, Colorado State University.

Howells started at *Cosmopolitan* early in March to prepare the May 1892 issue. He shared a large, airy office with other editors in the *Cosmopolitan* suite on the fourth floor of the Madison Square Bank Building, a triangular structure at the intersection of Broadway, Fifth Avenue, and Twenty-fifth Street. Howells contacted literary friends to submit stories and asked the executor of James Russell Lowell's estate for permission to publish poems. (Lowell was editor of *Atlantic Monthly* when he selected a poem by young Howells for publication in 1860.) Howells bought stories from Hamlin Garland, Thomas Janvier, Frank Stockton, and others; he also wrote a story. His first *Cosmopolitan* in May carried five stories, a Lowell poem, a frontispiece of Lowell, and five other poems—a total of forty-two pages. The June issue ran three stories and four poems, a total of twenty-six pages. July offered readers two stories and three poems, a mere eighteen pages. Where was the literary emphasis?[68]

Howells had quit.

Walker had given Howells freedom to pack the May issue with stories and poems, but Howells quickly learned that John Brisben Walker was the only editor. Howells edited stories and poems, Walker edited again. Howells chose stories and poems for publication, Walker reviewed the choices and accepted most, not all. The literary legend was not accustomed to supervision. Also, after the May issue Walker tightened space for fiction. Howells was altering the format. *Cosmopolitan* had grown tremendously adhering to Walker's format. It was a general magazine, not a literary magazine. Howells quit in early May, after the June issue had gone to press and only two months since becoming coeditor.[69]

Upon his departure, a humorous tidbit of undeterminable veracity made the rounds. "Mr. Howells hated the routine and wanted to get back to authorship," the *Journalist* reported. According to office gossip still heard several years afterward, Howells could not adjust to the work schedule. Walker insisted that everyone begin their eight-hour workday promptly at eight o'clock. Howells was a late-night person who rarely awoke by eight o'clock, much less started work, and many years of being an editor and an author had accustomed him to flexible hours. Howells was miserable, according to gossip, and the hours may have been a factor in his dissatisfaction.[70]

Their separation was amicable. Walker agreed to pay Howells $425 for each story chosen for publication. Howells wrote seventeen stories in the next two years. Because both men viewed Christian socialism as an alternative to the capitalism of robber barons, their kindred philosophy resulted in memorable serials by Howells, "A Traveller From Altruria" and "Letters From An Altrurian Traveller"; both ran consecutively from November 1892 through March 1894.[71]

The Altrurian fables recorded the reactions of a visitor to the United States from an isolated island nation where socialist principles governed life. Homos, the visitor, was eager to see America because Altrurians had heard it was a democracy dedicated to economic and social justice. Homos observed instead a hierarchy of classes based on wealth. He also learned that owners of business and industry regarded workers as mere instruments for personal riches. A stay in a rural community restored his optimism about America when he saw farmers and their neighbors helping one another and sharing. Disappointed by American city society and the plutocracy, Homos sailed home.[72]

Howells walked away from *Cosmopolitan* after a brief stay, but his association helped persuade Mark Twain of the magazine's commitment to literary quality. The two authors were longtime friends. *Century* and *Harper's* were Twain favorites for publication of his short stories, humor essays, and travelogues, although a letter to his agent candidly mentioned he did not "have any business to object to the Cosmopolitan if they pay as good rates." If the money was equal, however, Twain preferred stature. When the author received an offer of $10,000 from *Cosmopolitan* for a dozen articles about his travels in Australia and a similar offer from *Century,* Twain accepted the latter.[73]

Twain, though, always was grateful to the *Cosmopolitan* editor-publisher, who paid the literary legend top dollar, ranging from $400 to $600 per item. The magazine presented five stories from Twain during Walker's tenure. Twain had instructed his agent to accept whatever fee Walker or Richard Watson Gilder, *Century* editor, offered him. "I make no prices with Walker or Gilder—I can trust them," Twain told his agent. Walker, of course, admired Twain, and the editor-publisher sent the author a surprise bonus for a story when Twain was bankrupt. The gesture impressed Twain, who informed his agent about his delight upon opening the mail that had delivered a "letter from John Brisben Walker enclosing $200 additional pay for the article . . . this is the second time he has done such a thing." Twain also thanked Walker for the generosity. "By gracious but you have a talent for making a man feel proud and good," Twain wrote to the editor-publisher. "I like to work for you; when you don't approve an article you say so, recognizing that I am not a child and can stand it; and when you approve an article I don't have to dicker with you as if I raised peanuts and you kept a stand; I know I shall get every penny the article is worth." He signed the letter S. L. Clemens.[74]

Another temporary benefit to *Cosmopolitan* from coeditor Howells was the presence of a new contributor, Theodore Roosevelt. The young New York politician already had served three terms in the state legislature, had run and lost a campaign for mayor of New York, and was a member of a federal government commission supervising merit-based civil service employment. Howells regarded young Roosevelt as a fine public official. TR wrote "The Merit System In Government Appointments" for Howells's debut issue and contributed two more articles the next few years. TR's first article informed readers about the success of civil service employment for the federal government, which had eliminated the patronage system except for U.S. postmasters. Written exams and competency tests for skilled jobs had benefited the government and had helped citizens, TR noted. "It has proved a real boon to the better-educated colored people," he commented. "Under the spoils system the negro never got his share of the appointments."[75]

Cosmopolitan competed for literary stars, too. The top-tier magazines bid for authors whose books sold well or whose magazine stories were popular with readers. Story fees ranged from $100 to $500. Only the stars made this kind of money; new authors and middling talent generally received $5 to $10 per printed page, which usually ran six pages. *Cosmopolitan* sometimes paid a new author of promise $50 regardless of story length.[76]

Many of the era's important authors submitted stories to *Cosmopolitan*. Half of all fiction authors were "notables" of the era whose names appeared in *The Literary History of the United States*. Stories and novellas by Hjalmar Hjorth Boyesen continued to appear, as did work from Willa Cather, Stephen Crane, Henry James, Sarah Orne Jewett, Jack London, and Walt Whitman. Almost two-thirds of the authors published by *Cosmopolitan* were Americans. Foreign authors, primarily British and Russian, supplied fiction to a middle-class readership enthused by the opportunity to read H. G. Wells, Anton Chekhov, and Tolstoy, among others. The magazine paid the going rate for these literary stars and legends. Walker preferred nonfiction, but for commercial reasons *Cosmopolitan* published quality fiction to attract new readers and retain old ones.[77]

The magazine also gave dozens of unknowns their moments of fame. The selection process was collegial. Each associate editor took a manuscript from the office pile, read it, wrote comments on an evaluation sheet, and passed it to another associate editor. Walker read them all. Manuscripts were discussed on a weekly basis, but Walker had final say. "There is an idea abroad that the magazines are surrounded by literary cliques—special friends of the editor—and that through favor their manuscripts obtain places in the magazine," Walker informed readers. "Nothing could be further from the truth. The editor himself knows that any favoritism upon his own part will weaken the magazine and bring punishment. A favor to a friend may cost him several thousand subscribers."[78]

A slight majority of fiction represented the genre of literary realism. A scholarly examination of the magazine's fiction throughout the 1890s concluded it mirrored mainstream literary trends.[79]

Cosmopolitan published "Sally Ann's Experience," a story by Eliza Calvert Hall about injustice to women. Set in Kentucky and written in backwoods dialect, the story portrayed a social circle dominated by ignorant, ill-mannered men. State law mandated that all property owned by a woman prior to marriage became her husband's upon marriage. A married woman could not write a will bequeathing her assets or possessions to anyone should she die before her husband. Hall's fiction was based on reality. The depiction of a young woman whose fate hinged on the judgment of men inferior in intelligence and common sense created a sensation. The magazine continued to receive requests for reprints for several years and Theodore Roosevelt urged that schoolchildren should read it. Walker had admired its conversational tone and its true-to-life dialogue. It epitomized the spirit of American literature.[80]

Realism had its limits, though, even for John Brisben Walker. A six-part serialization in 1899 of *The Awakening* by Count Leo Tolstoy began with fanfare and ended abruptly after four months with an apology. Tolstoy had written an introspective novel, a presumably autobiographical story that was repentance for sins of youth and abuses of social inferiors his privilege had permitted. The central characters of the novel were a young nobleman and a young woman born to an unmarried manor servant. As teenagers, they had fallen in love during the nobleman's visit to the manor owned by two elderly aunts. The nobleman's mother had learned of the relationship and ordered her son home. A tender farewell between the young couple had "consummated her ruin," and a pregnancy had resulted. She was dismissed from manor service. Over time, the woman had been a prostitute and a thief, and then accused of murder.[81]

Tolstoy's writing was blunt, graphic, and quite realistic in its portrayal of caste, criminals, and the fate awaiting a woman whose poverty condemned her to hardship and mistreatment.

Walker, who had promoted the imminent publication of *The Awakening* prior to its premiere, apparently was nonplussed upon receiving the translation of the manuscript. He purged material pertaining to sex, prostitution, and the woman's treatment in prison. *Cosmopolitan's* expurgated version of *The Awakening* elicited no known protests from readers, but Tolstoy's agent in London and his agent in Saint Petersburg, Russia, publicly castigated *Cosmopolitan* for its censorship.

By the time all this occurred, the May installment of sixteen pages in the magazine was distributed by mail and to vendors and the June installment was on the presses. Walker exchanged letters with the London agent. No resolution was accomplished. The magazine ran a much abbreviated fourth installment. Then *The Awakening* disappeared from *Cosmopolitan.*

Instead of a fifth installment, Walker published a four-page explanation to readers titled "Discontinuance Of Count Tolstoy's Novel." Much of the explanation concerned specific provisions of the contract between Tolstoy and *Cosmopolitan,* and numerous paragraphs alleged that late delivery of the translation, incompleteness of the manuscript, and general literary misfeasance by Tolstoy and his agents had compelled Walker to edit the novel in the interests of his family readership. "It was claimed by the London agent of Count Tolstoy that the novel was a work of art and that it was sacrilege to change it in any way," Walker wrote. Not so, said Walker. The contract had stipulated "the novel itself is of unobjectionable character, and that it contains nothing which cannot be presented in a magazine entering the household."

Walker absolved the venerable Tolstoy of blame. "It is not believed that Count Tolstoy has had any part in this comedy of errors," the editor-publisher stated. Walker, who had fearlessly advocated the formation of laborer militias to battle the mercenaries of industrialists, dared not offend the presumed morality or sensitivity of his readership.[82]

Cosmopolitan and Walker were on safer ground with the futuristic science fiction of H. G. Wells. *The War of the Worlds* had its American debut in April 1897, a lengthy fourteen pages of text interspersed with a half-dozen illustrations. The British novelist was paid $150 for each of the nine installments that ran until December 1897. Wells had set the novel in England, naturally, where Martians zapped men, women, and children by the thousands with heat rays. Fantastic illustrations in *Cosmopolitan* depicted the Martians roaming the countryside in metallic orbs from which tentacles dangled. Walker, an aviation enthusiast and a person fascinated with futuristic scenarios, bet that his readers would appreciate the tale.[83] Years later, a disgruntled Wells complained to Walker in a letter that he had been "crudely victimized by both editors and publishers," an allusion to the payments he had accepted.[84]

Cosmopolitan was never the literary equal of *Atlantic Monthly, Century,* or *Harper's,* yet it was not mediocre. The experience with Howells might have prompted Walker to elevate literary content because the magazine added an Arts and Letters section of five pages in summer 1893. Each month the section provided a dozen book reviews and several brief essays on literature and poetry. The magazine, though, treated poems as filler material from the mid-1890s to early 1900s. Most issues offered two poems, and the only issues with three or four poems were those in which the bottom of pages needed text to fill space. The expansion of *Cosmopolitan* to an occasional 144 pages for editorial material early in 1893 allowed for an additional article and a story each issue, but not poems; until his final two years as editor-publisher, a period when his commitment to the magazine waned, Walker gave scant space to poetry.

Cosmopolitan was a complete package by the fourth anniversary of Walker's ownership. The magazine published articles, fiction, illustrations, photographs, poetry, reviews, and special sections of sufficient interest and quality to attract an ever-increasing number of subscribers and single-copy readers. Advertisers, too, considered the magazine a good buy.

The Turnaround

A magazine was a business. John Brisben Walker was a businessman. *Cosmopolitan* thrived.

Cosmopolitan had metamorphosed from a poorly managed, moribund enterprise in summer 1888 to an intelligently operated, prosperous entity by early 1893. Walker had taken a "rather purposeless publication," the *Journalist* remarked, and had given it an identity, while also imposing an effective managerial style and organizational system.[85]

Beyond the quality of what readers saw in its pages, *Cosmopolitan* moved into the top tier of magazines because its editor-publisher formulated a strategy to get it there. The same fundamentals—circulation and advertising—that had bedeviled Paul Schlicht by their cost and complexity also vexed Walker. The different outcome was attributable to perspective. Schlicht was a tactician, Walker a strategist.

Magazine circulation success depended on new subscriptions and subscription renewals. To obtain new subscriptions, Schlicht had dispersed canvassers on an ad hoc basis to cities in the northeast and central states, and established a network of community agents and reading clubs; by contrast, Walker saturated a city with canvassers until a specific number of subscribers was signed, and eliminated the network of community agents. To obtain renewals, Schlicht had reduced the price, and relied on the magazine's editorial format—except he fiddled around with it so much that readers wondered what material the magazine would publish; by contrast, Walker maintained price, which had the effect of affirming value, and retained a familiar format—except for the barely noticeable Howells interlude.

Walker had a flair for promotional campaigns. A *Cosmopolitan* charter train rolled into a city or town, its railroad engine and cars festooned with banners and flags. Canvassers pushed carts or rode wagons down the streets, each vehicle adorned with the *Cosmopolitan* name. One memorable campaign combined promotion with public benefit: *Cosmopolitan* financed a thousand college scholarships for a year to the top thousand sellers of subscriptions, boys and girls; a recipient could choose to attend Georgetown, Harvard, the University of Michigan, Vassar, Wellesley, or Yale with "free tuition, free board, free lodging and washing." (Archival records regarding tuition and room and board at several of these institutions indicated an annual cost of at least $160,000 to *Cosmopolitan*.) Could the magazine afford it, or was it another impulsive decision by the editor-publisher? Most magazines of the era received advertising revenue amounting to $2 per subscriber each year. Although this sum was not clear profit, the additional ad revenue generated from subscribers signed by college scholarship recipients could cover *Cosmopolitan*'s commitment if each person sold a minimum of a hundred subscriptions. Depending on the subscription renewal rate, the magazine then could subsidize the scholarships the remaining three years.[86]

Subscription premiums also differed. Schlicht had given functional, practical gifts for filing and organizing paperwork; Walker gave gifts for the mind. The *Cosmopolitan* premium for 1891–1893 was a memoir of the subscriber's choice from a set by General Ulysses S. Grant, General George McClellan, General Philip Sheridan, or General William Tecumseh Sherman. The cost was a year's subscription plus seventy cents. The two-volume Grant memoir sold retail at $7. Certainly, Walker got the memoirs at wholesale cost, but any choice was quite a premium for a $3 subscription, the new price effective autumn 1891.[87]

Circulation soared. Walker was careful not to specify an exact number to advertisers or ad agencies. Directory listings and promotional advertisements for *Cosmopolitan* referred to "copies sent to readers." This avoided the matter of actual subscriptions. But because Walker was an astute businessman whose own fortune was at stake, most copies printed each issue assuredly went to subscribers, along with a sensible percentage for free samples to be handed out by subscription agents. Whatever the proportion, the *Cosmopolitan* press run certified growth: 20,000 copies for January 1889; 40,000 copies for January 1890; 60,000 copies for January 1891; 100,000 copies for January 1892; 150,000 copies for January 1893.[88]

Tremendous circulation growth required more people at the magazine. The core staff of four department managers, five associate editors, and several proofreaders remained fairly constant, but processing new subscriptions and renewals kept many clerks busy while bookkeepers recorded financial information for advertisers and subscribers. Also, a cadre of office assistants classified and tracked hundreds of unsolicited manuscripts for articles and stories sent by would-be writers and authors. (*Cosmopolitan* received six thousand such manuscripts during 1892, of which approximately eighty were published.) Salaries alone amounted to thousands of dollars every month.[89]

Cosmopolitan benefited from economy-of-scale. Despite the doubling of editorial pages and exponential growth in circulation, the effective cost per copy was only eighteen cents for distribution, printing, production, editorial material, and salaries by early 1892. The magazine received fifteen cents for each copy sold by vendors, a loss of three cents, and cleared approximately seven cents a copy each month on renewal subscriptions. Commissions to subscription agents caused *Cosmopolitan* to lose a penny or two per copy on new subscriptions.[90]

Still, the only way for *Cosmopolitan,* or any magazine, to profit was to raise advertising rates or to sell more advertising pages. Any operational deficit did not include overhead expenditures for rent and promotional campaigns. Ad revenue was not easy to get. Walker had to overcome the inherent skepticism of potential advertisers and ad buyers for agencies who were leery of circulation claims by magazine publishers. Decisions to buy ad space in a magazine were based on perception of its quality and a presumption about its readership. This was an era prior to the advent of marketing surveys and statistical evidence on readership demographics. *Cosmopolitan*'s quality would be evident to potential advertisers and ad agencies, but Walker hoped to achieve credibility by citing to them the monthly press run of copies rather than actual paid circulation. *Cosmopolitan* announced in directory ads, "Books and Post-office receipts always open for inspection."[91]

Advertisers gradually accepted *Cosmopolitan*. Two years after Walker purchased the magazine, it carried a monthly average of 62 ad pages, then a monthly average of 74 ad pages the third year. Compared to other top-tier magazines, *Cosmopolitan* was doing well. *Century* ran an average 106 ad pages the same year, *Harper's* 102 ad pages, and *Scribner's* 82 ad pages.[92]

Cosmopolitan ad rates matched its circulation growth. The page rate of $60 for 1889 went to $125 in 1890 and $200 in 1892. The latter rate was $50 higher than a page in *Century,* a gesture of supreme confidence by Walker justified by his magazine's editorial quality and burgeoning circulation. Advertisers received a discount for a year's contract, and because each ad page cost money to print it resulted in estimated actual revenue to *Cosmopolitan* of $130 a page. The average of seventy-eight pages a month brought $10,100 monthly during 1893.[93]

Steady progress toward profitability verified the wisdom of Walker's strategy: an emphasis on nonfiction, with priority for timely articles and commentary; a focus on associating the magazine with the best literary names; continuous comprehensive promotional campaigns to build circulation; a willingness to raise subscription prices as a statement of editorial quality; and persistence to establish credibility with advertisers. *Cosmopolitan* had absorbed $360,000 of Walker's fortune, slightly more than half, before its finances turned around.[94]

A major reason for profitability was his decision in summer 1892 to buy printing presses and ancillary equipment—cutter, folders, binders—and to hire people to operate and maintain it all. "Not only is the machinery of the best," Walker informed readers, "but the workshop is of the brightest and healthiest, lighted by a hundred and forty-five windows, free to the sunshine." The magazine now controlled its printing quality and production schedule. If a worthy article arrived late or a recent momentous event merited commentary, new printing plates could be produced and the presses kept waiting at the editor-publisher's discretion. Of utmost financial importance, *Cosmopolitan* also saved money by eliminating the markup of three cents per copy charged by a contract printer, thereby reducing the cost of a copy to fifteen cents. Walker applied some of the savings to printing a color frontispiece regularly.

Cosmopolitan made an average monthly profit of $5,400 from late 1892 onward to the next summer.[95]

January 1893 was an occasion for celebration. *Cosmopolitan* was a bright star in the magazine universe. Reputable, popular, profitable. To the tens of thousands of Americans who held a copy of *Cosmopolitan* in their hands on the fourth anniversary of his ownership, John Brisben Walker immodestly proclaimed his magazine's role:

It is not easy to exaggerate the influence which the four great magazines, Harper's, Century, Scribner's and The Cosmopolitan, have exerted upon the civilization and progress of the United States. They have carried ennobling thoughts . . . into the most remote hamlets. As a consequence scarcely a home can be found that has not been refined, educated and made brighter and better by these magazines.[96]

3

Competition

Country Life

Commuters aboard trains that pass through Irvington to and from New York City to the south can see the big building on a small hill nearby. It is quite impressive, a faded white beaux-arts relic that stretches the length of a football field alongside the railroad tracks. Irvington residents call the old landmark the Trent Building, but for many years after its construction during the late 1890s it was the Cosmopolitan Building.[1]

John Brisben Walker bought a twenty-acre tract in Irvington for *Cosmopolitan* that overlooked the Hudson River during summer 1894 and a separate adjacent parcel for a homestead in May 1895 because he wanted to move out of Manhattan. The reasons were personal, philosophical, and financial. He had spent his childhood on a homestead in the country near Pittsburgh, and his adult years mostly in a small community in West Virginia and the frontier city of Denver; he was not a city person. Another reason for leaving the city was concern for his family. In April 1893, his son Randolph, age thirteen, had been knifed by "young ruffians" near Columbus Avenue and 101st Street while on an errand for his father. The boy was seriously wounded, an inch-deep gash to the stomach with "a considerable loss of blood." Randolph fully recovered, but his father preferred a safer environment elsewhere to the family's grand residence on Central Park West. Walker believed, too, that country life would benefit his workers and their families—tidy cottages rather than crowded apartments, streets shaded by trees, garden plots, and a walk to work down shady lanes. Also, operating a business in Irvington cost much less than in the city, and the practicality of owning property rather than leasing it made eminent sense.[2]

Walker chose Irvington in Westchester County because the small town offered everything he wanted and because it was only twenty-five miles by train from midtown Manhattan to the south; this would allow *Cosmopolitan* to maintain contact with advertising agencies, artists, and writers. *Cosmopolitan* created an enclave for its workers amid the estates of industrialists and their heirs. The mansions of William Rockefeller, a son of oil tycoon John D., and the sons of robber baron Jay Gould were nearby along the Hudson River. Walker went to their parties and played host to them at the mansion he built on a homestead in view of the Cosmopolitan Building, while his workers lived in their cottages a short distance away.[3]

Construction began in mid-1895 on the building designed by renowned architect Stanford White, who adorned it with a colonnade and rooftop glass domes, beneath which was a fourth floor not visible from the outside. White apparently admired Walker and his magazine because his fee for the Cosmopolitan Building design was a mere $413, hardly the usual bill for a partner in the prestigious firm of McKim, Mead and White. *Cosmopolitan* moved its editorial and printing operations to Irvington in 1896. The massive structure provided 85,000 square feet of space, or two full acres under one roof.[4]

Approximately 110 employees worked there. The interior of the building was airy and bright because of hundreds of floor-to-ceiling windows that brought fresh air and sunshine into the lower three floors, while the rooftop domes allowed skylight illumination of the top floor. The building housed twenty-one printing presses, each operated and maintained by a two-man crew. Other than the pressmen, the magazine employed bindery operators, engravers, folders, machinists, typesetters, clerks, and mailroom sorters. (Besides sorting hundreds of thousands of subscription orders, the mailroom handled 14,000 unsolicited manuscripts for articles and stories annually by the late 1890s.) Walker was true to his word regarding fair treatment for workers. *Cosmopolitan* was a union shop. Typesetters, pressmen, and electroplating operators had labor contracts with the magazine.

A railroad spur from the main track led to a loading dock beneath the building for delivery of tons of paper for each month's press run. A postmaster from New York City arrived in Irvington upon completion of the monthly press run to weigh the magazines for postage. Pallets of bundled magazines then were loaded onto freight cars parked at a siding. Copies of *Cosmopolitan* filled eight freight cars every month.

The twenty acres around the building resembled a country estate. The site featured a landscape of trees and shrubs, a white picket fence, and numerous benches and picnic tables for employees. A meadow separated the Cosmopolitan Building from the Walker residence.

Walker had encouraged, but not required, his employees to move from New York City to Irvington when the printing plant opened. An article informing readers about the magazine's rural site asked, "Why should a large force of employees be compelled to suffer all the disadvantages of city life—narrow, badly-lighted workshops, small tenements, hot streets, high rents, noise, and crowded schools for their children?" Most of the magazine's employees gladly moved from the city to Irvington. Walker paid them the same wages although the cost of living in rural Westchester County was less. Workers rented cottages, some with gardens, and they walked to work rather than rode trolleys or wagons. It was not a company town, either. "Each finds his own home without suggestion or interference from the employer," the article stated.[5]

The $60,000 investment in property and $300,000 for construction of the Cosmopolitan Building was an ultimate expression of Walker's confidence at the time he decided to move to Irvington. His magazine was the most popular general magazine in the nation, and it was profitable. Also, the Irvington site was a wise investment. Consolidation of the magazine's operations at one location eliminated rental payments for Manhattan sites, while the railroad spur saved on cartage costs by allowing direct delivery of paper and supplies and direct distribution of the magazine. *Cosmopolitan* saved approximately $1,600 a month.[6]

The savings were vital. Every year after 1895 the magazine's profit margin eroded. From the moment Walker committed the last of his Colorado fortune to creating a new home for *Cosmopolitan* until its occupancy, the dynamic magazine industry in the United States had spawned a new competitor, a new leader. *Cosmopolitan* confronted a most serious challenger.

Survival

Cosmopolitan had risen from obscurity to prominence by the sixth year of Walker's ownership, an incredible achievement that affirmed his belief that people wanted a modern magazine devoted to current events and ideas of significance. *Cosmopolitan* was the most popular general magazine in the nation by the mid-1890s, its monthly distribution rising to 200,000 copies, then to 250,000 copies, then to 300,000 copies. The old giants, *Century* and *Harper's,* slid or stagnated; both soon fell behind *Cosmopolitan* by 50,000 copies and within several years by 100,000 copies and more. Walker's magazine focused on modern curricula for colleges, military preparedness, America's place and role in the world—and whether the nation should be an imperial power by governing foreign territories seized during a war with Spain.[7]

The magazine's stay at the top was brief. *Cosmopolitan* had widened its lead over the older prestigious literary magazines, but a new competitor occupied second place by 1895: *McClure's.* A general magazine named for its publisher, *McClure's* began in June 1893, the first summer of profit for *Cosmopolitan.* The newer magazine, which also celebrated all things modern, took just two years to reach a circulation of 169,000 copies—an amount verified by a sworn statement from publisher Samuel S. McClure and published in the *Ayer* directory of publications. The suddenness of *McClure's* ascent had surprised everyone, most of all McClure, age thirty-six. His startup capital to launch the magazine in June 1893 was $7,300.[8]

McClure's was a fine magazine, all right, but it had soared to the top tier for a reason other than quality: price. At fifteen cents from a vendor and $1.50 for a year's subscription, *McClure's* had lowered the cost of quality to middle-class readers. *Cosmopolitan,* at twenty-five cents from a vendor and $3 a year to subscribers, was no longer the most affordable quality magazine.

McClure lacked sizable startup capital, but he had vast knowledge about what Americans liked to read. He had owned and operated a newspaper syndication service for several years. His syndicate bought articles and stories, sent them to newspaper editors who bought or rejected the items, and learned from editors which articles and stories readers had seemed to like. McClure also learned how cheaply many authors and writers would sell their material. Only the elite could dictate their own fees; the majority who hoped to make a living off their words were desperate for income. McClure initially relied on syndicated fiction and nonfiction to fill his magazine.[9]

McClure's was lively and timely. *McClure's* published many photographs each issue, which cost only one-tenth the amount to process and print as woodcuts, and it pioneered the photo essay in a section called Human Documents. Pictures of famous people—historic personages, literary legends, military commanders, statesmen—filled its pages, documenting their lives from childhood to prominence. Articles on science and profiles of contemporary notables were standard. Authors from Britain, some unfamiliar to Americans, were on its pages. A story by Conan Doyle appeared in August 1893, to be followed five months later with a story by the same author—now identified as A. Conan Doyle—that introduced a detective named Sherlock Holmes. Stories by Rudyard Kipling and Robert Louis Stevenson regularly appeared.[10]

The most brilliant decision by McClure was hiring an American writer living in Paris, moving her to New York, and assigning her to produce a serial biography of Napoleon. Ida Tarbell wrote a six-part series on the French icon, a meticulously researched and well-written serial that became a book. *McClure's* circulation doubled to 80,000 copies.

While the life of Napoleon was in *McClure's* from late 1894 to April 1895, Tarbell visited backwoods Kentucky and rural Illinois to interview people whose families and friends had known the Lincoln family when young Abraham was growing up seventy to eighty years earlier. Their recollections comprised the first account of Lincoln's boyhood. Her six-part series "Abraham Lincoln: A Life" graced the pages of *McClure's* from June to November 1895, later becoming the basis of a book regarded for decades as the definitive biography of young Lincoln. Tarbell was famous and respected, and *McClure's* was the newest bright star in the magazine universe. Its circulation jumped from 90,000 copies to 169,000 copies because of the Lincoln serial.[11]

One adverse effect on *Cosmopolitan* from *McClure's* was a decrease in monthly growth. The year prior to *McClure's* appearance the monthly growth of *Cosmopolitan* was an average of 4,000 copies; the year after *McClure's* began, the monthly growth was an average of 1,500 copies.

Walker had reacted promptly to *McClure's* premiere issue in mid-1893 by slashing *Cosmopolitan's* price 50 percent, selling at vendors for twelve and a half cents per copy (the United States Mint made two-penny and half-penny coins) and to subscribers for $1.50 a year. This undercut *McClure's* fifteen-cent cover price and matched *McClure's* subscription. The stratagem almost forced McClure to quit, which was Walker's plan. The rather small circle of magazine publishers in New York City was aware of the new publication's precarious startup condition. "I had thought that it would be a year or two before there was another cheap magazine in the field," McClure recalled. "Nevertheless, in one way and another, always on the edge of failure, we got through the hard fall and winter of '93–'94." One way was a sizable loan from an advertising agency, which bartered a deal for a 25 percent ad discount in *McClure's* for its clients. Another way *McClure's* kept going was trimming the magazine to eighty-eight pages of editorial material from its original ninety-six.[12]

The consequence to *Cosmopolitan* of its editor-publisher's impulsive response was a substantial loss of subscription revenue, to no avail because *McClure's* continued to grow faster than *Cosmopolitan*, testimony to the new competitor's appeal.

The quick reaction by Walker revealed his instinctive competitiveness and an awareness that both *Century* and *Harper's* had erred by refusing to meet *Cosmopolitan's* lower price upon its early success beginning in 1889. Those magazines lost circulation gradually and experienced serious financial problems. *Century* came close to death by the late 1890s. Their initial reluctance was understandable. *Cosmopolitan* had failed once, restarted, and then was sold to an unknown man from Colorado. But their price vanity permitted *Cosmopolitan* to establish itself, and neither of the prestige magazines ever deigned to reduce the vendor price of thirty-five cents or the $4 subscription. At the point when *Cosmopolitan* was their equal in readership, it was too late. To their publishers, price and prestige were entwined. Walker knew better.

Walker soon realized the price reduction was too drastic, but he was trapped. New subscriptions and renewals, which accounted for 90 percent of total circulation, were coming in at $1.50 a year, so the only option for Walker was to raise the vendor price to fifteen cents, same as *McClure's*.

Fortunately for *Cosmopolitan* and other magazines during the mid-1890s, paper was less costly. The explosion in magazine circulation had persuaded owners of paper mills to invest in machinery that dramatically increased output. The price fell from $87 a ton to $52 within several years; this saved *Cosmopolitan* two cents per copy—a $6,000 monthly benefit. Walker also tightened the production and printing budget. He restricted the magazine to an average of 124 pages an issue for the next few years, eliminated almost all woodcut illustrations, ran more photographs, and strictly rationed the number of color frontispieces. Ownership by *Cosmopolitan* of production machinery and presses helped constrain costs, too. These stringent controls sliced the production and printing cost of a *Cosmopolitan* copy to eleven cents—another $8,000 saved.[13]

With subscription revenue at the much lower price bringing the magazine slightly more than twelve cents per copy and vendors sending six cents to the magazine for each copy sold, the magazine managed to recover most of its production and printing costs, which included wages for several dozen machinery operators and pressmen. However, budget items for office salaries, editorial material, and mailing the magazine were substantial. The magazine employed two assistant editors, five associate editors, four department managers, and at least thirty office workers. Also, as a popular and prestigious publication, *Cosmopolitan* spent approximately $4,200 each issue on fees for authors, illustrators, photographers, and writers. Other necessary expenses for promotional campaigns further spread red ink.[14]

Cosmopolitan upped its page rate to $225 for advertisers in January 1894. The timing was not good. A severe economic depression, or "panic," affected citizens and businesses. The steady growth in ad pages turned into a small decline. At $150 actual revenue per page, a monthly average of seventy-one ad pages generated $10,700 each issue. Combined with the total savings on overhead, paper, production, and printing of $15,600 each month, advertising generated enough money for an acceptable profit despite the price war with *McClure's*. Advertisements, always important, now had become the lifeblood for magazines.[15]

Advertisers tolerated rate increases because *Cosmopolitan* and other quality national magazines reached a fantastic number of middle-class households, which had discretionary income to spend even though the depression made families hesitant to spend money. One major ad agency, J. Walter Thompson, dominated representation of major brands for placement in magazines, and its agents advised clients to buy space. Newspapers continued to receive the bulk of advertising revenue, but magazines delivered an upscale readership.[16]

The 1890s saw the introduction of national brands familiar today: American Tobacco Company, Coca-Cola, General Electric, Wrigley's Gum, Hershey's Chocolate, Kellogg's Cereals, Colgate & Company, and National Biscuit Company (Nabisco). To create brand identity and to stimulate sales, national consumer product companies poured money into advertising.[17]

Ads seen in *Cosmopolitan* demonstrated the variety of national products: Armour's Extract of Beef ("It's Flavor Finds Royal Favor"), Baker's Breakfast Cocoa, Hand Sapolio ("Delicate enough for baby's skin / Capable of removing any stain"), Hardman Piano, Ingersoll Watch Company, Mason & Hamlin Organs, Raleigh Bicycles, Rambler Bicycles (price, $125), Remington Typewriter, Royal Baking Powder ("Absolutely Pure"), Uneeda Biscuit ("Everybody Knows Uneeda Biscuit"), Union Pacific Railroad. Lesser-known and long-forgotten products also advertised: Drake & Company Home Law School and Yabe School of Jiu-Jitsu ("The Japanese National System of Physical Training and Self-Defense"). And, of course, ads for patent medicines, a product not yet regulated by the federal government: Wilson's Pure Cod-Liver Oil & Phosphates, Colton's Kidney Wort ("Permanently Cures Kidney Diseases, Liver Complaints, Constipation and Piles"). Only one magazine, *Ladies' Home Journal,* banned ads for patent medicines from its pages, an honorable stand adopted in 1893 by publisher Cyrus Curtis at the insistence of editor Edward Bok.[18]

Cosmopolitan clustered its ad pages at the front and back, similar to other magazines; one-third of ad pages usually were in front. Few were full-page advertisements, and for the many ads that shared pages there was no product separation. Competing brands of typewriters faced one another, as did competitors in bicycles, pianos, boots, and soaps. Today, magazines guarantee an advertiser it will not be near a competitor. Also, few advertisements contained any display elements other than the product itself. No happy, smiling customers and no imagery to suggest any psychic rewards from buying the product. Ads promoted functional, tangible aspects. Many ads provided wordy descriptions of the product's benefits or assurances of quality craftsmanship, ingredients, or packaging.

The fact that quality magazines carried abundant advertising for a profusion of products directed toward a continually greater number of middle-class readers was all the more impressive given what had happened to the national economy. The United States endured a severe, lengthy economic depression beginning in 1893. For four years, unemployment ranged from 11 to 14 percent, industrial production declined year by year, and the nation's total output was minus 2 percent from start to finish. However, middle-class occupational categories—managers, professionals, proprietors—expanded throughout the 1890s to constitute 6 percent of the total workforce.[19]

The majority of middle-class families lived in cities. Their income and desire for a home of their own lifted owner occupancy to one-sixth of urban residences, almost double the proportion at the start of the decade. The suburbs grew, too. Census reports for the largest metropolitan areas counted 10 percent of the populace residing in suburban communities. As homeowners, consumers, and citizens, the middle class was becoming politically aware. Magazines would serve a vital role into the early twentieth century informing readers about corruption, public health hazards, and reform efforts. Magazines were a middle-class favorite for decades prior to the rise of movies and commercial radio programs. At the peak of magazine popularity, the typical middle-class household subscribed to several periodicals.[20]

One reason for multiple subscriptions was the price war begun by *McClure's* and intensified by *Munsey's,* a former weekly that switched to monthly publication in 1891. *Munsey's* devoted its pages mostly to fluffy features and a focus on celebrities. It was a minor magazine until it took price-cutting a step further, dropping its vendor price to a dime. *Munsey's* was not a quality magazine, but it was a competitor of sorts in the readership marketplace; its circulation skyrocketed from 40,000 copies to 100,000 copies in three months. *Cosmopolitan* and *McClure's* finally matched the dime price in 1895, by which time *Munsey's* was at 600,000 copies. Naturally, annual subscription prices fell, too—for *Cosmopolitan* to $1.20 and *McClure's* to $1. These incredibly cheap prices spurred circulation growth for all magazines. *Cosmopolitan* and *McClure's* grew by 3,000 to 4,000 copies a month the next few years, although *McClure's* usually had the higher figure.[21]

Total circulation or distribution determined a magazine's fate. Advertisers could distinguish between quality magazines and mediocre magazines, but determining the difference among quality magazines was not easy. Numbers mattered. As a result, *Century* (150,000 copies) nearly ceased publishing by 1900 because its number of readers placed it far below *Cosmopolitan* (335,000) and *McClure's* (359,000).[22]

Historians have designated 1893 as the start of the Magazine Revolution, an era of tremendous circulation increases, advertising revenue growth, adoption of half-tone photographs, and timely articles. The founding of *McClure's* at the lowest price ever for a quality monthly magazine triggered a war with long-term consequences. Hundreds of thousands of people had subscribed to magazines for entertainment, information, and photographs. Most subscribers were middle class, and some magazines aided the development of political awareness and activism that inspired progressive political and social reforms. Until the 1920s, about 60 percent of middle-class households subscribed to at least one magazine.[23]

The Magazine Revolution produced magazines much more readable than the preceding Gilded Age periodicals. Halftone photographs, which conveyed authenticity and realism, were common in magazines by the mid-1890s. Page design was more innovative. Occasional oval photographs lent an openness to pages heretofore restricted to rectangular and square shapes. Type was set by hand to wrap around photographs centered in the page. Other creative elements appeared: cursive script headlines for monthly columns, with type inset to background illustrations; facsimile photographic reproductions of handwritten letters and documents, which accompanied articles on historical leaders and contemporary events.

The revolution solidified the dominance of advertising revenue. It became the primary source of income for magazines. Commercialism greatly diminished editorial elitism. Magazines for genteel readers slowly lost circulation and advertisers. Timeliness supplanted literary quality as magazine editors focused on events and contemporary social concerns. Writers with specific knowledge about a subject were commissioned to submit articles, a shift from the prior practice of asking essayists or intellectuals to pontificate.

Price reductions for subscriptions and single-copy sales exacerbated operational deficits, despite a decrease in the overall page count. *Cosmopolitan* had wrung a major concession from the national distributor, which lowered its fee to three cents per copy. Vendors pocketed a similar sum. At a dime cover price, the magazine received four cents for each copy sold, while each subscription renewal returned a dime per copy, and a new subscription, minus an agent's commission, brought a nickel. *Cosmopolitan* thus incurred a further monthly revenue loss of $7,000.

Walker had acted decisively to reduce overhead expenses. He spent the remainder of his Colorado fortune to construct the Cosmopolitan Building in Irvington, thereby eliminating all rental or lease payments, while also reducing cartage costs for delivery of paper and supplies because the railroad spur at the suburban site brought items to a basement dock. Also, the new site with its railroad spur allowed direct distribution of magazine copies rather than shipment to a postal station in midtown Manhattan. Each dollar saved was vital.

Price competition for readers hurt *Cosmopolitan* and other magazines, yet it was able to raise ad rates again in 1899, an imperative increase to $250 a page. Ad revenue that year, based on an actual receipt of $165 per page for eighty-eight pages a month, was approximately $14,500 each issue. Every month, profit diminished.[24]

Without the price war, *Cosmopolitan* probably would have boosted its editorial material to a minimum of 144 pages for competitive reasons. *Century* and *Harper's,* despite their continuing decline, continued to provide 160 pages to readers who paid $4 for a subscription. Walker had shown his commitment to match their quality, both in terms of editorial material and volume. Editorial material in *Cosmopolitan* from 1889 through mid-1891 was an average of 130 pages; from mid-1891 to mid-1893, it was 132 pages. Competition from *McClure's* and the price war dropped the average to 122 pages for the final ten years of Walker's ownership, with many issues at only 112 pages. Reduction of pages meant loss of space for one or two articles every month and perhaps a story, too. Readers got a cheaper magazine in more ways than one.

A Modern World

Walker could not make *Cosmopolitan* bigger, but he tried to make it better until he was distracted by other ventures toward the end of his tenure. *Cosmopolitan* was his podium. The magazine let Walker display his intellectual curiosity to whoever read it. As the editor-publisher, he was responsible for 198 issues from January 1889 to June 1905, and he personally approved for publication approximately 3,800 text items, of which nonfiction articles accounted for 58 percent of total pages and opinion or special topic columns, such as science and book reviews, occupied 6 percent; illustrations and photographs filled 9 percent of editorial pages.

The magazine covered every imaginable subject. Its attention mostly focused on national life and the need for society to prepare its citizens for the modern world. International events and the need for the United States to prepare for its global role received plenty of pages, too. An obvious influence on the magazine and others was the coming end of the nineteenth century, a demarcation between old and new. *Cosmopolitan* evinced steadfast optimism about the twentieth century, an epoch it was certain would produce constant human progress, beneficial discoveries in science, advances in technology, and the primacy of rational thought in politics and world affairs.

Preparation for a modern way of life required education, a passion of Walker's. *Cosmopolitan* published 106 articles on the subject during his sixteen-year ownership. Collegiate studies especially interested him. *Cosmopolitan* expressed a message that higher education was important for social purposes to advance democracy and economic opportunity. This clearly spoke to a middle-class readership. Enrollment at colleges and universities in the United States was very small at the start of the twentieth century, only one-fifth of 1 percent of the national population, which compared to 3 percent at the start of the twenty-first century. "In the intelligence of the greatest number lies the hope of good government and general prosperity," the editor-publisher declared in an essay.[25]

No admirer of the institutions of American higher education, Walker sought articles and commentary that explored alternatives to the traditional system. *Cosmopolitan* warned its affluent readers that many American colleges and universities were mired in the past and that curriculum reform must be adopted to ensure a practical, useful education for prospective leaders of business and government. Magazine articles advocated courses in modern languages rather than Greek and Latin, modern sciences rather than botany and zoology, modern literature rather than the classics, and modern subjects, such as economics and political science. Walker's education had blended classical coursework at Georgetown College with practical classes at the U.S. Military Academy. His successes owed some debt to the education he received, and *Cosmopolitan* never disparaged the intrinsic value of higher education.

The debate over practical versus classical education was not new. Since the 1870s, universities in several states initiated a broadening of curriculum to include practical studies useful to students who would embark on business careers or in technical occupations, such as architecture and engineering. Herbert Spencer, an English philosopher whose social utilitarian doctrine and advocacy of individualism had transmuted to Social Darwinism, was a proponent of modernism for British colleges and universities during the 1850s. Walker was an ardent advocate of Spencer's doctrine and *Cosmopolitan* articles urged prompt adoption of modern studies.[26]

Cosmopolitan articles wove criticism into otherwise laudatory profiles of various colleges and universities from 1889 to 1890. A historical feature on Cornell University repeatedly referred to founder Ezra Cornell's principles. "He had no use for the dead languages and no interest in them," the article stated. "He held it to be very unfair, on the part of the colleges, to compel a man to study what he did not want, as a condition for being permitted to study what he did want." Another article praised Columbia College in New York City for its tradition of scientific studies distinct from "more strictly academic studies." The college president, Seth Low, declared that curriculum revision need not "mean a reckless experimentation with every new educational nostrum," the article explained, "but a frank recognition of the demands of the age and a prudent adoption of whatever has endured the test of experiences."[27]

Princeton College was an example of modernism in higher education, according to *Cosmopolitan*. The newly renamed campus, which had been the State University of New Jersey, offered a course in "microscopical anatomy" and a degree in biology, among other scientific coursework. It was "rapidly adapting to the new conditions" of society, the magazine reported. The magazine described the curriculum at Georgetown University, which had "a course of studies to fully equip the young man for an entrance into any of the professions." No mention was made of its connection to Walker, who received an honorary doctorate from the university at its centenary celebration in February 1889.[28]

A seven-page profile of the University of Chicago specified revisions in curriculum that had given the university a reputation for radical thought. Revisions included new studies of economics, political science, and sciences such as chemistry and physics, the creation of an extension service to teach adult education classes at high schools in northern and central Illinois, and an academic schedule divided into four 12-week terms each separated by a week-long break, which was the only year-round university schedule in the nation. Faculty were required to teach three terms and students could enroll in as many as they wished. The University of Chicago faculty had resisted, but strong

Cosmopolitan moved to a spacious office suite in Manhattan a year after John Brisben Walker purchased the magazine. Within another year, Walker bought printing presses especially for quality work worthy of a fine periodical. *Cosmopolitan*, February 1890; source: Morgan Library, Colorado State University.

The prospect of continuing prosperity generated from numerous subscriptions and advertisements encouraged John Brisben Walker to buy property in Westchester County north of New York City and to commission Stanford White to design the magnificent Cosmopolitan Building. Construction was not yet done when *Cosmopolitan* publicized its new home during late summer 1897. *Cosmopolitan*, September 1897; source: Morgan Library, Colorado State University.

administrators had persisted. "It is comparatively easy to work the old tread-mill of academic routine and predict disaster to anyone who scorns to trudge along in the well-worn ruts," the writer commented. "But it should be remembered that (outside of the clerical profession) there is none which counts so many venerable fossils as that of the academic teacher." Modernists at other colleges and universities "ought to feel grateful to Chicago, for trying on so extensive a scale a new and most interesting experiment in education."[29]

The University of Michigan adhered to its core mission of academics, not athletics, which *Cosmopolitan* considered admirable. "Athletics have never had the prominence and systematic attention here which they seem to receive in the East," an article reported. The students had their choice among traditional and nontraditional majors: liberal arts, mechanical engineering, pharmacy, physics. *Cosmopolitan* endorsed physical exercise as an adjunct to daily studies, and the Michigan campus was an active place. "Rowing, bicycling, coasting, baseball, football, and lawn tennis are all popular," the article reported, and its writer offered a descriptive account of a weekend football scrimmage between freshmen students and sophomores.[30]

During winter 1896–1897, Walker toured college and university campuses in northeastern states, met with a dozen presidents, and requested essays from each on the direction higher education should take; nine agreed to his request. The pages of *Cosmopolitan* were the forum for a lengthy, lively debate that

An impressive structure, the Cosmopolitan Building overlooked the Hudson River in Irvington, New York. Passengers aboard railroad trains to and from New York City passed near the building, which still stands today and is known as the Trent Building. *Cosmopolitan*, September 1897; source: Morgan Library, Colorado State University.

Advertisers seeking to reach middle-class consumers filled dozens of *Cosmopolitan* pages by the late 1890s through early 1900s. Source: Norlin Library, University of Colorado.

Coast-to-coast travel aboard a train was expensive. The fare advertised in *Cosmopolitan* during the early 1900s would be the equivalent of $1,180 in 2010. Source: Norlin Library, University of Colorado.

included twelve articles spread across thirty-four monthly issues. Walker began the series "Modern College Education: Does It Educate In The Broadest And Most Liberal Sense Of The Term?" in March 1897 with an eight-page treatise on nine categories of curriculum reform. A crucial component was exposing students to career choices. "It would seem that too much time could scarcely be given to this most important matter," Walker commented, after mentioning the disdain among professors toward such advice. A career in business, law, medicine, or science was much more likely for a student than one in academe, Walker sensibly argued, and learning about careers would be beneficial to a student. "Should he not be compelled to hear lectures by at least two fair minded men upon each of the professions and upon the various kinds of business life," the editor-publisher suggested, "one arguing in favor of and the other against—so that all sides shall be presented?"

Walker recommended an "educational motto for the twentieth century":

Time For The Most Important Studies:
Omit The Least Important

"We are guilty of something like a platitude when we say that throughout his after-career a boy, in nine cases out of ten, applies his Latin and Greek to no practical purposes," Walker commented. "If we inquire what is the real motive for giving boys a classical education, we find it is simply in conformity to public opinion. Men dress their children's minds as they do their bodies, in the prevailing fashion."[31]

Daniel Coit Gilman, president of Johns Hopkins University, defended the traditional curriculum at colleges and universities by relegating technical and vocational education to the public schools. A lack of common standards for elementary and secondary schools was detrimental to society because many young men and women were incapable of succeeding at careers in business and industry. "It is not likely that American education will be satisfactory to the most thoughtful people, until it is far more systematic than it is at present," Gilman asserted. France and Germany had unified their standards, and each nation had advanced the level of learning to satisfy the needs of employers. "Comparing American youth with those of foreign countries, the most competent judges are of the opinion that the Americans have lost two or three years of time in their educational careers," Gilman concluded.[32]

Timothy Dwight, president of Yale University, recommended staying with a traditional curriculum. "It cannot be questioned that the main object of college education, according to the thought which has come down to us from the past, is a general preparation for educated life—and this is the true idea," Dwight stated. The nation needed "broadly educated men and men of largely developed thought-power; men who are not mere lawyers, or physicians, or able in business, or skilled in science."[33]

The final article was written by Walker, his prerogative, for the January 1900 issue. The question he posed was: if no college or university existed in the United States, what curriculum should be created? To find an answer he proposed to appoint a commission of "disinterested men of wisdom and learning, and generally sound judgment" whenever a new college or university was created in any state. The commission would rank courses of study by importance. Walker, by indirection, hinted that every existing college and university should review curriculum and accomplish reforms not possible because of faculty resistance. His hypothetical commissions would be composed of representatives from business, industry, and science whose neutrality was presupposed, a stark contrast to the ossified professors whose self-interest caused them to oppose reform. "The president of the college must, in the nature of things, be influenced by these special pleaders," Walker stated, explaining why reform was difficult.[34]

The editor-publisher concluded the article ungraciously by accusing every contributor to the series on higher education of having "ignored the points at issue" and "indulged in glittering generalities." His derogatory comment about the educators who had written articles followed their refusal to accept an invitation by Walker to attend a public forum tentatively scheduled at Harvard University. *Cosmopolitan* was to sponsor the event, which invited students to question the presidents in attendance. Also, the magazine had announced it would award $2,000 to the student whose curriculum proposal for modern studies was judged best by an independent committee appointed by the editor-publisher. Walker canceled the forum when the educators would not participate.[35]

While successive issues of the magazine carried articles from educators, readers were letting the magazine know they wanted access to higher education. "Many letters have been received from men and women," Walker reported in the August 1897 issue. Their message was a "desire for broader education than that given by the public schools" among adults who could not afford to enroll at a college or university for reasons of income or full-time work. Walker, a man of principle who set an eight-hour workday for his employees, decided to make higher education available to his readers.[36]

Cosmopolitan University was founded in August 1897. A free correspondence school modeled on the Chautauqua School self-education method, Cosmopolitan University promised a "course of studies with reference to the real needs of men and women in the various walks of life." To enroll, applicants submitted a statement about prior education, the reason for further study, and the courses they wished to take. "All instruction blanks, examination papers, official circulars, etc., will be furnished free," the *Cosmopolitan* announcement stated. Enrollment was not restricted to magazine subscribers.[37]

Prior to the announcement Walker hired a few professors in anticipation of a big response from the public. He also recruited Elisha Benjamin Andrews, the former president of Brown University, to direct Cosmopolitan University. Andrews recently had resigned from Brown because trustees had censured him for political activism on behalf of William Jennings Bryan, the unsuccessful Democratic presidential candidate in 1896. Brown spoke at public forums on behalf of the Silver Democrat.[38]

Bryan's candidacy had sharply divided the nation. He was considered a Populist, an essentially rural midwestern and southern political coalition that vilified banks, railroads, and industrialist robber barons. Bryan had pledged coinage of silver and a policy of bimetallism to enlarge the nation's supply of currency with dollars backed by silver and gold. Dollars backed solely by gold were mandated by financiers in Britain and continental Europe to secure their massive loans to American industry and railroads. Bryan's pledge was popular among farmers, ranchers, and rural communities in the central and western states where tight money caused by an outflow of gold to foreign creditors had created economic hardship, primarily steep interest rates and deflation of income. Conversely, Bryan's pledge was extremely unpopular among bankers and city residents who preferred the security and stability of dollars backed by gold. Bryan was regarded as a radical by many easterners and the middle class generally.[39]

Walker, too, supported Bryan. Although wealthy, Walker was a westerner who was suspicious of eastern bankers and financiers. His ideology was progressive, believing in humane labor practices and habitable city neighborhoods for the poor. Walker paid for rental of auditoriums and lyceums to stage rallies for Bryan at which bands played and politicians spoke, and he organized parades. Also, just prior to the November election Walker functioned as Bryan's campaign manager in New York City; he scheduled appearances for Bryan, who was the first presidential candidate ever to travel the nation on a campaign, and was the introductory speaker for Bryan at public events. Therefore, Walker was delighted to recruit Andrews to direct the new Cosmopolitan University.[40]

The timing of Andrews's resignation from Brown University, the announcement of his new position with Cosmopolitan University, and the connection of Andrews and Walker to Bryan afforded an opportunity for some nasty sniping by the *New York Times,* a nominally Democratic newspaper whose publisher dreaded the prospect of bimetallism. An editorial in the *New York Times* accused Andrews of duplicity: "For it seems that at the time when President Andrews offered his resignation to Brown he had already received a liberal offer to take the direction of Mr. Walker's new university to be conducted in connection with Mr. Walker's magazine." The *New York Times* publisher, Adolph Ochs, had purchased the daily with a minuscule circulation in August 1896. Ochs was careful to curry favor with the bankers and insurers whose loans of $300,000 financed the deal. (The newspaper did not endorse Bryan, choosing a Gold Democrat candidate instead; he received less than 2 percent of the vote in November.)[41]

Another *New York Times* editorial sarcastically commented that Walker "being the only Bryan man in New York" had placed Andrews on "a throne from which he can inculcate and promulgate the blessedness of the free and unlimited coinage of silver." The editorial urged Cosmopolitan University to establish an endowed chair for "Theory of Government to be occupied by Debs," meaning Eugene Debs, the labor union activist and socialist.[42]

The critical editorials on Walker and Cosmopolitan University caused a problem for Ochs. Spencer Trask, a New York banker who served both as director of a committee of lenders monitoring the finances of the heavily indebted *New York Times* and as an advisory committee member for Cosmopolitan University, was an acquaintance of Walker. Trask warned Ochs not to publish any more editorials on the subject. Ochs, however, demonstrated his independence by approving a third editorial about the university. This one ridiculed the idea of a magazine or any business operating a university: "Is there any insuperable obstacle to the establishment of an institution of liberal education in connection, say, with a restaurant?" One subject of study, the editorial suggested, could be "the most liberal instruction in the science of the proper adjustment of sandwich to beverage."[43]

Walker never acknowledged these criticisms. He had other problems. Andrews quit the presidency of Cosmopolitan University before the first correspondence courses began. Brown University trustees had agreed to allow Andrews to withdraw his resignation; they had yielded to a faculty protest about the threat to academic freedom posed by the censure of Andrews for his political activity. The Andrews decision was bad timing. The September 1897 *Cosmopolitan* carried a full-page photograph of Andrews accompanying a two-page article that praised his experience and ideas about education—delivered to readers the same week Andrews returned to Brown University.[44]

Now without a leader, Cosmopolitan University foundered. Walker hurriedly asked a retired professor to take charge. The more serious problem was the incredible response from *Cosmopolitan* readers and others: 700 applications arrived within two weeks of the announcement; a month later nearly 4,000 people had applied; at year's end, university enrollment was 12,000 students; and by May 1898 applications totaled 18,854 from men and women across the country. On the first anniversary of its founding, enrollment at Cosmopolitan University was 21,000 students.[45]

The magnitude of the financial burden the free university imposed on the magazine worried Walker. If he fulfilled the promises made in August 1897, *Cosmopolitan* itself could go bankrupt. The free university needed to pay salaries for faculty and clerical staff, finance the printing of thousands of booklets and examination papers, and buy postage for mailing a continuous stream of material to thousands of students. Cosmopolitan University hired eleven faculty to handle coursework in English, ethics, languages ("dead" and modern), mathematics, philosophy, physics, science. The average professor of the era earned $1,600 a year; if the correspondence university matched it, the annual faculty payroll would have approached $18,000. On top of that was payroll for clerks and other overhead.[46]

The creation of Cosmopolitan University might not properly be called impulsive, but obviously Walker had not thought things through—an enrollment limit, for example, might have been a wise policy. In the January 1898 magazine issue, a statement from the editor-publisher indirectly appealed for help: "The unexpected dimensions which the undertaking has assumed render these resources entirely insufficient for the services to be performed, in view of the daily growing lists of applicants. That there will be those, generous-minded and appreciative, who will comprehend the magnitude and importance of this work and be glad to render such aid as lies within their power, is not to be doubted."[47]

Walker ultimately confessed to *Cosmopolitan* readers that the university was a mistake. "Many difficulties have been encountered during the first year of The Cosmopolitan's educational work," Walker wrote a year after launching the institution. The magazine could not afford to continue it. The free university closed. Students had to pay five dollars, if they could, to continue their correspondence studies. Many did, and Cosmopolitan University continued to employ three professors for coursework into the early 1900s.[48]

The experiment convinced Walker a great demand existed for higher education. A *Cosmopolitan* essay by him asked Congress to appropriate money for a national university. "The friends of education in the press, in Congress, among the great universities and among the people are asked to give their earnest cooperation," Walker pleaded. No congressional action ensued.[49]

Preparation of the American mind for a modern world was one theme in *Cosmopolitan*. Another was preparation of the nation for its role in the world. The magazine published 138 articles throughout the 1890s on international events and royal governments in Europe, an average of slightly more than one per issue. Many *Cosmopolitan* articles focused on military technology and military capabilities of other nations. Walker had spent two years, off and on, as a West Point cadet and supposedly had performed military service in China, which made subjects regarding armaments, organization, and preparedness a matter of personal interest. Military subjects presumably were of interest to men.

The magazine published eighteen articles about the armies of Germany, France, Japan, Russia, and Sweden, and about the condition of the American military during the first four years Walker owned the magazine. Articles described the equipment, organization, standard of pay, and training of a nation's army, or specified the armor, engine capacity, and range of guns aboard warships. The unstated purpose was to inform readers about military capability in important nations; for readers who might have missed the point concerning comparable American readiness, *Cosmopolitan* ran a twelve-page article, "National Guard Camps Of Instruction And Their Faults," that lamented ineffective training, lack of artillery, and variance in readiness among the militia units.[50]

Walker arranged to meet with General Nelson A. Miles, the army's commander, to discuss developments in military technology. Their discussion resulted in an invitation from Miles for Walker to attend field tests of new artillery. At an April 1896 test on Long Island an accidental explosion blew apart a pneumatic breech assembly of an artillery piece just ten yards from where Walker sat as an observer. He and others nearby suffered temporary deafness. "All knew that the gun had burst," a newspaper reported, "and nearly everybody, after a moment or so of standing aghast, thought of possible consequences. Each looked for his neighbor and on the ground, as if expecting to see fragments of human beings." The gunner was seriously injured and two soldiers slightly hurt.[51]

Military mobility was dependent upon horses then, but Walker, an avid automobile enthusiast, believed the army should test motor vehicles. Walker designed a "rapid transit wagonette," capable of transporting six soldiers, for consideration by the army. Powered by a steam engine, the prototype did not do well. One model's engine boiler erupted hours after taking to the road, a second model caught fire on the journey, and a third took three days to drive from New York City to Washington, D.C. The wagonette was not adopted for military purposes because the army was "rather skeptical of its utility for field operations."[52]

Military subjects actually were germane during the 1890s. Crises had fomented war scares. Germany and the United States had a showdown in the western Pacific at Samoa early in 1889. Warships from each nation gathered in the principal harbor to lay claim to anchorage rights. Tensions heightened, but a severe storm inflicted damage on the warships before any incident occurred. A subsequent diplomatic conference did not resolve various conflicts involving assertions by each nation regarding de facto sovereignty over other islands in the Pacific.

Several years later Britain and the United States engaged in a war of words over a border quarrel between Venezuela and the British colony of Guyana during 1895–1896. The British sought control of navigation at the mouth of the Orinoco River, an inland passage to Venezuela. This worried the U.S.

Government, which saw the tactic as a precursor to outright seizure of land on Venezuela's side of the river. Britain had used similar methods in India, Burma, and Africa to expand its colonies.

The United States invoked the Monroe Doctrine to intercede in the dispute, relying on the assertion of hemispheric privilege to thwart a European colonial power in the Americas. Britain told the United States to mind its own business. A belligerent Senate refused to approve an arbitration treaty with Britain. A *Cosmopolitan* article referred to Britain's colony "causing so much trouble," described the territory in dispute, offered a complete lesson in the geography of Venezuela, and then concluded with hopes for "a satisfactory ending of a perplexing question." Walker wanted the British government to explain its motives. Realizing that no government official in London would dare respond to an invitation to write for *Cosmopolitan,* Walker decided to ask William Gladstone, formerly the British prime minister for a fourth time, to provide an explanation. His letter to Gladstone offered a $1,000 fee. The prime minister did not respond.[53]

An essay by Walker in May 1896 urged establishment of a World Court to arbitrate the border quarrel. The court could become permanent, an arbiter of other international disputes. "All the interests of civilization are tied up in the permanent abandonment of the old methods of settling disputes between nations," Walker argued. "If we progress it must be by peace and if we are to have peace it must be by international arbitration."[54]

The June 1896 *Cosmopolitan* carried an article provocatively titled "In Case Of War With England—What?" Walker again was the writer. Relying on his acquaintance General Miles, the editor-publisher outlined the nation's response to a formal declaration of war against Britain. Walker identified industrial centers that would produce weapons, discussed specific weaponry, speculated about a British invasion of Long Island, and predicted the defeat of Britain from economic factors, not military ones: "As the war progressed, England would suffer not only in her commerce and in her ships, but in the deprivation of some hundreds of millions of income which she draws from the mortgaged farms and factories of the United States. Her loss of an American market would be suffering at a thousand points. England would have killed her Goose of the Golden Egg." Britain and the United States indulged in combative rhetoric, but nothing happened. Diplomacy finally resolved the situation in November 1896.[55]

The border dispute incident between Guyana and Venezuela prompted Walker to send Julian Hawthorne, a notable author and essayist, to India to report on colonial malfeasance there that had exacerbated the death toll from famine. Grandly, *Cosmopolitan* anointed Hawthorne its "special commissioner" to investigate conditions in India. A special fete attended by thirty journalists bade him farewell, and Walker praised Hawthorne for agreeing "to undertake this dangerous mission," not an exaggeration because British colonials jailed visitors caught in off-limits areas in India. Hawthorne visited India for several weeks. His report to *Cosmopolitan* was dramatic, made more so by stark full-page photographs of Indian children, men, and women emaciated by starvation and gaunt from illness. Hawthorne portrayed a colonial nation ineptly administered, its raj rulers callously indifferent about famine and plague in the countryside. "The only persons of white blood in India who know what is actually going on are the missionaries," Hawthorne reported, "for they go about quietly everywhere, see everything, and cannot be deceived or put off."[56]

Walker took the unusual step of using the In The World Of Art And Letters column for a political commentary condemning Britain for its inhumanity in India. "England boasts that she is the richest nation on the earth," Walker stated. "While India starved, food was rotting in American granaries and could have been bought at prices never so low before. Upon what ground, then, does England, as a nation, justify its indifference while twenty millions of its people are perishing of want almost within sight of the English locomotives which could so easily transport a part of the world's over-abundance?"[57]

Walker made sure that everyone understood *Cosmopolitan*'s commitment to bringing such important news to its pages. "No task has been too difficult or costly if it promised substantial return to the readers of the magazine," Walker stated upon the return of his special commissioner. "The recent trip of Mr. Julian Hawthorne, to investigate the real conditions prevailing among the starving multitudes of India and determine the responsibility of civilization for so much misery, is an evidence of this policy."[58]

Walker distrusted Britain and disliked colonialism. The magazine presented information on hazards associated with British imperialism. "Peppered By Afghans" recited disastrous encounters with mountain warriors whose ambushes had killed hundreds of British troops in Afghanistan. "It is certain they are cruel, bloodthirsty and treacherous," the writer, a Brit, commented. "But again it is certain that they are patriots of the stanchest devotion; so strenuously and indomitably do they oppose and harass the invader that no power, however seemingly overwhelming, has ever succeeded in crushing their independence or even in maintaining a permanent foothold in their territory."[59]

Finally, an international crisis did ignite a war near the end of the decade. The United States fought a war with Spain. The war itself was brief, actually lasting only several weeks, but its aftereffects fostered sharp public debate and influenced foreign policy because victory won a prize—an island empire consisting of the Philippines and Guam in the Pacific Ocean and Puerto Rico in the Caribbean Sea. The core issue was imperialism, whether the United States should become a colonial power that governed foreign territory by fiat. The Democratic Party formally opposed annexation or governance of these islands during the election of 1900, although a national policy already was in effect. Policy makers in the Republican administration of President William McKinley, many senators, some prominent citizens, and a minority of newspapers endorsed the idea of controlling the islands. *Cosmopolitan* did not. Walker was no imperialist. Yet, the magazine lacked the fiery rhetoric of condemnation it had used against robber barons years earlier.[60]

The doctrine of Manifest Destiny had been resurrected prior to the Spanish-American War. Originally a doctrine referring to the extension of the nation's boundary across the continent, Manifest Destiny had evolved to a sense of American mission beyond the borders. Congressional speeches manifested the spirit of the times. "This race of ours—the Caucasian race—starting from the mountains of Asia, has gone ever westward, carrying civilization and blessing in its march," declared Senator Orville H. Platt, a Republican from Connecticut. "It halts now for a moment on the shores of the Pacific, looking out over the ocean."[61]

Expansionist ideology developed in the public sphere from mid-1893 onward. Frederick Jackson Turner, a historian at the University of Wisconsin, presented his thesis on the importance of the frontier in American life to a conference of historians during the Chicago World's Fair that summer. In his presentation, Turner had synthesized several concepts espoused by intellectuals and writers pertaining to the potential political and social consequences of the settlement of the American continent. Turner's thesis became known within academe and among intellectuals for his conclusion that "the frontier has gone, and with its going has closed the first period of American history."[62]

The first genuine test of American principle versus expansionist opportunity occurred a few months prior to Turner's speech. In mid-January 1893, a revolt by American property owners in Hawaii deposed the monarchy of Queen Liliuokalani. The insurrection was the culmination of several years of tension concerning economic policy and political power in a struggle between indigenous Hawaiians and Americans who owned pineapple and sugar plantations. While the revolt was in progress, sailors came ashore from the cruiser *Boston* in Honolulu harbor to protect Americans and their property from irate Hawaiians. Sanford B. Dole, a plantation owner, became president of a provisional government, which sought annexation by the United States.

President Benjamin Harrison and fellow Republicans in the Senate welcomed a delegation from the provisional government, and Congress received numerous reports from the Hawaii Special Commission, an entity composed of whites who owned property there. Americans owned two-thirds of the sugar and pineapple acreage on the islands, annual exports of these crops amounted to nearly 90 percent of Hawaii's commercial trade, and the U.S. Navy had secured from the monarchy prior to its overthrow the exclusive right to develop a permanent anchorage at Pearl Harbor. Naval strategists wanted a fortress for a fleet of warships to protect a string of coaling stations across the Pacific Ocean, to safeguard merchant ships en route to Asia, and to preempt Britain, Germany, or Japan from developing a naval base in Hawaii. Enough doubt existed about justification for the revolt itself and whether annexation of Hawaii should proceed that Democrats stalled a vote in the Senate until the inauguration of President Grover Cleveland in March 1893.[63]

Cleveland, a Democrat, refused to seek annexation. "Fair-minded people with the evidence before them will hardly claim that the Hawaiian Government was overthrown by the people of the islands or that the provisional government had ever existed with their consent," the president told Congress. "I mistake the American people if they favor the odious doctrine that there is no such thing as international morality, that there is one law for a strong nation and another for a weak one, and that even by indirection a strong power may with impunity despoil a weak one of its territory."[64]

Because the publication process for monthly magazines resulted in a lag between occurrence and coverage of an event, the first article about the situation in Hawaii did not appear until June 1893 in *Cosmopolitan*. Public ardor for annexation had waned because Japan made known its intention to monitor the political situation to guarantee fair treatment for the sizable Japanese population of Hawaii, a message that posed the risk of military confrontation. The *Cosmopolitan* writer spent most of the article describing the climate, topography, and lifestyle of Hawaii. Clearly, according to the writer, the islands had benefited from the arrival of white men. "The real history of Hawaii—using history in its strictest sense—does not go back much more than one hundred years," the article stated, referring to development of commercial agriculture in Hawaii and establishment of Anglo-Saxon society. The transformation of island life engendered resistance from Hawaiians, although progress was inevitable because "the only uncertainties were when the aboriginal population would cease to struggle with the invading white man, and of what nationality the white man who should conquer, would be."[65]

Cosmopolitan informed its readers that the revolt and subsequent unrest had disturbed the natural tranquility of the place. "Those who have known the genial, easy-going Kanakas as the favored children of nature, made for the enjoyment of the passing hour, may well feel that all this talk of revolt, new constitution, provisional government and the rest, is a barbarous and prosaic intrusion into paradise," the article explained. Still, the requirements of the modern world superseded those of the indigenous residents. "It is sad when the real interests of a country are not identical with the supposed interests of the natives," the writer acknowledged. "But the main fact of the situation, namely, that the native stake in the good government of the country is small as compared with that of the foreign population, must be faced, before the difficulty can be finally settled." Commerce and competition among nations compelled the United States to control Hawaii, *Cosmopolitan* told its readers.[66]

The Hawaii question lay dormant for more than a year until Senate Republicans revived it. "We should at least control those islands," Senator Henry Cabot Lodge of Massachusetts told Congress. "Our institutions should be predominant" and "the islands should become a part of the American Republic," Lodge declared. The senator compared British policy with American. "My criticism is that we do not exhibit the same spirit, the true spirit of our race, in protecting American interests and advancing them everywhere and at all times," Lodge said, a racial superiority theme that would be common in magazine articles. Lodge described the Japanese: "They are an element in the population disposed to be turbulent and to make trouble, and that they are regarded as very dangerous by all the people of the white race, English and Americans alike."[67]

Opponents of expansionism did not dispute the necessity for competing against European imperial nations in economic terms, nor did they dispute an American mission. They argued that annexation or governance of territory beyond the continent betrayed American ideals, which had renounced European imperialism. "The fact that this island [Hawaii] is weak, that they are a feeble folk, neither rich nor numerous, is only an additional reason why the Government of this nation should exhibit toward it the deference and delicacy of treatment demanded by the highest principles of justice and fair dealing," said Senator David Turpie, a Democrat from Indiana. Opponents also came from the ranks of liberal and reformist Republicans. For the United States to become an imperialist power, they believed, the nation would be no different from the morally corrupt societies of Britain, France, Germany, and Russia. These sentiments would appear in articles published by *Cosmopolitan* and two of its direct competitors, *Century* and *McClure's*, during the debate on imperialism sparked by the Spanish-American War.[68]

Turner ultimately gained a measure of public recognition when the *Atlantic Monthly* featured a further explanation of his frontier thesis in its September 1896 edition. The nine-page article written by Turner reviewed at length the beneficial effects of historic territorial expansion across the continent on economic and social development in different regions of the nation. Turner predicted the consequence of a closed continent: "Failures in one area can no longer be made good by taking up land on a new frontier." Turner believed the situation temporary, however, because "the demands for a vigorous foreign policy, for an interoceanic canal, for a revival of our power upon the seas, and for the extension of American influence to outlying islands and adjoining countries, are indications that the movement will continue." This was a reference to speeches in Congress and popular essays of the day that demanded an active international role by the United States.[69]

Expansionists echoed Turner's statements in the pages of *Cosmopolitan*, *McClure's*, and *Century*. Opponents of expansion called themselves anti-imperialists, and their words appeared in these quality magazines. The debate about the nation's future was a perfect moment for the magazines. *Cosmopolitan* and *McClure's* each did their best to discuss the most relevant, most crucial topic on the national agenda; *Century* switched gears to enter the competitive fray by presenting timely articles and essays, completing its transition to a general magazine.

Several years earlier, *Cosmopolitan* had explored the concept to construct an interoceanic canal in Nicaragua. The article analyzed the strengths and weaknesses of various proposed routes through the region. Nicaragua itself was perfect because "the general nature of the country seemed to promise that the continent might successfully be pierced by a canal." The background to the Nicaragua locale concept was the failure of the French to finish a canal across Panama.[70]

The prospect of a Nicaragua canal renewed the effort by expansionists in Congress and President William McKinley to annex Hawaii upon his inauguration in March 1897. They cited the need for an American naval base and coaling station on the main ocean route to Japan and China. Among the most vocal was Theodore Roosevelt, a newly appointed assistant secretary of the navy.[71] *Century* mentioned the connection between annexation and the canal. "The Hawaiian Islands will afford a resting-place for ships, and their importance will be immeasurably increased by the opening of the canal," the author stated. *Cosmopolitan*, which had indicated several years previously that Hawaiians were unable to govern the islands in a modern world, now was less enamored of assuming responsibility. The magazine ran a scare headline, "Shall We Annex Leprosy?" above an informative article on a leper colony at Molokai; the message was that leprosy did not affect the general population. Apparently lacking a substantive anti-imperialism piece, Walker decided to publish something, anything, to make readers doubt the wisdom of governing Hawaii.[72]

The revolt in Hawaii and the initial debate on its annexation, Turner's frontier thesis, and public awareness of the advantage of an isthmian canal prepared Americans for the greatest crisis, and opportunity, of the 1890s: Cuba. Spain had governed Cuba since the early 1500s. Cubans had rebelled unsuccessfully against colonial rule, but a rebellion that began in 1895 was widespread and a serious threat to Spain. Sympathetic Americans donated money for weapons and ammunition, which were ferried to Cuba by smugglers. Cuban guerrillas attacked Spanish army outposts, burned huge tracts of sugar cane, ripped apart railroad tracks, and forced Spain, a weak and poor nation, to send tens of thousands of soldiers to Cuba. American businesses with property in Cuba wanted protection, and some agitated for military intervention.

   Editor-publisher Walker believed in military preparedness, but he was not a warmonger. *Cosmopolitan* reacted promptly to the start of the Cuban insurgency. In a commentary section of the August 1895 issue, *Cosmopolitan* published "Our Duty To Cuba, The Republic," a two-page essay favoring intervention, of sorts, in Cuba. "Marvelously little interest seems to have been felt in what the Cubans are doing," *Cosmopolitan* stated. "Nevertheless, the time is ripe for the interference of the United States in the affairs of Cuba." *Cosmopolitan* proposed not military action but payment by the U.S. government to Spain of $200 million to buy independence for Cuba. The money could be repaid by export fees on Cuban crops, primarily sugar and tobacco. The United States would create a Cuban republic. "Every germ of republican liberty should be nurtured," *Cosmopolitan* recommended. Walker sent an emissary to Madrid to make the offer. His plan did not conform with the wishes of the Cleveland administration, which did not want responsibility for Cuba, and no formal proposal to buy Cuba's independence was discussed. (*Cosmopolitan* made another offer to Spain in July 1896, this one for $100 million—an apparent markdown to interest the U.S. Government, but it was not seriously regarded either.)[73]

   Cosmopolitan published its proposal on Cuba several months prior to sustained and sensationalized newspaper coverage of the Cuban insurgency by the *New York Journal,* the *New York World,* and other newspapers. The magazine based its interventionist appeal on the ideals of liberty and independence, omitting reference to the substantial American economic investments placed at risk by insurgent raids. American bankers, railroad companies, and plantation owners repeatedly had asked the U.S. Government to pressure Spain to negotiate with the Cubans, and to demand that Spain assign soldiers to protect property from attacks, which Spanish officials assured they would do.[74]

   No magazine articles or commentary regarded the destruction of American property as a valid reason for intervention in Cuba, although the McKinley administration definitely was upset about the havoc from summer 1897 onward. The United States became more assertive toward Spain concerning protection of American property in Cuba. "Spain's inability entails upon the United States a degree of injury and suffering which can no longer be ignored," the U.S. secretary of state advised the American ambassador in Madrid. "Assuredly Spain can not expect this Government to sit idle." The ambassador then met with his counterparts from Germany and Russia to alert them to American dissatisfaction with Spain, a courtesy in the event military action was taken. "American citizens had invested large amounts of money in the sugar and tobacco plantations," the U.S. ambassador reported. "The sugar plantations of Cuba are necessary to the food supply of the United States."[75]

   Spanish suppression of the rebellion was brutal. Tens of thousands of farmers and their families were forcibly moved to fortified encampments to separate them from the rebels. Starvation and illness killed many Cubans in the camps. The newspapers of William Randolph Hearst and Joseph Pulitzer attempted to inflame public opinion with melodramatic articles and occasional outright fabrication. War was possible.[76]

Walker asked his acquaintance General Miles to explain to *Cosmopolitan* readers circumstances that might bring war. The June 1896 issue provided an informative seven-page article by the general, or possibly ghostwritten by an aide, that listed examples of military actions by England and the United States both with and without a formal declaration of war. Circumstances relating to commerce and security most often brought war, the general noted, but a nation faced internal threats, too. "Yet war is not the most serious thing which can come to a nation," Miles stated. "There are many evils transcending those of modern warfare among civilized nations. Among these can be mentioned national dishonor, the degeneration of a people, political corruption, absence of patriotism, moral depravity—national, state, and municipal."[77]

An evil that worried Walker was warmongering by politicians and McKinley administration officials, among them Theodore Roosevelt, an assistant secretary of the navy. TR, enamored of the strategic concepts put forth by Admiral Alfred Thayer Mahan, lobbied Congress for money to create a modern fleet of warships. TR also sided with expansionists, especially on annexing Hawaii. Walker thought *Cosmopolitan* readers needed to know the motives of people who sought to make the United States a major military and global power. His article pertaining to the possibility of war with England immediately followed the one by General Miles. Walker assailed those who would profit by a greater, permanent military. "A large and powerful class of armor manufacturers have discovered extensive self-interest in the furnishing of a navy for the United States," Walker commented. "All large monied interests invariably command extensive press interests, and the changes have been rung upon the importance of a navy, until the public has been blinded. The pride of the Jingo voter has been touched and the congressman is free to favor this new industry."[78]

If anything, the editor-publisher feared a conflagration ignited by war with Spain. Britain and Germany were predators in his opinion. As colonialists, they were immoral, mercenary, and untrustworthy. The drama of the Cuban rebellion, the prospect of war with Spain, and the debate about imperialism awakened the literary Walker. A four-part serial, "A Brief History Of Our Late War With Spain," appeared in *Cosmopolitan* from December 1897 to February 1898. Its author was anonymous, but assuredly it was Walker, given its thorough details on weaponry, military tactics and strategy, economic aspects of war, and its scope.

A fantasy of fifty-six pages, "A Brief History Of Our Late War With Spain" imagined Britain and Germany sending an army of 100,000 soldiers to Canada for an invasion of the United States. The British fleet would bombard American port cities. Fortunately for the American people, though, wiser heads had spent millions of dollars on coastal defense fortifications to repel the warships rather than a U.S. fleet certain to be sunk by the British. And, money saved by not building warships instead had purchased artillery and machine guns for the army, which defeated the invaders from Canada. The war ended with the United States victorious: Montreal captured, Canada annexed, an autonomous American canal zone in Nicaragua, and Cuba liberated by American troops. The conclusion envisioned an earthly paradise:

Unhappy Cuba, decimated by the heroic struggles through which it had achieved freedom, was now to begin a new life. . . . With its wonderful resources of climate, soil and mine, the Gem of the Antilles was sought as a home by the intelligent of all countries. Especially from the United States, now that order was assured, came an immigration of the most desirable character. England, Ireland, Germany, Switzerland and Norway.

Although written as a satire to pass judgment on the rational and irrational rhetoric of proponents and opponents of American territorial expansion, the lengthy serial also encapsulated various economic, political, and social topics pertinent to the debate on the nation's future prosperity and security, vis-à-vis its international role. *Cosmopolitan* ended the serial on a realistic note, admonishing expansionists to limit their quest for empire. "For the United States of America, no Hawaii, none of China, none of Africa, but all of North America," the anonymous author asserted.[80]

The fourth and final installment of "A Brief History Of Our Late War With Spain" appeared in *Cosmopolitan* of February 1898. The timing of the serial proved eerie. Its conclusion ran the same month the battleship *Maine* exploded and sank in Havana harbor, killing 266 sailors and serving as pretext for real warfare against Spain.

The "splendid little war," a description ascribed to John Hay, the U.S. ambassador to Britain, lasted from spring through midsummer. At a cost of some 5,300 dead Americans, almost 90 percent of them killed by tropical diseases and poor sanitation rather than bullets or shrapnel, the United States acquired Guam, the Philippines, and Puerto Rico from Spain, while Congress separately authorized annexation of Hawaii. The formation of this island empire provoked fervid discussion on America's international policy and national principles, usually within the context of the American sense of mission, Anglo-Saxon racial superiority, and Social Darwinism among nations.[81]

The explosion of the *Maine* in Havana harbor and subsequent declaration of war against Spain in April, accompanied by the Teller amendment that disclaimed "any disposition or intention to exercise sovereignty, jurisdiction, or control" over Cuba, propelled the subject of imperialism onto the pages of *Century, Cosmopolitan,* and *McClure's.*[82]

Ten days after the war declaration, U.S. Navy warships commanded by Commodore George Dewey sank the Spanish fleet in Manila Bay, clearing the way for army infantrymen to occupy the city several weeks later. *McClure's* rushed into print a seven-page article on the agricultural and mineral wealth of the Philippines. Ignoring the legal and political facts, namely that the war was not over and U.S. policy not formulated, the article assumed the future of the Philippines was indisputable. "Manila is the capital of our new colony, and the 400 islands of the Philippine group, with their 8,000,000 inhabitants, the materials to be used in our first great colonial experiment," *McClure's* reported.[83]

The *McClure's* author candidly recognized the likelihood of resistance by Filipinos to a new master, referring to "wild tribes who are there to dispute our possession. The gems of the Pacific are as yet rough diamonds, and the cutting is going to be harder than the acquisition." Also, a nationalist movement led by Emilio Aguinaldo had quickly formed an independent government. Filipinos fought American troops from February 1899 until July 1902; about 4,200 U.S. soldiers and an estimated 20,000 Filipino insurgents died.[84]

Cosmopolitan, alone among the three magazines, had perceptively informed readers before the war started that Spain also had dealt with periodic rebellions in the Philippine Islands, an indication that Filipinos might not welcome another foreign master. A fourteen-page article in October 1897 summarized the government-church partnership that had ruled Filipinos for three hundred years. Prominently mentioned, in the racial connotation of the era, was Filipino resistance to Spanish colonialism. "Small wonder, then, that the indolent and peace-loving natives, led by more energetic and restive half-castes, have risen repeatedly against the hand that oppresses them," the *Cosmopolitan* author noted.[85]

Cosmopolitan articles discussed the advantages and disadvantages of imperialism, usually within the context of racial superiority. The prospect of a rich commercial trade with China seemed probable, according to a six-page review of opportunities for Americans who could emulate the British and Germans established in coastal cities. Western ambition and expertise practically guaranteed success because the Chinese lacked essential traits. "They have had no incentive to progress and morality," according to the *Cosmopolitan* article. "The consumption of narcotics gratifies the Oriental craving for apathy and escape from consciousness. Western people typically desire fullness of life, exhilaration of spirits, expansion of self-consciousness—hence their love of stimulants." China could not match the West. "The ancient empire stands where it stood when Europe awoke to modern ideas," the article stated.

Cosmopolitan judged Hawaii and the Philippines essential for access to China, but warned readers that imperialism meant the nation must assume the indefinite burden of governance. "The people of the Philippine Islands are divided into at least three races, all Oriental, and each hostile to the others . . . they are utterly incapable of self-government," the author wrote. "Nobody will pretend that Hawaii is designed ever to become a state, or the Philippines are designed to become a state. It is the idlest dream to speculate upon the time when the inhabitants of either of these countries will be fit for the proper discharge of the duties of citizenship under our system."[86]

Attitudes in the *Cosmopolitan* article closely resembled official U.S. Government opinions, evident in a State Department report that described Filipinos as "inferior and unfit to rule." Policy makers believed American administration of the islands would impose "no burden of any kind" and "would help the island." The *Cosmopolitan* article provided a different perspective. "There can be no escape from the proposition that we shall stand stamped with dishonor in the face of the world if we annex the Philippines," the magazine asserted. "Dazzled with Oriental dreams, America must have immense standing armies, multitudinous fleets, and sink the Republic in world-wide imperialism."[87]

In September 1898, *Century* devoted fifteen pages to arguments for and against imperialism. An anti-imperialist essay by Carl Schurz, a nationally known Mugwump, or liberal Republican, employed the same racial judgments the *Cosmopolitan* author used, but expressed in a hyperbolic style. Schurz argued that imperialism was indefensible, thus all territory acquired by the United States must be granted statehood. "Immense territories inhabited by white people of Spanish descent, by Indians, Negroes, mixed Spanish and Indians, mixed Spanish and Negroes, Hawaiians, Hawaiians and mixed blood, Spanish Philippinos, Malays, Tagals, various kinds of savages and half-savages," Schurz wrote, "not to mention the Chinese and Japanese—at least twenty-five millions in all, and all of them animated with the instincts, impulses, and passions bred by the tropical sun; and all those people to become Americans!"[88]

Senate approval of the peace treaty with Spain in early 1899 ended the imperialism debate for *Century, Cosmopolitan,* and *McClure's.* The attention to international events, the war with Spain, and the imperialism debate attracted readers to *Cosmopolitan.* Circulation increased 10 percent from the time of the declaration of war through the Senate vote on the treaty with Spain, reaching 335,000 copies.[89]

Falling Star

McClure's briefly passed *Cosmopolitan* during 1896, distributing an average 259,000 copies monthly to *Cosmopolitan*'s 250,000 copies. The next year *Cos-*

mopolitan regained first place with 300,000 copies to *McClure's* 278,000. But from 1899 through 1905, *McClure's* was the top general magazine and *Cosmopolitan* second, usually behind by 20,000 copies even at its peak distribution of 350,000 copies in 1903.

Intense competition affected all the top-tier quality magazines. *Century,* a successful literary magazine aimed at a genteel readership, gradually added nonfiction articles to each monthly edition, paring fiction and poetry over the years until achieving a rough parity between journalistic and literary material. It never lowered its price. At the beginning of the 1890s, *Century* had a circulation of 198,000 copies; by 1900, circulation had declined to 150,000 copies and it would continue to slide. *Harper's* held remarkably steady at 150,000 copies monthly, but only after it eventually lowered its subscription to $3 a year. *Scribner's* bottomed at 70,000 copies in 1898, then staged a comeback to reach 175,000 copies in 1905 with an emphasis on articles about contemporary events.[90]

Economists would argue that competition benefited everyone, but an argument could be made that competition among the quality magazines adversely affected readers. *Cosmopolitan* and *McClure's* could have offered readers more articles, more photographs, more stories because each magazine could have printed additional pages if reasonably priced at twenty-five cents for a single copy and $3 for a subscription. What articles never were published, what subjects never were explored because of economic constraints? *McClure's* might have failed miserably had it competed at *Cosmopolitan's* price, or it might have succeeded because of its quality. And a prosperous *Cosmopolitan* would have become better than ever because Walker would not have settled for less.

The ultimate effect of the price war forced magazines to rely almost entirely on advertisers for financial support. The first generation of editor-publishers retained editorial integrity, according to Walker. *Cosmopolitan* remained "at all times untrammelled by any adverse advertising influence and free to consider the best interests of the whole people," Walker assured his readers. The historical record affirmed his statement: no references to brand products, no coy allusions to well-known ad phrases or slogans, no evidence of articles rejected or withheld because of content that might displease an advertiser. Still, *Cosmopolitan* did not publish any exposé articles on patent medicines nor did it ban their advertisements, which *Ladies' Home Journal* had the integrity to do. The ads in *Cosmopolitan* for quack products that contained undisclosed amounts of alcohol and narcotics to dull pain sometimes filled four to five pages, which by the early 1900s amounted to a monthly sum of a thousand dollars—sufficiently vital to sustain the magazine.

4

Distraction

Country Life

William Jennings Bryan visited New York City during early summer 1897. It was a chance to thank important city Democrats for their support the previous year, and perhaps to let them know that despite his loss to William McKinley he might try for the presidency again in 1900. At age thirty-seven, Bryan planned to be a political figure for a long time. He relied on a coterie of staunch believers in New York City because the rest of the state was a stronghold of opposition to the Silver Democrats; Bryan had received 40 percent of the state's votes compared to 47 percent nationwide.

The Boy Orator of the Platte started his political rounds Saturday with breakfast at dawn, then took a passenger train to Irvington to see the man whose enthusiastic assistance had been a boon to the presidential campaign. The train arrived at the Irvington station near eight o'clock. Bryan, followed by a few reporters, walked up an adjacent hill past the Cosmopolitan Building and across a meadow to a white, two-story mansion. "Mr. Walker was not expecting Mr. Bryan, and was just getting up when he arrived," according to the *New York Times*.[1]

The first fact perhaps was accurate, but the second fact was questionable. John Brisben Walker did not sleep past dawn. He awoke at sunrise, then worked in bed for two hours or more opening and answering mail, reading manuscripts of articles and stories, writing directives to associate editors, and awaiting his male secretary to report promptly to the bedroom at eight each workday for dictation of memorandums and instructions on the day's tasks. "He would be impatient to begin the day's work," recalled a secretary, one with literary aspirations whose work Walker never accepted for publication. "There was no nonsense tolerated in Mr. Walker's presence." Saturday was no exception. It was a workday, and the weekly editorial conference consumed the afternoon.[2]

In the meantime on this particular Saturday, Walker and Bryan conducted political business. "They walked out on the tennis lawn, and talked for some time," the news article reported. Walker was no political novice, but the caustic public roasting from the *New York Times* the previous autumn had exacted a personal toll. One sardonic editorial had warned people about the "Popocratic" political organizer, using slang for the fusion of Populists and Democrats. "Now, Mr. Walker, barring his temporary aberration of mind on the silver question, is a most estimable and trustworthy citizen," the newspaper commented, before declaring that Walker "can delude himself with the notion that justice requires" silver coinage. "The only safe course for sound-money men to pursue in this campaign is to beware of John Brisben Walker."[3]

During the 1896 campaign, Walker had organized rallies and scheduled appearances for the Democratic candidate in New York City. Bryan had visited Walker's home in Irvington for dinner and an overnight stay several weeks prior to the November election. Democratic leaders and Bryan supporters had convened at Irvington for the day to meet Bryan, the first presidential candidate to travel the country on a campaign. One of the supporters at the campaign session was William Randolph Hearst, the young publisher of the *New York Journal,* a lackluster newspaper until the sensationalist from San Francisco purchased it in autumn 1895. Hearst and Walker were acquaintances who also were active in a municipal government reform organization in New York City to break the hold of Tammany Hall politicos. *Cosmopolitan* had remained mute on the presidential contest, however. Walker was a realist, aware that most *Cosmopolitan* readers lived in eastern states and big cities. He would not endanger his magazine by openly allying it with Bryan.[4]

No doubt his activism on behalf of Bryan had caused some discomfort among business associates in Manhattan. Walker was a charter member of the Up-Town Club, an organization of businessmen that included Simon Brentano, Charles Tiffany, and executives of Macy's, Stern Brothers, Lord & Taylor, and numerous banks. Also, some neighbors in Westchester County scarcely were silver types. Men of wealth who campaigned for Bryan were shunned socially. *New York Times* editorials during summer 1896 referred to Walker's support of Bryan when criticizing and ridiculing the concept of Cosmopolitan University.[5]

The magazine had not abandoned Manhattan completely upon completion of interior work at the Cosmopolitan Building in summer 1897. Its advertising representatives and accountants occupied an office suite in midtown. Walker rode the train into the city each weekday to visit the suite, talk business with those who would still speak with him after his fiscal apostasy, and meet with prospective contributors of articles. Walker preferred country life, though; his childhood home was rural, the cities in West Virginia and Colorado were unlike eastern cities, and he was an outdoors person who enjoyed hiking and riding horses.

Irvington was a forty-minute train ride from the city. It was a proverbial horse-and-buggy community in the mid-1890s, although horseless carriages were an occasional sight on the road to Tarrytown alongside the Hudson River. Walker was fascinated by motor vehicles—also known as "motocycles" and "auto-mobiles." Whenever he saw a motor vehicle on the road that passed by his property he asked for a ride; and Walker learned how to drive with the aid of helpful owners who let him navigate roads, pastures, and golf courses in the area. Walker sensed that these vehicles were the future of transportation.[6]

The Future World

Machinery, science, technology—all were beneficial to humans, all essential to human progress in the pages of *Cosmopolitan*. Throughout most of the 1890s, a five-page section, Progress Of Science, celebrated the wondrous advances of the era: electricity for home and industry, x-rays, pasteurization, agricultural fertilizers, radio, automobiles, motion pictures, and the aeroplane. Walker personally wrote articles describing futuristic scenarios, and he commissioned articles from engineers, intellectuals, and scientists to write informative articles to enlighten *Cosmopolitan* readers. His fascination with marvelous inventions inspired a fervent optimism that the perpetual betterment of human life was possible. *Cosmopolitan* sponsored competitive events to encourage technological innovation and awarded cash prizes to inventors and thinkers. The magazine publicized these events to promote itself and to persuade readers about the bright future that awaited their children and grandchildren. Yet, his obsession with future technology ultimately ruined Walker financially and crippled *Cosmopolitan* to such an extent that a new owner intervened to restore it to prominence.

Aviation was the magazine's first foray into futurism. A *Cosmopolitan* issue of summer 1896 depicted a college campus in 1901, the sky above speckled with bi-wing gliders, each piloted by a man or woman student, circling and drifting above an open grassy quadrangle, where from the roof of a tall tower other gliders launched by dropping toward the earth and swooping upward. "Just what the results to the human race would be if the navigation of the aerial currents could ever be successfully accomplished, it would be impossible to predict," noted the writer, John Brisben Walker.[7]

Cosmopolitan commissioned a contest for an authority on aviation to write an article for the May 1892 issue. Walker set the stage for the presentation with an essay "The Problem Of Aerial Navigation." (The term "navigation" did not apply to point-to-point travel but to the art of flying itself, from becoming airborne to controlling yaw and pitch in flight to returning safely to earth.) *Cosmopolitan* would pay $250 to the person who submitted "the most valuable paper suggesting the best methods of accomplishing navigation of the air," $100 to the second-best essay writer, and $150 for best paper on the effects of "successful aerial navigation upon the moral and material interests of the world."

The editor-publisher expressed his vision of air travel: "To London would mean embarking in a comfortable way at eight a.m. and arriving without the discomforts of sea sickness or bad air by noon of the following day. Leaving New York at sun-up, one would arrive at Denver in time for a late dinner, having passed over the most charming panorama without fatigue and comparatively without danger."[8]

Walker informed readers that Thomas A. Edison, the inventor, agreed to be a consultant for evaluating essays to receive the prizes. Edison "in response to an offer by The Cosmopolitan of $100 per hour for services" had told Walker, "I freely give my services without pay, and the use of my laboratory too if you need it for experiment."[9]

An authority explained the science of aviation to *Cosmopolitan* readers a month prior to the winning essay. Samuel Pierpont Langley, secretary-director of the Smithsonian Institution, referred to experiments by Octave Chanute on aerodynamics and research in meteorology and predicted immediate answers to all existing questions about the mysteries of flight. "The physicist and the engineer will find, then, a new profession here to occupy him later," Langley wrote. Flight was a certainty. "Recent experimentation has rendered it as certain as anything proved and tried can be, that if we only move fast enough, even thin air will resist sufficiently to sustain us."

Langley alluded to flying machines constructed of sturdier material than canvas and wood used for present prototypes. "It has been demonstrated that machines, even if they are built of the heavier metals, such as steel, can be sustained in the air with an expenditure of power certainly within our ability to command," he asserted. Flight was possible "at a great speed," but the obstacle to be overcome was to "guide such machines aright in the desired horizontal path and that we can descend with safety in them."[10]

The winner of the $250 prize was Hiram S. Maxim, inventor of the machine gun and builder of a steam-engine flying box that had flown almost a mile. His four-page article in June 1892 discussed the ratio of horsepower-to-weight necessary for flight, fuel consumption, and speed. Maxim also spent many paragraphs explaining what rudders did and the importance of the craft's center of gravity for lift. A safe arrival required "a large field" with the craft "having approached the field so as to be facing the wind," which would permit a landing "so that all shock would be avoided."[11]

The November 1892 issue carried the second-place essay by John P. Holland, a naval engineer who had designed the first practical submarine and would design the first submarine accepted by the U.S. Navy in 1897. Holland proposed propellers of a specific angle mounted on engines producing eight hundred horsepower to be attached to wings on either side of a fuselage. "Very interesting experimental tests of a thin, flat plane against concaved planes with convexed backs and sharpened edges were made," Holland explained. "The thin, flat plane inclined fifteen degrees gave a lift equal to 4.5 times the drift."[12]

What must be considered here was the willing participation by Langley, Maxim, and Holland, each one a person of repute and dignity, to provide *Cosmopolitan* readers with intelligent, technical information about flight. The magazine was a worthy forum.

Walker continued to promote aviation. He admonished Congress and the public for apathy. "Professor Langley should have had a Congressional appropriation for his work, but has been compelled to work along in a small way owing to the limited resources at his command," Walker wrote in July 1896. "When hundreds of thousands of dollars are being spent upon all sorts of frivolous and unimportant things, it seems incredible that the sum of one hundred thousand dollars cannot be raised for such a purpose."[13]

As he would do for public education, Walker volunteered the resources of *Cosmopolitan* for aviation. "To begin, The Cosmopolitan Magazine subscribes five thousand dollars to a fund, to be expended under the charge of experts, in solving the problem of aerial navigation." The magazine would post its money "provided the additional sum of ninety-five thousand dollars shall be subscribed within six months to the stock of The Cosmopolitan Aeronautical Association." People who bought stock would do so "without any expectation of profit or return of any kind, but simply with a view to furthering the solution of the problem of aerial navigation."[14]

No further word was written about The Cosmopolitan Aeronautical Association. The public was not altruistic.

The subject of aviation was an excuse for the *New York Times* to again put a spotlight on Walker, this time in January 1904. The editor-publisher had arranged a dinner at the Waldorf-Astoria Hotel to honor Langley, a recognition of the scientist's research contributing to the first successful heavier-than-air flight by the Wright brothers the previous month at Kitty Hawk, North Carolina. The newspaper reported: "The aeroplane was discussed much after the fashion of some sort of an automobile, and the speakers dwelt confidently upon the time in the near future when the flying machine would be constantly hitched up to the bay window of the rich man, ready to take him to his downtown office or to Europe." Walker, the reporter noted, predicted that by 1930 aeroplanes "would be the safest means of travel."[15]

The next day an editorial ridiculed Walker. "The curious fact, however, is that there are still many bright and imaginative people who believe that the practical flying machine is imminent," the *New York Times* commented. "For example, Mr. John Brisben Walker permits himself to go on record as a prophet. When gentlemen come together to promote a common fad across the walnuts and the wine, there is no possible objection to their indulging in any amount of airy persiflage; but they should not expect those who have not dined with them to take them quite seriously."[16]

It cannot be determined whether personal or political animosity motivated *New York Times* publisher Adolph Ochs to chastise Walker. This time Walker responded. The newspaper published his full-column letter three days afterward. "My own prediction as to the speedy construction of a merchantable machine was based upon the efforts now being made by scientific minds the world over," Walker stated.[17]

Walker wrote another rejoinder to the *New York Times* for the March 1904 issue of *Cosmopolitan*. "The Final Conquest Of The Air," a tribute to the Wright brothers, opened with this paragraph: "The pettiness of the human mind, the cowardice of man, has never been so well illustrated in any phase of the world's development as in the slow evolution of the flying-machine. Every man who attempted to advance the art of aerostation risked the ridicule of the unintelligent world, risked the criticism of conservative minds, and even grave doubts as to his mental quality."[18]

On more earthly subjects, Walker's faith in the future was nowhere more evident than the attention and space given to expositions, commonly called world's fairs. *Cosmopolitan* conveyed awe and wonder at the achievements of engineers, mechanics, and scientists with its articles about the Columbian Exposition of 1893 in Chicago, the Pan-American Exposition of 1901 in Buffalo, and the Louisiana Purchase Exposition of 1904 in St. Louis. "The Cosmopolitan has represented from the beginning the belief that, with the closing of the nineteenth century, the human race is destined to make rapid strides towards a new and higher civilization," Walker asserted.[19]

Two articles preceded the Chicago event. The first used a highly unusual stream-of-consciousness writing style, a technique popularized by journalist Tom Wolfe seven decades later. The *Cosmopolitan* writer described the Loop at closing time in late afternoon:

Cabs, carts, hacks, wagons, trucks, grips, gongs, gamins, bells, yells, shouts, swear words, shrill-voiced newsboys, dago fruit sellers, rushing street urchins tumbling over everybody; gum-chewing, giggling shopgirls; bewildered, bundle-laden rustics; pallid, weary-looking typewriters; elbowing, jostling, toe-treading clerks and counter jumpers; hulking street loafers, furtively eyeing the club-brandishing policemen; everyone going full tilt, every man for himself and the devil take the hindmost. Collisions, shocks, wild plunges for hats that go skimming among the tramping feet; crash in the street, locking wheels, declamatory policemen, blaspheming driver, slang, billingsgate, uproar, clatter, ear-piercing screams—some woman's small boy under the wheels—no, he isn't, only stooped to pick up an apple.[20]

The second article boasted about the grandness of the exposition. On a site of 974 acres, the Chicago event was ten times the size of the Paris Exposition of 1889. The exposition featured landscape architecture by Frederick Law Olmsted and a basin into which flowed water from Lake Michigan, and the nighttime brightness of the electrifying all-electric White City.[21]

Finally, the September 1893 issue: its introductory article was written by Walker, followed by ninety-four pages of text and several dozen photographs or illustrations, and a final article written by former president Benjamin Harrison, who congratulated exposition organizers and the American public for an event certain to impress the world.

Walker was no detached observer. He admired the majestic buildings and enthused about the demeanor of the crowds. "No monarch in the history of the world ever had such palaces erected," he exclaimed. "And these palaces are not the whim of one man for the pleasure of himself and his courtiers, but the first great creation of a government intended originally to be of the people, for the people, and by the people, a government that perhaps has not yet attained that ideal, but promises in the early future to scientifically solve the problems of distribution." The people earned praise, too. "What a change has come over our civilization in the past twenty-five years! Such a crowd, anywhere in the United States, before the sixties or seventies, would have been the scene of endless personal conflicts, of drunkenness. Yet here were only happy, smiling faces, women and children moving with perfect freedom."[22]

New agricultural equipment, including a multi-row harvester, was on display; General Electric built a Tower of Light with its dynamo visible to spectators; a schedule of exhibitions of steam-driven machinery and fiery molds demonstrated efficient industrial production; and an electric train rolled along a perimeter track. *Cosmopolitan* published 40,000 words. It wasn't enough.

The December 1893 issue presented seventy-two pages summarizing the Chicago exposition's significance. Its writer, Paul Bourget, a French novelist, believed the most noteworthy aspect was the concentration on agricultural and industrial progress by every participant nation from Asia, Europe, and the Americas. No nation flaunted military progress. "Think, again, what this absence of military pomp means: the reign of law instead of war; what it promises of peace, of sinew for industry instead of for murder!" The writer prophesied, "This is the age of cooperation."[23]

Mark Twain contributed a short story, "Travelling With A Reformer," a tale of his intention to visit the White City, but his diversion to Boston because of a companion who had "a passion for reforming petty public abuses." He and

Twain stood patiently at a telegraph desk "trying to get the attention of one of the young operators, but they were all skylarking." The companion helped himself to a telegram blank, scribbled a note on it, and handed it to a skylarker. It was addressed to the president of Western Union Telegraph Company, the lad's employer. "When he read it he lost color and began to apologize and explain," Twain wrote. The rest of the journey consisted of the companion rectifying bad manners and bad behavior.[24]

For the 1901 event in Buffalo, *Cosmopolitan* dispatched a veritable squad of writers to record their impressions of the Pan American Exposition—fourteen in all, plus the editor-publisher. The result was ninety-eight pages of text, which featured dozens of photographs. An enthralled Walker told readers about a future urban metropolis of boulevards, trees, parks, and buildings of moderate height to permit the sun to light the daytime streets: "Who believes that the people of the second half of our new century will be content to live in those abominations of desolation which we call our great cities—brick and mortar piled higgledy-piggledy, glaringly vulgar, stupidly offensive, insolently trespassing on the right to sunshine and fresh air, conglomerate result of a competitive individualism which takes no regard for the rights of one's neighbor?"[25]

Improvement to city life was important to reformers of the era. American cities were filthy places, their municipal services inefficient and contracted to bidders who bribed the politicians signing the contracts. Many city residents lived in squalid poverty. The quality magazines, *Cosmopolitan* and *Century* among them, often published articles that presented ideas for the figurative and literal cleanup of cities. Walker, whose ideas for municipal transit systems and cooperative apartment complexes for poor people *Cosmopolitan* promoted, saw the displays at expositions and world's fairs as feasible creations of an urban paradise.[26]

Walker and *Cosmopolitan* outdid themselves in September 1904. The entire magazine of 144 pages described the World's Fair in St. Louis. The editor-publisher wrote every article, every photo caption. The effort produced approximately 60,000 words of text. Walker had dictated to "two stenographic secretaries," usually while he walked through exhibits during an eleven-day visit in late June. A photographer took two hundred pictures for publication. Writing, editing, and coordinating the tasks associated with an entire issue devoted to a single topic took so much time that the introductory article from Walker incorrectly stated the number of pages—128—when it actually amounted to 144. He overlooked the mistake when he closed the issue by explaining it was "necessary to increase the number to one hundred and forty-four pages."[27]

Most impressive to him were classroom teaching demonstrations, active smelters, active well-digging, a metal clamp that automatically and correctly instructed a counter clerk to slice a proper amount of cheese, and ongoing scientific lectures on a fantastic array of subjects. "Science is even invading the realm of the mind and undertaking to point out the germs of good and evil," Walker observed. "Science is taking the drunkard from the gutter and releasing him from the slavery of the alcoholic germ."[28]

A lecture by an educator offered an opportunity for Walker to cite statistical evidence of the nation's inconsistency in schools. Colorado appropriated $7.60 per capita for its schools, "the maximum for any state." New York spent $5.70 per capita. "Again the eye rests on some of the Southern states," Walker noted— per capita expenditures of eighty-nine cents in Louisiana, ninety-one cents in Tennessee, and ninety-eight cents in Georgia.[29]

Automotive demonstrations warranted praise. A "freight-carrying automobile truck" was a "steam-car without tracks" that showed why railroads were obsolete, if only the barons of finance would see the future. "But so conservative is the human mind and so stupid is capital," Walker declared, railroads controlled transportation. "The exhibit of this class of car is surprisingly small at St. Louis," he stated. "It should have been one of the most notable."[30]

Articles mentioned a variety of manufacturers, including Edison Electric, International Harvester, Remington, and Westinghouse. Walker assured his readers that *Cosmopolitan* would not benefit financially from these references, "It is unnecessary for The Cosmopolitan to say that no word of mention in any part of this number is paid advertising."[31]

An extra 151,000 copies of *Cosmopolitan* were printed for the special World's Fair issue. It was not a perfect issue. To write all the articles and captions consumed Walker's time from mid-July to early August. The writing was fine, but photographs were placed on pages without regard to adjacent text; sometimes, the scene of an exhibit or a building had no relationship and a reader was left to search the magazine for relevant information. No matter its flaws, a cloth-cover souvenir issue sold for fifty cents to nonsubscribers. Not all the extra copies were bought, because *Cosmopolitan* offered them as premiums to new subscribers a year later.[32]

Troubles

Cosmopolitan for January 1896 announced a $3,000 prize to the builder of a vehicle that would win a roundtrip race from city hall in lower Manhattan to Ardsley Country Club near Irvington. (The prize would be equivalent to $70,000 in 2010 dollars.) The winner would be judged on speed, ease of driving, cost, and "simplicity and durability of construction." The stunt was partly promotional, partly personal—John Brisben Walker wanted to align *Cosmopolitan* with modernity and to persuade his readers that the technology of motor vehicles was practical.[33]

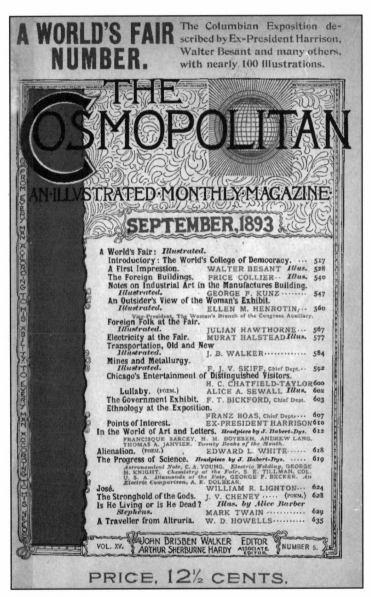

Cosmopolitan devoted many pages to lengthy articles about each World's Fair while John Brisben Walker was editor-publisher. The socialist motto, "From Every Man According To His Ability, To Every Man According To His Needs," adorned the cover of *Cosmopolitan* throughout most of Walker's ownership. *Cosmopolitan,* September 1893; source: Morgan Library, Colorado State University.

he Horseless Carriage Competition.—The indications are, at this writing, that the test of horseless carriages which will be made under the auspices of THE COSMOPOLITAN, on the 30th of May, in competition for a Prize of $3000, will attract the widest attention. The Committee of Judges who have already accepted, is probably the most distinguished that has ever consented to act upon the occasion of the trial of a new and useful invention. It consists of

NELSON A. MILES, The General of the Army.

WILLIAM P. CRAIGHILL, Chief of Engineers, U. S. Army.

H. WALTER WEBB, Vice-President N. Y. Central & H. R. R.R. Co.

JOHN JACOB ASTOR, Esq.

The interest which these gentlemen have shown in accepting places upon this Committee is indicative of the importance of the subject. The contest itself will receive international attention in both military and civilian circles.

A roundtrip automobile driving contest sponsored by *Cosmopolitan* in 1896 attracted many entrants for the midtown Manhattan to suburban Irvington circuit. The prize would be the equivalent of $70,000 in 2010. *Cosmopolitan*, April 1896; source: Morgan Library, Colorado State University.

Duryea Motor Wagon Company won the money; its vehicle made the trip to the country club in an hour and five minutes, returning to city hall "in even shorter time." Judges for the contest were General Nelson Miles, commander of the army; Chauncey Depew, president of New York Central and Hudson River Railroad; John Jacob Astor; and two other men. They awarded the prize to recognize "the important part which the new horseless carriage must play in the life of the twentieth century, and the impetus its perfection must give to the building of new roads at the end of the present century," an article stated.[34]

Spectators were skeptical about the new mode of transportation. The Duryea and other vehicles got stuck in a turnaround area—a plowed field—adjoining the country club. "The occupants of carriages were compelled to dismount and assist the motors in their work, creating an unfavorable impression in the minds of the onlookers," *Cosmopolitan* reported.

The preceding January the magazine had published a seven-page article with ten photographs detailing the various experimental engines in development for the motocycle, a vogue name for a motor vehicle. Battery, "gasolene," and steam engines competed for selection. "The question of the practicality of the motocycle, or horseless carriage, as a desirable, rapid, and safe means of conveyance has gone beyond the speculative state," *Cosmopolitan* asserted.[35]

Several other articles and Progress Of Science column items noted developments in motor transport. A photograph in one article showed a bicycle with a motor mounted between the pedals. An illustration of a "bicycle railroad" depicted a single-track overhead suspension train with individual passengers standing inside walk-in cubicles. Another illustration of a "freight trolley" resembled a present-day monorail. *Cosmopolitan* welcomed the future.[36]

An article by Walker, "Some Speculations Regarding Rapid Transit," compared expenses for motor vehicles with other forms of transit and mentioned a social benefit. "With asphalted streets, the cost of operating numberless eight-seated, low-running vehicles, under a carefully planned organization, ought not to be greater than the present cost of cable cars," he predicted. "This would mean the disintegration of the great companies who now control street car transportation in the large cities, and everywhere prove so corrupting an element in the city elections. No mere cab company can ever become a menace at the polls."[37]

Walker also opposed construction of the New York subway system. His commentary in the *New York Times* dismissed the idea that private automobiles and motor buses would clog the city. "The plea that the streets would be crowded by such an excess of vehicles is not tenable," Walker wrote. "It would only be necessary to regulate the traffic to each street so that it would pass in but one direction. This would enable a stream of vehicles to travel at an extremely rapid rate."[38]

Walker, ever the entrepreneur, let his fascination with motor transport evolve to participation in the industry. A visit to a Boston exhibition of vehicles in autumn 1898 introduced him to the Stanley Steamer, an eponymous vehicle recently engineered by twin brothers from Massachusetts. Walker surprised the brothers with an offer in February 1899 to buy a partnership in their company. They did not want a partner. He persisted, and in April 1899 offered to buy the company. To dissuade him, the brothers set what they considered an unreasonable price of $250,000. Walker did not hesitate. However, he had no cash because his fortune was invested in the Cosmopolitan Building and equipment for *Cosmopolitan*. The Stanleys gave him ten days to come up with the quarter-million dollars.

None of the wealthy scions in his neighborhood wanted to front the money to Walker for the acquisition. He did find a willing investor whose estate was up the road from the *Cosmopolitan* site, and the man supplied the cash to acquire the patent rights to the Stanley steam engine. The contract prohibited the brothers from manufacturing their own steamer for a year. Walker was half-owner of the new venture, the Locomobile Company; his half would come from a loan for the purchase of property and construction of a factory in West-chester County.

True to form, Walker was impossible to work with and the partnership dis-solved within a few months. The partner retained the Locomobile name and the Stanley factory in Massachusetts.[39]

Walker obtained a mortgage from a New York City bank for land and a fac-tory in North Tarrytown, not far from Irvington. The loan enabled him to buy six hundred acres for $164,000. Stanford White designed the factory. To begin production, Walker had to buy equipment that cost tens of thousands of dol-lars. The Irvington acreage and Cosmopolitan Building were collateral for an equipment loan from Travelers Insurance of Hartford, Connecticut. *Cosmo-politan* itself was not encumbered by the loan. Walker also incorporated the Mobile Company of America; later, he would create its successor, the Mobile Rapid Transit Company, with four sons as partners.[40]

Early in 1900 the factory began production of a fifty-mile-per-hour steam-er runabout priced at $650, a six-passenger steamer sedan for $2,000, and a steamer omnibus, or delivery vehicle, also for $2,000. To demonstrate the agil-ity and power of the Mobile sedan, Walker shipped the car to Colorado by train, then drove it up a narrow trail almost to the top of Pike's Peak; the trail became a footpath, preventing the car from proceeding. It was the first motor vehicle to accomplish the feat, and not without considerable risk. "The road was in frightful condition," Walker told the *New York Times*. "Going back was like coming down a toboggan slide."[41]

It was at this point Walker tried and failed to sell the army on the idea of a steamer wagonette as a troop transport. His steamer vehicle was an idea in need of a mechanic. The wagonette was unreliable and took too long to build up steam for the engine.[42]

Now was the time for retribution by New York City politicos whom Walk-er had irritated with his participation in municipal government reform. Tam-many Hall controlled the city, and its operatives played hardball. First, police began arresting Mobile Company omnibus drivers on their regular delivery routes into the city from North Tarrytown. The traffic tickets cited omnibus drivers for lacking an engineer's license. Walker protested that an engineer's license was unnecessary because each vehicle had an automatic transmission that did not require any special skill other than steering. An omnibus was hard-ly a railroad engine. The New York legislature eventually amended the law to eliminate the engineer's license for steam vehicles, for which an examination was mandatory, and instead require a driver's license.[43]

Next, the six Mobile Company wagonettes that operated in lower Manhattan were stopped by the city marshal, who enforced licensing of businesses. Accord-ing to the marshal, the wagonettes were a bus service, not a taxi service. Walker said the wagonettes were for-hire, meaning a person on the street waved them over for a ride. Walker conceded that the wagonettes ran a regular roundtrip route from Wall Street to the Waldorf-Astoria Hotel, Grand Central Station, and Pennsylvania Station. The city marshal insisted the route made it a bus service. Walker told the drivers to remove exterior signboards that listed the destinations, but the city marshal refused to relent. Mobile Company was compelled to buy a bus license.[44]

Automobiles needed paved roadways. Walker organized the National Highway Commission in 1900. A private organization, the commission lobbied state legislatures to fund networks of highways. Walker sent letters to Congress advocating a coast-to-coast national highway.[45]

He also was a founder of the National Association of Automobile Manufacturers the same year. The association's membership reflected the character of the infant industry, its two dozen participants small manufacturers located in Massachusetts, New Jersey, New York, and Pennsylvania.[46]

Never a person to delegate authority, Walker handled every detail concerning Mobile Company and *Cosmopolitan*. The magazine suffered from his inattention. Associate editors reviewed manuscripts, commented on them, and waited for Walker to respond. Ideas for articles awaited approval. Weeks passed and the stacks of manuscripts in editorial offices grew taller. His personal secretary noted the decline in the magazine's status. "The Cosmopolitan was an old plaything with him, and in his preoccupation with motors he forgot, from then on, many details connected with his editorial work," the secretary observed. "The household magazine which he had started languished because of his inordinate interest in the greater venture, and his editors were in despair."[47]

Walker's instinct about motor vehicles was correct, of course, but he was dead wrong about the steam engine. Gasoline engines were better for many reasons, not least of which was ease of operation. No boiler to refill, no burner to clean, no separate container for boiler fuel, and no problems with leaky valves and feeder pipes. Steam engines were much cheaper to run, namely because water was free, but the internal combustion engine was ready to run upon ignition and peppier on the road. These factors and the high prices for Mobile Company runabouts and touring wagons doomed the venture.

The steamer company was in desperate shape by autumn 1902. A promotional campaign to attract investors from the general public at $100 a share to raise $400,000 attracted few people. The final blow was the formation in March 1903 of the Automobile Trust, a consortium of gasoline-engine vehicle manufacturers—Olds, Packard, Pierce, Stevens-Duryea, and others. Members of the trust pledged to share hundreds of patents for engines and transmissions, which were available for nominal fees, and also agreed to quash all pending patent-infringement lawsuits involving other members of the trust. The

Automobile Trust permitted rapid growth in the industry for gas-powered vehicles. The steamer was dead. Mobile Company had sold six hundred steam vehicles, and that was it.[48]

Mobile Company ceased production. Its corporate successor, the Mobile Rapid Transit Company, manufactured a few dozen wagonettes that did not sell. The factory and property in North Tarrytown were leased by Maxwell-Briscoe Motor Company. (The factory ultimately was bought by Chevrolet, which then became part of General Motors. The factory, frequently expanded and modernized, remained operational until the mid-1990s, when it was razed.) Following a subsequent misadventure on Walker's part in real estate development in North Tarrytown, he sold the factory and property for $350,000. This enabled him to retire the bank mortgage, but not a final $40,000 of the Travelers Insurance loan, which still held a lien on the Irvington site. The man from Colorado who had arrived in New York with a fortune of at least $620,000 in autumn 1888 now lacked cash to clear the title on *Cosmopolitan*'s home.[49]

Adrift

The last half of Walker's tenure at *Cosmopolitan* witnessed a profound change in his political ideology. The friend of laborers who fought for them on the pages of his magazine became a defender of industrialists. Cartels were efficient, and the men who created them were obeying the dictates of natural progression.

A commentary by Walker criticized proponents of an income tax rate of 7 percent on individuals who earned more than $500,000 a year—an interesting about-face from the editor-publisher who formerly had advocated an income tax on industrialists. Among the industrialists who would pay the top rate was John D. Rockefeller. Walker protested on behalf of the oil tycoon. "The common opinion is that such a man is a legitimate object for attack, to be taxed and badgered with the hope that he may be made to disgorge," Walker wrote. "An attack upon him is an attack by one part of the public upon another part of the public. It is nothing more nor less than civil industrial war."[50]

The difference in Walker's attitude was most obvious nearly a decade after the Homestead tragedy. In autumn 1892, an irate John Brisben Walker had excoriated "rich Romans" whose "bands of fighting bullies" and "gladiators" were responsible for deaths at Homestead, Pennsylvania, and other scenes of labor violence. The righteous anger in "The 'Homestead' Object Lesson" arose from the battle between Pinkerton security guards and laborers on strike at a steel mill owned by Andrew Carnegie. In autumn 1903, Walker made amends.

The editor-publisher reviewed a book about the life and career of Carnegie, whose steelworks at Homestead were among the many foundries and mills recently combined by financier J. P. Morgan into the largest trust of all, United States Steel Company. Walker's was no ordinary book review of one or, at most, two pages; it was twenty pages divided into two consecutive issues of *Cosmopolitan*. The extended review glorified Carnegie for efficient management and bold decisions to create ancillary ventures that forged the steel his workers produced. The review also excused the steel baron for the acts of chicanery and unfair pricing practices specified in the book, citing prevalent standards. Walker admitted in his review of "The History Of The Carnegie Steel Company" to admiration for Carnegie, and described a personal meeting many years previously where Carnegie emphasized the importance of reinvesting profit to continuously adopt new technology. "They were my first insight into the methods which have made Mr. Carnegie so successful," Walker remembered.[51]

On the matter of the Homestead strike and deaths, the book review blamed Henry Clay Frick, manager of the mills. Frick "became hardened in dealing with men who were ever ready to take advantage," Walker wrote. "Mr. Frick organized an army of private detectives, fitted up a gunboat and in the night moved up to Homestead."[52]

Labor leaders were selfish, Walker commented, more concerned about keeping their ten-dollar-a-day steward jobs than serving the workers they represented. The leadership was confrontational. Violence was inevitable.

Carnegie, though, was not responsible for the Homestead tragedy, Walker implied, because he had delegated complete authority to Frick. The entire book, according to Walker, was based on conversations between the writer and Frick, an attempt to sully Carnegie's reputation resulting from a financial dispute. "The leaning . . . is evident throughout the book in favor of Mr. Frick," Walker stated. "Doubtless Mr. Frick, who, since the famous lawsuit with Mr. Carnegie, has been reported as feeling strongly against the latter, was only too glad to furnish all necessary data. This affords a very interesting illustration of the lack of diplomacy which prevails in the offices of some of the great corporations amongst those accustomed to the exercise of much power."[53]

Finally, Walker judged the creation of United States Steel Company at the instigation of Morgan. "Undoubtedly his conception of the uniting of the various interests in the steel industry was a correct one," Walker wrote. "Under the old conditions there would have been fierce competitive war which would have resulted disastrously to the companies and to the public."[54]

This was published several months prior to his own experience with the Automobile Trust, and it followed years of ferocious competition against other magazines, notably *McClure's*. Perhaps a Magazine Trust would have proven beneficial, with each publication agreeing to sell for twenty cents at vendors and for $2.40 a subscription. Whatever his rationale for believing Carnegie and Morgan were benevolent, Walker was seriously out of touch with public sentiment. Perhaps his devotion to the Mobile Company had isolated him from political currents, but the Progressive movement was very much alive. The traditional classic liberalism of American life and politics, which rejected the idea of governmental regulation of businesses because private enterprise was private property, was yielding to public disenchantment and disillusion with the powerful cabals of financiers, manufacturers, and processors that controlled the national economy. Reform and regulation were on the agenda.[55]

Wisconsin had elected a Republican progressive governor; President Theodore Roosevelt had ordered the Justice Department to sue a railroad holding company for violating the Sherman Antitrust Act; and *McClure's* had begun publishing a nineteen-part series by Ida Tarbell exposing the machinations of John D. Rockefeller's Standard Oil Company. *McClure's* had led all magazines in the crucial enterprise of exposé journalism. For several years during the early 1900s magazines crusaded against government corruption, fraudulent insurance companies, business monopolies, and unsafe medical products. Reformers were organizing across political party lines into a coalition dominated by urban activists and therefore were more effective than the rural populists of the previous decade. Magazines that went to middle-class readers assisted reformers.[56]

Cosmopolitan stood aside. McClure had hired an able team of journalists to produce exposés; Walker did next to nothing. Months after the legendary January 1903 issue of *McClure's* launched exposé series, *Cosmopolitan* seemed to take the opposite side. *Cosmopolitan* in August 1903 defended meatpackers, an industry notorious for substandard practices. An article entitled "A Pound Of Meat" praised American meatpackers for "the sanitary end of the manufacture" of beef and pork. "No laws could enforce greater efforts toward cleanliness," the writer asserted. The article also assured readers that government inspectors were vigilant, ensuring that no diseased cattle ever were butchered for human consumption. "Should the inner organs show infection, that animal is instantly condemned, and the entire carcass is cooked up for grease and fertilizer," the article explained. "This loss is gladly borne by the packer, and should the Government give up this inspection, he would use every effort to have it reinstated." In 1906, a novel by Upton Sinclair, *The Jungle*, would paint a different picture.[57]

(Curiously, Walker volunteered to inspect slaughterhouses in Chicago within weeks of publication of *The Jungle*. "I have left no stone unturned and have spared no effort to secure, at first hand where possible, the real facts of the meat situation in so far as they related to the house of Swift & Company," Walker wrote in the preface to "Condition Of The Chicago Packing House And Stock Yard," a report he submitted to President Theodore Roosevelt in October 1906. Walker faulted Swift & Company for low wages and long hours for women and for allowing too few work breaks for cutters. He also recommended hiring more sanitation inspectors. Other than that, Walker reported that the processing of meat posed no threat to public health.)[58]

During the momentous shift in public perception that now regarded industrialists and mercantilists with apprehension and suspicion, *Cosmopolitan* published a "Captains Of Industry" series portraying rich and powerful autocrats in preponderantly positive prose—an incredibly lengthy series in monthly installments from May 1902 to March 1904. This stupendous output of capsule biographies profiled 138 corporate executives, entrepreneurs, and scions of American gentry, each one staring or glaring at readers from a portrait-style photograph. The series filled 206 pages of the magazine. Among those profiled were Andrew Carnegie, Thomas Edison, Henry Flagler, Meyer Guggenheim and sons, Edward Henry Harriman, William Randolph Hearst, John D. Rockefeller, Charles Schwab, Gustavus Swift, William K. Vanderbilt, George Westinghouse, and William Whitney. Decisions by these men set prices for many consumer products, lessened competition among manufacturers and transportation companies, and determined the pay and working conditions of millions of people. *Cosmopolitan* alluded to controversies, but did not hold the men responsible. Their ambition, intelligence, and perseverance were celebrated.[59]

Of the sensationalist, warmongering Hearst, the profile writer declared, "The actual intention of W. R. Hearst, through his newspapers, is to fight persistently the cause of genuine democracy—not merely the Democracy of a political party, but the real democracy upon which the government is founded." No reference was made to the Hearst brand of irresponsible journalism, personal vendettas, and opportunistic orchestration of exposés that coincided with the publisher's political career. The writer of the *Cosmopolitan* profile was Arthur Brisbane, editor of Hearst's *New York American and Journal,* a connection Walker evidently did not consider a disqualification. Brisbane complimented his boss for being unlike the sons of other wealthy families. "He has succeeded in spite of wealth," Brisbane wrote, a reference to the father, George Hearst. The father was owner or a partner of an empire of copper, gold, and silver mines that included a founder's stake in the Comstock lode in Nevada, Homestake in the Dakotas, and Anaconda in Montana. No mention was made about the father appointing his son editor-publisher of the family's newspaper, the *San Francisco Examiner,* at age twenty-four in 1887, or that the purchase of the *New York Journal* in 1895 was financed by a loan from his mother, who controlled a trust fund enriched by the deceased father's mining shares. The profile delivered an unintentionally prophetic statement, "Of many great newspapers and great editors this has been the history: they began poor and radical, they ended rich and conservative."[60]

Cosmopolitan became less serious the last three full years of Walker's tenure. Its promotional ads boasted about stories and photographs, not about articles on contemporary events. The magazine carried an average of six stories an issue during 1901–1904, an allocation of nearly forty-five pages each month, or almost 40 percent of total pages. This proportion was approximately double the allocation for fiction three years earlier. Articles still accounted for sixty pages a month, but had the previous ratio prevailed the magazine would have carried eighty pages. A back-of-the-book photographic section of four to six full-page photographs displayed beautiful women in artistic poses, always fully dressed, and an occasional scene of a child at play or a family together on a lawn.

Walker was not the editor-publisher he once was. Walter Hines Page, a famous editor of the era who had worked at *Atlantic Monthly, Forum,* and *World's Work,* spoke to journalists at a Sphinx Club dinner in New York City and described the ideal magazine editor. "I would name moral earnestness as the point of first importance for the American magazine editor who seeks to make the ideal magazine," Page said. "He should not think that a magazine ought to have anything to do with literature. The making of a magazine is not literature; it is journalism. Those editors who are trying to get out monthly literature are making dull magazines." Walker was in the audience.[61]

Walker, attempting to recover from his financial bind, started a new magazine, *Twentieth Century Home,* in February 1904. A son, James Randolph Walker, was editor. It focused on home décor, architecture, and fiction for women. Photographs appeared on almost every page—furniture, interiors of rooms, lighting fixtures. Advertisements for relevant products closely resembled items in the photographs. To attract subscribers to the new magazine, the premium was the 1904 World's Fair issue of *Cosmopolitan.* The new publication ceased in May 1905.

In desperation, Walker tried to sell his last tract of riverfront land in Denver to the city. He disguised the intent to sell four hundred lots as a gift, publicly proclaiming that the land was worth a million dollars but Denver could have it for $600,000. A local newspaper commented that if the city paid the asking price of $1,500 per lot it "would cause the average real estate dealer to burst with envy." An editorial sarcastically remarked that Walker "may be a shade too generous and too much inclined to throw away his money" by selling for such a low price; instead, the newspaper suggested, he should find a private buyer who would pay full price. Denver did not buy the lots.[62]

At age fifty-seven, Walker contemplated the future as owner of a formerly prestigious and popular magazine now far from the top. His fortune was gone. He had no prospects for financial recovery. Monthly distribution for *Cosmo-*

politan had fallen perilously by early 1905, down to 230,000 copies. Advertisers were aware of its diminished vitality and stature; the magazine carried a monthly average of seventy-two ad pages, which generated actual revenue of $11,200. *Cosmopolitan* was in a downward spiral.[63]

Walker contacted Brisbane. *Cosmopolitan* was for sale if William Randolph Hearst was interested. The asking price was $400,000. The amount reflected the magazine's fall.

Hearst bought *Cosmopolitan* in May 1905.[64]

Walker would tell friends and family he sold the magazine for a million dollars, seemingly a favorite sum of his. Hearst told his associates he paid $400,000—payable in five annual installments. Considering the circulation decline and drop in ad pages at *Cosmopolitan,* it was likely Hearst told the truth.[65]

Failures

Cosmopolitan was gone, but the magnificent building in Irvington remained in Walker's hands. For some reason, none of the money from Hearst repaid the Travelers Insurance loan; a lien remained on the Cosmopolitan Building, which was leased to other businesses for several years. In 1915, Travelers Insurance forced a sale to retire the loan. Walker received $40,000 from the proceeds. The stately Cosmopolitan Building was sold by the new owner to a metals manufacturer the same year for $100,000. Then it briefly was a movie studio. A cycle of vacancy and tenancy followed. A variety of commercial, manufacturing, and multipurpose tenants occupied the place. The building stands today, known as the Trent Building. It overlooks the railroad tracks that had carried bundles of *Cosmopolitan* magazines to subscribers and vendors.[66]

Walker used at least $100,000 from the *Cosmopolitan* sale to buy several thousand acres of mostly mountainous terrain and hilly ravines west of Denver. The lifetime entrepreneur then embarked on several ventures that all ended in failure. First, he developed hilltop lots in the rugged tract of land near Denver for houses, accessible only by a cable car; few people were interested in such a remote location. Next, he worked with mechanics to invent an asphalt paver for multilane highway work; it was a complex, unreliable machine that was never manufactured. Finally, he tried a few small real estate developments in Colorado; none was profitable.

In the meantime, Walker started construction on a presidential summer residence at Mount Falcon, his personal tract of hilltop property southwest of Denver. The residence was meant to be available to presidents and their families during summer to relax in the fresh, cooler air of Colorado as an escape from the stifling heat of Washington, D.C.—all for free. One night a lightning bolt from a thunderstorm struck the partially built residence, or an arsonist set a blaze, and the structure burned to its stone foundation. Walker lacked the money to build anew.

He also owed back taxes on a gorgeous, scenic piece of land called Red Rocks. The site of a natural amphitheater with wonderful acoustics, Red Rocks was host to operas, symphonies, and other outdoor events from the early 1900s to 1920s. Walker negotiated with Denver to take the property in lieu of taxes for a park. The city refused, but Red Rocks later was deeded to Denver and is a city park famous for its beauty, hiking trails, and outdoor concerts.[67]

Walker, a widower, moved to Brooklyn late in the 1920s to live with a son. John Brisben Walker died there in July 1931, at age eighty-three.[68]

His contribution to magazine journalism has received some attention from scholars, always in comparison to *Century* and *McClure's*. Most scholars compared *Cosmopolitan's* fiction to *Century* and *Cosmopolitan's* articles on current events and science to *McClure's,* but the scope of *Cosmopolitan's* editorial material and Walker's personal agenda exhibited in magazine articles on educational reform, humane treatment of laborers, and the international role of the United States were not recognized. *Cosmopolitan* was a prominent, serious, quality magazine for many years during his ownership.

The magazine was not a political pulpit. Walker did not align *Cosmopolitan* with either Republicans or Democrats, although he was a political activist. The magazine truly was nonpartisan on most subjects, and when it favored an action or a policy it did so because Walker believed in it. For sixteen years, his personal preferences determined everything that appeared on its pages. *Cosmopolitan* sought to educate and inform its readers, to make them sufficiently knowledgeable about events that they might be better citizens.

5

Sensation

Privilege

Of the eleven biographies written about William Randolph Hearst, two described him as something of a saint: generous, honest, idealistic, kind, loyal. The first was written by the wife of a former Hearst editor, the second by one of his own sons. Nine other Hearst biographers agreed the man had some positive traits, but their descriptions of less than saintly characteristics established his personality for eternity: irresponsible, reckless, selfish, vain, vindictive.

Vanity—"his indomitable refusal to shrink from publicity," according to a biographer—brought him success in journalism. Hearst's newspapers proudly proclaimed his ownership, always on the editorial page and sometimes on the front page, too, above the nameplate. Hearst was certain his name sold papers. In summer 1905, there was no reason not to believe his name would help sell *Cosmopolitan* upon its entry to the Hearst media empire. The magazine needed a new identity, something to alert the public to its different format and style. Strangely, though, the name of William Randolph Hearst was not associated with *Cosmopolitan*. Instead, International Magazine Company was the listed owner; neither was Hearst one of the three executives named on the masthead. Twelve years passed until Hearst proclaimed ownership of *Cosmopolitan* in its pages.[1]

Evidently, his vanity yielded to sensibility because Hearst intended *Cosmopolitan* to be an orator for him. A national publication, *Cosmopolitan* could shout his ideals and ideology, his invective and spite to a readership generally unaware of its connection to Hearst. The publisher whose newspapers were known for sensationalism and vitriol had astutely decided to separate *Cosmopolitan* from the Hearst brand, aware that not everyone admired or liked his journalism and politics, especially the American middle class.[2]

William Randolph Hearst wanted to be president of the United States. Hearst acquired *Cosmopolitan* when he was a second-term Democratic congressman representing a working-class district in Manhattan, although his absences from 83 percent of congressional roll calls indicated the district was not represented well. Hearst had come surprisingly close to the Democratic nomination for president in 1904, but the refusal of William Jennings Bryan to endorse him had doomed his quest. Hearst regarded the decision as disloyal because his newspapers had touted Bryan for president in 1896 and 1900, had sponsored rallies, and had vilified William McKinley and the Republicans. Then in autumn 1905, Tammany Hall Democrats cheated Hearst, an independent candidate, out of becoming mayor of New York City by flagrant ballot-box fraud. In 1906, Hearst was the Democratic candidate for governor of New York and lost by a margin of only 4 percent.[3]

It was noteworthy that *Cosmopolitan* never reported the campaign or election results for governor of New York, a highly uncharacteristic silence by a Hearst publication whenever the publisher was on the political stage. Neither did *Cosmopolitan* publicize his sponsorship of a national independent party and presidential candidate in 1908, or his ultimately futile attempt to maneuver the Democratic presidential nomination his way in 1912.

Hearst in those years was not the media baron most people know about now. At the point his political dreams yielded to reality, Hearst owned nine newspapers, four magazines, and International News Service (INS). Twenty years later, just before the Depression era gutted his media empire, Hearst owned twenty-eight newspapers, nine magazines, INS, a newsreel company, several radio stations, and a book publisher. *Cosmopolitan* was the Hearst flagship magazine early on, a prominence it would lose during the Depression, although it remained his favorite until his death. Given its reputation for quality and its sizable middle-class readership, *Cosmopolitan* was quite a prize for Hearst upon its acquisition from John Brisben Walker.[4]

Hearst newspapers appealed to laborers and lower-income workers—clerks, craftsmen, mechanics. People who bought his newspapers did so because they enjoyed the selection and presentation of news—a daily menu of crime, disaster, scandal, and tragedy written in melodramatic prose and topped by lurid headlines. Strident editorials, which ranted about every imaginable subject and warned about real or imaginary cabals, were colorful ribbons on the daily package of news. People who did not buy Hearst newspapers because they detested the sensationalism had other choices; early in the twentieth century, each city that was home to a Hearst newspaper had at least another three daily newspapers. His influence on public opinion, a matter of speculation under any circumstances, therefore was limited to the five cities where Hearst newspapers published and where they shared the media marketplace with other dailies: Boston, Chicago, Los Angeles, New York, and San Francisco.

Cosmopolitan was a classy complement to those rabble-rousing newspapers. The dailies succeeded by entertaining readers with sensational journalism, by recognizing the legitimate grievances of workers, and by crusading for decent living conditions in the slums. Newspaper cartoonists, columnists, editorial writers, and reporters followed the edicts of editors who followed instructions from Hearst. During this phase of his life, when Hearst was a progressive Democrat, his newspapers persistently campaigned for an eight-hour workday, the cleanup of tenements, additional trolleys for public transit, community hospitals, sanitary water and sewer systems, garbage removal, and establishment of schools in working-class neighborhoods. Each campaign adhered to a formula: news stories day after day on men, women, and children affected by the situation; front-page cartoons criticizing or ridiculing the people responsible for the situation; repetitive editorials demanding a solution to the situation and punishment of the scoundrels; columnists lavishing praise on heroes or heaping scorn on villains; and relentless publicity promoting each campaign via billboards, posters, flyers, and advertisements. Republicans usually were targets, although city-machine and southern Democrats also were occasional villains.[5]

Hearst, who became publisher of *Cosmopolitan* at age forty-two, was a journalistic showman. Lively prose and plentiful photographs soon enlivened the magazine and promptly increased monthly circulation to 400,000 copies by early 1906. *Cosmopolitan* relied on articles and commentary from the best reporters and columnists working for Hearst newspapers; their hyperbole and disregard for factual accuracy or fairness were assets. Magazine editors modified the newspaper format to suit a monthly publication. Rather than several days of articles on a single subject, the magazine published months of articles in a series; rather than cartoons, the magazine created symbolic imagery from composite illustrations that combined drawings and photographs; rather than editorials, the magazine presented commentary to condemn villains, praise heroes, and propose solutions. Publicity methods were the same, only on a national scale.

Cosmopolitan, of course, also competed for attention and influence in the national magazine marketplace. Numerous middle-class households subscribed to several magazines simultaneously. Still, because *Cosmopolitan* was not openly affiliated with Hearst it had the potential to accomplish his purposes: namely, to undermine the credibility or sully the reputation of political opponents and to promote an agenda. It was a publisher's privilege.

Until just before his fiftieth birthday, Hearst and *Cosmopolitan* had shouted anger and outrage to an ever-increasing readership. Then, as suddenly as it had started, the shouting ended. "I got cured of politics mainly by realizing that I could accomplish what I was after better in my own line of activity than in a line that I was not so familiar with," Hearst told a *Cosmopolitan* editor years later. "However, I have never stopped telling the politicians what they should do."[6]

Cosmopolitan quit politics during the election year of 1912 and became yet another kind of magazine the moment Hearst's political ambitions ended.

Notoriety

William Randolph Hearst realized that his new magazine must transform its editorial format immediately. *Cosmopolitan* became an agitator for reform. The dormancy induced by the inattention of Walker had slowed response by the magazine to events and topics of relevance to the middle class. Competitors, notably *McClure's,* had kept pace and prospered. *Cosmopolitan* published articles in serial format that touched on many subjects from 1906 to 1912, the period of the magazine's sensationalism: accusations of corruption, incompetence, and thievery against various governors, mayors, and U.S. senators; denunciations of the robber barons and their economic cartels; insults to President Theodore Roosevelt; demands to end child labor; suspicions about the Mormons; questions about the choice between prohibition of alcohol versus temperance. Hearst also sensed when readers tired of exposé journalism, and he rapidly converted *Cosmopolitan* to a fiction format. Although he was not editor of the magazine, Hearst approved for publication every article in *Cosmopolitan* and closely edited each month's issue, sending his critiques to an editor. The magazine became a profitable centerpiece of Hearst's media empire and his personal favorite for decades.

Prior to its purchase by Hearst in summer 1905, *Cosmopolitan* was a laggard in exposé journalism. While the travails of the steamer car venture had preoccupied John Brisben Walker, causing him to ignore or simply miss the shift in public opinion regarding industrialists, manufacturers, and mercantilists whose collusion caused inflationary prices for many consumer products, other magazine publishers had acted on the opportunity arising from the political awakening of the American middle class. Exposé articles in magazines informed readers about detrimental effects of illegal and unethical business practices, threats to public health from unsanitary food and unsafe medicine, and pervasive corruption that permeated city, state, and national governments. Exposé articles informed citizens about financial connections between legislators and their patrons—banks, insurance companies, railroads. Many state legislators and members of Congress received lucrative contracts and jobs from private businesses while holding public office or were former executives and lawyers for corporations.[7]

The election of a Republican progressive governor, Robert La Follette, in Wisconsin and the insurgency of some Republicans in Congress against arch-conservatives of both political parties, along with progressive policies put forth by TR, created the Progressive coalition. Reformers and everyone with a social conscience supported an effort to achieve some sort of balance to protect the public from an economic autocracy neither accountable nor responsive to any-one. The public, particularly the middle class, received from a handful of maga-zines much useful information about the way business did its business. Not all profited from the newly popular genre of exposé journalism, but *McClure's* was the model to emulate.[8]

Exposé journalism had lifted *McClure's* to first place among general maga-zines in circulation and advertising. Its distribution of 400,000 copies a month attracted advertisers who bought an average of 150 pages an issue. *McClure's* famous January 1903 issue signaled the start of the exposé era, although it and other magazines actually had published exposés for several months. However, the January 1903 issue of *McClure's* had presented another installment of Ida Tarbell's exposé of the Standard Oil Company, an exposé by Lincoln Steffens of government corruption in Minneapolis, and an exposé by Ray Stannard Baker of labor violence among coal miners and strikebreakers.

McClure's perfected the exposé series. The Standard Oil exposé finished at nineteen installments in autumn 1904. Relying on court documents filed in lawsuits and interviews with independent oil drillers and refiners, the Tarbell masterpiece was instrumental in the eventual breakup of Rockefeller's oil com-pany that had dominated distribution, production, and prices of petroleum for twenty years. Exposés by Steffens of municipal corruption constituted the famous "Shame Of The Cities" series. Baker was the master of exposés; his ar-ticles on railroad rate-fixing and rebates to prime customers aided enactment of a federal law to strengthen the Interstate Commerce Commission.

McClure's exposé articles revealed putrid conditions of life in city tenements. Tuberculosis was an urban scourge. Epidemics caused by raw sewage and filthy water sickened entire neighborhoods, infant mortality rates in all cities was horrific, and medical doctors were not required to have formal education or practical training to practice in many states. One exposé article embarrassed Trinity Episcopal Church in Manhattan. A rich church for rich people, the church was a slumlord with a vast territory of tenements.[9]

The public appreciated *McClure's*. Its subscriptions and vendor sales aver-aged 375,000 copies monthly for 1905 and 414,000 copies monthly for 1906.[10]

Exposés by other magazines—*Everybody's, Collier's*—disclosed deception by major insurers that defrauded beneficiaries of life insurance policies by not paying full death benefits and funneling payments by policyholders to executives and directors for interest-free loans. Wall Street manipulators were a target, as were financiers who duped investors. And railroads, always railroads, were the satanic forces of the era. Their lobbyists routinely bribed state legislators to approve noncompetitive freight rates, right-of-way easements for new routes, and tax-free or nominally taxed status for miles upon miles of railroad tracks. Railroad lobbyists on Capitol Hill regularly bribed senators to quash legislation to regulate the industry. (One practice had a serious adverse economic impact on rural businesses and farmers. Freight rates for point-to-point shipments within a state's boundaries prohibited discounts to bulk shippers, such as oil companies and grain processors. To evade these restrictions, railroads commonly paid off-the-books rebates, or kickbacks, to bulk shippers to get the contracts for large volumes of freight. Railroads then recovered the hidden rebates by charging an assortment of fees to small-volume shippers, such as for coupling cars on a siding or loading freight in a rail yard.)[11]

A few brave newspapers had revealed scandalous conditions and corruption in some cities, but many were timid or susceptible to bribery. Exposé magazines, by linking similar conditions and endemic corruption across the country, educated the public about the scope of the problems.

Hearst wanted *Cosmopolitan* to join the fray. His newspapers in New York City fought the good fight against Tammany Hall, and his other newspapers generally raised hell whenever the railroads received special treatment from legislators. *Cosmopolitan* could inform readers throughout the nation about corporate chicanery and official malfeasance. It could also settle the score with political opponents, especially Theodore Roosevelt and Republicans generally. Hearst, who never lacked imagination, decided to focus on the network of corruption in the U.S. Senate. Party politics aside for Hearst, a Democrat, it just so happened that Republicans were the majority party in the Senate: fifty-six of the ninety seats.[12]

During winter 1905–1906, *Cosmopolitan* editor Bailey Millard persuaded David Graham Phillips, at age thirty-eight a former newspaper reporter and successful novelist, to write a series on corruption in the Senate. Phillips was reluctant. He had written a few pieces for *Cosmopolitan* the last year of Walker's ownership to finance his fiction work, and a return to journalism would delay a novel in progress. Phillips therefore set a fee for writing the series that he could not imagine *Cosmopolitan* paying. Incredibly, Millard agreed to it. Hearst approved the project, authorizing payment for a first-rate writer and two researchers. One thing about Hearst the publisher: money never mattered.[13]

When the researching and writing for the series began, five senators were under indictment for a variety of corruption crimes; many of the other eighty-five had prior professional connections, usually as lawyers, to the numerous insurers, railroads, and trade associations that directly benefited from federal laws and policies or, equally important, from a lack of laws and policies. For years, proposals to regulate railroad rates and performance, to monitor financial reserves and practices of insurers, and to collect information on corporations engaged in interstate commerce had passed the House of Representatives but not the Senate. Also, Congress set tariffs on a range of imports to protect domestic manufacturers and producers, which added appreciably to the price of imports—50 percent or more on many items by the late 1890s. Tariffs allowed domestic manufacturers and producers to keep prices high on their items, which then could not be undercut by cheaper imports. Cotton, lumber, metals, shoes, sugar, and wood pulp—the ingredient for paper for all uses, including newsprint and coated stock for magazines—were protected items. Both the House and Senate provided protectionist tariffs to manufacturers and producers within their districts and states.[14]

The Senate was the main impediment to reform, however. Members of the House of Representatives were elected by male-only voters in the forty-five states, but senators were appointed to terms by state legislators. Some states conducted primary elections by each political party for nominations to the Senate; legislators of the majority party then affirmed the winner of the primary—in theory, anyway, but a legislator was not honor-bound to uphold the people's choice, honor being the key word. In quite a few states, legislators expected payments for their votes and a minority party's primary winner sometimes could buy enough votes from majority party legislators to win a Senate seat. A Senate seat for Rhode Island allegedly sold for $200,000 paid to state legislators, and a Wisconsin senator bought a term for $112,000. The bribes were repaid many times over because protective tariffs and exorbitant railroad rates generated revenues of tens of millions of dollars each year, a hidden tax on consumers.[15]

The February 1906 *Cosmopolitan* alerted readers to its forthcoming series, "The Treason Of The Senate." A three-page editorial, accompanied by a full-page photograph of a grim David Graham Phillips, termed the inflammatory title "fit and logical," and it promised the series would identify senators who "have betrayed the public to that cruel and vicious Spirit of Mammon which has come to dominate the nation." The series lived up to the promise, but Phillips refrained from directly attacking TR. The president was very popular, and he was a reformer.[16]

The cover of *Cosmopolitan* for March featured a full-profile illustration of a beak-nosed, white-haired man looking left, his bushy white sideburn sharply contrasting a dark shadow of his face extending down the center. The cover's left-center displayed a four-line stacked cover blurb, "The Treason Of The Senate," with a byline for David Graham Phillips below. Inside, a commentary preceded the debut installment. "Money makes the Senate go," the opening sentence declared. "The Senate of the United States has ceased to exist, and in its stead we have the House of Dollars." A lengthy litany of Senate obstructions of necessary reforms ensued. The commentary concluded, "Washington must be saved from Wall Street, and the popular election of senators would be a most important step in that direction."

Then came the sixteen-page showpiece. The introduction of the article, and each of the subsequent eight articles, quoted the first sentence of Article III, Section 3 of the U.S. Constitution: "Treason against the United States shall consist only in levying war against them, or in adhering to their enemies, giving them aid and comfort." Those enemies, of course, were the robber barons and the trusts, the term for economic cartels that controlled specific industries or sectors.[17]

The focus of the opener was New York's senators, both Republicans. One was a sometime sponsor of Theodore Roosevelt during his rise from a reformist state legislator to governor to selection as vice president for William McKinley. The senator, Thomas Platt, had prodded TR to get into national politics, perhaps simply to get him out of New York, where he was a reformer who had organized a cadre of Republicans somewhat independent of the insurers, manufacturers, and railroad owners that controlled the state's party organization. Platt had coordinated TR's nomination as vice president, a position certain to lessen his political influence. The assassination of President McKinley in September 1901 had instead placed TR in a most influential position; his election in November 1904 against a nondescript Democratic candidate—a candidacy Hearst believed was his, if not for Bryan's disloyalty—offered an excellent opportunity to advocate reforms. TR cautiously attempted to strengthen government regulation of the cartels.

The *Cosmopolitan* series eventually would acknowledge that Republican conservatives hindered President Roosevelt, but the first installment limited its scope to an exposé of New York's senators. Phillips briefly summarized Platt's background as a senator, then dismissively referred to Platt as sickly and demented, not worth investigating despite allegations he had received enormous fees from insurers. "Platt cannot live long," Phillips wrote. "His mind is already a mere shadow."[18]

The bulk of the article took aim at Chauncey M. Depew, the senator whose profile illustration was on the magazine cover and whose photograph sat squarely above the constitutional definition for treason. This was the same Depew who had judged the automobile race from Manhattan to Irvington staged ten years earlier by John Brisben Walker. Depew then was president of the New York Central and Hudson River Railroad, a Vanderbilt family business. Depew continued to serve as a railroad company director for the Vanderbilts, receiving a salary while senator. Phillips had an easy target. Depew not only was on the Vanderbilt payroll, but the New York attorney general had alleged financial impropriety by the senator during an investigation of Equitable Life Assurance Society. Equitable Life had paid excessive compensation to directors, who also had loaned themselves company money to create subsidiary businesses. Equitable Life paid an annual $20,000 "retainer for legal services" to Senator Depew, who had received a $160,000 loan, too.[19]

Nothing in the article truly was new. The two researchers for Phillips had gathered material from newspaper articles about formal investigations of the senators, and the article constructed a biographical timeline of the private and public careers of both. In fact, very little information in the entire "Treason Of The Senate" series was revelatory. Every senator profiled in the series had a known record of conflicts-of-interest, a known business or professional relationship with corporations, and a personal fortune built on favoritism. The value of the series was publication itself. Newspapers of the era rarely paid attention to scandals or investigations of public officials beyond their own territory. A scandal involving a senator from Indiana, for example, would receive plenty of ink in Indiana newspapers, but none in Minnesota or Pennsylvania. Citizens in many states were unaware of political scandals elsewhere. Magazines served a very useful purpose by consolidating and connecting separate incidents of apparent corruption or favoritism, then presenting the details to readers everywhere. Magazines explained the scope of corporate influence and political corruption, demonstrating how bribery, favors, and secret partnerships were common throughout the hierarchy of government from city to state to federal.

A legend about the "Treason" opener has endured. A friendly biographer, whose 1936 book appeared several months after bankers removed an elderly Hearst from corporate leadership because of his financial irresponsibility, intended to show that Hearst cared more about factual accuracy than his critics presumed. The biographer passed along an anecdote told by a longtime executive associated with Hearst since the early 1900s: Hearst had not seen the first "Treason" article until reading a galley proof for the March issue the night the presses rolled at Cuneo Printers in Chicago; he judged it weak because it lacked sufficient evidence about Senator Depew's shady background; Hearst hurriedly contacted the executive to stop the presses and rapidly rewrote portions of the article, inserting material on the known responsibility of Depew for massive cost overruns during construction of a new state capitol in Albany during the 1870s—overruns that subsidized kickbacks from contractors to Depew and Republican legislators; also, Hearst instructed editors to insert excerpts of transcripts from testimony on the Equitable Life scandal and photographs of letters from an Equitable Insurance executive that incriminated Depew with references to favorable legislation. The new version was typeset and the presses restarted.[20]

It certainly was a great story, and the anecdote from the friendly biographer became a standard reference by historians. However, the sequence described by the biographer conflicted with statements in the February editorial that promoted the March debut of the "Treason" series. "The Cosmopolitan had hoped to present Mr. Phillips' opening chapter in this February number, but the work of preparation and revision of this exhaustive series has been such that, at the last moment, it has been found impossible to do so," the writer stated. "It was also necessary, in order to make an elaborate and convincing presentation, that the first chapter should be illustrated in a striking manner, with whatever facsimiles of letters and public documents might be secured. This has also occasioned delay." The editorial guaranteed readers that the series opener would roll off the presses on "February 15th, the date of publication of the March Cosmopolitan."[21]

To be fair to the biographer and the executive who told the tale, it was possible that Hearst saw the galley proof for the February issue, canceled the press run, and ordered standby editorial material to replace the pages occupied by "Treason." Because of the time required to obtain and photograph the relevant documents, then prepare printing plates, especially to engrave illustrations, and send hundreds of thousands of magazine copies through the presses, folders, and binders, it was improbable that the scenario described by the anecdote could have happened.

The first installment of "The Treason Of The Senate" indeed was more than text. *Cosmopolitan* displayed nine photographs and two facsimiles of typewritten letters. Depew's grand homes in Washington, D.C., and rural New York, plus his brownstone townhouse in Manhattan, were pictured; photographs of Cornelius (Commodore) Vanderbilt and his son William H. Vanderbilt carried a caption statement that they had "owned him [Depew] mentally and morally." Depew was a railroad lawyer for the Vanderbilts for decades. "No one would pretend for an instant that he sits in the Senate for the people," Phillips wrote. "The Vanderbilt interests ordered Platt to send him the first time; and when he came up for a second term the Vanderbilt-Morgan interests got [him]." All in all, Phillips portrayed Depew as a slavish, venal corporate toady and political plodder.[22]

An editorial accompanied the first installment. "There in the Senate Chamber is the center of the conspiracy which has defrauded us of our rights," *Cosmopolitan* declared. "The senators as a rule are either direct representatives of the trusts or political bosses by the grace of the trusts. The problem before us is to select our own bosses for ourselves and make the senators our representatives. Popular election seems to be the obvious reform."[23]

Although dated March 1906, *Cosmopolitan* arrived by mail to subscribers and at vendors in late February. The White House received a copy. President

Roosevelt promptly sent a letter by courier to Hearst's *New York Journal* bureau near the White House. Addressed to Alfred Henry Lewis, the bureau chief, TR's message began, "Don't you want to come down here some time when I can have an hour's talk to you?" TR bluntly stated the reason for the invitation: "I have just been reading the Cosmopolitan. There is no need for me to say that so far as in one article or another corruption and fraud are attacked, the attack has my heartiest sympathy and commendation; but hysteria and sensationalism never do any permanent good. Now some of the articles in the Cosmopolitan consist of nothing but a mixture of hysteria and mendacity." Unknown to the president, Lewis already had written a direct attack solely on Platt for the April issue.[24]

William Randolph Hearst, publisher of several large newspapers, purchased *Cosmopolitan* during the summer of 1905. Hearst used the magazine to further his political ambitions, and he changed the magazine's editorial format to sensationalistic journalism. Photograph by Linedinst, 1904, courtesy of the Library of Congress.

A novelist, newspaper reporter, and occasional magazine journalist, David Graham Phillips angered President Theodore Roosevelt with the "Treason of the Senate" series in *Cosmopolitan* during 1906. TR referred to exposé journalists as "muck-rakers," a pejorative description. Photograph, undated, from the George Grantham Bain Collection, Library of Congress.

The April issue of *Cosmopolitan* placed "The Treason Of The Senate" spotlight on Senator Nelson Aldrich, a Republican from Rhode Island who was chairman of the Senate Finance Committee and whose daughter was married to John D. Rockefeller Jr. The finance committee set tariffs, which were the primary source of revenue for the federal government, and appropriated money to government agencies and departments. Phillips provided these facts to allege corruption: Aldrich owned a trolley franchise in Providence; Aldrich "invited" a major sugar producer to invest in the franchise; Aldrich sponsored a sugar tariff to add 40 percent to the price of imported sugar. Phillips declared, "How Aldrich must laugh as he watches the American people meekly submitting to this plundering through tariff and railway rates and hugely overcapitalized corporations!"

The article listed six senators on the finance committee who collaborated with Aldrich, again mentioning Platt ("corruptionist and lifelong agent of corruptionists"). Each senator owed allegiance to a railroad company or Standard Oil. Phillips wisely listed specific consumer products that cost more than justified because of tariffs, which enabled readers to understand the price they had to pay for protectionist legislation: $10 extra for a sewing machine; five cents a pound extra for borax; $1.40 extra for a keg of nails; $12 a ton extra for steel rails. Aldrich and his allies awarded mail contracts to railroads at triple the freight rate private businesses paid. Phillips concluded the Aldrich article, "Treachery has brought him wealth and rank, if not honor, of a certain sort."[25]

The Platt attack began next. "His day has been a day for weasels to succeed," Lewis wrote. "No matter what he is about, he arrives always by the side entrance and leaves by the back stairs. He prefers moonlight to sunlight, midnight to noon, and, in making his journeys of politics, adopts the back alleys and keeps clear of the streets."

The article carefully differentiated between the vile Platt and the president. Lewis praised TR for his reform efforts: setting policies and standards for the federal civil service while a federal commissioner; a two-year stint as New York City police commissioner beginning, but not really accomplishing, a cleanup campaign of the department; a righteous campaign against corrupt legislators when governor of New York; presidential initiatives to regulate railroads and monitor monopolies. But had this rise to the presidency been on merit or manipulation, assisted by fate? "There was never the moment when the sly, secret, timid one from Tioga [Platt] did not go plotting," Lewis asserted. "He moved him [TR] to the Navy Department to be rid of him as police commissioner." TR returned from combat in Cuba during the Spanish-American War a war hero and was elected governor of New York. "Platt became subsequently dexterous," Lewis explained, "and rid himself of the Albany presence of Roosevelt by making him vice president."[26]

The career progression supposedly engineered by Platt suggested that Roosevelt either was unaware of his sponsor's motives or a willing accomplice to his sponsor's schemes. Lewis intended to denigrate Platt, but had insulted TR—or had he meant to do both? Hearst dreamed of being the Democratic candidate for president in 1908, which was not farfetched when the exposé series on the Senate started. Any opportunity to undermine the incumbent Republican served to benefit Democrats.

TR retaliated. For personal and political reasons, TR believed it necessary to rebuke *Cosmopolitan*'s exposé journalism. Journalists had helped him throughout his career, and the president realized their importance to build public

The May 1906 *Cosmopolitan* was the most dramatic magazine cover for the "Treason of the Senate" series. Source: Morgan Library, Colorado State University.

support for reform. He also realized the *Cosmopolitan* articles damaged the Republican leadership in his home state and depicted the Republican-led Senate as a den of thieves.

The *Cosmopolitan* series coincided with an attempt by a handful of Senate progressives, led by newly selected Senator La Follette, to enact crucial legislation strengthening the Interstate Commerce Commission. The Hepburn Act, passed almost unanimously by the House, authorized the commission to review railroad rates, assess their merit, and approve or revise. The railroads were furious. They could control most state legislatures and set whatever rates they wished. The idea a federal entity might lower rates or require justification for rate increases was unacceptable. The railroads expected to defeat the Hepburn Act outright or to amend it to impotence in the Senate. TR needed a coalition of Republican progressives and moderates, joined by Democrats who were not doctrinaire about the party's commitment to states' rights, which rejected as unconstitutional most federal laws affecting domestic commerce. Significantly, a Republican president could not rely on the fifty-six Republican senators simply to cooperate and pass his legislation. A coalition was necessary to attain a majority of forty-six votes for passage of the Hepburn Act. In that regard, the premise of the "Treason" series—that the Senate did not serve the public's interest—was correct.[27]

Roosevelt's angry tirade against "The Treason Of The Senate" gave exposé journalism its historic label: muckraking. The word came from a scene in a Christian fable, *Pilgrim's Progress,* written by John Bunyan in England late in the seventeenth century. In the fable, journeyers encounter a man with a "muck-rake" standing in a room, scraping sticks and straw from the dirt, his gaze downward; although the man with the rake was offered a celestial crown, which symbolized admittance to heaven, he would not look upward to the crown; he saw only a world of muck at his feet. TR applied the symbolism of the scene to the situation.[28]

To TR, Phillips and Hearst were men with muckrakes; they did not look upward toward the promise of the Hepburn Act, but instead gazed downward on a minority of corrupt senators. TR chose retaliation to demonstrate to aggrieved Republican senators his loyalty to the party and to the Senate as an institution, with the hope that some of them might agree to approve the Hepburn Act in a useful form.

TR tested his muckrake speech at a Gridiron Dinner in March, when his anger at the Platt article in *Cosmopolitan* was raw. The dinner was an annual event in Washington, D.C., attended by editors and reporters. They applauded the denunciation of their peers. No newspapers reported the speech because it was an off-the-record event.[29]

FILING TOWARD THE COLLIERIES INSTEAD OF TOWARD THE SCHOOLHOUSES

Illustrations by Warren Rockwell

The Hoe-Man in the Making

By EDWIN MARKHAM

Author of " The Man with the Hoe, and Other Poems"

Little Slaves of the Coal-Mines

Cosmopolitan was an important participant in the effort to protect children from exploitation and hazards in the workplace. The "Hoe-Man" series ran for several months during 1906–1907. *Cosmopolitan*, November 1906; source: Morgan Library, Colorado State University.

The Cosmopolitan's Readers Agree That This Disgrace Must Go

HILD LABOR must go. Thousands of letters received by the new Child Labor Federation join in demanding its abolition. With unanimity the writers insist that an industrial civilization which depends upon child labor is a sorry form of civilization; the speedier changed the better for the human race. promise of childhood into gold, is the burden of that never-ceasing song. Under the circumstances, has ever mankind listened to a croak more hideous? Was ever a death-chant so despairingly relentless, like a wild wail from out of the nethermost depths, petrifying the very senses? The sentence it decrees is writ deep. Death to the child; first, mental death in ignorance and degradation, and deprivation of all that should make a child's life normal and

Editorials accompanied articles about hazardous and horrific conditions affecting child laborers. *Cosmopolitan* urged readers to join the crusade to protect children. *Cosmopolitan*, November 1906; source: Morgan Library, Colorado State University.

Ray Stannard Baker, whose solid exposé articles for *McClure's* on railroad rate-fixing and favors to public officials in every state, usually free passes for travel by them and their families anywhere along the route, learned about the Gridiron Dinner speech from friends. Baker also heard that the president meant to repeat the speech at a subsequent public event. Baker wrote TR to ask him to relent because "attacking the magazines" would "give aid and comfort to these very rascals" who blocked reforms. TR responded promptly, "I feel that the man who in a yellow newspaper or in a yellow magazine (I do not think it worth while to say publicly what I will say to you privately, that Hearst's papers and magazine are those I have in mind at the moment) makes a ferocious attack on good men or even attacks bad men with exaggeration or for things they have not done, is a potent enemy of those of us who are really striving in good faith to expose bad men and drive them from power."[30]

(Top left) Cosmopolitan created composite photographs for various special exposé series. This multipart serial on Mormon wealth featured several composite sensationalistic photographs. *Cosmopolitan,* March 1911; source: Morgan Library, Colorado State University.

(Top right) Cosmopolitan continued with exposé journalism after other magazines had abandoned it. Referring to a phrase supposedly uttered by William "Boss" Tweed of Tammany Hall notoriety, the "What Are You Going To Do About It?" series dealt with the crusade to ban alcoholic beverages, political corruption, and social injustice. Source: Morgan Library, Colorado State University.

In mid-April, TR spoke to the public at a ceremonial placement of the cornerstone for a new House of Representatives office building:

Now, it is very necessary that we should not flinch from seeing what is vile and debasing. There is filth on the floor, and it must be scraped up with the muck-rake; and there are times and places where this service is the most needed of all the services that can be performed. But the man who never does anything else, who never thinks or speaks or writes, save of his feats with the muck-rake, speedily becomes not a help to society, not an incitement to good, but one of the most potent forces for evil.

Gross and reckless assaults on character, whether on the stump or in newspaper, magazine, or book, create a morbid and vicious public sentiment, and at the same time act as a profound deterrent to able men of normal sensitiveness and tend to prevent them from entering the public service at any price.

The men with the muck-rakes are often indispensable to the well-being of society, but only if they know when to stop raking the muck, and to look upward to the celestial crown above them, to the crown of worthy endeavor.[31]

Baker, Tarbell, and other veteran exposé journalists were saddened by the president's speech. "The Chicago Tribune, on the next day, listed the names of the writers, whether sensational or not, all together, as being cast into outer darkness," Baker wrote. The journalist lost faith in TR. "I could never again give him my full confidence, nor follow his leadership."[32]

Cosmopolitan responded to the president, too. A clever title, "The Man With The Hose," introduced commentary by an associate editor of the magazine, who sarcastically noted, "It is a new theory that the man with a muck-rake is responsible for the muck."[33]

Roosevelt was not the only progressive upset with the Senate exposé. Progressives feared that the corrupt alliance of politicians and monopolists could deflect legitimate reform efforts by associating them with the sensationalism and irresponsibility of muckrakers. Some progressives also denounced *Cosmopolitan*. Among the criticisms was the accusation that the magazine was profiting from the "Treason" series at the expense of credible journalism. *Cosmopolitan* acknowledged its new popularity and refuted the profiteering motive. "Our growth in circulation merely goes to show that there are more liberty-loving people in America than there are lovers of slavery," a commentary declared. "Indeed, we would far rather profit by leading people to liberty and to light than by leading them into darkness by the devious paths of the Wall Street policy, which is the Standard Oil policy, which is the bribery policy, which is the policy of corrupt officialdom, the hotbed of treason against republican ideals."[34]

Presidential rebukes of the magazine did not alter the tone of the Senate series. *Cosmopolitan* insisted it was trying to help the president. The May issue of *Cosmopolitan* went to subscribers and vendors displaying a cover illustration of an American eagle shackled to a chain, its wings poised for flight but unable to fly, and above the illustration was "The Treason Of The Senate" blurb. This installment criticized Democrats and Republicans, referring to a "merger of interests" by both political parties to protect the economic cartels. "Every traitor senator, whatever else he represents in the way of an enemy to the people, always represents some thief or group of thieves through railways," Phillips insisted. "For the railway, reaching everywhere, as intimate a part of our life now as the air we breathe, is the easy and perfect instrument of the wholesale looter of investors and of the public, and is also the natural nucleus and subsidizer of a political machine."[35]

The series continued through November. Photographs showed senators leaving the Capitol and walking on the street, a sharp contrast with the usual portraiture of solemn senators at their desks; the "Treason" photographs made senators more human, and thus more corruptible—a point driven home by photographs of the mansions and estates where senators written about by *Cosmopolitan* resided. The nine installments of the series filled a total of 106 pages in *Cosmopolitan*, with an additional eleven pages of commentary from the magazine's editor or associate editors. Seventeen senators were listed as traitors. A special damnation—"betrays Roosevelt"—labeled Senator Philander Knox, a Republican of Pennsylvania. Knox, the U.S. attorney general during TR's first term, reluctantly litigated the Northern Securities antitrust lawsuit and had presented a weak argument to the Supreme Court. Justice Oliver Wendell Holmes had written that Knox's brief was so poorly phrased the Supreme Court had the impression it was "two small exporting grocers" colluding to restrain trade rather than a consortium of powerful railroads.[36]

One senator apparently evaded widespread identification in an article that accompanied the October installment of the "Treason" series by buying advertisements in *Cosmopolitan*, according to research by a scholar. Senator John F. Dryden, Republican of New Jersey and president of Prudential Insurance Company, was the focus of "Our Millionaire Socialists," an eight-page exploration of his ownership of a trolley franchise surreptitiously financed by Prudential policyholders. The October *Cosmopolitan* went to vendors on schedule in mid-September. Then it was removed from racks and shelves without an explanation. Two weeks passed, and the October *Cosmopolitan* reappeared at vendors, but without "Our Millionaire Socialists" in it. Instead, a fiction piece and a poem occupied the pages. The writer of the Dryden article was a researcher for Phillips. Two years later, he reported in a socialist magazine that *Cosmopolitan* had received a $5,000 contract for Prudential Insurance advertisements while the October issue was on the presses and copies of the early run already had gone to vendors.

The scholar who investigated the allegation did find several copies of the original October 1906 issue in public libraries that had "Our Millionaire Socialists." Copies of the same issue at dozens of other public and university libraries did not contain the article. Although the allegation of a payoff surfaced in 1908 while Hearst was the financial sponsor of a national independent political party, newspapers of the day ignored it—an inexplicable decision by numerous editors and publishers who competed against his newspapers and others who should have relished a chance to attack his integrity. The fact that the allegation was made by a socialist publication probably diminished its credibility.[37]

The "Treason" series was perfect for the typical Hearst promotional campaign. A masterful promoter of his newspapers, Hearst applied his usual tactics to *Cosmopolitan*. Signboards, posters, and newspaper ads touted the series. Newspaper editors throughout the nation received complimentary copies of *Cosmopolitan* during the entire run of the series. An editorial note from the magazine's editor granted newspapers permission to reprint copyrighted material on the condition that *Cosmopolitan* received credit. Practically every issue of the magazine itself published commentary to praise the series and to tout upcoming revelations.

Letters written by Roosevelt to confidants and political allies revealed his anger and frustration toward Hearst and *Cosmopolitan*. Political partisanship by the Democratic publisher and the socialist writer was the motive for the series on the Senate, not a desire for reform. "[Phillips] certainly makes no serious effort to find out the facts," TR insisted in a letter. "He either is or ought to be well aware of the fact that the average congressman, the average legislator, the average man in public life, is a great deal more afraid of the labor vote than of corporations."[38]

The president also sent letters damning *Cosmopolitan* to editors of other magazines. *Saturday Evening Post* editor George Horace Lorimer received one: "You doubtlessly know that many entirely honest people firmly believe that Mr. Phillips, in accepting the money of Mr. Hearst to attack the public servants of the United States, was actuated merely by a desire to achieve notoriety and at the same time to make money out of the slanders by which he achieves notoriety." *Forum* editor Lyman Abbott received another: "The Cosmopolitan is owned by Hearst, and, with articles in it from men like David Graham Phillips, is the friend of disorder, less from principle than from the hope of getting profit out of troubled waters."[39]

Cosmopolitan did prosper from the series. Hearst ordered an extra 30,000 copies printed for the March issue—and it sold out. An extra 50,000 copies for the April issue sold out, too. The magazine's monthly distribution soared by nearly 100,000 copies at the end of the series in November 1906, a convenient finale just prior to the congressional elections and general elections in the states. After sixteen months of Hearst ownership, *Cosmopolitan* distributed 500,000 copies to subscribers and vendors. Many middle-class citizens may have responded to the series because of their concern and suspicion about the steady increase in prices for basic items. Inflation was a problem throughout the early 1900s, and monopolists certainly set prices to benefit themselves.[40]

Cosmopolitan's success as a muckraker and the tremendous popularity of other muckrakers troubled some peers. *The Critic*, a literary journal, disparaged *Cosmopolitan*, *McClure's*, and the exposé genre while "The Treason Of The Senate" series ran. "Under the guise of exposing graft, corruption, or whatever the title we may be pleased to give it, some of the mediums of publicity have magnified petty faults and grossly exaggerated conditions merely for the sake of commercialism—to increase their circulation," a commentary declared. "The cheap magazines and yellow press are not reformers—and that the masses will learn very soon."[41]

Between the start and finish of the series in *Cosmopolitan,* the Senate passed the Hepburn Act. It was heavily amended, the most serious revision restricting the Interstate Commerce Commission from acting on its own to review railroad rates and instead allowing the commission only to respond to complaints. Despite its watering down by the Senate, the Hepburn Act was a significant step. Reform took time, but the Northern Securities antitrust lawsuit by the Roosevelt administration, the establishment of a Bureau of Corporations to gather data on big businesses, and creation of the Food and Drug Administration to ensure safer products for human consumption were evidence of progress during TR's presidency from autumn 1901 to winter 1909. It was not until 1913 that the Sixteenth Amendment implemented a federal tax on corporations and individuals, while the Seventeenth Amendment that took effect the same year mandated direct election of senators by voters.

Of lesser importance, but noteworthy because of its relevance to the "Treason" series, was a decision by TR to investigate a statement in the April 1906 installment about excessive railroad rates charged to the postal service for transporting mail. Congress ordered the U.S. Post Office to renegotiate lower rates in March 1907. *Cosmopolitan*'s role was not mentioned.[42]

Over the years, critics have passed judgment on "The Treason Of The Senate" series. Some said it was long on accusations and short on facts; not so. Phillips built his case by going back decades to show a pattern of favors granted, obsequious service, and special relationships between senators and the monopolists. The *Cosmopolitan* articles firmly connected corrupt state legislators with corrupt U.S. senators, and declared that the systematic corruption was on behalf of railroads, insurers, and economic cartels.

"The Treason Of The Senate" series did on a lesser scale what "The History Of The Standard Oil Company" by Ida Tarbell in *McClure's* had done previously. Both series documented patterns of behavior. Tarbell had spent months traveling to different states to review lawsuits filed against Standard Oil and John D. Rockefeller for details about kickbacks, rebates, price-fixing, and financial skullduggery that created the oil monopoly; she also sifted through reams of documents kept by regulators in several states to find facts pertaining to railroad rates charged to Standard Oil and the volume of oil shipped by rail. Tarbell proved her case. Phillips, by contrast, relied on two researchers to supply facts, and they did a fine job establishing probable cause for the culpability of certain senators.

Phillips explained to *Cosmopolitan* readers the longtime duplicity of these senators, listing their clients when they were lawyers or their business associations when private citizens. Phillips also contrasted their public speeches with their decisions to modify or weaken legislation while in committees and their votes on legislation. Phillips identified specific pieces of reform legislation that never made it out of committee and detailed the costs of tariffs to consumers.

Some critics faulted Phillips for histrionic prose and excessive exclamation marks. His prose was overly dramatic, to express outrage. Phillips hoped his prose would inspire anger among Americans who read the series. Journalistic objectivity was a pretense far in the future. The acceptable style of the day was storytelling: scene-setting, drama, villains.

Phillips also conveyed an attitude common to the era's exposé journalists. They believed that Americans did not comprehend the depth of corruption or the power of the robber barons and their monopolies, and that citizens were unaware of the economic effects corruption and monopolies had on their lives. Phillips created a dramatic narrative predicated on valid presumptions about patterns of association, collusion, and consequence.[43]

"The Treason Of The Senate" series launched further exposés, each of them a series, by *Cosmopolitan* the next five years. Whatever the personal or political motives of its publisher, *Cosmopolitan* would help its middle-class readers learn about the lives of less-fortunate Americans and about the corporate-political alliances that impeded economic and social justice.

Crusades

If the researchers for David Graham Phillips also had investigated absenteeism in Congress during the 1905–1906 session to document dereliction of duty, William Randolph Hearst might have topped the list of public servants who did not serve their constituents. Hearst never was a conscientious congressman. He proposed legislation, but did not marshal it through committees. He missed numerous roll-call votes, generally because his own business interests had priority over the public's interests. Hearst sponsored legislation that had absolutely no chance of passage, including an eight-hour workday and direct election of senators, solely to claim credit.[44]

Hearst realistically appraised the status of a junior minority party congressman, which was very low. The seniority system ruled. Not surprisingly, Hearst figured he had more power as a newspaper and magazine publisher. His newspapers and *Cosmopolitan* advocated a progressive agenda. *Cosmopolitan* was especially vital to the cause of reform. Inspiring or provoking the middle class to action was the magazine's mission.

Eradication of the atrocity of child labor was a priority item on the agenda. With the Senate series having pumped up readership, *Cosmopolitan* started "The Hoe-Man In The Making" series to inform readers about conditions, pay, and treatment of boys and girls whose employment in dangerous and dirty jobs was a national disgrace—the moral equivalent of slavery.

President Roosevelt asked Congress in 1906 for money to finance a special report by the Bureau of Labor on children employed by manufacturers, mines, textile mills, and other employers that exposed boys and girls to hazardous or strenuous work. The census of 1900 had determined that one of every four children between the ages of ten and fourteen—1.3 million boys and girls—worked to bring home income for their families. The children's pay ranged from a dime to a dollar a day; their workday varied from six hours to fourteen hours. Children under the age of eighteen comprised a tenth of the American workforce. Each year an estimated 50,000 of them were killed or injured on the job. Congress refused to appropriate money for the special census report.[45]

McClure's had published an article in 1902 on child laborers in coal mines. Ten years before that, Jacob Riis had published a book, *How the Other Half Lives*, on poverty in New York City. Riis was a photographer, and the power of his book originated from many images of children, men, and women living in destitution, working in sweatshops or doing piecemeal labor in their tiny tenement apartments. Photographs of homeless children sleeping in stairwells and on street grates sparked an effort by wealthy New Yorkers to improve sanitation and housing. Still, by the start of "The Hoe-Man In The Making" series in *Cosmopolitan* no magazine had given extensive space to the subject.[46]

The title of the series alluded to a popular poem, "The Man With The Hoe," by Edwin Markham. Published in 1899, the poem was an ode to common laborers in the Industrial Age—men whose unbelievably hard labor in factories and foundries exhausted them every day, wearing them down physically and mentally. Markham described the man with a hoe:

> The emptiness of ages in his face
> A thing that grieves not and that never hopes
> Whose breath blew out the light within this brain?
> Is this the Thing the Lord God made and gave
> To have dominion over sea and land
> To feel the passion of Eternity?
> Through this dread shape humanity betrayed
> Plundered, profaned and disinherited
> Cries protest to the Powers that made the world
> A protest that is also prophecy.

Markham's poem foretold that the protest would culminate in violent revolution.

Bailey Millard, then editor of a Hearst newspaper in San Francisco, heard about the poem, which was being read as a sermon in many churches in California. The newspaper published it. Newspapers everywhere reprinted it, and the poem became a Sunday sermon in churches across the land, a plea to congregants and parishioners to demand humane conditions and treatment for workers. Millard, upon becoming *Cosmopolitan* editor for Hearst, commissioned Markham, a schoolteacher, to write a series on children who toiled at jobs only adults should do.[47]

Markham devoted each installment of "The Hoe-Man In The Making" to a different industry: "The Child At The Loom"; "Child-Wrecking In The Glass-Factories"; "Little Slaves Of The Coal-Mines"; "The Grind Behind The Holidays"; "The Sweat-Shop Inferno;" "The Smoke Of Sacrifice." The series ran from September 1906 to February 1907, its first three installments concurrently with "Treason." Descriptions of work performed by children, whether fastening spindles of thread to a rapidly spinning loom or stabbing a thick needle through heavy fabric to stitch a coat together or staggering down an alley with a bundle of tobacco leaves atop shoulders or shoving wood into a furnace hour after hour, told the men and women reading *Cosmopolitan* about the toll on a child of a day's labor. Markham spared no details:

They are doubled over the coal-breakers, breathing black coal-dust; they are racked in the cotton-mills, breathing damp lint; they are strained in furniture-factories, breathing sawdust; they are parceled in glass-factories, breathing dust of glass; they are crowded in soap-factories, breathing dust of alkali; they are twisted in tobacco-factories, inhaling the deadly nicotine; they are bent over in dye-rooms, soaking in poisonous dyes; they are stooped in varnishing-rooms, absorbing noxious fumes; they are stifled in rubber-factories, where they are paralyzed with naphtha; they are choked in match-factories, where they are gangrened with phosphorous; they are huddled in type-foundries, where they are cramped with the poison of lead.[48]

Greed created the situation, Markham explained. "The factory, we are told, must make a certain profit, or the owners will complain," he wrote. "The factory blasts the moral nature, blights the mind of the child, and sows through his body the seeds of disease." And in each installment Markham hammered home the theme that workers sought relief from the bottle to dull the pain of continuous labor and suppress the humiliation of being treated as less than human. "While yet in the first sap of youth, they are flung out to the society of lewd and hardened men," Markham stated. "What wonder that the gambling-hole and the drinking-joint are their frequent havens?"[49]

Children worked the machinery at southern textile mills. "Many of the mills of the South are owned by New England capitalists, the machinery having been removed from the North to the South, so as to be near the cotton fields, near the water-power, and, shame to record, near the cheap labor of these baby fingers," Markham stated. It was all-day indoor work for children who changed the whirring spindles while the looms operated. "This new slavery of the mills is worse than the old slavery of the cotton fields," Markham insisted. "For the negro of the old days was well fed and sure of shelter; he did his work under the open sky, singing as he toiled. But the slavery of the white women and children sucks life dry of all vigor and all joy."[50]

Markham visited a glass manufacturer. "Go to the glass-works, and, amid the roar and the glare and the torrid heat, gaze on the scorching and shriveling children clustered about the red-hot hives of the furnaces," he wrote. "By night and by day they are there, running constant chance of being burnt and blinded by fragments of molten glass splintering through the room, always breathing the powdered glass sleeting through the air." Glassmakers relied on boys to carry hot glassware on an asbestos shovel to a blower for shaping. Each boy scurried a hundred feet from oven to blower and back seventy times an hour, "always in a Sahara of heat, always in a withering drift of glassy dust."[51]

Machinery was not available to strip tobacco leaves from stalks for cigars, so children performed that task in the tenements and sweatshops of New York City and other cities. "Young girls got the work, accepting two dollars and fifty cents a week, less sixty cents for carfare," Markham informed readers. An estimated twelve thousand children labored to separate tobacco for rolling, their workday usually ten hours. "Now the United States consumes nearly nine billion cigars a year, and sixty million dollars a year are spent for this fleeting pleasure," Markham wrote. "Is tobacco so necessary to human welfare that we should sacrifice childhood for it?"[52]

If appeals to conscience were not sufficient, Markham tried scare tactics. An article about families that earned money sewing garments in tenements passed along this story: "Settlement workers tell me of a child, dead of diphtheria, that was kept three days in a closed room, while a stream of visitors, some bringing their sewing, passed in and out by day and night. An epidemic of diphtheria in a wealthy village a hundred miles from New York city was traced by chance to the 'knee-pants' purchased from a traveling-agent selling the sweat-shop goods of New York. Misery scatters widely her seeds." Markham also advised readers that New York health investigators had traced outbreaks of "pink eye," or conjunctivitis, to middle-class families whose clothes came from garment workers in the tenements.[53]

Cosmopolitan supplemented three of the six Markham articles with editorials. The first announced the formation of the Child Labor Federation, organized and financed by the magazine. "It asks you, readers of the Cosmopolitan, to help it in this work and to interest your friends, acquaintances, and the people of your locality," an editor wrote. "It costs nothing to join. Remember, all these movements tend to sway legislation in favor of the child-workers." The second editorial directed the many readers who wished to donate money to the effort to send their contributions to the National Child Labor Committee, a longstanding organization the new Child Labor Federation would assist. The final editorial bluntly stated, "Child labor must go."

Cosmopolitan appealed to parents, "You have boys and girls of your own; when you see them grouped happily about the Christmas dinner, can you feel satisfied with yourself if you do not give a thought to the millions of other children to whom Christmas brings only the reminder that they are wage slaves?" It ended by restating that membership in the Child Labor Federation was free.[54]

"The Hoe-Man In The Making" series ended in February 1907. The next session, Congress approved the request by Roosevelt for a special census report it had previously rejected. Gradually, because of advocacy by the National Child Labor Committee and Child Labor Federation, various states enacted laws limiting the type of work and hours of work for children under the age of fourteen. Finally, the federal government established the Children's Bureau in 1912 to monitor employers of child labor involved with interstate commerce.[55]

Concern for laborers extended beyond the borders. *Cosmopolitan* published a three-part series during autumn 1906 on the plight of workers constructing the Panama Canal. Articles described the lack of sanitary water, open sewerage ditches, and incompetent management of the enterprise. The fact that the Panama Canal was the crown jewel of American imperialists, chief among them TR, lent a dual purpose to the series.

Nicaragua was the preferred canal site for many years until a French corporation that had abandoned its effort to cross Panama with a lock-and-dam system agreed to appreciably lower its price for the route. However, Panama was a province of Colombia, which refused to sign a treaty with the United States. Conveniently, in November 1903 a rebellion in Panama created an independent country that was granted diplomatic recognition immediately by the Roosevelt administration. The new country agreed to a treaty, and the Senate ratified it in February 1904. Two years passed without much progress. Disease, usually yellow fever and malaria, killed hundreds of workers and families until medical researchers gained control.[56]

Cosmopolitan reported that things were still chaotic a month before Roosevelt was to visit Panama, the first time any president had visited a foreign country. According to the first article, incompetence was the order of the day. "When a man tells you on the Isthmus that he is an engineer you don't know whether he has tended a soda-water fountain or run an elevator," the writer commented. Derelict equipment lay in ditches and swamps, railroad tracks sagged and buckled, and concrete bridge abutments broke apart within weeks of completion. Water pumped from wells was awful. "The water is tainted with the cesspool and latrine refuse," the writer explained.

A tropical location was not the problem. "One of the most healthful cities of the tropical world" was in British Guyana, and "Georgetown is as free from fever and dysentery as any city of the United States," according to the article.

The article accused Roosevelt of lying to the public in a report that "assured the country that there was an abundance of water, a splendid reservoir with some five hundred millions of gallons bubbling over the dam daily." The writer had walked through the "alleged reservoir," an empty swamp.[57]

American supervisors had brought racial prejudice with them to direct predominantly black laborers. Because many laborers were from the Bahamas, Jamaica, and other British colonies, they protested mistreatment and abuse. "There is no color line" in British colonies, the writer stated.[58]

The article described wood pilings of poor quality that split or splintered when pounded into soil. Mechanical dredges and steam shovels constantly malfunctioned. Companies had received government contracts without any proof they could do the work. "We have, in the past two years, also spent extravagantly and already are rearing monuments recalling those of the famous Tweed ring of New York," the writer insisted. "There is not a single man connected with the Panama Canal to-day who before his appointment would have been selected by a private corporation for analogous duties. The chairman of the Canal Commission and the chief engineer are men of railway and financial training; and for the man of railways to be the boss of waterway problems is like putting a cavalry colonel in charge of a man-of-war."[59] Some, perhaps most, *Cosmopolitan* readers would have remembered that Roosevelt was a cavalry colonel in Cuba.

A subsequent *Cosmopolitan* commentary reprinted a notice from a canal official ordering supervisors and property managers at job sites to "give such buildings a coat of paint or whitewash and clean up and improve the surroundings at once" for the president's visit. The magazine published the circular to verify the accuracy of the articles, which TR and Elihu Root had ridiculed. "At any rate, the enforced whitewashing of Empire must stand as testimony in favor of [the magazine's] statements," an editor asserted.[60]

TR was furious, of course. His letter to William Howard Taft, the secretary of war, seethed: "Have you looked at the Cosmopolitan? It is crammed full of the usual type of slanderous falsehood, and one of the most infamous is the leading one." However, the president also asked Taft to organize a committee to investigate. As a result, the Army Corps of Engineers took control of construction in early 1907. The original congressional appropriation for the Panama Canal was $140 million; the final cost was $325 million upon completion in 1914.[61]

"Money makes the Senate go," a *Cosmopolitan* commentary had declared at the start of "The Treason Of The Senate" series. Rich corporations and rich people bought the laws they desired or blocked the reforms they abhorred. Until ratification of the Seventeenth Amendment in 1913, the rich accumulated wealth without hindrance and bequeathed it unencumbered by an inheritance tax. *Cosmopolitan* sought to explain the vastness of personal fortune among American tycoons and to demonstrate the connection between the economic elite and the cartels that dominated the national economy. Magazine articles wanted readers to understand how the system worked.

"Owners Of America," a ten-part series of periodic articles from early summer 1908 through summer 1909, concentrated on a person or family whose privilege owed its existence and sustenance to a cartel. The ten were, chronologically: Andrew Carnegie, steel; Thomas Ryan, municipal water and trolley franchises; J. Pierpont Morgan, finance; the Vanderbilt family, shipping and railroads; Charles M. Schwab, steel; John D. Rockefeller, oil; the Armour family, meatpacking; the Swift family, meatpacking; E. H. Harriman, railroads; the Astor family, real estate. The profiles of Hearst-owned *Cosmopolitan* could hardly have contrasted more starkly with the "Captains Of Industry" series John Brisben Walker had published. "Owners Of America" dealt candidly with controversies affecting each of the rich men or families.

More explanatory than exposé, "Owners Of America" objectively chronicled the path to wealth of each and painstakingly guided readers through a maze of favoritism, manipulation, and tariff protection that enriched each. Although the series primarily summarized previous exposés by magazines and newspapers, it served as primer on the scope of official corruption fed by payoffs from businesses.

The writer, Alfred Henry Lewis, applied wit and sarcasm liberally throughout each of the five installments he supplied for the series. Lewis was a muckraker who specialized in documenting legal problems affecting robber barons. His articles for newspapers and magazines relied on lawsuits and court documents. *Cosmopolitan* frequently commissioned articles by Lewis during its exposé phase, including the piece on Senator Platt that angered President Roosevelt. Lewis also was a genuine misanthrope. "The public is most somnolently thick," he declared near the start of the Carnegie article. "Of all the inane lambs that ever gamboled in plain sight of the wolves, the public is the most bleatingly witless."[62]

Then Lewis moved on to Carnegie, the wealthiest man in the world. Lewis rehashed familiar biographical material on Carnegie for much of the article.

Born poor, Carnegie became rich by hard work, shrewd decisions, a keen intelligence that saw opportunity others did not see, and a resolute determination that intimidated partners and competitors alike. A practitioner of vertical integration, Carnegie "needed iron-ore, wherefore he owned iron-mines . . . needed coal, wherefore he owned coal mines . . . needed coke, wherefore he owned coke-ovens . . . needed money, wherefore he owned banks." Lewis noted that the steel tariff of 40 percent afforded him a generous markup and immense profits selling to American customers, while a lucrative navy contract to manufacture steel plates for warships paid Carnegie triple the price private shipbuilders did. "Why? Because the public buys armor plates."

Now fabulously wealthy, Carnegie disbursed his money to do good. The article praised the robber baron for his philanthropy, but wondered about his altruism. "Sentimentally Mr. Carnegie is eager for a world's approval," the writer commented. "To this laudable end he builds libraries, and has piled up nearly seventeen hundred of them in England and Scotland and America. One and all they are carefully 'Carnegie Libraries.' His is no light to be hidden, whatever the accumulation of bushels."[63]

Next, Lewis educated the magazine's readers about municipal franchises awarded to private companies. "Franchises—street-railway franchises, gas franchises—are favored of the gods," Lewis wrote. "The courts say that a fortunate recipient, getting them for nothing, may capitalize them for millions. The courts say also that, although capitalized for millions, and a proper basis of dividends, the public may not list them for taxation." This era preceded the passage of laws transferring ownership of gas, sewer, and water systems and public transit to municipal government. Franchises often went to contractors who gave company stock to anyone and everyone in city or county government who had the slightest part in awarding a license; and if corrupt officials did not want stock, they got cash instead.

Utility pipes were buried beneath surface easements granted by government and tracks were laid on streets owned by government, but the franchise company reimbursed the community with a nominal percentage of revenue collected in fees from citizens and businesses based either on usage volume or a flat rate. Trolleys owned by franchises contributed a percentage of revenue, too. Quality of service was at the discretion of the franchise holder. With a legal monopoly, profits were enormous; stockholders were amply rewarded.

Thomas Ryan held franchises in New York City. "Tammany Hall is as a dog for his hunting, and he breaks city councils to his money-will as folk break horses to harness," Lewis stated. "At least he is honest in the New York city sense. To be honest in the New York city sense is to be sternly opposed to every robbery in the proceeds whereof you are to have no personal share."[64]

J. Pierpont Morgan's specialty, according to Lewis, was stock-watering. Morgan bought manufacturers and railroads, merged them, and issued stock far in excess of actual value. Upon formation of the merged entity, Morgan sold most of his stock, reaping a hefty profit, and kept a smaller, though still significant, collection of stock for future trading or manipulation. "An artist of stock-company hydraulics, he was a wonder-worker when it came to water," Lewis explained. "Given a dime and a chance to visit the nearest hydrant, he'd return you a ten-dollar gold piece." The writer riffed on an anecdote about Sir Henry Morgan, "an admiral of buccaneers" in the West Indies during the 1700s, then slyly referred to J. Pierpont Morgan's yacht, the *Corsair*.

Morgan engineered many mergers, formed holding companies, and controlled the gigantic new entities by converting his bank's loans that had financed everything to ownership stock. His shrewd assessments of efficient and inefficient practices resulted in formerly unprofitable enterprises becoming immensely profitable, and Morgan himself received compensation inconceivable to most people. The House of Morgan arranged loans for governments, financed the purchase of rights to the Panama Canal and its construction, and on more than one occasion rescued Wall Street banks from their own ruin caused by greed and recklessness.[65]

Lewis was at his most educational leading *Cosmopolitan* readers through a steel deal engineered by Charles M. Schwab and financed by Morgan. Starting with $7.5 million to buy Bethlehem Steel, Schwab and Morgan floated $40 million in stock and $26 million in bonds to form a new entity, with each man profiting by several million dollars. The lesson was: the rich help themselves.[66]

Arthur Brisbane, the Hearst newspaper editor and his sometime partner in New York City real estate purchases, contributed an installment of "Owners Of America," on the Swifts of Chicago slaughterhouse fame. Brisbane admired the fathers and sons of both families because of their dedication to the family enterprises and their innovation in machinery. Brisbane vouched for the sanitation and safety standards at the stockyards, contrary to the portrayals in *The Jungle*, a novel by Upton Sinclair published in 1906. Of the author whose book horrified a nation, Brisbane wrote: "Mr. Sinclair acted as a little girl does when she walks into the garden and finds a green slug eating her pet tomato vine. Sinclair really discovered the slaughterhouse. It was quite new to him. Sinclair discovered that the place in which eight or nine million animals are disemboweled in one year is not an absolutely tidy, sweet-smelling resort. The squeals of the pigs and the patient resignation of the cattle were too much for him."[67]

In its profile of the Astor family, the last installment of "Owners Of America," *Cosmopolitan* damned with praise. "Theirs is a clean fortune," the writer advised. "It is tainted with none of the scandals and high-handed methods of outlawry

that have characterized the building of many great estates." The article then listed the vast Astor properties of tenements, sweatshops, luxury apartments, and
blocks of retail space in Manhattan. And it just so happened that a prime piece
of property "directly opposite" the proposed Pennsylvania Station in midtown
Manhattan was purchased by the Astors a scant time prior to the railroad's announcement it would be built. "It is this shrewdness and keen insight which has
been one of the chief factors in building up the enormous Astor fortune through
succeeding generations," the writer concluded sardonically.[68]

A hidden owner of America, according to *Cosmopolitan,* was the Church of
Latter Day Saints. An editor introduced a three-part series on the Mormons—
"The Viper On The Hearth," "The Trail Of The Viper," "The Viper's Trail Of
Gold"—promising "a full realization of what Mormonism really means; how
it has already cinched its slimy grip upon the politics and business of a dozen
states." Mormon ownership of a railroad in Oregon and a position on the Union
Pacific railroad's board of directors received attention, as did the church's sizable cash deposits in banks owned by Morgan and unspecified substantial investments in major American corporations. Mostly, though, the series written
by Alfred Henry Lewis delivered invective.[69]

Lewis cited the Oath of Blood Atonement, a pledge of vengeance inscribed
at the temple in Salt Lake City that vowed "to avenge the blood of the prophets [Joseph Smith and a son] upon this nation," meaning the United States. To
gain statehood for Utah, Mormon leaders approved a manifesto forsaking polygamy; but the custom of multiple wives persisted. "Now the Gentiles threaten
them with an amendment to the national Constitution, taking the business
away from the state courts and making polygamy an offense punishable in
the federal courts," Lewis wrote. Mormon residents in eight western states—70
percent in Utah, 30 percent in Idaho, 10 to 20 percent in Colorado, Oregon,
and elsewhere—voted as a bloc and effectively controlled the state legislatures,
Lewis stated. A subsequent commentary by Lewis accused President William
Howard Taft of political expediency on a visit to Salt Lake City where "he flattered the Mormons, who are always Mormons and never Americans."[70]

Mormons meant to avenge the deaths of their prophets and their persecution by Gentiles by ruining the economy of the United States, Lewis warned.
The substantial investment by the Mormon Church of the annual tithes from
hundreds of thousands of the faithful would be a weapon to smite persecutors.
"At a nod from the Mormon prophet panic will sweep business like a storm,
prosperity be laid on its beam-ends and commerce blown as flat as any field of
turnips," he declared. "All this is being planned and looked forward to by the
Mormon Church."[71]

A fascinating element of the series was the composite illustrations of photographs and drawings depicting Mormon leaders and representations of the

church. Vipers, of course, adorned many illustrations, their bodies coiled around a Gentile mother and children, or slithering across a page to a temple. An octopus embedded with the face of the prophet Joseph Smith, grandson of the martyr prophet, grasped a dozen senators on the Capitol steps. The combination of Lewis's vituperative text and vivid illustrations intended to evoke fear and hatred. The *Cosmopolitan* series exemplified the trademark Hearst sensationalism.

Sensationalism was absent, however, on another subject: the alcohol problem. *Cosmopolitan* explored aspects pertaining to a national debate about whether to ban all alcoholic beverages or to impose temperance by limiting availability to beer and wine only. The prohibition campaign had intensified since the 1890s under the guidance of a coalition of churches, industrialists, Progressives, and women's organizations. The coalition had persuaded legislatures in several states to allow local option referendums, either by county or municipality, thereby permitting residents to choose whether to go dry or remain wet.

Clergy sought a ban on alcoholic beverages for moral reasons, industrialists for economic reasons because drunken workers were less productive, and Progressives and women's organizations for social reasons because drunkards created a wide range of problems for communities. Proponents of prohibition believed a correlation existed between a father's alcohol consumption and a shortage of money to buy food and pay rent, which forced children into the workforce to bring income home for basic necessities. The Anti-Saloon League, the Women's Christian Temperance Union, and other activists prodded state legislators to approve statewide bans or make local option referendums possible. A general effort arose to enact federal legislation to prohibit all alcoholic beverages.

Wrapped up in the prohibition movement was public recognition that licensing and regulation of the liquor business had corrupted local governments and law enforcement departments. Tavern owners bribed policemen and deputies to ignore the after-hours trade that violated closing times stipulated by liquor licenses, and the illicit manufacture of booze was permitted in return for payoffs. Also, solicitation by prostitutes was commonplace inside taverns and on nearby streets.[72]

Cosmopolitan broached the prohibition versus temperance debate with laudable evenhandedness, probably because Hearst had no vested interest in the subject. He abstained from alcohol, a choice made while a student at Harvard University where he did drink heavily his freshman year, but by his sophomore year he decided sobriety was better. Harvard expelled him anyway for not attending, or completing, classes. Besides, as a publisher Hearst hardly could avoid contact with drinkers in his newsrooms. He was not contemptuous or scornful of them. According to one of Hearst's sons, many a journalist found a place to sleep atop a roll of newsprint near the presses when drinks after deadline made it difficult to navigate home.[73]

Cosmopolitan articles displayed a bias toward temperance, but did not ridicule proponents of prohibition. Arthur Brisbane introduced the subject in "The Fight Against Alcohol." Brisbane offered an overview of the moral and social arguments against imbibing alcohol, an assessment of the problem of intoxication, and an explanation about medical research on the effects of alcohol. "Interesting in to-day's cold, calculating war on alcohol is the fact that it does not follow any outbreak of drunkenness," Brisbane wrote. "On the contrary, it crops out in a civilization in which the excessive use of alcohol has steadily diminished. The whole world agrees that all but temperate use of stimulants should be condemned." Scientists had not found "any food value, except in small doses" of alcohol. Brisbane noted concerns in Europe about alcoholic beverages, too, except there the public mood preferred temperance. Brisbane's article preceded commentary by two guest writers—a prohibition proponent and an owner of a famous brewery. "Intelligent readers, after interesting discussion, will form their own opinions," Brisbane remarked. "It is quite likely that each will put down this magazine with his opinion what it was before, but stronger."[74]

The first commentary by a self-described "total abstainer" filled three pages. Its message was succinctly imparted in three sentences, however: "He who takes the first glass does not possess the moral power to resist the second glass which he had to resist the first. Therefore, the only sound doctrine is, 'Decline the first glass.' This is the doctrine of total abstinence in a nutshell."[75]

The second commentary was by Gustave Pabst, owner of the nation's largest brewery, best known for its Blue Ribbon beer. Pabst framed the choice as a contest for Americans between "finding temperance in their will-power" or to "confess defeat and put upon themselves a strait-jacket to make up for their lack of character." Successful men were "moderate drinkers of light wines or beers," Pabst asserted. The most advanced nations in the world—Germany, Britain, America—favored temperance, not prohibition. Nations that prohibited alcohol were second rate. "Among Mohammedans, the Turks especially, we can study the effects of legal prohibition," Pabst stated. "They are a race of prohibitionists, and we hear of them only by the reports of outrages, fanatical murders, and massacres that come to us from time to time, or from tragedies in their harems where women are slaves. Has prohibition, with them, meant moral uplift?"[76]

Another *Cosmopolitan* article examined the success of prohibition in southern states. Georgia had gone dry, at least publicly. Taverns were gone. State law, however, allowed locker clubs. A club rented individual storage bins to men for bottles of liquor and a key to unlock the bin; tables in a nearby lounge were available for drinking liquor, either alone or with others who had keys to storage bins. Cities in Georgia had dozens to hundreds of locker clubs with membership at each ranging from a few hundred men to almost two thousand. "Public opinion is assaulting these strongholds with increasing persistency and force," the writer reported, noting local attempts to challenge the legality of locker clubs in court. Other information in the article mentioned positive effects from prohibition in Georgia. "Landlords speak of better rents and prompter payments, employers of labor describe an advance in home life and home comfort among workingmen," readers learned.[77]

A final article basically reiterated the futility of either choice. "The attempt to change drunkenness into temperance is bound on the face of it to fail," the writer argued. "It is not the slight stimulation, but the excessive, that the drunkard wants, and to tickle his palate with the straw of temperance is but to inflame the more this finally victorious appetite." Yet, a ban on alcohol was doomed. "The attempt to enforce prohibition by legal means will surely fail, and the present success of prohibition all over the country and abroad will have a reaction marked for a time by new excesses."[78]

The coalition of organizations determined to eradicate alcohol placed it on the ballot in several states from 1908 to 1911. Twelve states adopted prohibition within their boundaries and almost every state accepted local option referendums. But voting did not eliminate the conflict between dry and wet factions. *Cosmopolitan* described a lynching in Newark, Ohio, a crime committed in summer 1910 following a shootout between enforcers from the Anti-Saloon League and customers at a tavern. The league's enforcers had attempted to seize liquor bottles from the tavern, which openly flouted the county's dry law. An enforcer had shot and mortally wounded the tavern owner. A mob dragged the enforcer from a cell at the local jail and hanged him from a streetlamp. "Out in the Middle West to-day there is warfare," the article explained. "It is a warfare between the 'wets' and the 'drys'—a warfare in which the participants Jesuitically maintain that the end justifies the means." The incident had resulted from blatant lack of enforcement by either the sheriff or the mayor, who was a regular patron at the tavern. The militant Anti-Saloon League had decided to close the tavern on its own, hoping a demonstration of resolve would persuade the four dozen other taverns in town to shut down.[79]

The tragic event in Ohio was a flashpoint resulting from the frustration reformers felt when their battle against the corruption and immorality permeating all levels of government seemed futile. Years of exposé journalism, reformist campaigns, and a victory at the municipal or state polls here and there had not accomplished much permanent improvement. A hopeful sign was the growing appeal of Progressives, from which blossomed a full-fledged national campaign in 1912. To get there required further prodding.

Cosmopolitan in 1906 had informed its readers about corruption in the U.S. Senate, and had updated its perception of the web of sinister alliances with a series of articles at intervals from July 1910 to November 1911. The magazine reviewed the battles for reform in cities—Chicago, Pittsburgh, San Francisco—and in the states of Colorado, Illinois, Ohio, Oklahoma, Mississippi, and Wisconsin. The ten-part series, "What Are You Going To Do About It?" reiterated familiar examples of misconduct and payoffs, but also offered uplifting tales of angry citizens in revolt.

The title "What Are You Going To Do About It?" served a dual purpose: to challenge readers to become active politically in their hometowns and states; and to remind them about one of the great crusades of journalism—the valiant fight by cartoonist Thomas Nast, *Harper's Weekly,* and the *New York Times* against Tammany Hall and "Boss" William Tweed during the early 1870s. The title supposedly was a quote from Tweed. Legend had it that a *New York Times* reporter asked the Boss about the newspaper's evidence of bribery, kickbacks from construction contracts, and a multitude of ghosts, or nonexistent workers, on the municipal payroll; the Boss snarled in response, "Well, what are you going to do about it?" Nast seized on the quote and used it as a standard caption for his cartoons as an example of Tammany Hall's arrogance and attitude of invincibility. ("Supposedly" is the operative word because no *New York Times* from the period in question, early July to mid-August 1871, actually contained the quote. Two newspaper editorials referred to a statement from a Tweed crony, "Well, can you do anything about it?" A letter to the editor referred to Tweed saying, "Well, what can they do about it?") Each installment of the magazine series challenged readers by concluding, "What are you going to do about it?"[80]

The series, six installments of which were written by Charles Edward Russell, one of many known socialists employed by Hearst and a contender for the Socialist Party presidential nomination in 1916, primarily led readers through the fundamentals of machine politics. Pittsburgh was captive to the Magee-Flinn network of political hacks. "It is at all times a badly governed city," Russell commented. "The machine holds the city government in its hands like putty. Councilmen that obey orders get saloon licenses, or city, county, or state jobs, or bits of subcontracts, or bits of profitable businesses, or slices of the money-making deals the machine is always engineering."

Citizens, including business owners and reformers, formed the Voters League to fight the Magee-Flinn machine. The Voters League devised a trap. One of them posed as an out-of-town paving contractor interested in bidding on street work. The pseudo-contractor met individual councilmen in a hotel room to discuss how business was done with city government, and implied that a payoff was certain for assistance. Unknown to the councilmen, listeners from the league had drilled a small hole in the wall from an adjacent room, holding a hearing-cup to the hole for a stenographer to record the conversations.

The Voters League printed and distributed transcripts of the session for newspapers, churches, and civic associations. "It was an astonishing document, implicating about two-thirds of the members of the councils and some of the foremost bankers and business men in the city," Russell noted. The bankers had paid bribes to receive long-term deposits of city revenue.[81]

An article on the Illinois legislature described in fine detail a hotel conference where individual legislators each received a bribe of nine hundred dollars to vote for a Republican, William Lorimer, as U.S. senator. Fifty-two Democrats abandoned their party's winner of the primary election for senator—a nonbinding choice by voters—and fifty-five Republicans ignored the fact that Lorimer had not won their party's primary election either. Lorimer went to the Senate.[82]

The Colorado political machine controlled by Senator Simon Guggenheim, a Republican and a wealthy owner of ore smelters and mines, handed out money on election days with instructions to recipients to vote for specific candidates. "As many as eight thousand fraudulent votes have been available in Denver for whichever party was slated by the Interests to win," Russell stated. Workers at mines in the mountains and lumber camps were told how to vote or lose their jobs; the ballot tally affirmed their obedience.

Colorado reformers spoke at churches, Sunday suppers, and county fairs to ask citizens to pressure legislators to approve laws allowing referendums, recall elections, and the direct primary election to replace caucuses. "Public education on these points had been complete," Russell explained. "They sickened of the whole business and demanded sweeping reforms." These proposals passed into law.[83]

Cosmopolitan credited Senator Thomas Gore, Democrat of Oklahoma, for single-handedly stopping a swindle of Indians on reservations in western states. Gore revealed excessive payments to a law firm purportedly representing Indian tribes negotiating mineral and oil rights with private companies; not only were the tribes cheated, but the Department of Interior was billed $1.7 million by the lawyers for representation. "The duty of the government is to protect these wards," Russell declared. "It is a duty frequently underperformed."[84]

George Creel, a respected journalist and later a notable Progressive, wrote two installments of "What Are You Going To Do About It?" The first dealt with an Ohio county where hundreds of voters each had received twenty dollars every election day to help swing state elections to the Democrats or Republicans, depending on who paid the cash. Fortunately, a courageous prosecutor persisted in exposing the payoffs, and a change of venue to another county produced nineteen indictments. Creel's second article profiled James Vardaman, a reform governor in Mississippi. Vardaman was cheated out of the Senate seat by legislators who selected the candidate preferred by oil and lumber companies that had incredibly cheap leases on state land. Vardaman accomplished some significant reforms during his term: ended the practice of letting private landowners use convicts from state prisons as free labor; required banks to submit competitive interest-rate bids for deposits of state revenue; refused to renew lumber and oil leases at previous payment rates. "Such, then, were the activities that made Vardaman the wrong sort of Democrat," Creel noted. (The article also mentioned Vardaman's "negrophobia"; the governor regularly proclaimed his belief that blacks should not be allowed to vote.)[85]

A historian called *Cosmopolitan*'s "What Are You Going To Do About It?" series the "last of the important series on graft which the muckrakers produced." Each installment was an impressive four thousand to five thousand words, equivalent to fifteen to eighteen typewritten pages. The conclusion of the series in late 1911 marked the demise of exposé journalism. Other magazines that had relied on exposés—*McClure's, Collier's, American*—had seen evidence from circulation stagnation or a decline in readership that the public was less interested and also had encountered resistance from advertisers who were wary of sponsoring controversial publications.[86]

Cosmopolitan had specialized in political corruption, a reflection of its publisher's personal ambition. As a Democrat, Hearst hoped to benefit from "The Treason Of The Senate" articles on Republican senators Depew and Platt that appeared in the months preceding his candidacy for New York governor. As a Democrat with presidential aspirations, Hearst believed he would benefit from articles that connected businesses to the shame of child labor, government corruption, and unfair financial advantages accrued from favoritism, manipulation, and tariffs. Hearst avoided problems with Democrats because *Cosmopolitan* stayed away from exposés pertaining to corruption among labor union leaders and the intimidation by violence that unions directed against employers and nonunion workers; *McClure's* published several exposés on these subjects.

Cosmopolitan did not join the crusade against vile patent medicines, many of which contained high percentages of alcohol and some of which contained addictive narcotics, nor did the magazine examine deceptive business practices of insurers and Wall Street stockbrokers, which other magazines revealed.

Certainly, *Cosmopolitan* helped reformers educate the public with articles showing the web of relationships among local, state, and national governments and powerbrokers in the private sector. The magazine undoubtedly raised political awareness among its middle-class readership and inspired community activism by some.

Payback

Hearst used *Cosmopolitan* to punish his political enemies, a list that included anyone who had thwarted his quest for mayor of New York City, governor of New York, and president of the United States. The person at the top of the list was Theodore Roosevelt.

William Randolph Hearst envied Theodore Roosevelt. Five years older than Hearst, TR had steadily progressed up the political ladder, with a brief detour for the Spanish-American War. TR had a desk job as assistant secretary of the navy when the battleship USS *Maine* exploded from unknown factors in the harbor at Havana, Cuba, in mid-February 1898. War was declared in April, and TR immediately resigned to organize a regiment of volunteer cavalrymen mainly from the Rocky Mountain region. The regiment, nicknamed the Rough Riders, served in combat against Spanish soldiers in Cuba. Commissioned as a colonel, TR led the Rough Riders on an assault against an entrenched position at the top of San Juan Hill near the city of Santiago. His bravery and leadership in combat rightly earned him public adulation. Meanwhile, Hearst had half-heartedly volunteered for military service in Cuba, too, but his contribution was limited to loaning his yacht to the navy and reporting the war with a coterie of reporters as companions.[87]

Republican leaders in New York recruited Roosevelt to run for governor in November 1898. Never a patient man, Hearst wanted the Democratic nomination despite having resided in the state only three years. He believed his two newspapers in the city could persuade enough voters to cast ballots for him to overcome Republican strength elsewhere in the state. Hearst vainly attempted to persuade Tammany Hall to support his nomination; the powerful city machine rejected his request.

In 1904, Hearst garnered 40 percent of Democratic Party convention delegates to support his nomination for president and might have challenged the incumbent President Roosevelt if the publisher had gotten an endorsement from William Jennings Bryan. Hearst decided the only chance he had for the Democratic presidential nomination in 1908 was to become governor of New York, the nation's most populous state. Hearst, the politician, probably had benefited somewhat from the "Treason" series in *Cosmopolitan* because several months prior to the November 1906 election the magazine had pilloried two figureheads of the state's Republican Party, senators Platt and Depew. Middle-class readers throughout New York might have switched party allegiance temporarily because of the negative portrayals.

Hearst had begun his campaign for governor as the candidate of an independent political party he organized for his mayoral effort in 1905. Large, enthusiastic crowds attended his speeches, perhaps some in attendance because lively music from a marching band preceded his speeches and an impressive display of fireworks concluded them. Hearst was always the showman.

His obvious popularity in New York City and in industrial areas elsewhere in the state prompted Tammany Hall to offer Hearst the Democratic nomination for governor. The publisher so desperately wanted to be governor that he accepted, pragmatically becoming partners with the political gang that had stolen the mayoral victory from him.[88]

President Roosevelt and the state's Republican leadership feared a Hearst victory. The president genuinely believed Hearst was a demagogue. Hearst's newspapers had for years hammered away on the contrast between rich and poor. The squalor of the slums and the harsh conditions of laborers were compared to the extravagant lifestyles, ostentatious displays of wealth, and idleness of the heirs of rich families. Now, the series on the Senate in *Cosmopolitan* was telling its middle-class readers that the rich controlled government to the detriment of everyone else. TR's muckrake speech the previous April had alluded to Hearst. The president decried newspaper and magazine articles that portrayed owners of corporate enterprises as immoral and insensitive, stating that such journalism "divides those who are well off from those who are less well off" and that it encouraged a resentment that "will be fraught with immeasurable harm to the body politic."[89]

Roosevelt dispatched Elihu Root, the U.S. secretary of state, to defeat Hearst. Root, a venerable figure among Republicans in New York, denounced Hearst for his fondness of music halls, friendships with theater actors and actresses, reputation for late-night partying, and irresponsible journalism.

However, the most serious, and effective, denunciation by Root was a reminder to audiences that a *New York Journal* editorial might have persuaded an assassin to shoot President McKinley. The editorial, published many months prior to the September 1901 tragedy, had referred to political assassinations in Europe that had freed nations from despots; the editorial urged that "the killing must be done" in the United States—an allegorical recommendation to kill with votes, not bullets. Public outrage toward Hearst and the *New York Journal* for the editorial immediately after McKinley's murder forced the publisher to rename the newspaper the *New York American*. Audiences gasped when Root told them President Roosevelt believed the editorial had "inflamed" the assassin to commit murder. The accusation undoubtedly dissuaded enough voters from choosing Hearst to cause his defeat.[90]

Hearst lost the election for governor to Charles Evans Hughes in November 1906 by a mere 60,000 votes out of 1.5 million cast. The defeat eliminated Hearst from contention as the Democratic presidential candidate in 1908; a back-to-back loser for mayor of the nation's largest city and governor of its most populous state, Hearst had no chance to win the presidency and would have to wait until 1912.

Roosevelt was the first target for payback. The "Treason" series was the first volley. The "Panama Canal" series was the second. The third was an article that in itself was quite innocuous; it was the headline that smeared TR.

The April 1909 issue of *Cosmopolitan* returned to the TR-Platt connection, but in a much more sensational way. On the cover was a blurb across the top: "Platt's Reminiscences: The Nomination Of Roosevelt, Is The Hero Of San Juan A Coward?" To anyone who has ever stood in a supermarket checkout line and scanned the *National Enquirer* or *Star,* the *Cosmopolitan* blurb was the perfect tabloid headline—a teaser. It alleged something the article inside did not report, a phrase taken out of context.

Senator Platt had retired from public office the previous month, and had purportedly dictated his memoir to a lifelong friend; no manuscript existed, but someone passed along transcriptions of the senator's dictation. *Cosmopolitan* printed several excerpts, but mostly summarized memoir material pertaining to key political decisions affecting congressional legislation and nominations for public offices that Platt had arranged or approved. The thirteen-page article was replete with recollections of conversations involving national and state politicians familiar to readers of the era—among them James Blaine and Marcus Hanna.

The text provided an insider's perspective on the crucial political decision to persuade Theodore Roosevelt to accept the Republican nomination for governor in 1898. First mentioned on the ninth page of the article was a meeting at a hotel in Manhattan of Republican powerbrokers with their prospective nominee, at which TR was told his opponents had obtained an affidavit declaring he was not a citizen of New York. A startled Roosevelt admitted he had declared residency in Washington, D.C., upon becoming an assistant secretary of the navy to avoid liability for state taxes. He realized the document and his nonpayment of taxes could deny him the nomination for governor. Nervous and emotional, TR told Platt he would withdraw his name from consideration. Platt and other leaders at the meeting preferred not to act in haste; they wanted to confer with key delegates to the upcoming Republican state convention, including Senator Chauncey Depew, to assess reactions to this information. Platt needed to persuade Roosevelt not to withdraw. Knowing that TR was a fighter, Platt purposely provoked an instinctive response by asking, "Is the hero of San Juan a coward?" TR replied, "No, I am not a coward."[91]

That single remark was the basis for the cover blurb. Naturally, a Hearst-style promotional blitz preceded distribution of the April issue using the tabloid-style blurb as the centerpiece. A *New York Times* headline, "Roosevelt Afraid In

1898, Platt Says: Senator Declares President Shrank From Governorship Fight In This State," accurately summarized a lengthy article that thoroughly explained the incident. Still, it was publicity for the upcoming *Cosmopolitan* and that was all that mattered. Many people who saw posters and flyers emblazoned with the "coward" blurb probably did not learn the background.[92]

Platt died early in 1910, which gave *Cosmopolitan* an excuse to run an entire chapter of the memoirs. Anecdotal and unapologetic, Platt defended the Republican Party in New York by mentioning numerous distinguished public officials from the ranks, although the credentials of some were questionable, including Roscoe Conkling, a staunch opponent of reform, and Chauncey Depew. One sentence concerned *Cosmopolitan*'s publisher, whose name was not listed on the magazine's masthead, and TR: "It was Roosevelt who sent Elihu Root into New York State to save Hughes, when it was feared that William R. Hearst, the Democratic candidate for governor, would defeat him." Four years after the election, *Cosmopolitan* at last had printed the name of its publisher—without mentioning his ownership of the magazine.[93]

Cosmopolitan had another opportunity to target TR in 1912. The former president decided to run again and almost snatched the Republican nomination from the incumbent president William Howard Taft. A variety of decisions by Taft concerning tariff reform and antitrust enforcement had alienated "standpatter" Republicans and Progressives. TR accepted the nomination of the newly created Progressive Party, bumping aside the longtime leader La Follette to become the party's first presidential candidate. Roosevelt had interested the Progressives since his role as negotiator between traditional Republicans and so-called insurgents prior to the 1910 congressional elections.

Hearst quickly sensed a possible comeback in the making for Roosevelt and visited Taft at the White House, then shocked Democrats and Republicans alike with a formal statement that praised the president, although it enabled him to jab the former president, "He is doing the things that Roosevelt should have done but did not do." Hearst accused TR of having "fairly neglected" while president to implement the limited reforms passed by Congress.[94]

A commentary in *Cosmopolitan* of October 1912 began with praise for the spirit and new ideas of the Progressive candidate. Then the positive tone abruptly switched to one of concern. "Colonel Roosevelt's new party has also the greater or less distinction of getting nearer to the Socialist party than any other political organization of the quarter-century," the commentary warned. "And he and his lieutenants fully expect to enlist the support of thousands of Socialists who have no expectation of winning under their own Presidential candidate, but hope to enact into legislation some essential elements of their creed by supporting the third party." The pairing of TR with socialists was certain to alarm middle-class readers. It also was disingenuous considering that socialist journalists employed by Hearst wrote some of the *Cosmopolitan* exposés.[95]

Roosevelt lost to Woodrow Wilson, finishing ahead of Taft. The 1912 election marked the end of TR's political career, and of Hearst's. The publisher tried to persuade Democrats to consider him for the 1924 presidential nomination, but few responded.

Redirection

Cosmopolitan had regained first place among general magazines during 1906 with the readership surge from "The Treason Of The Senate." The magazine's average monthly distribution was 450,000 for 1906, compared to 414,000 for *McClure's. Scribner's,* once a top competitor and occasional muckraker, was at 175,000 copies and *Century,* never a muckraker, stayed at 150,000 copies that year.[96]

The popularity of exposé journalism peaked in 1906. *Cosmopolitan* had carried two to three exposés each month the last half of 1906, but other magazines published few exposés. Perhaps the criticism of muckrakers by President Roosevelt had dissuaded some editors and publishers, or perhaps the public had lost interest. Monthly circulation for the leading muckrakers stagnated, then slightly decreased as the first decade of the twentieth century ended. *Cosmopolitan* and *McClure's* settled at 425,000 copies monthly during 1909.[97]

Significantly, *McClure's* lost its star crew of Tarbell, Baker, and Steffens at its peak because of a disagreement with Samuel McClure concerning his commitment to the magazine. The three crusaders resigned in 1906 to buy *American,* joined by the business partner of McClure. *American* published several exposé series annually for a few years, which propelled monthly circulation to 250,000 copies at the start of 1907 and to 287,000 copies for 1909. *McClure's* developed few exposés after its prime journalists departed.

Muckraker magazines also offered ordinary articles dealing with education, international events, medicine, and science to provide readers with plenty of informative material. Fiction, too, was a valuable, if minor, component. However, the allocation of pages for fiction in muckraker magazines began to increase each year. Editors and publishers saw that circulation had flattened out. It seemed wise to adjust the format. *McClure's* drifted into popular culture articles and fiction. *American* emphasized fiction more than nonfiction when it was sold in 1911.[98]

Cosmopolitan altered its format, too. Circulation had stagnated since the end of 1906, hovering between 415,000 and 450,000 copies. The magazine had raised its cover price to fifteen cents in 1908, the first rise since 1895. Price may have foreclosed some circulation growth, but the majority of the magazine's circulation was by subscription, which remained at a dollar.

An editorial format change for *Cosmopolitan* showed that a higher price was not an impediment. Although the exposé era for *Cosmopolitan* formally ended in late 1911 at the close of the "What Are You Going To Do About It?" series, the effort was an anomaly in a magazine that was two-thirds fiction. The transition from nonfiction to fiction had started in autumn 1909. Articles and fiction reached parity the next year. Fiction dominated from mid-1911 onward.

Initially, the decline of exposé journalism and nonfiction articles in *Cosmopolitan* might seem connected to the broader trend affecting other magazines. Realistically, though, it was the keen journalistic intelligence of William Randolph Hearst, a man who knew how to get the public's attention and who knew when the public was not interested. Hearst shifted *Cosmopolitan* to fiction while the magazine still was popular, and in the process made it more popular, thus preserving it. Hearst no longer needed his flagship magazine to be his orator. His political career was of lesser importance to him by autumn 1910, a point at which only a truly obtuse person would have continued to pursue the presidency.

The decision to redirect *Cosmopolitan* was brilliant. The most popular authors of the era, including some of the best, appeared on its pages: Ellis Parker Butler, Robert W. Chambers, George Randolph Chester, Dorothy Dix, O. Henry, Rudyard Kipling, Jack London, Booth Tarkington, H. G. Wells, Edith Wharton, P. G. Wodehouse. Illustrations by Frederic Remington and Charles Dana Gibson adorned stories and frontispieces. *Cosmopolitan* spent incredible sums of money for individual stories, serials, and excerpts from novels, and to sign a select few authors to long-term exclusive contracts. Jack London initially earned $600 to $800 per installment for a serial. (The equivalent amount in 2010 would be $13,000 to $17,500.) Later, a five-year contract guaranteed London fifteen cents a word through 1916, or approximately $1,350 for each story or serial installment; sometimes, he submitted five or six items a year and made $7,000 to $8,000.[99]

In 1911, a popular author whose work had appeared in all the top magazines, Robert W. Chambers, wrote "The Common Law" and submitted it to *Saturday Evening Post*. The editor rejected it for its impropriety. Chambers centered the story's risqué plot on an artist and his relationship with a nude model, while a subplot concerned an unmarried couple who lived together. *Cosmopolitan* eagerly bought it and promoted it in newspaper advertisements. Circulation soared by tens of thousands of copies. Each time a Chambers serial ran, circulation went up. *Cosmopolitan* paid Chambers $18,000 for eight installments of a subsequent serial, and commissioned Charles Dana Gibson to illustrate it for $10,000.[100]

David Graham Phillips, who had quit writing nonfiction upon completion of "The Treason Of The Senate" series, returned to the pages of *Cosmopolitan*, albeit posthumously. Phillips was murdered by a mentally ill man who believed himself to be the real-life counterpart to a character in one of the author's novels and was angry about the portrayal. Shortly before his murder at age forty-three late in January 1911, Phillips had completed *The Price She Paid,* a novel about a woman singer whose ambition became all-consuming. *Cosmopolitan* paid the author's estate $7,000 to publish the novel in eight installments from October 1911 to May 1912. An editor wrote a fine two-page tribute to Phillips. "The novelist and the preacher were yoked together in his mentality," *Cosmopolitan* stated. "His novels were ribbed with moral purpose. Even in his reform articles, he saw good and evil moving as in a spectacle or story."[101]

Famous authors responded to the generous rate of twenty-five cents a word that *Cosmopolitan* offered the top tier. A typical premier story covered ten to twelve pages with six thousand words and several illustrations. Fees to prominent authors that averaged $1,500 paid dividends to the magazine. People wanted stories. The diminution of nonfiction articles sparked a rise in readership. The number of copies to subscribers and sold by vendors was 440,000 each month for 1911, not much different from the total at the end of the "Treason" series five years earlier; in 1914, the monthly figure was 800,000 copies; and during 1916, the last year of peace prior to American entry into World War I, the monthly amount was 1.06 million copies. Fiction had trumped reality. Despite a subscription price increase to $1.50 a year in autumn 1911, stagnant circulation was a memory. *Cosmopolitan* outdistanced its former competitors, specifically *McClure's* and *Scribner's.*[102]

Hearst reaped tremendous profits because larger circulation justified higher advertising rates. A full page cost an advertiser $448 in 1908, $784 in 1912, and $840 in 1916. Advertisers rushed to buy because ad agencies such as J. Walter Thompson, the nation's foremost shop, pushed their clients into magazines to enhance brand identity. *Cosmopolitan* carried a monthly average of 138 ad pages in 1908, 126 ad pages in 1912, and 124 ad pages in 1916. The average number of ad pages declined because of the steep rate increase, which smaller manufacturers and producers could not afford. Actual ad revenue rose sharply from $43,900 monthly in 1908 to $70,100 monthly in 1912, and $73,800 monthly in 1916. The annual average profit for *Cosmopolitan* during its 1905 to 1911 exposé period was $110,600; the annual average profit during its fiction era from 1912 to 1916 was $348,400.[103]

Hearst did not abandon politics per se. He enjoyed playing powerbroker and having a national podium for his personal agenda. So, in 1911, Hearst bought a middling monthly magazine, *World To-Day,* to continue attacks on politicians he envied or disliked, namely Theodore Roosevelt, Woodrow Wilson, and William Jennings Bryan. He renamed it *Hearst's Magazine* in April 1912, shortened it to *Hearst's* in June 1914, and ultimately titled it *Hearst's International* in May

1922—the last three title choices irrefutably affirmed a biographer's judgment that Hearst exhibited an "indomitable refusal to shrink from publicity."

Hearst's Magazine published another exposé series by Charles Edward Russell, a *Cosmopolitan* stalwart. The exposé on the Lumber Trust explained arrangements by the major corporations to limit harvesting of trees so prices would remain artificially high, to the detriment of consumers. Also, smaller lumber companies often were driven out of business because of cutthroat practices by major corporations, which included temporarily dropping prices for wood products to force smaller operators either to quit or to accept a buyout from a larger operator. The series was noteworthy because it appeared in 1912, long after other magazines had ended their exposé efforts.[104]

Politics was the mainstay of *Hearst's Magazine* throughout the 1912 election campaign. Its most sensational exposé showed the extremes to which Hearst would go to seek revenge against TR, who was the Progressive Party presidential candidate. Hearst had resurrected a scandal from 1908 that his newspapers thoroughly reported concerning bribes paid to a Republican senator by Standard Oil Company for favorable legislation to evade regulation. The newspaper articles in 1908 were based on letters somehow obtained by Hearst that specified the amount of the bribes.

The four-year-old scandal became a series in *Hearst's Magazine* generally titled "The Standard Oil Letters," which ran from June through November 1912—with the final installment, which went to readers three weeks prior to the election, displaying the byline of William Randolph Hearst. The series rehashed the bribery accusations. Standard Oil had tried to prevent antitrust action during TR's presidency by influencing a powerful senator from Ohio to intervene. Magazine articles also hinted that TR met with Standard Oil emissaries to discuss amending the government's antitrust lawsuit to weaken its impact.

The series reaped publicity for the magazine from newspapers across the country. It also prompted an investigation by the Senate to ascertain how Hearst got the letters. They had been stolen from a Standard Oil Company executive's office, photographed, and returned to the office file. Hearst denied that any money was paid for the letters.[105]

The sensationalism of its nonfiction articles boosted Hearst's eponymous magazine from a monthly circulation of 80,000 copies at its purchase to 316,000 by the start of World War I. *Hearst's Magazine* occupied the former domain of *Cosmopolitan* and permitted Hearst to dabble in national and international topics while freeing *Cosmopolitan* to generate the profits he sought to finance various business and personal ventures.[106]

Cosmopolitan was the flagship magazine, and crucial to Hearst's media empire. Its revenue and profits persuaded him to buy other magazines, which would constitute the financial center of the complex corporate structure that governed his newspapers, radio stations, a movie production studio, a newsreel company, and a book publisher. Prior to buying *Cosmopolitan* in May 1905, Hearst had owned only *Motor* magazine, a small publication for automobile owners, an elite group at that time. Hearst bought *Motor Boating* in 1907, both *World To-Day* and *Good Housekeeping* in 1911, and *Harper's Bazar* in 1912. (The spelling changed to *Bazaar* several years later.) During the Depression era of the 1930s, Hearst's magazines enabled the empire to survive while its newspapers lost millions of dollars. Without the magazines, Hearst would have gone bankrupt.

Cosmopolitan had entered the Hearst empire with a mission to assist its publisher in his quest for political power. Its mission upon his fiftieth birthday in 1913 was to make money. A directive to an executive stipulated that profits from magazines must furnish the Hearst family a salary of $10,000 a month. Hearst planned to build a castle on the coast in California and would scour Europe for artistic treasures; both endeavors absorbed a fortune funneled from his profitable media entities.[107]

Cosmopolitan mattered very much to him financially, but it also was a magazine of which he was proud. From his hilltop residence near the Pacific Ocean at San Simeon, through the Depression era and World War II, William Randolph Hearst would monitor the decisions of *Cosmopolitan* editors, critique each cover, and review the contents every month. Soon, the magazine would list his name on the masthead—and eventually on the cover itself.

6

Consolidation

Struggle

"Cosmopolitan is a problem."[1]

It was December 1932. A letter from the Manhattan office of the general manager of magazines bluntly stated the financial situation to William Randolph Hearst at his castle in San Simeon, California. *Cosmopolitan,* the flagship among nine magazines published by Hearst, was beset by common and uncommon circumstances: national economic conditions at the start of the Depression era had reduced advertising revenue severely for almost all magazines, and the outlook was bleak; the personal vanity of the publisher had sacrificed *Cosmopolitan*'s distinct identity as a premier fiction magazine by merging it with a lesser general periodical, *Hearst's International;* money from *Cosmopolitan* and other Hearst magazines had subsidized the publisher's lavish lifestyle to the detriment of their quality; the magazines also had covered expenses for several unprofitable Hearst newspapers; and a recent corporate power struggle had ousted the *Cosmopolitan* editor whose sense for popular fiction during a dozen years had attracted an affluent, steadfast readership. This adverse combination of a poor economy, ego, selfishness, fiscal mismanagement, and corporate intrigue had placed *Cosmopolitan* in a precarious position.

"Going into the first six months of 1933 business does not look good," the letter from general manager Richard Berlin warned Hearst. "We feel that further drastic economies are in order." Among the cutbacks Berlin implemented specifically for *Cosmopolitan* were thinner paper (thirty-pound weight, down from forty-pound weight), which reduced paper tonnage consumption by 25 percent to save $200,000 annually, and fewer color illustrations, which lowered printing costs $50,000 annually.[2]

The stock market crash on Wall Street in October 1929 had triggered a general economic collapse in the United States fully evident two years later and seemingly irreversible by the end of 1932. Subsequent to the disastrous drop in stock prices, businesses and manufacturers had dismissed millions of employees and also had reduced salaries and wages for millions of others who remained on the payroll. Virtually no social safety net existed, so government aid did not replace lost income. Consumer spending withered. With fewer customers buying merchandise and products, American manufacturers and retailers slashed advertising expenditures. Magazines suffered enormously. Data from 1929 to 1932 reveal the extent of the financial disaster:

- for 1930, the top sixty-five monthly magazines gained 0.3 percent aggregate advertising revenue from the prior year;
- for 1931, the same magazines lost 14 percent aggregate ad revenue from the prior year;
- for 1932, the same magazines lost another 31 percent aggregate ad revenue;
- aggregate advertising revenue for these magazines decreased a horrendous 42 percent from 1929 through 1932.[3]

Cosmopolitan for the same period fit the industry pattern, except for a higher initial gain:

- for 1930, the magazine gained 8 percent advertising revenue;
- for 1931, the magazine lost 17 percent ad revenue from the prior year;
- for 1932, the magazine lost another 32 percent ad revenue;
- advertising revenue for the magazine decreased 39 percent from 1929 through 1932—from $4.611 million the year of the Wall Street crash to $2.82 million the year Franklin D. Roosevelt was elected.[4]

Total advertising pages shrank accordingly. *Cosmopolitan* carried an average of ninety-eight ad pages monthly in 1929 compared with fifty-nine pages monthly in 1932, while ad rates remained the same. Many magazines lowered ad rates to adjust to the economic crisis and to reflect an overall one-tenth decrease in readership resulting from numerous people not renewing subscriptions, but Hearst and his executives held rates steady. Unlike other magazines, *Cosmopolitan* had retained its readers because executives had anticipated the long-term effects of the Depression; in June 1930, the magazine cut its cover price from thirty-five cents to twenty-five cents and its subscription price from $4 to $2.50 a year. The price reduction was a bargain for readers, and a candid recognition by executives that *Cosmopolitan* had lesser value—the decrease in advertising had trimmed its average monthly page count from 226 in 1929 to a decidedly thinner 162 pages in 1931.

Of course, *Cosmopolitan* was not the only magazine owned by Hearst adversely affected by the Depression. *Good Housekeeping* incurred a 19 percent decrease in advertising pages during 1932, *Harper's Bazaar* dropped by 27 percent, and the upscale *Town & Country* was down an unprecedented 47 percent. Profits at all Hearst magazine publications declined $670,000 for the year, a slide of nearly 40 percent. Still, the magazines fed profits to the corporation even during the worst years of the Depression.[5]

Despite the severity of the Depression, Hearst persistently siphoned money from all his businesses—cattle ranches, gold and silver mines, magazines, a few profitable newspapers, some radio stations—to continue construction of two grandiose residences in California, one at Wyntoon in northern California south-southeast of Mount Shasta and the other at San Simeon on the central coast north of San Luis Obispo. Construction of a Bavarian mansion and village at Wyntoon cost an estimated $1.3 million through the early 1930s. The epic edifice at the 270,000-acre San Simeon estate (420 square miles of land) cost at least $8.9 million from 1919 to the late 1930s: $4.7 million for the 115-room castle on the hilltop; another $2.7 million for a museum's worth of classic paintings, statuary, and tapestries from Europe; at least $800,000 on the Neptune Pool and Roman Pool, one inlaid with marble and the other with mosaic tile; approximately $550,000 for a cluster of roomy villas adjacent to the castle; and $150,000 for a five-mile paved road, septic tanks, and water system. Other costly items for which no accurate estimate ever was made included a zoo with a menagerie of African wildlife and an airport alongside the coast for private aircraft. Construction, maintenance, and operation of both residential complexes absorbed immense sums of money during the 1920s and most of the Depression era.[6]

Also, surplus cash from the magazines kept several Hearst newspapers alive far longer than feasible. Between the start of the Depression and the start of World War II in December 1941, the magazines funneled $24 million to the newspapers.[7]

Because the newspapers were a financial drain, the magazines also functioned as primary sources of personal allowances and salaries for the Hearst family throughout the 1930s. His estranged wife, from whom he had separated in 1922 in order to live with his mistress Marion Davies, received an annual allowance of $60,000 until later in the Depression when it was halved. A son, John Hearst, earned $38,000 annually as a magazine executive despite his failure as an advertising salesman and lack of qualifications for a managerial job. John performed so poorly he was sent to California to sell ad pages in *Cosmopolitan* to movie studios, but a dismal performance there compelled his father to beseech Richard Berlin to take him back. "I am sure you could find a place for him on the magazines and that you would find him much more satisfactory than he ever was before," Hearst wrote. "He is more of a man now and is settled into his stride." John was then thirty-one years old. Hearst himself received a $60,000 salary from the magazines while his other businesses contributed $440,000—making the publisher the highest paid executive in the nation for 1935.[8]

The publisher's lavish lifestyle, his insistence on sustaining unprofitable newspapers, and the financial obligation to the Hearst family diverted money the magazines needed for better quality paper, additional color illustrations, and higher fees to compete for popular authors and writers.

Finally, an internal power struggle between Berlin and Ray Long, the legendary Jazz Age editor of *Cosmopolitan*, ended with Long's resignation in autumn 1931. Long, a middle-aged man who addressed Hearst as "Dear Grandpa" in many business telegrams of the 1920s and who received "your grandpop" responses from the sixty-something publisher, spent enormous amounts of money to publish the most popular contemporary authors. Long also bought numerous manuscripts simply to keep competitors from publishing them, and some manuscripts sat on shelves in *Cosmopolitan*'s office suite for years until space was available in the magazine. Berlin considered Long wasteful even during prosperous times. His campaign to undermine Hearst's confidence and respect for Long achieved its purpose. Subsequent to his departure, *Cosmopolitan* slowly drifted into mediocrity as a general magazine that mixed fiction with nonfiction. His successor winnowed the massive surplus of manuscripts to fill its pages for many months and then coped with Berlin's tight budgetary controls.

Cosmopolitan was alternately profitable, marginally profitable, and slightly unprofitable from the early 1930s to 1941. Its circulation grew somewhat, but advertisers drifted in and out depending on economic conditions. World War II restored the national economy and the magazine prospered again.

The Depression era drastically changed life for William Randolph Hearst. It stripped him of power, depleted much of his fortune, and diminished his media empire. His selfishness and irresponsibility had overwhelmed the corporate web that controlled his businesses, leaving the multitude of entities $126 million in debt to banks and paper suppliers by the mid-1930s. Bankers and creditors deposed Hearst to collect their money. For eight years, until repayment of the enormous debt, other people controlled his empire. A committee of bankers and creditors scrutinized expenditures and revenue to ensure that every penny of profit repaid debt.

The committee appointed Richard Berlin president of the magazines. Hearst realized he had no authority in the interim, but he wired directives and requests to Berlin via Western Union telegrams, most sent at the cheaper overnight rate. Berlin could comply or ignore them at his discretion. He handled the situation with tact, aware that when the bankers and creditors relinquished control Hearst would return to the top position. Meanwhile, Berlin demonstrated exceptional ability, especially a willingness to sell or shut several unprofitable newspapers. The committee of bankers and creditors promoted Berlin to the presidency of Hearst Corporation in 1943, a position he retained after retirement of the debt in March 1945.[9]

Cosmopolitan survived the Depression, but lost its flagship status to *Good Housekeeping,* which became dominant in circulation and profit. This would have serious ramifications later.

"Middlebrow"

Cosmopolitan entered the Jazz Age with a reputation among authors for generous fees and popularity among millions of Americans for enjoyable fiction serials, short stories, and novellas. Its editor spent money virtually without restraint until the Depression. It always had competitors, but it was unique until the mid-1920s because its roster of authors and illustrators ranked among the most commercially successful of the era. Each issue of *Cosmopolitan* delivered to its readers the writings and artwork of the biggest names in popular culture. It was a format so perfect that it could have lasted for many years. Then, William Randolph Hearst ruined it because he refused to allow his namesake magazine to disappear. His decision to merge *Hearst's International* with his personal favorite forfeited *Cosmopolitan* its distinctiveness. The odd merger caused circulation to stagnate, and the cumbersome cover title insensibly placed *Cosmopolitan* below that of the smaller, lesser quality magazine. The merger was the start of *Cosmopolitan*'s decline. It was the victim of three men with too much ego and not enough foresight: William Randolph Hearst, Ray Long, Richard Berlin.

Ray Long was *Cosmopolitan* editor from December 1918 to October 1931, a period that established it as the premier popular fiction magazine in the nation. The list of authors *Cosmopolitan* published regularly during Long's tenure comprised a literary Who's Who of the era. Among those whose work appeared in at least ten issues of *Cosmopolitan,* and some whose writing was in twenty-five or more issues, were these bestselling novelists and storytellers from the Jazz Age: Frank R. Adams, Samuel Hopkins Adams, Michael Arlen, Faith Baldwin, Rex Beach, Louis Bromfield, Ellis Parker Butler, Robert W. Chambers, Irvin S. Cobb, Theodore Dreiser, Edna Ferber, poet Edgar Guest, Rupert Hughes, Fannie Hurst, Peter B. Kyne, Ring Lardner, Sinclair Lewis, W. Somerset Maugham, Gouverneur Morris, Mary Roberts Rinehart, Arthur Somers Roche, Damon Runyon, Rafael Sabatini, Adela Rogers St. Johns, Booth Tarkington, Louis Joseph Vance, P. G. Wodehouse.

Their serials and stories were illustrated by popular artists, including Howard Chandler Christy, Harrison Fisher, James Montgomery Flagg, and Charles Dana Gibson.

Several on this list were previous *Cosmopolitan* stalwarts from the years prior to World War I—Chambers, Hughes, Morris, Wodehouse—and most authors chosen by Long his first few years as editor already were known to the public. Long infrequently showcased unknown authors in *Cosmopolitan*, instead relegating some of them to *Hearst's International*, a placement Long could authorize because he also was editor-in-chief of International Magazine Company, the entity that operated Hearst magazines. Near the end of his career with *Cosmopolitan*, Long did introduce several unknown authors to readers, including a few Russian exiles who had fled to Paris because their critical and satirical depictions of life in the newly communist nation made them likely candidates for persecution when Stalin became the supreme leader.

Not on the *Cosmopolitan* list of authors were F. Scott Fitzgerald, whose manuscripts Long let *Hearst's International* publish, or Ernest Hemingway, who Long decided was unsuitable for affluent middle-class readers. Long let Fitzgerald know *Cosmopolitan* would pay him $1,750 for a story on acceptance, a fee worthy of a star author, but the editor either rejected every manuscript or else shunted it to the lesser magazine. "Long hates me," Fitzgerald wrote a friend. The *Cosmopolitan* editor also refused an opportunity to run serial installments of *The Great Gatsby* prior to its publication in 1924. Long never specified why he rejected Fitzgerald, although the author had his own explanation. "Long is a sentimental scavenger with no ghost of taste or individuality," Fitzgerald informed Ernest Hemingway.[10]

Hearst hired Long to make *Cosmopolitan* more popular than it was, not to make it a literary magazine, and he rarely doubted the judgment of his editor. Long believed his own literary preferences matched those of middle-class people. "I felt that I was an average American, with the reading taste of the average American," Long explained. "Any reading which entertained, or instructed, or thrilled me would entertain or instruct or thrill enough other average Americans to produce circulation in sufficient quantity to enable the magazine to sell advertising profitably."[11]

Jazz Age magazine readers were middle class. They earned or lived in households with above-average incomes, most had graduated high school, and some had college degrees at a time when only one-eighth of adults had completed high school and few of those went to college. Enrollment at public colleges and universities tripled during the 1920s. This indicated a broadening base of American families able to afford higher education.[12]

Long astutely sensed shifts in public taste and reduced a specific literary genre in anticipation of it being overdone, thereby publishing fewer mysteries or ethnic tales or adventure pieces or romances whenever their popularity was about to wane. For example, Long rejected stories by Damon Runyon for many years because he thought the characters and situations stale; when

Runyon later submitted manuscripts involving colorful, sentimental, wise-cracking characters and their misadventures along Broadway, Long bought them for *Cosmopolitan*. Long also had a knack for knowing when a genre was ready for a comeback. He resuscitated the career of author Bruno Lessing, who wrote fiction about Jewish neighborhoods in lower Manhattan.[13]

Cosmopolitan circulation surged soon after Long became editor, but his real value was sustaining a readership among city and suburban subscribers whose higher incomes made them prime targets for advertisers. Long offered them mainstream quality fiction, not cheap fiction.

Long, age forty when Hearst hired him to edit *Cosmopolitan*, was not a man of letters formally. He graduated high school in southern Indiana during the mid-1890s, a rare accomplishment for males of that period, and worked for an Indianapolis newspaper. His career break came in 1912. A publisher in Chicago hired Long to edit *Red Book* magazine, a mediocre periodical with a circulation of 225,000 copies. Long changed its format from a blend of fiction and non-fiction to almost exclusively fiction, added a photography section devoted to images of beautiful actresses from motion pictures, and increased the number of illustrations accompanying stories. *Red Book* soared, its monthly circulation reaching 405,100 copies at the end of 1918, although Long boasted years later he had raised it to 600,000 copies.[14]

Hearst and his executives noted the impressive success *Red Book* achieved and intermittently negotiated with Long about taking control of *Cosmopolitan*. Long required a higher salary than they were willing to pay, and whenever Hearst would belatedly agree weeks or months later to an amount, Long then would name a higher figure. Finally, Long got what he wanted in autumn 1918 because Hearst was eager to remedy the stagnant circulation that afflicted his flagship magazine, which had stuck at approximately one million copies monthly for two years. No salary was publicized; however, based on subsequent references it possibly was $60,000 a year (equivalent to $840,000 in 2010 dollars).[15]

Long quickly converted *Cosmopolitan* to an almost all-fiction format. It had relied heavily on fiction for several years, but Long boosted the allocation for serials and stories from 80 percent to 95 percent of total editorial pages. (*Cosmopolitan* pages were bigger after World War I. The magazine had adopted the new standard size for the industry of 8½-by-12 inches, replacing the previous size of 7-by-10 inches.) Editors prior to Long had relied on eight to ten authors for most fiction, believing that readers preferred material from familiar names. Long broadened the list of regular authors to twenty, usually publishing at least eight of them in each issue and rotating fiction into the magazine from numerous other authors of lesser fame. Long also introduced The Stage To-Day, a four- to six-page section of full-page photographs mostly of movie and stage actresses, with an occasional photo of an actor. Long mixed so-called women's fiction consisting of personal drama, family crisis, and romance with men's fiction involving adventure, crime, and intrigue; also, he chose fiction with ethnic characters, historical settings, and humor. Science fiction rarely appeared.

Cosmopolitan already ran numerous illustrations, a Hearst trademark. Long, though, favored freestyle images with text flowing over and around them rather than boxy, squared artwork with adjacent text. Pages at the front and middle of the magazine therefore looked more open and readable compared to previous designs. Meanwhile, the back-of-the-book section lacked illustrations altogether, a common magazine policy for a section reserved for continuation of articles and stories from the front and middle.

To select material that initially filled an average of 86 editorial pages each month and subsequently expanded to an average of 112 pages within two years, Long read manuscripts six hours each weekday and ten to twelve hours during his usual three-day weekend from Friday through Sunday. This reading regimen permitted him to peruse a quarter-million words weekly, according to his own calculation—equivalent to a thousand typewritten pages. Long was a speed reader, having learned a reading method suggested to him by President Theodore Roosevelt, whom he had interviewed as a young journalist. TR told him he scanned a line at a time. "I didn't understand at first," Long wrote, "but I began trying. The result was that I read a book in much less than half the time required by the average reader; and yet, of necessity, I must read it more carefully than the average, because if I liked it, I'd buy it; if I rejected it, I might overlook a bet." Associate editors at the magazine and authors credited Long with excellent recall of material.[16]

Long was a confident editor who tactfully, yet firmly, insisted to authors that *Cosmopolitan* would not publish their manuscripts unless he approved every word. Many editors of quality magazines edited manuscripts prior to publication, but they were sensitive to authorial ego and sometimes would not mandate revisions if an author of repute resisted. Long mandated revisions regardless of the stature of an author.[17]

Long applied his charm to Fannie Hurst, an author whose stories had been very popular for several years and who typically refused to rewrite her manuscripts. During one of his marathon reading sessions soon after becoming *Cosmopolitan* editor, Long discovered that the magazine owned an unpublished manuscript by Hurst. He liked it, but thought it needed improvement. Aware that Hurst did not do revisions, Long asked her permission "to eliminate the first page of the manuscript" and begin the story with a descriptive passage on another page. Long assured her he was not "trying or planning to teach you how to write short stories," but "if you will permit me to make these changes, you will come very close to hearing more about this story than any you have ever published." Hurst agreed to the revision. It was the start of a mutually beneficial relationship.[18]

For favorite authors who lacked story ideas, Long created storylines with characters and set deadlines for completion. Long helped authors through writer's block, too. One author of a serial already running in *Cosmopolitan* told Long he could not decide how it should end. Long hurriedly sent the author an outline of scenes and an ending, which the author gratefully accepted.[19]

Long also encouraged authors to try new forms of writing. Hurst appreciated advice from Long, and when the editor suggested she should write a novel instead of another short story Hurst decided to do it. The result was *Star-Dust: The Story Of An American Girl*. *Cosmopolitan* serialized the novel starting in March 1920. (It was scheduled to start in February, but a printers' strike prevented publication of *Cosmopolitan* that month.) Long gave Hurst star treatment: the first installment carried a full-page profile illustration of the author drawn by Harrison Fisher, the magazine's famous cover artist; illustrations by James Montgomery Flagg, a noted popular artist of magazines and posters, accompanied each serial installment. Long authorized payment of $17,500 to Hurst for the *Star-Dust* serial.[20]

Besides his rapport with authors, Long conversed with *Cosmopolitan* readers through monthly promotional items on the contents page and brief biographical sketches of authors inserted in back-of-the-book continuation pages. These snippets fulfilled two functions of a typical Hearst editor: publicity and salesmanship.

"Cappy Ricks will be at it again in September," Long wrote in the August 1919 table of contents, referring to a familiar fictional character created by author Peter B. Kyne. "He's gone to Camp Kearny and taken up his K. of C. duties with all the zest of his youthful old soul. He takes a train-load of circus animals and freaks off the hands of the army." Long assured readers the forthcoming work by Kyne "is one of the best Cappy Ricks stories." Another time, Long avowed that a serial concerning an outdoorsman's life was revelatory and significant. "Behind it is the sincerity and earnestness of a man telling what happened within himself—the sort of sincerity and earnestness that makes Cosmopolitan America's Greatest Magazine," Long wrote. "These articles give an understanding that comes home to everyone, city-dweller and country-dweller alike. They are the sort that Cosmopolitan takes pride in publishing, because they are big, vital, full of real meaning, and give greater joy to life."[21]

A blurb by Long for a serialization of a new novel led to a sales pitch: "This announcement will create an unprecedented demand for the issue which it may not be possible fully to supply. We suggest, therefore, that those Cosmopolitan readers who are not regular subscribers enroll as such at once, or, at all events, place orders for the magazine with their news-dealers at an early moment. The news-stand stacks of Cosmopolitans will melt away as never before." The editor frequently reminded *Cosmopolitan* readers of their special status. "If it is the best, Cosmopolitan publishes it," Long promised. "That is why nearly everybody worth while reads Cosmopolitan."[22]

Biographical sketches by Long on the magazine's back pages humanized authors. An item on Arthur Somers Roche mentioned "he wanted a quiet place to work" so the editor "suggested Miami Beach, beautiful, restful, colorful Miami." Roche could not work there. "He moved to Palm Beach, which has all the placid calm of Forty-second and Broadway," the editor noted. "Was his story peopled with beauties in bathing suits and Harper's Bazar men in flannels? Not a bit of it. His heroine works in a department store and his hero is conductor of a surface car! But the story is a corker." The item adroitly referred to a corporate sibling magazine, which changed its spelling to *Harper's Bazaar* later. Long reintroduced readers to Bruno Lessing, whose fiction had not appeared in the magazine for a while. "He's the world's greatest expert in slap-stick humor," the editor stated. "His stories of East-Side Jews have been a feature in American fiction for years. He's coming to Cosmopolitan as a regular contributor."[23]

The purpose of these tables-of-contents promotional blurbs and back-of-the-book sketches was to pique the interest of readers, persuade single-copy buyers to subscribe, and reinforce the notion that *Cosmopolitan* was an extraordinary magazine for extraordinary people.

Authors of the era wrote for other magazines, too. Names in the *Cosmopolitan* tables of contents appeared also in monthlies such as *American, Ladies' Home Journal, McCall's, McClure's,* and *Red Book,* or weeklies such as *Collier's, Liberty,* and *Saturday Evening Post.* The result, naturally, was a bidding war for the best and most popular masters of fiction, a valuable commodity for magazines during an era when movies and radio programs were not yet serious competitors for fictional entertainment. *McCall's,* for example, offered $70,000 to Edna Ferber, author of several bestsellers, to write a twelve-part serial.[24]

Many magazines entered the bidding war because subscriptions and newsstand sales depended on quality fiction. Middle-class Americans then were avid readers of books, magazines, and newspapers. They might attend movies and listen to radio, but reading was a habit. Readership for periodicals grew fantastically during the 1920s, and kept growing until the mid-1960s. Much of this growth was attributable to the expansion of the American middle class. The Jazz Age era, a colloquial term for the 1920s that referred to important cultural and social changes, yielded a middle class that included one-sixth of all households, almost double the proportion from the early 1900s. National magazines remained an efficient form of media for advertisers to reach potential customers with disposable income.[25]

One statistic that demonstrated the effect of middle-class expansion on magazines was the number of periodicals with a circulation of a million-plus copies. At the start of the twentieth century, two magazines circulated a million or more copies—one being *Ladies' Home Journal* and the other *Comfort,* a cheaply printed publication for rural housewives. At the midpoint of the 1920s, nineteen magazines surpassed a million circulation—one being *Cosmopolitan*—and six others circulated more than two million copies, while none exceeded three million copies. Aggregate circulation for national magazines spiked from 128. 6 million copies per issue early in the decade to 202 million per issue when Wall Street crashed, a 57 percent increase.[26]

Revenue from advertisers also permitted magazines to compete for authors. Advertisers spent money to buy space aplenty in national magazines throughout the 1920s. Total advertising revenue for all consumer magazines rose from $119.9 million to $185.723 million. This 55 percent growth occurred despite the arrival of a new national communications medium useful to national advertisers: radio. The two major radio networks of the era—Columbia Broadcasting System and National Broadcasting Company—hardly were challengers to magazines at the end of the decade, although commercial sponsors of some programs already had seen positive results. Radio would divert a percentage of ad revenue as the Depression persisted because many Americans stayed home and listened to the free entertainment coming from a tabletop receiver or console. Radio networks emerged as economic competition when an initial phase of economic recovery from the Depression occurred during the mid-1930s, by which time Mutual Broadcasting System also was on the air.[27]

Cosmopolitan thrived within months of editor Long taking command. The editorial format devised by him proved his worth because readership and advertising revenue rapidly moved upward. Circulation went from 1.051 million copies monthly in 1919 to 1.404 million copies monthly the next year, a superb one-third increase that placed *Cosmopolitan* ahead of *American,* its nearest competitor. Half of all copies circulated were sold at newsstands. Prior to Long the magazine had sold 70 to 80 percent of newsstand deliveries, but the Long formula resulted in an average sales rate of 92 percent.[28]

Higher circulation and an exceptionally affluent readership allowed the magazine to raise its basic full-page ad rate from $1,060 in 1919 to $2,840 in 1923. Advertisers bought an average of eighteen additional pages each issue during that period, a one-fourth increase to eighty-eight ad pages. *Cosmopolitan* added approximately $1.31 million actual ad revenue comparing Long's fifth year with his first.[29]

Less than a year after hiring the new editor, Hearst promptly drafted a new contract for Long that raised his salary by one-third. Then the publisher boosted *Cosmopolitan*'s cover price a dime to thirty-five cents in August 1920 and set the annual subscription price at $4, twice the previous rate. At thirty-five cents, *Cosmopolitan* separated itself from common magazines, which cost fifteen to twenty-five cents at newsstands. It was a strategy meant to declare *Cosmopolitan's* status as a quality magazine.[30]

Hearst had miscalculated. It was too much too soon. Newsstand sales plummeted and subscription renewals decreased. Total circulation actually receded for two years. It bottomed out at a monthly average of 983,400 copies, a substantial reversal unlike any since Hearst had acquired *Cosmopolitan* from John Brisben Walker in summer 1905.[31]

To recover its readership, *Cosmopolitan* launched various promotional campaigns, including an innovative summer-only subscription for $1, and by summer 1922 announced a price rollback to $3 for an annual subscription. The magazine also gave a premium of a new novel to any subscriber who recruited someone else to subscribe. These tactics and its fine fiction helped restore circulation to 1.127 million copies monthly by early 1925.[32]

A positive effect of the price debacle was the creation of a loyal, affluent readership for *Cosmopolitan* willing to pay extra for a magazine it liked. Ad executives for the magazine analyzed addresses of subscribers and discovered that they could demonstrate to potential advertisers its somewhat wealthier readers. Ad sales representatives for *Cosmopolitan* delivered a 220-page handbook filled with statistical tables and geographic distribution charts to executives at advertising agencies, manufacturers, and other providers of consumer products. An impressive two of every seven subscribers resided in wealthy sections of big cities (such as Park Avenue in Manhattan, the Gold Coast of Chicago, Beacon Hill in Boston, Chestnut Hill in Philadelphia) and in wealthy suburban communities (such as Palo Alto, California; Greenwich, Connecticut; Lake Forest, Illinois; Brookline, Massachusetts; Maplewood, Missouri; Bryn Mawr, Pennsylvania; Wauwatosa, Wisconsin). "In these communities it costs more to live and people pay more for the privilege of better living," the handbook advised advertisers—and potential advertisers. "Residents of such communities are most typical of what we mean by the expanded class market of the United States. Cosmopolitan's circulation is class market circulation."

This early effort at demographic analysis also emphasized snob appeal. Magazine executives touted the fact that only one of every sixteen *Cosmopolitan* subscribers lived in "industrial or mining centers"—such as Hammond, Indiana; Bayonne and Trenton, New Jersey; North Tonawanda, New York. The clear message was that ads would not be wasted on blue-collar readers.[33]

Advertisers took notice. Ad pages did not decline despite the circulation loss. *Cosmopolitan* carried an average of ninety-four ad pages monthly by mid-decade. *Cosmopolitan* continuously raised its page rates throughout the 1920s, yet the magazine thickened with advertising. Many pages of advertisements exhibited upscale items, such as automobiles, jewelry, refrigerators, silverware, and vacation packages via ships and trains. Among the advertisers were Atwater Kent Radio (consoles), Bailey Banks & Biddle (jewelry), Canadian Steamship Lines, Chevrolet, Ford, Holmes & Edwards Silver, Premier Vacuum Cleaner, Studebaker, and Travelers Insurance. No liquor advertisements were seen, of course, because it was the Prohibition era.

The circulation decline did not affect the magazine's profitability. Revenue from advertisers seeking to sell to the class market and income from subscribers who paid $3 a year and single-copy buyers who paid thirty-five cents actually allowed *Cosmopolitan* a sizable profit for 1923 of $1.15 million.[34]

Hearst realized that Long was a real asset, so amidst the circulation dive the editor received another new contract, this one providing a one-fourth increase in salary that took him to $100,000 a year.

The *Cosmopolitan* circulation setback also never affected the editorial budget because Hearst pampered his flagship magazine. The magazine continued to bid competitively for authors. Long guaranteed lucrative fees to certain authors from his first day on the job. A star author typically received $1,000 to $2,500 for a story and $7,500 to $20,000 for a serial of six to ten installments. At least two authors, Cobb and Kyne, commanded fees of $4,000 per story or serial installment. Long consistently provided readers with stories and serial installments from eight to ten famous authors each issue and another two to six fiction pieces from lesser authors.

An analysis of tables of contents throughout Long's tenure revealed that *Cosmopolitan* published dozens of authors only once or a few times, an indicator that they never attained the popularity Long deemed necessary to rotate them into the magazine on a regular basis, or that their subsequent manuscripts did not meet his standards. Lesser authors usually received $500 for a story.[35]

Fees to artists who illustrated fiction varied from $1,000 for a single story to $5,000 for a serial. Some artists earned incredible sums from *Cosmopolitan*. Harrison Fisher drew almost every *Cosmopolitan* cover at a fee of $3,000 each throughout the 1920s and until his death in summer 1934. Fisher also illustrated serials for star authors at fees ranging from $5,000 to $10,000. The magazine recouped some of this expense by offering for sale at twenty-five cents apiece cover replicas of the "Fisher Girls," whose beautiful, elegant, fashionable, and wholesome images adorned *Cosmopolitan*. The magazine also sold sets of serial illustrations by Flagg and Gibson for $2.[36]

An interesting aspect of *Cosmopolitan* covers from the 1920s through the Depression era was that illustrations were irrelevant to the magazine's content: no dramatic depictions of the issue's top adventure story, mystery, or romance; no fictional character from a story or serial; no celebrity or prominent person. The names of top authors frequently were shown, and sometimes a terse blurb referred to a profile of some well-known person. Other than that, the magazine sold itself on the basis of its title.

Hearst let Long spend extravagantly because some *Cosmopolitan* expenditures were offset in more substantive ways than selling reprints of magazine covers and illustrations. Movie producers of the era in New York City and Hollywood bought rights to numerous stories and serials selected by Long for publication in *Cosmopolitan*. Payments varied widely depending on the stature of the studio and the popularity of the author, with movie rights selling for a few hundred dollars to several thousand dollars. Specific amounts for movie rights were not recorded, but total payments would have made a significant contribution to the corporation during any year.

Initially, authors did not receive a penny for movie rights from Hearst. Most publishers agreed upon purchase of a manuscript to share ancillary revenue with the author. Hearst and Long insisted that the International Magazine Company owned a manuscript outright. The Authors League of America in 1921 criticized the policy and requested Hearst to conform to standard industry practice. Long defended the nonpayment policy and denied that he compelled authors to relinquish their claims to ancillary rights, a statement the Authors League rebutted. Hearst would not respond to the Authors League. An impasse lasted for months. Then, Hearst relented to avoid a possible boycott of his magazines by some popular authors, including *Cosmopolitan* regulars Rupert Hughes, Arthur Somers Roche, and Louis Joseph Vance, all of whom were active in the organization. Long maintained rapport with the authors, and he was host at subsequent literary fetes.[37]

Hearst also was an early practitioner of synergy, a term popularized decades later to denote the benefits of multimedia cross-ownership by a corporation. Hearst founded Cosmopolitan Productions, a movie company, in 1919 to develop material for the screen from his magazines. Hearst also created Cosmopolitan Book Corporation to publish short-story collections and novels from magazine fiction. Synergy worked like this for a select few fiction items: a story or serial installment in *Cosmopolitan* would be tagged by Long for development as a book or potential movie; columnists and feature writers for Hearst's twenty-eight newspapers and syndication service would publicize the story or serial and its author; Cosmopolitan Book Corporation would publish a collection of the author's short stories or a novel based on a serial; the book would receive publicity from Hearst newspapers, syndication service, and *Cosmopolitan* itself; Cosmopolitan Productions would produce a movie based on the fiction material; and, finally, reviewers employed at Hearst newspapers, syndication service, and *Cosmopolitan* would tout the movie to millions of readers.

Not every story or serial merited such treatment, but much fiction from *Cosmopolitan* became books and/or movies until the Depression crippled Hearst's

Ray Long was a popular *Cosmopolitan* editor, and prominent among literary and theatrical people in New York City during the 1920s. His sense of what Americans would like in fiction made the magazine very popular and prosperous, although his management style and generosity to authors caused his downfall. Photograph by Doris Ulmann, 1925, courtesy of Knight Library, University of Oregon.

(Opposite, top) Harrison Fisher, the artist who created almost every *Cosmopolitan* cover illustration for twenty years until the mid-1930s, commanded an incredible fee for his work. His lucrative contract was a factor in the demise of Ray Long. Photograph by Lumiere, 1917, courtesy of the Library of Congress.

(Bottom right) Amelia Earhart became *Cosmopolitan* aviation editor for a few years starting in 1928. Hired by Ray Long to boost readership because of her fame and celebrity value as a pilot, Earhart brought attention to the magazine but had no appreciable effect on subscriptions or newsstand sales. Underwood & Underwood photograph, 1928, courtesy of the Library of Congress.

media empire. Prior to the fiscal crisis, Cosmopolitan Productions released twenty to twenty-four movies a year—all of them scripted from fiction chosen by Ray Long in his dual role as *Cosmopolitan* editor and as the vice president who supervised *Good Housekeeping, Harper's Bazaar,* and *Hearst's International.*[38]

In reality, Cosmopolitan Productions was a cog in a corporation financial shell game. When the movie studio paid International Magazine Company for rights to fiction it was transferring money from one corporate entity to another. Cosmopolitan Productions lost an estimated $7 million during its twenty-year existence, and a portion of the continuous debit was attributable to fees paid to Hearst's magazines for movie rights.[39]

Long was a synergizer extraordinaire. The section he created, The Stage To-Day, regularly ran photographs of actors and actresses at Cosmopolitan Productions. Each full-page photograph carried a caption that named the latest movie and role of the person pictured. Among the photographs displayed in *Cosmopolitan* for January, February, and June 1923 was Marion Davies. No other movie or theatrical personality received such attention that year. Davies was a capable actress and popular with the public, but she also was the mistress of William Randolph Hearst—a relationship never hinted at in *Cosmopolitan* or any other Hearst publication. Hearst lived at San Simeon with Davies while his wife lived in a grand residence in Manhattan with their sons. The caption for a Davies photo in the February 1923 issue mentioned her latest movie and declared that she "renders an interpretation whose beauty and gay winsomeness makes memorable one of the greatest love stories ever screened."[40]

Long was especially good at identifying stories and serials that would be bestsellers. A serial by Kyne published as a novel by Cosmopolitan Book Corporation in 1922 sold 500,000 copies. Long edited the manuscript for the novel, too, which required a train trip to northern California to visit the author. Long notified Hearst's personal secretary by telegram that he would be close to San Simeon. "Have to see several writers on Coast and work with Kyne on his novel," the message stated. "Please advise Chief and tell him if he wants his grandson in weekend party at Ranch or elsewhere said grandson will be delighted." Hearst replied, "Grandson is cordially invited to attend all functions that occur while he is in the West."[41]

Fiction was the reason for *Cosmopolitan*'s popularity. Still, six to ten pages each issue carried nonfiction. Nonfiction was undistinguished into the mid-1920s. A commentary or homily occupied one page and two or three articles filled the others. Long was not a crusader. The nonfiction he selected was disparate: profiles of prominent Americans in business and public life; religion; child-rearing; cultural and social trends; international events. Rarely did a nonfiction piece exceed four pages.

An exception to the usual nondescript nonfiction fare was a series of articles by Winston S. Churchill, the British politician and occasional government official when conservatives had the majority in Parliament. A middle-aged man with not much of a political future during the interwar years, Churchill augmented his income writing for British and American magazines. (Not to be confused with Winston Churchill, an American novelist of the era whose work also had appeared in *Cosmopolitan;* Lord Churchill signed his nonfiction pieces with his middle initial—an informal arrangement he suggested to the other Churchill, who had no middle name.) The magazine ran eight articles by the Briton. Lord Churchill mostly wrote about his Boer War adventures as a young correspondent thirty years earlier in South Africa, but he also discussed aviation and military strategy predicated on the lessons of warfare from World War I. *Cosmopolitan*'s top rate for a nonfiction article was $1,500 during the 1920s.[42]

At mid-decade, *Cosmopolitan* was popular and profitable. Long focused on popular fiction, commissioned illustrations to accompany almost every story and serial installment, and paid generous fees to bestselling authors. His formula worked.

William Randolph Hearst had other plans for *Cosmopolitan,* however.

Merger

"The main thing is to differentiate Hearst's from Cosmopolitan," a letter from William Randolph Hearst at San Simeon instructed K. M. Goode, editor of *Hearst's* in New York City. "This is very difficult to do because while Hearst's used to imitate everything that Cosmopolitan did, now Cosmopolitan imitates everything that Hearst's does, and the consequence is that there is bound to be a similarity in publications."[43]

Hearst's was a direct competitor of corporate sibling *Cosmopolitan.* It made no sense, of course.

Whose fault was it? The letter from Hearst to Goode in early 1921 admitted no personal responsibility for the situation, yet the publisher was to blame. Hearst had changed the format of *Hearst's* just prior to World War I because its nonfiction format and emphasis on exposé journalism had resulted in stagnant circulation. On his orders, *Hearst's* gradually had enlarged its fiction component. By the start of the 1920s, it had more fiction than nonfiction—the *Cosmopolitan* model. Circulation had climbed steadily if not spectacularly for several years from the mid-300,000s to low 400,000s.[44]

Hearst's circulation then stalled again because Long used his authority as a vice president of International Magazine Company to strengthen the appeal of

Cosmopolitan by taking the top names in fiction for it and consigning literary newcomers to *Hearst's*. Long also assigned better-known artists to *Cosmopolitan*, leaving *Hearst's* to share lesser talent with *Good Housekeeping* and other corporate magazines clustered in leased offices around midtown Manhattan. Goode complained to Hearst that the namesake magazine was at a disadvantage. Hearst, however, deferred to Long's decisions.[45]

Goode suggested an editorial strategy for *Hearst's* that would concentrate on international topics. The editor listed several ideas, including a series of "general special" articles on postwar political unrest in Europe where communists, socialists, and reactionaries battled in the streets for political power in several nations. Goode also thought the magazine should bid on the memoirs of Georges Clemenceau, the premier of France during World War I. Goode wondered, too, if *Hearst's* should publish a series of articles with each installment on an individual country, such as Czechoslovakia, Germany, and Poland.

Hearst appreciated the potential for international coverage in *Hearst's*. "I want to ask you particularly to see what can be done in the way of making the magazine the medium for the discussion of international economic relations—financial, industrial, commercial, etc.—by important people who will really contribute something to the discussion," he ordered Goode. Hearst also enthusiastically endorsed a proposal by Goode to change the title to *Hearst's International*.

Goode recommended exclusivity for *Hearst's International* on events and topics outside the United States to give it a separate identity from *Cosmopolitan*. "Generally speaking Hearst's to have the monopoly of the foreign field," a letter from Goode urged. "Cosmopolitan to develop more along domestic lines. Hearst's to aim its chief appeal primarily at men; Cosmopolitan never to shoot over the head of the average woman."

Hearst agreed to the concept for *Hearst's International*, except the gender differentiation proposal. "Here is a distinct opportunity for difference, and that to my mind is much more important than living up to the name," the publisher explained. "I do not mean by that Hearst's should appeal only to men, but that it should surely appeal to men; nor that Cosmopolitan should appeal only to women, but that it should be certain that its articles did interest the women."[46]

The new emphasis on international topics did not help the Hearst namesake. Circulation hovered at 440,000 for a year. Hearst was impatient. He replaced Goode with Norman Hapgood, a veteran muckraker who had written exposés on patent medicines for *Collier's* and had edited magazines. Hapgood produced exposés for *Hearst's International* on the virulent anti-Semitism of Henry Ford, which comprised a seven-part series during 1922, and on the resurgence of the Ku Klux Klan. The public apparently was not interested in exposé journalism, however. Circulation of *Hearst's International* slipped to 390,000 copies monthly by autumn 1924.[47]

Hearst had invested a significant sum to promote the revamped magazine and commission writers for international articles. If everything else had gone well within his media empire, Hearst could have continued throwing money at *Hearst's International* no matter what, which was his usual way of doing things. However, the failure by Goode and Hapgood to gain circulation came at a bad time. Newspapers owned by Hearst in some cities, notably Boston and Chicago, were losing readers and advertisers to competitors—and their financial losses were substantial. Also, Hearst was starting to spend considerable amounts of cash from his corporation to subsidize two pet projects: construction of the San Simeon castle and production of movies at Cosmopolitan Productions in Manhattan.

Various corporate executives previously had warned Hearst that expenses exceeded income. He finally listened to them, up to a point. In order to spare serious cutbacks at San Simeon, Hearst agreed to two major changes for his media empire. First, Cosmopolitan Productions would close its movie studio and movies would be financed by Cosmopolitan Productions but produced at Metro-Goldwyn-Mayer in Hollywood, which also would be a distribution partner to place movies for showing at theaters. Second, *Hearst's International* would merge with *Cosmopolitan* effective March 1925.[48]

---

182   *Cosmopolitan for February, 1925*

Coming Next Month...

Two magazines in one... both for the price of one

BEGINNING with the *March* issue, HEARST'S INTERNATIONAL will be combined with COSMOPOLITAN. ~ ~ ~ Bringing these two magazines together merges editorial resources of unprecedented strength. The result will be a periodical unique in publishing endeavor.

It can truly be said that never before has there been published in a single magazine such a wealth of fiction, entertainment and inspiration, or such a fine presentation of the work of many famous illustrators, and all with a mechanical beauty beyond anything heretofore seen in magazines of large circulation... Order your copy of this new magazine now... at your newsdealers, or mail the coupon below.

William Randolph Hearst refused to let his namesake magazine die, so he merged it with the more popular *Cosmopolitan*. The merger initially slowed *Cosmopolitan*'s steady readership rise. *Cosmopolitan,* February 1925; source: Memorial Library, University of Wisconsin-Madison.

Time, a newsweekly not yet two years old, commented on the forthcoming merger in December 1924: "Persons who buy both the International and the Cosmopolitan do so primarily for the fiction and illustrations and these are almost identical in the two magazines. Asked to distinguish a difference, few readers point out that the Cosmopolitan's are of slightly greater fame and salary than the International's. Even this faint distinction is confused by the fact that many of these authors write for both magazines, and that what they write is invariably the same—'high-life' escapades, 'low-life' escapades, apartment-house romances, love at first sight—all manner of Tillie-the-Toiler skits in the popular, fiction-factory formulae, excellent literary trash and 'what the public wants.'" The disdain by *Time* for mainstream fiction perhaps was attributable to its corps of editors, all graduates of Ivy League colleges.[49]

The combined circulation of the magazines was 1.517 million—with *Cosmopolitan* providing three-fourths of it. Four years after the merger, circulation was 1.565 million copies, a 3 percent gain. By contrast, *Cosmopolitan* had grown 16 percent from the end of 1922 until the merger date while it recovered from the effects of the price increase. In one sense, though, the fact that circulation did not decline after the merger indicated that most readers of the formerly separate magazines accepted the new publication.[50]

Vanity determined the name of the newly merged magazine. Standard practice after a magazine merger was to combine both titles on the cover temporarily, with the smaller publication listed in smaller type until readers adjusted to the new identity, at which point the dominant title would prevail. Long assigned an artist to design a new cover for the March 1925 issue. The artist was aware *Cosmopolitan* was the larger magazine, the better magazine, and the magazine that made money. Naturally, the artist placed *Cosmopolitan* in large lettering at the top and reserved a small space below it for *Hearst's International.*

Staffers at *Cosmopolitan* apparently had talked about what happened at a meeting to review the design, and their comments inspired the recently founded *New Yorker* to report, with tongue-in-cheek exaggeration, the reaction of the San Simeon lord: "Unfortunately, when this proposed cover was shown to Mr. Hearst, so report has it, the publisher made an ascent so truly vertical as to be of great interest to the experimental branch of the Army Air Service. A new design had to be formed. Eventually, the chief's assent was given, and presently the approved cover blossomed on the newsstands of the nation; where, lo, *Hearst's* name led all the rest, even so high sounding a one as *Cosmopolitan.*"[51]

(In letters and memorandums to Long and executives of International Magazine Company afterward, Hearst himself referred solely to the *Cosmopolitan* title, never to *Hearst's International.* Replies from executives to this correspondence usually cited only *Cosmopolitan.*)

Each magazine lost its editorial identity because of the merger. Hapgood was not retained and returned to newspapers, thereby removing a voice for serious journalism at the new publication. Long preferred lightweight articles, and *Hearst's International combined with Cosmopolitan* avoided controversy for the remainder of his tenure and for many years afterward. *Cosmopolitan* itself sacrificed its reputation as a purely fiction magazine, compelled to mix a larger presence of nonfiction articles on popular culture, prominent people, and features concerned with contemporary social trends along with stories and serials.

Promotional ads for the dual title prior to the merger emphasized the bargain that readers would get: "Two magazines in one . . . both for the price of one. Bringing these two magazines together merges editorial resources of unprecedented strength. The result will be a periodical unique in publisher endeavor." To entice customers at newsstands who presumably bought both *Cosmopolitan* and *Hearst's International,* the ad touted a subscription deal: "Special Offer! The next 3 issues of this great combined magazine for $1."[52]

Long retained the usual *Cosmopolitan* fiction contributors, but economic factors forced him to pare fiction pages subsequent to the introductory phase of the merger, a period when the intent was to convince readers that nothing had changed except the name of their favorite magazine. The new publication did change. Long cautiously restored fiction to a higher percentage of editorial pages within several years, usually keeping it at approximately 80 percent.

The immediate effect of the merger was an expansion of twenty pages to accommodate extra nonfiction articles. Rather than the pre-merger offering of two or three articles each issue, *Hearst's International combined with Cosmopolitan* often ran six to eight articles with photographs. (To save space and to reflect the magazine's name used in corporate reports from 1925 to 1952, further references will be to *HI-Cosmopolitan* rather than *Hearst's International combined with Cosmopolitan.*)

The long-term effect of the merger was a gradual transformation to a general magazine format, except it was a reversal of the format under John Brisben Walker thirty years earlier that had placed priority on nonfiction. This time around, nonfiction served as filler.

Long handled the merger adroitly. He did not bury nonfiction in back pages or otherwise assign it secondary placement. He let associate editors display large photographs for effect, which was quite an adjustment for a magazine that was copiously illustrated with fictional characters and scenes.

Yet the editor evidently was disenchanted. One year after the merger Long informed Hearst that Scripps-Howard Newspapers had offered him a job, while also letting Hearst know that a Hollywood movie studio wanted to hire him and that a rival magazine publisher did, too. Long preferred the newspaper organization. "This has the advantage of taking me into a field where I will not be competing with your magazines," he wrote. "My contract expires in October 1927, but I am appealing to the friendship you've always shown for me when I ask if you don't think, since I intend to leave then, the thing to do is for me to leave this October."[53]

Hearst did not want to lose the editor of his vulnerable flagship publication. Long had proven his ability to craft a successful editorial format under a variety of circumstances. He negotiated with Long, who wanted an ownership stake in the International Magazine Company. Hearst would not agree to that, but he did include a contract provision for a yearly bonus linked to circulation growth. Of utmost significance, though, Hearst relinquished his title as president of International Magazine Company to promote Long to the position. The editor-president still would edit *HI-Cosmopolitan,* supervise *Good Housekeeping,* and coordinate selection of material for Cosmopolitan Book Corporation, but Long also would have higher status within Hearst Corporation. The deal was sealed by autumn 1926, and Hearst praised Long in a telegram confirming the contract's terms. Long was elated. His letter to Hearst began, "Dear Grandpa, that's the finest telegram any wandering son ever got." Hearst responded: "Your letter was very nice, Ray. Come out and talk to your Grandpop. Bring the folks."[54]

Despite his aversion to serious journalism, Long welcomed any opportunity to open *HI-Cosmopolitan*'s pages to serious people. This produced an interesting array of articles, and generated much free publicity for the magazine.

Benito Mussolini, the fascist dictator of Italy, was paid to write articles explaining his philosophy, policies, and programs. No fee for the articles was disclosed. Long did not edit Mussolini, who was a good writer and presented his positions with candor.

Mussolini's first article, "Woman," appeared in *HI-Cosmopolitan* of August 1928. "Man is in full possession of woman's liberties and measures them to her as a merchant does a piece of cloth," Mussolini wrote. "Her very nature imposes upon her a willing submission to the power and strength of the male." Newspapers and magazines commented on his patronizing attitude toward women, calling it "antifeminist." Articles by Mussolini in October 1928, July 1929, and August 1930 pertained to marriage, birth control, and science versus religion. "Italy, under Fascism, stands firmly against all birth control," Mussolini stated in "I Tax Bachelors." "The family without children is one of the saddest episodes in human life. The nation's conscience must be moved against the purposely childless couple."[55]

Long hired the famous pilot Amelia Earhart as aviation editor of *HI-Cosmopolitan* the same month Mussolini made his debut. It was strictly a publicity stunt on behalf of the magazine to take advantage of the sudden public interest in aviation. Charles Lindbergh had flown solo across the Atlantic Ocean to Paris in May 1927 and Earhart was famous for long-distance flights in twin-engine airplanes. The original magazine contract stipulated that Earhart would fly to a different city every month for a year, speak to a civic organization on behalf of *HI-Cosmopolitan,* and write an article describing each flight and visit. Earhart decided after signing the contract that this schedule was too demanding, especially because she had several other obligations associated with aviation. Long agreed to accept monthly articles on any topic regarding flying. The arrangement lasted until summer 1932 upon expiration of the contract signed by Long, who had since resigned.[56]

Earhart submitted articles frequently the first year, then sporadically thereafter, some of which were "Try Flying"; "Here Is How Fannie Hurst Could Learn To Fly"; "Is It Safe For You To Fly?"; "Shall You Let Your Daughter Fly?"; "Why Are Women Afraid To Fly?"; "Clouds"; "Mrs. Lindbergh"; "Mother Reads As We Fly"; "Your Next Garage May House An Autogiro"; "Flying Is Fun!" Almost every article featured a large photograph of the photogenic Earhart with an airplane nearby or in the air above her; some photographs were obviously composites that added or blended images, such as a sky filled with airplanes.[57]

The obvious intent of her articles was to persuade readers that flying an airplane, or traveling in one, was safe. Many people needed to be convinced because commercial aviation was a fledgling enterprise beset by conditions that made it an adventure not everyone enjoyed: airplanes lacked the capability to fly above storms, which resulted in scary turbulence; weather forecasting was spotty, which caused lengthy delays due to fog and snow; in-flight mechanical problems were common, which sometimes forced an airplane to return to an airport or hurriedly find an alternative landing site.

Most articles by Earhart were repetitive. Each referred to federal requirements for pilot licenses, advances in weather forecasting, improvements in radio communications, and standards of professional conduct for pilots. One article that differed was "Why Are Women Afraid To Fly?" in the July 1929 issue. Earhart described her disappointment at the reluctance of women to travel in airliners, although she knew that girls were fascinated by airplanes. She believed that this enthusiasm would be lost because schools discouraged girls from taking classes involving electrical and mechanical skills. "My point is that aviation is being sold to boys much more effectively than it is to girls," Earhart wrote. "So often response is only education. More often such instruction is barred, and they are shunted into cooking and sewing classes without a choice."[58]

"Ambivalent" best described the pilot's feelings about *Cosmopolitan.* Earhart and her promoters needed the salary to finance her flights across the country and to buy an airplane for long-distance travel. She also endorsed a variety of products, including luggage and cigarettes, to earn money. Hearst was an unpopular man to many people, and Earhart realized that she might be tainted by association with his journalistic reputation. Her unease was evident in a letter written in January 1930 to Anne Morrow Lindbergh, wife of aviation hero and legend Charles Lindbergh. Earhart wanted an interview for a *HI-Cosmopolitan* article. "I have been asked by Cosmo to write something of you for publication," she informed Morrow Lindbergh. "I flatly refused at first, and then decided to check off pros and cons (to you) . . . You may dislike the magazine ownership. (However, it really stands on its own feet distinct from the newspapers.)" Morrow Lindbergh agreed to the interview, which appeared in the July 1930 issue.[59]

Long expressed his admiration for Earhart and other women pilots in a magazine commentary that same month. "Some of the newspapers seem to get a lot of fun out of calling the women's cross-continent airplane race 'the powder-puff derby,'" the editor wrote. "That sort of humor makes me tired. One of the contestants is Amelia Earhart. If you know anything about flying at all, you know that what she has accomplished requires more than courage, more than training. It demands a cool head, a brain quick in emergencies but slow in taking chances." Long mentioned another woman pilot registered for the race and cited her similar qualities. His commentary concluded, "I know quite a few fellows posing as he-men who might emulate these women to their own great advantage, and to the advantage of those who pay their salaries—even if they have to buy a couple of powder puffs to accomplish it."[60]

Mussolini and Earhart garnered attention from newspapers and magazines for *HI-Cosmopolitan* though neither of them did much for circulation. Hearst was dissatisfied. He needed the extra revenue that a larger readership generated. "It is undeniable that circulation has a very definite influence on advertising and certainly has a very definite influence on the results of advertising," Hearst reminded Thomas J. White, the corporation's general manager.[61]

Hearst was impatient with Long. His admiration for the editor had waned by the late 1920s. *HI-Cosmopolitan* was an expensive publication with inconsistent profits. Long constantly upped its editorial budget, yet circulation was uneven; months of strong sales at newsstands were followed by months of weak sales. Year-to-year statistics verified the rollercoaster effect at newsstands: sales for 1925 fell 6,000 to 15,000 copies compared to similar months of the prior year; 1926 sales fell another 49,000 to 53,000 copies for comparable months; 1927 sales rose 28,000 to 46,000 copies; 1928 sales fell 14,000 to 81,000 copies.[62]

Also, Long had ordered magazine executives to renew the practice of giving premiums to subscribers, a policy Hearst disapproved of—except to correct mistakes of his own, such as raising the price of *Cosmopolitan* too much too soon. Premiums included free hardcover books from Cosmopolitan Book Corporation, a free series of Harrison Fisher cover reprints, and free subscriptions to people who got others to subscribe. The expense of premiums reduced subscription revenue precipitously. Hearst noticed.

"In our anxiety to get more circulation, we have practically given the magazine away," Hearst complained to White. "The present subscription circulation is in direct violation of the rules and instructions set up for all of our magazines." Advertisers were suspicious of circulation dependent on below-cost subscriptions. The *HI-Cosmopolitan* gimmickry threatened to undermine its reputation as a quality magazine.[63]

Hearst and White communicated by letter and telegram about prodding Long to enliven the magazine. "The Cosmopolitan, while not in the least abandoning its fiction character could have a certain number of more or less seriously interesting features," Hearst proposed. The publisher missed the controversy sparked by the old *Cosmopolitan* of his early years and the later exposés by *Hearst's International.* "Features that we run in the magazine now are fairly entertaining but in a sense casual," Hearst emphasized to White. "They do not mean much. They simply relieve the fiction."[64]

The historical record does not reveal specific ideas for "seriously interesting" articles Hearst might have recommended to White, but a reply to the publisher from his corporate general manager contained an unusually frank cautionary note urging restraint. "[In] our search for striking articles we would not become too sensational, such as, for example, political scandal, etc." White advised a responsible strategy to the sensationalist who had relied on exposé journalism and political-payback articles the first half-dozen years he owned *Cosmopolitan.*[65]

Long engineered a brief reprieve from grandpa's ire with a startling exclusive: the autobiography of President Calvin Coolidge. The quiet, reticent Coolidge had stunned the nation in summer 1928 by announcing he would not accept nomination for a second term by Republican delegates at the national convention. Coolidge was vice president when President Warren Harding died in August 1923 and had completed the final eighteen months of the term, then was elected president on his own and inaugurated in March 1925. No limit existed on presidential terms, but Coolidge believed a full second term that would bring his occupancy of the White House to ten years would be detrimental to the country and bad for him personally.

Long, to his credit, perceived a Coolidge autobiography as just the thing *HI-Cosmopolitan* needed to spur circulation. Reacting spontaneously to a rumor that Coolidge planned to write an autobiography, Long contacted the president to discuss a magazine serial from which a book would result. It was unusual for a magazine to solicit a presidential autobiography during a presidency. Long sold Coolidge on the idea that *HI-Cosmopolitan* was a quality magazine because of its cover price of thirty-five cents. The president agreed to deliver the first chapters of the manuscript prior to the March inauguration of his successor, Herbert Hoover.

Besides the certainty of terrific newsstand sales for *HI-Cosmopolitan*, prestige would accrue to Hearst himself for publishing the autobiography of a respected former president. No payment to Coolidge was disclosed, but a Hearst Corporation financial report for May 1929 indicated the former president received $75,000 for the serial (equivalent to $900,000 in 2010 dollars). Cosmopolitan Book Corporation distributed the Coolidge autobiography in November.[66]

Long was ecstatic when Coolidge agreed to the serial. He informed Hearst by telegram, "Unless I am all wet April Cosmopolitan will be most extraordinary magazine we ever issued."

Coolidge divided his autobiography into five-thousand-word installments for *HI-Cosmopolitan*. Long hurriedly read the early installments. "Astounding that man ordinarily so reserved could deal so frankly with most intimate thoughts, motives and events," Long informed Hearst by telegram.[67]

Both men agreed secrecy was crucial to prevent competitors from learning about the presidential autobiography and rushing unauthorized biographies of Coolidge into print before the *HI-Cosmopolitan* serial started in April 1929. "Please don't mention to any newspapermen," Long advised Hearst—a rather ironic bit of advice.

Long kept it secret from magazine readers, too. Each month the magazine's table-of-contents page highlighted the next month's big story with a large-type promotional blurb, but the page for March 1929 mentioned nothing. Long unleashed an ad blitz the moment the magazine was mailed for delivery to subscribers and bundled for newsstands. *HI-Cosmopolitan* spent $58,000 for newspaper ads and radio commercials to promote the first installment by Coolidge.[68] The April issue displayed a full-page photo of Coolidge. It just happened to show a presidential inscription—"To Ray Long"—and a signature, too.

Coolidge had not given the American people any reason why he decided not to run for reelection. His statement the previous summer simply declared, "I do not choose to run for President in 1928." His first serial installment in *HI-Cosmopolitan* explained the rationale for his decision: "It is difficult for men in high office to avoid the malady of self-delusion. They are always surrounded by worshipers. They are constantly, and for the most part sincerely, assured of their greatness. They live in an artificial atmosphere of adulation and exaltation which sooner or later impairs their judgment. They are in grave danger of becoming careless and arrogant."[69]

HI-Cosmopolitan made news with the surprise publication of Coolidge's memoir. Major newspapers across the nation reported the event on front pages, including the *New York Times,* the *New York Herald Tribune,* and the *Chicago*

Tribune. Editorials in several newspapers praised the magazine. "Ray Long received a sheaf of congratulatory messages on securing Coolidge articles from editors, advertisers and agencies all over the country," White informed Hearst by telegram. "Every indication of the most complete sellout in magazine history."[70]

Advertisers were indeed pleased. Hearst Corporation executives received numerous letters and telegrams from ad agencies and clients. It was good business to advertise in a magazine that an admirable former president deemed a proper place for a memoir.[71]

Public response was strong, but not overwhelming. The magazine circulated 1.785 million copies containing the first Coolidge installment, an increase of 220,000 copies from the March issue. Eight successive installments ran, with the second one spiking at 1.85 million copies. By the end of summer, circulation had slipped to 1.6 million copies. The Coolidge serial was something of a brief newsstand sensation without any sustainable circulation benefit.

White worried about another cycle of up-and-down circulation at *HI-Cosmopolitan*. "We would be heartily in favor of the continuation of articles of proven circulation value like those by Mr. Coolidge," White wrote to San Simeon. "The credit for the Coolidge article undoubtedly should go entirely to Ray Long but whether he can continue to secure a series of articles approaching this without having some specialist on his staff is a question."[72]

Long was not aware that Hearst and White now were searching for an associate editor who would develop special articles, such as additional autobiographies or memoirs and journalistic exposés. White already had contacted a former editor of *McCall's*, Harry Payne Burton, to offer him the job of managing editor for *HI-Cosmopolitan*. The plan was for Burton to be the development specialist and Long to concentrate on literary material. This was heavy-handed treatment of a Hearst favorite, and undoubtedly White first had cleared the offer to Burton with the publisher. Burton, who had expanded the circulation of *McCall's* by several hundred thousand copies to 2.45 million by 1929, sought a salary that White thought unreasonable and the plan to forcibly assist Long with the magazine was put on hold temporarily.[73]

Meanwhile, Long tried to duplicate his Coolidge exclusive. He contacted prominent statesmen—among them the ever-elusive Clemenceau and World War I military commander John J. Pershing—to persuade them to publish memoirs in the magazine. Neither of them signed with the magazine, nor did any other luminaries.

The magazine's circulation and desirable demographics pleased advertisers even if Hearst and his executives wished for better. The ad rate for the dual title rose several hundred dollars each year the rest of the decade, culminating in a page cost to advertisers of $4,800 for 1930. A distinctive carryover

category of ads in *HI-Cosmopolitan* was the special section for private prepara-
tory academies and schools, certainly an indicator that the magazine retained
its readership among affluent families. This special section displayed an average of sixteen pages of ads each month. Total advertising volume fluctuated after the merger, primarily caused by occasional economic downturns preceding
the October 1929 crash. The higher ad rates countered any revenue loss that
might have resulted from a temporary decrease in pages whenever the national
economy weakened.[74]

The corporation did benefit from the merger. *HI-Cosmopolitan* typically was
profitable annually for the last half of the 1920s, although the amount varied
widely from a low of $122,000 to a high of $599,200.[75]

Long prospered, too. His peak annual salary and bonus reportedly totaled
$180,000.[76]

Ouster

Acquaintances and journalists described Ray Long as "dynamic" and "dap-
per." The latter adjective was especially apt because the editor's wardrobe included forty suits made by a London tailor and innumerable shirts created by
a Paris tailor. Long apparently treated authors well and was liked—except by F.
Scott Fitzgerald and others whose fiction the editor rejected. Biographies of authors and articles in magazines and newspapers have nothing bad to say about
Long. The editor had every reason to be nice, of course. He controlled a popular, prominent magazine, was the recipient of the highest salary of any editor of
the era, and essentially was the duke of a fiefdom within the Hearst empire.[77]

To the dismay and envy of corporate executives, Long answered only to
Hearst from his start in December 1918 through early 1929. His promotion to
International Magazine Company president in 1926 shielded Long from interference. Hearst was a permissive publisher who let editors and executives spend
money practically without restraint if they produced exceptional profits. However, when profits were marginal or the bottom line was red Hearst would act
promptly through intermediaries to impose budgetary controls. At his newspapers, Hearst tolerated financial losses because the dailies were political weapons. At his magazines, Hearst demanded profits.

Long's *Cosmopolitan* was profitable and its subsequent iteration as *Hearst's
International combined with Cosmopolitan* contributed to the corporate treasury, but the magazine was an erratic performer. Profit for 1928 was $385,900—
a 40 percent dive from the prior year. Some of the shortfall was attributable to a
slight drop in ad pages, but editorial expenses had soared by $131,000 from the
previous year, a one-third increase. Long believed bestselling authors deserved
the best fees, regardless of the magazine's economic circumstances.[78]

Hearst was eager to improve *HI-Cosmopolitan* at the start of 1929. Long had failed to attain a circulation of two million copies, which the publisher had set as a goal, whether realistic or not. The merger was old news to readers and advertisers. Hearst wanted *HI-Cosmopolitan* to grow and make a consistent profit. He was receptive to imposing cost controls at his flagship magazine.

White argued that the editorial budget of *HI-Cosmopolitan* "should come under the control of the Finance Committee just as we in the business organization report to the committee." Long would have to explain and justify his decisions. "From year to year editorial costs of all kinds continue to advance," White told Hearst. "No doubt logically, but in the interests of sound organization there should be both control and budgetary forecast in as far as practicable with regard to editorial expenditures." Hearst concurred. Ten years of autonomy for Long ended.[79]

The corporate finance committee mandated an itemized annual budget from the editor and formal proposals for any extraordinary expenses, such as hiring a celebrity aviation editor or paying the nation's president for an autobiography. Long protested the intrusion on his editorial domain. "They don't understand the magazine business and they construe instructions from you in ways and to degrees am sure you never intended," Long complained by telegram to Hearst. "Result has been upsetting to me at times. Would like to come to California and talk things over." Grandpop did not reply.[80]

A more serious threat to Long than the corporate finance committee emerged at the same time. Hearst and White decided to hire a general manager specifically for the magazines. Technically, Long's position as president placed him above a general manager. In reality, the Hearst hierarchy was unlike any other. Its corporate segments had few clear lines of authority. Hearst and White determined that a general manager of International Magazine Company would monitor business operations of the magazine and report directly to them, not to Long. The general manager would function as a corporate watchdog for the magazines.[81]

Their choice for the job was Richard Berlin, a superb advertising sales representative for International Magazine Company for a decade. He was a nononsense person, intense, and absolutely loyal to the Hearst Corporation. Long had unwittingly boosted Berlin's career in August 1927 when he met him while searching for a person to energize the ad sales staff for the magazines. Long promptly had arranged for Hearst to meet Berlin at San Simeon when both traveled to California on a business trip. "If we come to Ranch might not be a bad idea to bring him so you could study him at close range," Long suggested by telegram.[82]

Discussions with Berlin about the general manager's job began in January 1929. Hearst invited him to San Simeon again for a lengthy conversation about the responsibilities of general manager. Hearst and White concluded that Berlin should focus on strengthening advertising revenue and devising a strategy to bolster newsstand sales. Hearst apprised White of the talk with Berlin, "He says furthermore that problems on Cosmopolitan are editorial and price problems, both absolutely beyond his control." Berlin, an astute corporate infighter, was aware that Hearst had lost confidence in Long. He told Hearst that Long would resist advice and the "situation on Cosmopolitan with Ray would be so delicate as to make any accomplishment utterly impossible." Hearst assured Berlin that Long had promised to improve the magazine.

Berlin also suggested reducing the cover price of *HI-Cosmopolitan* to twenty-five cents. This indicated he had been briefed by White prior to meeting with Hearst; White had pushed for a price cut, insisting it was the only way to attain the circulation goal of two million copies. Hearst rejected the recommendation. "Before we try publishing a 25-cent magazine, let us see if we cannot sell a really good 35-cent magazine," he told White.[83]

Hearst debated whether to appoint Berlin publisher of both *HI-Cosmopolitan* and *Good Housekeeping*, thereby placing him above Long. "It would disturb Ray Long considerably if he were made publisher there," Hearst's telegram advised White. They decided Berlin should be general manager of the magazines. Berlin accepted the job and started in March.[84]

The new general manager proceeded to gather data on *HI-Cosmopolitan*'s editorial expenses, newsstand sales, and general finances. Berlin analyzed expenses and revenue for the previous year and also compared the data with 1923 to match results. Berlin forwarded his report to White, who sent it along to Hearst in California. The report documented several key developments during Long's tenure:

- the magazine was losing money in 1929 at the rate of approximately $21,000 to $23,000 a month compared to the prior year;
- circulation of 1.6 million copies was divided evenly between subscriptions and newsstand sales, a violation of corporate policy limiting subscriptions to one-third of total distribution;
- a five-year analysis of circulation revenue disclosed that a $909,000 surplus had become a $282,000 deficit, because of premiums to induce subscribers;
- a five-year analysis of newsstand returns of unsold copies revealed an increase from six percent to eighteen percent, a clear sign the magazine lacked its former appeal;
- a five-year analysis of editorial salaries for associate editors, copy editors, and clerical assistants recorded a monthly payroll rise from $6,700 to $15,100 for additional personnel, a sum hardly justified by the one-third increase in editorial pages;
- a five-year analysis of fees for manuscripts and illustrations recorded an increase from $37,000 per issue to $64,000 per issue, a reflection of generous payments rather than a greater amount of material.[85]

A noteworthy problem relevant to editorial expenses was the large inventory of unpublished manuscripts and illustrations accumulated by Long. Hundreds of stories sat on shelves in *HI-Cosmopolitan* offices, and a backlog of no fewer than thirty covers by Harrison Fisher awaited publication at $3,000 apiece. Berlin also discovered "over 40 contracts involving payments of slightly over a million dollars a year" for authors and artists, some of which were two- and three-year pacts.[86]

Aware that he was under siege, Long defended the backlog of Fisher magazine covers and editorial expenditures. "When I came in with Cosmopolitan I found we had forty covers," Long informed Hearst by telegram. "In Nineteen Twenty One changed contract limiting him to twelve per year." Long had trimmed the backlog of covers by only ten after a decade, despite having the authority to place Fisher's artwork on the cover of *Good Housekeeping*. A letter from Long justified the necessity of multiyear contracts for authors and artists. "One reason for the high prices for fiction these days is McCall's," Long wrote to Hearst. "They spend money like drunken sailors. Their first move may be to raid Cosmo for writers and artists. If we hold the people we have, or get the people we should in future, it may cost more than it does now."[87]

A letter written by Berlin to Hearst much later pointedly, and sardonically, reminded Hearst about the editor's extravagance, "Do you remember in those good lush Ray Long days when we had over a million dollars in inventory in Cosmopolitan?" The evidence Berlin presented to Hearst did demonstrate mismanagement and financial irresponsibility by Long. The same criticisms could have applied to Hearst, of course.[88]

Berlin analyzed *Cosmopolitan* operations to match expenses with results. His report commented that "newsstand circulation has remained almost stationary" since 1923 despite the tremendous rise in the editorial budget. Basically, Berlin proved to Hearst that the successful formula Long devised during his first few years with *Cosmopolitan* had failed ever since. Not surprisingly, considering the conversations Berlin had with Hearst and White when discussing what his job would entail, the new general manager of magazines recommended a solution for *HI-Cosmopolitan* that would include his "close supervision of costs with expenditures reduced, newsstand returns decreased and subscription circulation supplanted by newsstands."[89]

White approved. He demurred, however, on whether stagnant circulation adversely affected ad revenue for *HI-Cosmopolitan*. White noted that placement of advertising remained strong, except for occasional weakness related to economic conditions. "The magazine advertiser and the agencies purchasing magazine space appear now to be less impressed by volume than by those who buy the book," White wrote, referring to the distinctive readership demographics.[90]

Hearst received the report and accepted its recommendations. Hearst was exasperated with Long, but still admired him. "There is no editor that half-way compares with him when he is really on the job," Hearst told White by telegram. The implied message was to let Berlin handle the business end and permit Long some time to make the magazine livelier.[91]

HI-Cosmopolitan never made front-page headlines again while Long was editor. He tried and failed to replicate the Coolidge exclusive. He tried for controversy by publishing an article that advocated an unwed woman's right to raise a child. Hearst was livid. The publisher had not seen the magazine's page dummies on schedule prior to printing; his telegram to Long was stamped RUSH for delivery to the editor who was aboard a train: "This article gives me cold chill. I think it will lose us many readers of better class. Don't think it has any place in Cosmopolitan and if not too late will you please cut it out. Never mind any inconvenience or expense necessary to omit article. I think it does not do any good to print articles that attract the more reputable and wholesome readers and then when we get them with Coolidge articles offend them with articles of illegitimate child kind." Long replied, "Awfully sorry, but presses already running and therefore impossible to eliminate article without serious delay on news stands." Whether any readers ever reacted angrily to the article is not recorded.[92]

The relationship between Hearst and Long deteriorated. With the information from Berlin on the huge inventory of unpublished manuscripts, Hearst monitored Long carefully. Berlin sent Hearst monthly budget summaries. One summary provoked an outburst by telegram from Hearst to Long: "I know you have to pay large prices to get the best stories but I think we could save a lot of money by not buying more than we surely can use. If we keep down editorial expense as closely as possible we will have more money for promotion."[93]

Long reacted sharply. "Your telegram terribly discouraging," his return telegram stated. "Someone is using propaganda. Anyone who tells you we buy for Cosmopolitan any article or story for which we have no definite use is liar." The tone of his telegram and refutation that a huge inventory of editorial material existed suggested Long himself did not realize how many stories he had shelved.[94]

An immediate reply from Hearst soothed his editor, yet reiterated the need to stay within budget: "For God's sake don't be disturbed. I see by reports that stuff on hand is constantly increasing and I thought we might be able to save some money that way if we can. You certainly are temperamental."[95]

Hearst quarreled with Long about business policy, too. Long urged the publisher to lower the newsstand price of the magazine to twenty-five cents, which White and Berlin had recommended. Perhaps the editor finally realized that both executives were critical of his management and he sought to win their favor, or perhaps Long hoped a lower price might get circulation closer to the two million copies Hearst demanded.

Long also pushed the idea of letting major advertisers place full-page ads next to editorial pages without paying extra for the privilege. This contradicted standard magazine pricing policy that charged a 50 percent premium for placement adjacent to a page of editorial text. Common wisdom of the era regarded an advertisement next to an article or story as likelier to attract the attention of readers. Hearst disapproved. "I am not objecting to the full pages but I am objecting to the cut-rate, and it is practically cut-rate when the Advertising Department does not get the extra price which extra position demands," Hearst wrote.[96]

HI-Cosmopolitan never approached a circulation of two million copies. It started 1931, a Depression year, a few thousand copies shy of 1.7 million. Its archrival *American* had outpaced it since the *HI-Cosmopolitan* merger and now led by 530,000 copies. Advertising revenue would plunge $853,000 for the year, a one-sixth decrease from the 1930 amount. The flagship was floundering.[97]

Perhaps it was coincidence, but an article in *Fortune* conveyed to its readers an entirely different story about the situation. *Fortune,* a recent startup by Henry Luce of *Time,* went to executives willing to pay a $1 cover price for a finely written, beautifully designed monthly devoted to business topics. Its readership consisted of people who decided where to advertise the products and services their companies provided. *Fortune* of March 1931 profiled Ray Long. It was flattering—praise for his editing style, his acute awareness of public taste in fiction, his roster of bestselling authors, and his stewardship of a highly profitable publication popular with advertisers. Long gave due credit to William Randolph Hearst, but *Fortune* readers got the idea it was the editor who was responsible for the magazine's success.[98]

Whether the *Fortune* article was arranged by Long to prevent further intrusions by Berlin and to signal Hearst that the identity of *HI-Cosmopolitan* was inseparable from its editor cannot be ascertained from the historical record. Whatever the genesis of the *Fortune* profile, it did not affect the inevitable; four months after its appearance, Long resigned the presidency of International Magazine Company and as editor of *HI-Cosmopolitan.*[99]

Harry Payne Burton replaced him.[100]

An eminent journalism historian speculated decades ago that Hearst asked Long to resign because of the *Fortune* article. The historian wrote, "It may be surmised that the president and editor-in-chief of the International Magazine Corporation sometimes took a little too much credit to suit the top boss." This speculation became the basis for a standard explanation why Long quit the magazine, and it has appeared in several media history books.[101]

This original speculation and subsequent repetition of it lacked perspective provided by letters, memos, and telegrams available in the Hearst archives at the University of California–Berkeley. An extensive examination has found evidence that Hearst's displeasure with Long preceded the *Fortune* article by two years and pertained to concerns about editorial and managerial performance, especially fiscal judgment. Perhaps the *Fortune* piece was the last straw, but if *HI-Cosmopolitan* had attained a circulation of two million copies and a consistently high profit Hearst probably would have tolerated a moment in the spotlight for Long.

Upon resigning, Ray Long formed a partnership to publish books. A few months later, for unknown reasons, he disappeared to sail the southern Pacific Ocean; his lengthy absence caused the bankruptcy of the partnership. Long returned from the eighteen-month sojourn to work a succession of temporary jobs in California with small magazines and a movie studio. It was a downward spiral. At age fifty-seven, Long committed suicide in Beverly Hills, California, almost exactly four years after his resignation.[102]

Survivor

The expulsion of Ray Long effectively placed Richard Berlin at the head of International Magazine Company, an entity that soon became Hearst Magazines. His tight control of budgets and pressure on ad sales representatives sustained magazine profits throughout the Depression despite wild variations in revenue. The national economy recovered somewhat by the mid-1930s and then slumped again; only the American military buildup that began in 1940 to prepare for war sustained economic growth.[103]

Berlin had promptly slashed *Cosmopolitan*'s monthly editorial budget of $74,000 by 60 percent. This forced the new editor, Harry Payne Burton, to withdraw from bidding on new manuscripts by bestselling authors. Burton depleted the inventory of unpublished manuscripts within two years, then managed to sign a few bestselling authors while relying on lesser-known storytellers for most fiction. Burton ran serials and stories by Pearl Buck, Agatha Christie, Paul Gallico, Ernest Hemingway, and Ellery Queen. His treatment of Fannie Hurst, though, contrasted dramatically with that of Long. Burton was slow to respond to her letters when he delayed publication of a story by her and he demanded extensive rewriting. Months would pass after publication until she received payment. Hurst stopped writing for the magazine within several years.[104]

Berlin may have dictated such treatment. He relentlessly pared expenses, and his primary targets were the generously paid authors and artists Long had signed to contracts. Authors soon learned that the economic reality of the Depression and the new management regime meant lower fees and piecemeal placement of their work. Burton bought fiction on a story-by-story and serial-by-serial basis. Berlin did not renew most contracts Long had arranged with authors and artists; the million-dollar pacts had dwindled to $150,000 at the start of the 1940s. Berlin bragged to Hearst that *HI-Cosmopolitan* paid its editor "a yearly salary of $25,000"—a sum that made its recipient "very happy."[105]

Berlin set his sights on Harrison Fisher, the cover illustrator making $3,000 for each magazine cover. Hearst received a letter from Berlin accompanied by a recent *HI-Cosmopolitan* cover drawn by Fisher; the general manager argued that hairstyles, jewelry, and clothing of the cover girl were hopelessly old-fashioned. Berlin hoped to issue an ultimatum to Fisher to draw contemporary women, but he knew better than to act on his own initiative. It was wise. Hearst evidently agreed that the Fisher Girls hardly were contemporary because he spoke with Fisher by telephone and insisted on updated appearances, to which Fisher concurred. Hearst then advised Berlin to deal tactfully with the artist should a modern look take some time to accomplish. "Fisher can do good work and to my mind more satisfactory work than anybody else you can get," the publisher wrote in a two-page letter. "He is a trade-mark and I do not like to change our trade-mark. I do not think we should make Fisher go around in circles or draw in circles or accept in the details of his work any minor ideas of other people. The important thing, and the only important thing, is to have him be modern and keep up with modern ways and fashions. I impressed it upon him vigorously."[106]

Fiction continued to be the trademark of *HI-Cosmopolitan*. Burton developed the concept of a four-book magazine that divided each monthly issue into separate departments. Book 1 was a novella of twelve to fourteen pages, followed by two or three stories of varying length, two serials of eight to ten pages, and several nonfiction articles of two to four pages. Book 2 was a full short novel of sixteen to twenty pages. Book 3 was a nonfiction book excerpt of six to ten pages. Book 4 was a truncated novel of twenty-four to twenty-eight pages. Total editorial material filled eighty to ninety-six pages.

Nonfiction, which comprised approximately one-fourth of editorial material, was more timely under Burton. President-elect Franklin D. Roosevelt discussed his plan for economic recovery in January 1933. Articles on life in the Soviet Union and economic trade with the Soviets, preparations for national defense, opportunities for college education, and profiles of prominent people were presented.

Historians have always concentrated on Hearst's ownership of newspapers and have barely mentioned his magazines. His daily publications cemented his reputation for sensationalism and vindictiveness. His magazines varied in quality and purpose, but for the most part they were useful sources of information and reputable by the 1920s. Readership for most of his magazines was solidly middle class or higher on the economic ladder.

His magazines usually made money, too, unlike many of his newspapers. Despite his reputation as a newspaperman, Hearst appreciated the profit potential of magazines. Although unwilling to close unprofitable newspapers, Hearst did not hesitate to shed magazines. He bought existing magazines throughout the 1920s and 1930s to expand the financial core of his empire. Some were specialty magazines for specific categories of readers, such as *American Architect* and *American Druggist*. Some were for upscale readers, such as *Harper's Bazaar, House Beautiful,* and *Town & Country*. And in what must have pleased him greatly, Hearst bought a nearly bankrupt *McClure's* in 1926—the magazine that had deposed Walker's *Cosmopolitan* from its leadership of general magazines thirty years earlier and the magazine that Hearst's *Cosmopolitan* had competed against on exposé articles twenty years before. Hearst directed the transformation of *McClure's,* which had changed its format many times since its muckraking days, into a romance magazine. Two years later, he sold it because it was not profitable. *McClure's* merged and disappeared in 1929. (Two other former competitors from *Cosmopolitan*'s early days also were Depression era deaths: *Century* in 1930; *Scribner's* in 1939.)[107]

The mandatory cost-cutting policy supervised by creditors and lenders contributed to magazine profitability the last half of the 1930s. Some Hearst magazines briefly lost money because of the economy's gyrations throughout the Depression, and there were a few years when two or three very profitable magazines covered the losses of others. Berlin proudly reported annual profits for the magazines ranging from approximately $1.13 million to $2.52 million. *HI-Cosmopolitan,* however, was not the prize earner; its average annual profit was one-fourth the amount *Good Housekeeping* earned—in 1938, for example, *HI-Cosmopolitan* made a mere one-sixth the profit of the now-dominant magazine. This disparity would determine the postwar future of *HI-Cosmopolitan*.[108]

The magazines subsidized the newspapers, a situation that aggravated Berlin. Upon his promotion to corporate general manager, and with the full support of the creditors who scrutinized every decision, Berlin began to discard unprofitable Hearst newspapers. Some were closed, some merged, some sold. Hearst, reduced to the role of bystander, complained about the policy. Berlin frankly told the publisher why those newspapers were expendable: "In the past decade the magazines earned over $20,000,000, no part of which we were permitted to retain for expansion or construction. Every year we made plans to expand the magazines. We wanted to promote them liberally, but in each instance we had to modify, defer, or eliminate entirely the plans because of the demands on the part of the newspapers." Berlin forwarded a supplemental list of another $4 million subsidy the magazines had diverted recently to newspapers. Hearst did not protest further.[109]

Berlin, despite his business sense, also lost a magazine to the Depression. He had persuaded Hearst in 1934 to purchase *Pictorial Review,* a very popular women's publication. It did not make money, though, and Berlin closed the magazine in 1939. *Pictorial Review* had a circulation of three million–plus copies at its death, which was the largest magazine ever to fail to that point—and the only Hearst magazine to die from Depression economics. Its closure clearly demonstrated that Berlin would not tolerate a money-loser, even one that he had sponsored.[110]

Berlin was more than a financial steward of the corporation from the mid-1930s through World War II. He was Hearst's alter ego. Fiercely loyal to the elderly publisher, Berlin led the fight to prevent the movie *Citizen Kane* from being shown in theaters and, failing that, to ensure that the movie received no publicity. *Citizen Kane* was the creation of Orson Welles, a young actor-director-producer of stage plays and radio shows. It portrayed an egomaniacal media mogul who was born rich and became richer from sensationalistic newspapers. Charles Foster Kane died a lonely man in the isolation of a dark castle named Xanadu. Obviously, Welles had created a fictional portrait of a man similar to William Randolph Hearst.

Hearst, though, was still alive—and furious. Berlin ordered Hearst newspapers not to review the movie and not to accept ads for it. The same order applied to magazines, with the added stricture not to publicize any movie from RKO, the studio that made *Citizen Kane.* This last ban came from Hearst himself, who had instructed Berlin by telegram to "omit from any of our magazines any reference in text or illustration relating to any moving picture produced by R.K.O." Berlin personally met with Hollywood executives to orchestrate a campaign to block the movie from booking in theaters owned by various movie studios. Berlin also had lunch with George Schaefer, the RKO manager. "He disclaimed knowledge that Welles had been doing the picture with the life of the Chief as a background," Berlin informed Hearst's personal secretary. "I further told Schaefer that he had a good Leftist for a partner in Orson Welles." Berlin also delightedly informed Hearst about rejecting a full-page ad for *Citizen Kane* in *HI-Cosmopolitan;* Berlin enclosed a copy of the RKO ad, with a note that the studio would have paid $5,300.[111]

The ad rate for RKO was evidence of the effect the Depression era had on *HI-Cosmopolitan,* which epitomized magazines generally. Berlin had postponed ad rate increases for *HI-Cosmopolitan* since 1931 despite its slight circulation increase from an average of 1.7 million copies monthly during Long's final year to 1.854 million copies monthly at the start of World War II in December 1941. Of total circulation, two-thirds still came from subscriptions—a violation of corporate policy for which Berlin had criticized Long in 1929 and had displeased Hearst.[112]

By the start of the war, Berlin had done nothing to reduce the magazine's reliance on subscribers. However, his stringent budget controls had reduced the quality of *HI-Cosmopolitan*. A letter asked Berlin, "Do you think the fiction in Cosmopolitan is as notable as it used to be?" The questioner was William Randolph Hearst. "Every story had distinction," Hearst wrote, "and indeed no great story appeared otherwhere than in Cosmopolitan. Now we have occasional good stories, but we seem to have lost the supreme position we had. What do you think is the matter?" Berlin did not reply.[113]

Wartime was a boon to media generally and to the Hearst Corporation. The war years generated some new advertising directed toward consumers earning good wages in a full-employment economy, but many ads served to remind people that businesses were winning the war and someday would again make products for a civilian society. Prosperity permitted *HI-Cosmopolitan* to restore its cover price to thirty-five cents in August 1942. Wartime circulation for *HI-Cosmopolitan* sometimes exceeded two million copies a month—too late for Hearst to enjoy. Infirm and past the age of eighty, Hearst never would control his media empire again.

7

Transition

An End

At age eighty-two, William Randolph Hearst was eager to resume authority for his newspapers and magazines in the closing months of World War II. A robust wartime economy had revived most remnant publications (eleven newspapers had closed, merged, or were sold), his businesses were creditworthy again, and his goal was to restore luster to his favorite publication. "I would like to see Cosmopolitan a very great quality magazine," Hearst informed his nominal subordinate Richard Berlin by letter from San Simeon. "I think we should have all the best stories, no matter what we have to pay for them. Of course we must have wonderful illustration, because appearance is so important and the general impression of quality is conveyed largely by the illustration. I would like to recommend more full color picture pages, to give a sumptuous look to the publication."[1]

These were ideas, not directives. Berlin was president of Hearst Corporation, a position attained by virtue of financial acumen and managerial toughness. He had reshaped the corporation to stave off bankruptcy, negotiated with creditors and lenders, arranged substantial loans to forestall a shutdown in operations when suppliers of paper would not extend credit further, and otherwise proved a capable leader. Subordinate executives met corporate profit goals or else he fired them—the opposite of Hearst's hesitancy to fire people whose intelligence or personality he admired or liked. Berlin judged a person on performance. Neither was Berlin a sentimentalist; he regarded the bottom line as inviolate and decided the fate of a publication based on its profit potential. Hearst, during his banishment from corporate leadership, had protested to no avail Berlin's predilection for "liquidation" and cost-cutting. "We have got to promote liberally and intelligently, and we have got to provide something to promote—something notable in fiction and in features," he urged Berlin.[2]

Hearst now hoped to revive the magazine's reputation, which was very popular despite its mediocre editorial quality. During the eight-year exile creditors and lenders imposed on him, Hearst had never stopped reviewing each issue. He had closely critiqued the content and style of *HI-Cosmopolitan*. His descriptive details of specific items suggested that he spent many hours at San Simeon reading his favorite magazine. Letters and telegrams to Berlin identified illustrations Hearst disliked and liked, articles he thought were overlong or not long enough, authors and writers he admired, and cover designs he enjoyed. ("I do not like the illustration of page 28. It seems rather crude." "I do not like the Dixon articles. They seem too much like Sunday paper stuff." "I do not think we do so well with pages 24 and 25, where even two colors are used to very poor effect.")

"These are just impressions as I turn the pages of Cosmopolitan," Hearst wrote to Berlin during summer 1945. "Perhaps you will find some of them useful." His signature by then was a thin, shaky scrawl.[3]

Berlin usually did not respond to specific comments from Hearst. He humored the old man by acknowledging remarks on relatively minor topics, such as selection of photographs and length of articles. If a Hearst critique faulted an editor's judgment, Berlin would agree to a reprimand; it was a management style for which Berlin was known and a reason why successors to Ray Long never had similar autonomy. Berlin dictated editorial policy along with business policy. A *Town & Country* editor had argued with Berlin about the magazine's editorial format—the editor preferred classy literary pieces and artistic page design; Berlin wanted "decorative pages with color plates of sumptuous homes." When the editor resigned in April 1947, Berlin explained to Hearst that the editor did not "conform with our ideas." Hearst scrawled a note on the letter, which was his reply by telegram, "I am delighted that you have accepted Mr. Bull's resignation."[4]

Hearst complained by telegram in summer 1947 about a cover. "I don't blame the artist for the Greer Garson cover as much as I do the editors of Cosmopolitan," he stated. "They put the Cosmopolitan, the leading high-class magazine of the Nation, in the cheap movie magazine class—and used the picture of a passé actress at that." Berlin's reply telegram concurred: "I feel exactly as you do and have already told the editors. There will not be a repetition."[5]

Upon the dissolution of the committee of bankers and creditors when debts were repaid, Hearst was named chairman of the corporation's board of directors, a symbolic position and title for an elderly man in frail health. Berlin remained president of Hearst Corporation. He continued to treat Hearst with respect and tact and also habitually ignored directives and requests from the remote magnate in California. Berlin was quite secure in his job because bankers and other creditors whose loans were vital to ordinary operations and future corporate expansion considered him a practical and responsible person. William Randolph Hearst, of course, had proven himself the opposite.[6]

Perhaps no more obvious evidence of the lesser status accorded Hearst was the cover nameplate of his flagship magazine. The typeface for *Hearst's International* at the merger in March 1925 was thirty-six points, or a half-inch high; twenty years later the typeface had shrunk to a barely legible twelve points. Meanwhile, the *Cosmopolitan* typeface visibly dominated at eighty-four points. Berlin could not remove the founder's name altogether, but it was sensible to minimize it given the public perception of Hearst as a self-indulgent ogre who had maintained his royal lifestyle throughout the Depression regardless of the consequent astronomical indebtedness of his corporate empire, unemployment for thousands of employees, and severe wage reductions for those who remained on the payroll.

Cosmopolitan was Hearst's favorite magazine, so Berlin did agree to a request to upgrade to forty-pound paper, which sharpened clarity of text and photographs. Other improvements were not approved for a few years, however. Most story illustrations on inside pages were duotone rather than full color, and color photographs rarely adorned articles. Berlin kept the magazine on a tight budget.

The elderly Hearst also communicated a wish for the magazine to Berlin that was anathema to the former ad sales representative—a request Berlin could never honor considering his obligation to make a profit. "I suppose I am prejudiced or prudish but I don't like so many whiskey advertisements in Cosmopolitan," Hearst wrote in autumn 1945. "Do you not think it is rather offensive in a dignified publication like Cosmopolitan?" A telegram from Hearst in December 1947 was more insistent: "A great many respectable publications refuse to take liquor advertisements." Liquor ads accounted for approximately 11 percent of *Cosmopolitan* advertisements from the mid-1940s to early 1950s— hundreds of thousands of dollars annually.[7]

Hearst sent the latter telegram regarding liquor advertisements from a Los Angeles residence, not San Simeon. At age eighty-four, his frailty necessitated quick access to medical specialists. His critiques of *Cosmopolitan* became sporadic at the end of the 1940s. Hearst's publications functioned without his guidance, and editorial directives usually were disregarded. Berlin continuously strengthened the financial security of the media empire year by year.[8]

William Randolph Hearst died at age eighty-eight in mid-August 1951.

Hearst's International disappeared from the magazine cover's nameplate in April 1952.

Cosmopolitan had its identity back.

But its future was uncertain. *Cosmopolitan* was neither the flagship magazine nor a personal favorite of Richard Berlin.

Mediocrity

Television threatened most national magazines from the mid-1950s onward, and it killed some giants. Advertisers liked the cost efficiency of commercials purchased during prime-time network programs because the expense to reach each thousand viewers was lower than many magazines could match and no magazine could compete with the sheer number of people who watched an episode of *I Love Lucy* or *The Honeymooners.* Also vulnerable were some magazines that lacked a specific readership demographic category sought by advertisers, such as especially affluent readers or a narrow age category for either men or women, and other magazines that lacked an editorial focus relevant to advertisers of certain products, such as fashion or family or travel. *Cosmopolitan* was a magazine that had no specific readership demographic desirable to advertisers and no editorial focus attractive to specialty advertisers. Diversion of ad dollars to television and a rather bizarre corporate strategy combined to strangle *Cosmopolitan* financially into the 1960s.

A clear sign of the magazine's lower rank within the Hearst Corporation was the appointment of *Good Housekeeping* editor Herbert Mayes to a dual position as supervisory editor of the lesser sibling publication. It was a reversal of the role assigned to Ray Long by Hearst three decades earlier. This time, Berlin chose the *Good Housekeeping* editor to focus on the successful larger magazine while making sure the smaller, less profitable former flagship stuck to its budget. Mayes ran both magazines until the runaway success of *Good Housekeeping,* which reached a monthly circulation of 3.5 million copies, required his full attention and necessitated selection of an editor-in-chief for *Cosmopolitan.*[9]

Mayes evaluated two contenders for the job: John O'Connell, the executive editor, and David Brown, the managing editor. Much to the disappointment of associate editors, O'Connell got the job. Brown, age thirty-four, was perceived as brighter and an innovator. Brown quit early in 1952 and moved to Hollywood to become a movie studio producer responsible for developing literary items. Several years afterward he married Helen Gurley, an ad agency account representative.[10]

O'Connell inherited a limited editorial budget that restricted *Cosmopolitan* to buying fiction mostly from unknown authors, with enough money for an infrequent purchase from a bestselling author. *Cosmopolitan* fiction now comprised half of all editorial material, representative of the decline in fiction among magazines of the era. Fiction lacked the appeal it once had because paperback books were an affordable alternative for readers and because television, which was becoming a fixture in American homes throughout the 1950s, offered fictional entertainment for free—its indirect cost hidden in the prices of products and services advertised during commercial breaks.[11]

Nonfiction articles lacked any particular emphasis in *Cosmopolitan*. Topics included profiles of politicians and their wives, the threat of nuclear war and need for military preparedness, and contemporary subjects, such as education, health care, inflation, juvenile delinquency, and urban crime. From late 1951 to early 1953, O'Connell included articles specifically pertinent to women: "Fatigue And Your Husband's Success"; "What To Tell Your Teen-Age Daughter About Sex"; "When Should Your Husband Change His Job?"; "Are Nice Girls Safe In The Service?"; "Secretaries Can Be Choosy, Too"; "Hollywood's Four-Week Beauty And Charm Course." Readers did not find the magazine worth buying. Circulation ebbed, despite an annual million-dollar promotional budget to tout its relevance to married couples.[12]

Another problem was that *Cosmopolitan* had intruded on *Good Housekeeping*'s editorial turf as a women's magazine. *Good Housekeeping* carried numerous service-oriented columns and feature articles pertaining to child care, family fashions, household budgeting, housekeeping, meal planning, and nutrition, but it also offered articles similar to those O'Connell published in *Cosmopolitan*. This editorial duplication harkened back to the similarity of *Hearst's* and *Cosmopolitan* prior to the focus on international topics, and title change to *Hearst's International*, at the start of the 1920s. O'Connell reverted to a general editorial format to avoid conflict with *Good Housekeeping*.

The brief foray during the early 1950s into women's topics signified what has become a popular misconception that *Cosmopolitan* was primarily a women's magazine for most of its existence. It was not. It began life in 1886 as a family literary publication with fiction for men and women, fiction for children, and articles on household chores for women, but quickly reduced its women-only content. It certainly was not a women's magazine during the ownership of John Brisben Walker from 1889 to 1905, nor during the exposé era of Hearst from 1905 to 1911. Its fiction format until the 1920s had no evident gender preference, and the statement by Hearst in 1921 that *Cosmopolitan* should not exclude men but instead "should be certain that its articles did interest the women" demonstrated its purpose as a general fiction magazine. Fiction throughout the Depression era showed no dominant gender preference and nonfiction was for both genders considering its newsy, serious slant.

Significantly, too, advertising pages from the 1880s through the mid-1950s exhibited no apparent gender bias. Ads were a thoroughly mixed assortment touting apparel for men and women, automobiles, beer, book clubs, feminine hygiene products, household appliances, life insurance, liquor, mouthwash, soap, toothpaste, and travel. Finally, none of the annual directories of publications that served as guides for advertisers had listed *Cosmopolitan* in the family, home, or women's categories; it was variously designated a literary, general, or standard magazine.

Cosmopolitan was a mediocre magazine, and its decline seemed irreversible. Readership was eroding and advertisers were abandoning it, too. Despite the economic prosperity of the 1950s and overall advertising surge for mainstream media, *Cosmopolitan* was thin. Ad pages averaged seventy-eight pages a month, which approximated the count for the early Depression years, and editorial pages were down to seventy-four pages. Advertisers were aware that demographics for *Cosmopolitan* after World War II pegged its readers as solidly middle class, not the affluent readership that Ray Long had attracted to the magazine. An indicator of the demographic shift was the skimpiness of the monthly directory for private academies, camps, and schools, which had shrunk to six pages an issue, compared with sixteen pages prior to the war.

Adding to the magazine's problems was an escalation in the cost of its most basic ingredient: paper. The postwar economy had generated an incredible demand for paper of all kinds, ranging from business and office forms to catalogs to school textbooks and to newspapers and magazines fatter with ads than during wartime. Most magazines covered the higher paper cost by selling more ads or raising prices for subscriptions and single-copy purchases. *Cosmopolitan* could do neither because of its already precarious position.[13]

Berlin decided to experiment with *Cosmopolitan*. His strategy was radical: no promotional newspaper ads, radio commercials, or door-to-door canvassing for new subscribers; no discount for a subscription compared to the newsstand price; no special discounts for two- and three-year subscriptions; no renewal reminders to subscribers—the magazine simply would not arrive in the mail if a person forgot when the subscription expired. *Cosmopolitan* was on its own. The rationale was the elimination of any financial obligation to subscribers should *Cosmopolitan* became unprofitable and Berlin decided to kill it; standard practice among publishers was to fulfill the unexpired subscriptions of a dead title by providing another magazine.

The bizarre strategy would determine, if *Cosmopolitan* survived, the size of its core readership, allow a precise demographic profile to emerge, and permit the magazine's ad sales representatives to pitch it to advertisers seeking to reach whoever those particular readers were.[14]

Not surprisingly, the strategy had a dire effect. By the late 1950s, total circulation plummeted by half to 866,700 copies in five years. *Cosmopolitan* subscriptions withered from approximately 900,000 to only 136,900. Readership stayed flat into the 1960s while loyal readers continued to buy the magazine at newsstands at thirty-five cents a copy—a price in effect from 1942 to 1966. Single-copy sales peaked at 840,000 copies and subscriptions almost disappeared, sliding to a mere 31,000. *Cosmopolitan* earned approximately three cents per copy on the twenty-one cents it received from distributors, but because an average of 140,000 copies did not sell each month the magazine merely recovered its total printing and distribution expenses.[15]

Advertising revenue kept *Cosmopolitan* alive. The rate for a full-page ad dropped to $2,400 by the mid-1950s. At that bargain rate many advertisers stayed with the magazine despite its rapid circulation descent. The magazine was thin, with an average of fifty-six ad pages and seventy-four editorial pages late in the decade. The lack of advertising resulted in an unusual situation for *Cosmopolitan* compared to other magazines: editorial pages outnumbered ad pages. Berlin and other executives realized that if the magazine was too skimpy people would not buy it.[16]

Cosmopolitan was a decidedly nondescript magazine. It lacked an editorial focus. It lacked style. "Nothing seemed particularly strong," said Harriet La Barre, an associate editor at *Cosmopolitan* for twenty years beginning in the early 1950s. "We really didn't have a purpose. None of the editors knew what to do." *Cosmopolitan* was imperiled. Cultural and social trends greatly affected the economics of magazines during the 1950s. The postwar baby boom created more interest in articles on children, education, family life, and home décor. The enlargement of the American middle class generated by expansion of the white-collar workforce and better income for millions of unionized employees at aircraft manufacturers, automobile makers, defense contractors, and transportation companies, plus the growth of electronics and technology sectors, resulted in a potential readership of incredibly diverse interests.[17]

Cosmopolitan's very lack of specificity detracted from its appeal to readers, who sought useful information relevant to their situations, and to advertisers, who sought exposure for products and services to likely potential consumers: baby food and diapers to young mothers who read family magazines; bowling shoes and golf clubs to men who read sports magazines; brokerage and financial firms to readers of business magazines; apparel and makeup to the women's magazines. General magazines did not offer any definite type of reader, and in that regard competed with network television programs.

Prime-time television programs began to siphon ad revenue from magazines. The prosperity of the urban middle class offered a consumer target of unprecedented size for advertisers. Tens of millions of dollars spent by national advertisers, especially for automobiles and household appliances, paid for commercials on television rather than ads in magazines. Network television programs exposed far greater numbers of people to sales pitches for products and services than any magazine could match. One of the only advantages over television commercials that magazine ads could offer was color; television was essentially black and white until the 1960s.[18]

The phenomenal surge in ad revenue spent on television programs was stupefying: $171 million in 1950, ranking it last of the four mainstream media; $1.025 billion in 1955, a sixfold increase that propelled it to second place behind newspapers; $1.59 billion in 1960, also second to newspapers. On a proportional basis, television received 3 percent of all advertising revenue in 1950, 11 percent in 1955, and 13 percent in 1960; magazines received 9 percent of all advertising revenue in 1950 and 8 percent in both 1955 and 1960. Statistically, television nabbed twenty-five cents of every additional dollar spent on advertising while magazines attracted six cents.[19]

Editorial specialization was beneficial to a magazine, a factor some editors and publishers did not recognize for years. Thirteen magazines with a circulation above a million copies died during the 1950s, but each lacked the specificity that advertisers demanded. *American,* the former exposé magazine that had adopted a predominantly fiction format prior to World War I and had surpassed *HI-Cosmopolitan* in circulation by the 1930s, died during summer 1956—its circulation above two million copies. *Collier's,* a popular weekly general magazine, died in 1957—its circulation above three million copies. *Woman's Home Companion,* a venerable magazine devoted to traditional fare befitting a readership of disproportionately older women, died the same month as *Collier's*—its circulation also above two million copies. Readers obviously supported these magazines. Advertisers did not. Television was more effective and efficient for reaching general consumers.[20]

Some general magazines played the numbers game against television. Publishers slashed subscription prices to build circulation, then approached advertisers to impress them with the numbers. It was an ill-advised tactic, and hopeless. A popular comedy, *I Love Lucy,* was seen in seventeen million households on a weekly basis at mid-decade. No magazine came close.

Specialization was salvation. New titles appeared, some of which were *Playboy,* 1953, an upscale men's magazine; *TV Guide,* 1953, a weekly with daily program listings and articles about celebrities and topics concerning television; *Sports Illustrated,* 1954, an upscale weekly; *Car and Driver,* 1955; *Bon Appétit,* 1956, for gourmets; *American Association of Retired Persons Magazine,* 1958.

Television affected magazines adversely another way. Fewer people were buying them. Approximately five of every eight adults subscribed to or bought a magazine early in the television era; this soon would decline to four of nine adults, a proportional decrease of almost one-third. The days when four or five magazines rested on a coffee table in the living room were coming to an end.[21]

Finally, by the late 1950s *Cosmopolitan* had an identifiable format. "We were a general woman's magazine," La Barre said. "Not a magazine for any specific type of woman, just any woman. That made us not a very special magazine." But it was special enough to avoid competing with *Good Housekeeping. Cosmopolitan* would not focus on family or household topics or anything directly connected to its corporate sibling's format. Instead, it would try to appeal to married women by including topics of general interest to couples. La Barre remembered that within the hierarchy of the International Magazine Building, commonly called the Hearst Building, *Cosmopolitan* was a lowly place to work. "We put out a good magazine," she said. "Nobody seemed to care."[22]

Its editorial slant toward married women changed the ads seen in *Cosmopolitan*. Formerly plentiful pages of advertisements for automobiles, beer, liquor, wine, and cigarettes yielded to pages selling books, cosmetics, perfume, and shampoo. The liquor ads that had so disturbed William Randolph Hearst amounted to only two or three pages each month at the end of the 1950s, or approximately 5 percent of the total. Steady newsstand sales impressed advertisers willing to pay $3,400 for a full-page ad, a higher rate for lower circulation justified by continuous increases in the cost of paper and ink.

The general women's magazine format developed by O'Connell included a special separate section of articles in every issue and a new department, Service, which featured columns on medicine, new consumer products, and family travel advice. The special separate section contained several articles relating to a single topic and ran as a package at the front of the magazine, comprising thirty-six to forty-two pages, interspersed by ads. Each topic was intended to interest women primarily, but might also interest men. It was not greatly different from Hearst's philosophy of the 1920s. Hearst's editors then relied on fiction, however, and O'Connell had to emphasize nonfiction.

Examples of special sections and their articles that *Cosmopolitan* offered from summer 1956 through 1964 included Beauty ("Modern Science And The Beauty Business," "Have A New Figure By Summer," "Elizabeth Arden—The Woman," "What The Beauty Salon Can Do For You"); New Pleasures ("Should You Belong To A Country Club," "The Lost Art Of Loafing," "Anyone Can Own A Boat"); Travel ("Sketchbook Of The Orient," "Send Your Teenager Abroad," "Thirty-Eight Pounds Of Fashion," "Our Spectacular Two New States—Alaska, Hawaii"); Morals To Murder ("Why They Killed The People They Loved," "Do Women Provoke Sex Attack?," "Our Moral Climate"); International Set ("The Royal Chambermaids," "Pretenders To The Thrones," "Great Families Of The World," "The Sport Royalty Loves Best"); Psychiatry And Emotions ("Middle-Age Divorce," "Fertility Diets," "Trade Homes—Trade Lives," "'I Committed My Daughter'"); Good Health ("Are Woman Troubles Out Of Style," "Cancer And Your Emotions," "Deafness—The Battle Almost Won," "My Victory Over MS"); Residences ("The Good Life In Shaker Heights," "Frontier Living In 1963," "Can Moving Make You Healthier?").

Some aspects of *Cosmopolitan*'s editorial material emulated the widespread format of popular women's magazines later excoriated by Betty Friedan in a landmark feminist book, *The Feminine Mystique*, published in 1963. Friedan, a former writer for various women's magazines, including *Cosmopolitan*, argued that editorial material purposely reinforced the imagery of advertisements to sanctify "the trivia of housewifery." Women's magazines promulgated "the mystique of feminine fulfillment," a concept that a married woman, especially a suburban housewife, should be gratified performing household tasks and assuring the happiness and comfort of her family. Friedan limited her critique to the women's magazines known as the Seven Sisters: *Better Homes and Gardens, Family Circle, Good Housekeeping, Ladies' Home Journal, McCall's, Redbook, Woman's Day.* Advertisements, too, reinforced the messages of the articles—the happy homemaker whose mission in life was clean clothes, lustrous hair and skin, perfect children, and tasty dinners.[23]

The Seven Sisters were immensely popular and profitable publications for middle-class women, primarily those who were homemakers with families or married women who balanced careers with family responsibilities. Average monthly circulation of the Seven Sisters ranged from 3.7 million copies (*Redbook*) to 8.3 million copies (*McCall's*). Advertisements each month filled an average of 70 pages to 120 pages. Hearst Corporation owned one of the Seven Sisters, *Good Housekeeping,* which was the corporate flagship for revenue and profits. (The corporation would buy another of the Seven Sisters, *Redbook,* during the early 1980s.)[24]

O'Connell also introduced an editorial layout plan that few magazines then practiced: the no-jump, or continuation, style. Standard practice in magazines was to continue an article or story from the front of the magazine to the back, requiring a reader to turn from page thirty-three, for example, to page ninety-nine and successive pages to finish the text. O'Connell believed readers would prefer to simply turn pages without searching for a continuation page. (Actually, O'Connell had revived the *Cosmopolitan* no-jump style that existed from 1886 to World War I.) It was a minor improvement and hardly the kind of thing that would boost circulation.[25]

Robert Atherton replaced O'Connell in 1959 and continued the format. Atherton enlivened the covers of *Cosmopolitan* by presenting photographs of celebrities—Hollywood actors and actresses, television performers, celebrity authors, and singers. Atherton added an entertainment section inside the magazine to feature two celebrity profiles each issue, one of a Hollywood star and the other a television star. The expansion of entertainment profiles reduced fiction pages still further. Fiction dwindled to two or three stories and a novella each month by the early 1960s, occupying approximately one-third of the editorial pages.

To stretch the editorial budget for the purchase of fiction by bestselling authors, Atherton relied heavily on stories from beginners eager for publication in a national magazine, no matter that the payment generally was $300 to $800 (equivalent to $2,100 to $5,600 in 2010 dollars). Joyce Carol Oates, Philip Roth, and Kurt Vonnegut Jr. were among authors whose early work appeared in *Cos-*

mopolitan. "Every so often we had enough money to pay really grand," La Barre said. The top fee of $3,000 frequently purchased a mystery manuscript for a novella in the back pages. Mysteries by John D. MacDonald, Ross MacDonald, and Ellery Queen regularly appeared.[26]

La Barre was fiction editor time and again from the mid-1950s into the late 1960s, alternating the job with stints as articles editor. She had started at *Cosmopolitan* as a manuscript reader. "I looked at the slush," La Barre said, referring to unsolicited manuscripts. "We shared a slush pile with *Good Housekeeping.*" Her promotion to fiction editor brought perquisites. "A lot of drinking, a lot of eating," La Barre said. "Mostly drinking." Literary agents for established authors usually submitted fiction to larger magazines and often would try to place a manuscript with *Cosmopolitan* only when better magazines had rejected it. "You were out lunching a lot of time with agents who were pitching you writers' work," she said. "You wasted a lot of time going to these interminable lunches."[27]

Atherton also saved money by assigning associate editors to write some nonfiction articles using pseudonyms. "He didn't want us looking like a small publication," La Barre said, "so we made up names to look like we had a lot of writers."[28]

The magazine rarely printed color photographs other than on the cover. Its page design was boxy and dull, its editorial material scattershot and occasionally repetitive—and its circulation trend inching downward. No wonder, considering that Hearst Corporation spent no money promoting it and none improving it. The magazine was caught in the classic cycle of all doomed periodicals: bouts of cost-cutting, which diminished quality still further; lack of support by the owner, which lowered staff morale; lack of editorial purpose, which affected readership.[29]

Perhaps another sign of *Cosmopolitan*'s lack of stature within the corporation was the decision to move it from the Hearst Building to offices nearby in the General Motors Building, above a showroom for cars. Other magazines, with growing circulation, needed room for additional staff. The relocation during summer 1964 occurred when circulation had fallen below 800,000 copies, the lowest in fifty years. Advertising was down to a monthly average of twenty-nine pages, the lowest since the magazine's infancy the previous century.

Cosmopolitan lost money during 1964. A *Life* article estimated the deficit at perhaps $1.5 million for the year, although this probably was rumor. Richard Berlin would not have permitted such a loss to occur; he would have killed *Cosmopolitan* first.[30]

However, nobody doubted that Berlin was ready to let *Cosmopolitan* die. It was common knowledge inside the Hearst Building and at the magazine office above the GM showroom.[31] "Everyone knew we were on the way out," La Barre said.[32]

Bestseller

Helen Gurley married David Brown, the former managing editor of *Cosmopolitan*, in 1959. At age thirty-seven, she was an account executive at a major advertising agency's branch office in Los Angeles and he was a production executive at a Hollywood movie studio. Upon her marriage, she preferred the designation Mrs. Brown, but her business stationery and personal correspondence stated Helen Gurley Brown. In this, she was ahead of the feminist preference initiated during the 1960s for retaining a woman's family surname upon marriage.[33]

Three years after marrying David, Gurley Brown quit her job at the ad agency. She could afford to. Her book, *Sex and the Single Girl*, a how-to advisory on dating and romance for career women, was a bestseller. The book was a reminiscence of her experiences as a single woman in Los Angeles from the early 1940s to late 1950s, consisting of a collection of anecdotes, replete with reconstructed dialogue and first-name-only characters. The message was that a woman should enjoy her career and romance, should flirt and have affairs, should expect and accept gifts from men, and should marry a man whose income would support her in comfort and style.

Gurley Brown had grown up in a small town in Arkansas, moved with her widowed mother and crippled sister to Los Angeles prior to World War II, worked a succession of menial jobs, and then attended a business college to learn shorthand and secretarial skills. Gurley Brown advanced her career to advertising copywriter and account executive on the basis of excellent writing skills, clever phrasing for ad campaigns, and an awareness that a woman must work harder than a man to prove her ability. "I was always able to write," Gurley Brown said. "The men I worked for depended on me to say exactly what they wanted to say. Memos, business letters, all sorts of correspondence. That's what kept me employed."[34]

Gurley Brown was a media entrepreneur: celebrity author of *Sex and the Single Girl;* host of a syndicated radio program; writer of a syndicated newspaper column (Woman Alone). She and husband David wanted to create a long-term career for her that would outlast the temporary fame. Together they wrote a prospectus for a new magazine, *Femme*—her ideas, his organization of the presentation. The prospectus was ready to show publishers in autumn 1964. "David knew everyone in publishing in New York," Gurley Brown said. David Brown knew editors from his earlier career with *Cosmopolitan* and *Liberty* magazine.[35]

Gurley Brown was a reader of magazines and saw an opportunity for a publication directed toward a readership group that no publisher cared to serve: young career women in their twenties and thirties, some of whom were single and some married without children. *Femme* would not be a family magazine or a traditional women's magazine or a fashion magazine or a magazine for affluent, sophisticated women. It was for "pink-collar" women, those who were office clerks and managers, secretaries and executive assistants, retail clerks and saleswomen—not cashiers or assembly-line workers in light industry and not executives or academicians.

"More than being ignored, the woman on her own—unless she is young enough to fit into the *Mademoiselle* and *Glamour* market (which presumes she will not remain on her own)—is swept under the editorial rug as a group nobody is particularly eager to acknowledge, much less talk to," Gurley Brown declared in the *Femme* prospectus. "When dealt with at all in women's magazines, these girls are often patronized and treated as objects of pity—rejects of our 'twosome' society."[36]

The Seven Sisters definitely were not for unmarried working women, and no valid reason existed for editors and publishers to incorporate editorial material for them. Readers and advertisers were happy the way things were. The only magazines specifically directed toward young women were *Glamour* and *Mademoiselle*. *Glamour* was very much a fashion magazine for working women, not the *Vogue* crowd. *Mademoiselle* was for young women from their late teens to early thirties who attended college or had graduated college. It emphasized fashion and quality fiction, but also contained secondary material on careers, dating, and contemporary social topics.[37]

The prospectus for Gurley Brown's magazine stated its premises for editorial content:

- *Femme is for women who like men.* "Women have stronger sexual desires as they grow older."
- *Femme is for women who like themselves.* "They want to progress financially, physically, emotionally."
- *Femme is optimistic, affirmative, upbeat.* "When it deals with a subject, it will deal in specifics and not in loose principles and generalities."
- *Femme is bold.* "Because women really are bold. In the interest of truth, *Femme* cannot pretend that women are not the equals of men—mentally, physically, and emotionally. *Femme* sees no reason to dwell on this subject, however—the equality of women—but only to acknowledge it by the selection of editorial material."[38]

The prospectus presented data on the number of single, divorced, and widowed women in the United States. It also listed general categories of potential advertisers.

Gurley Brown did not accompany her husband on visits to publishers. She did not know the magazine business and she had no experience as an editor. David Brown showed the prospectus to Dell Magazines and Fawcett

Publications, but both publishers expressed no interest in *Femme*. It was late 1964 and magazines were coping with competition from television for advertisers and the public's attention. *Femme* had a specific readership in mind, but startup costs for a new magazine were formidable: a staff of editors and ad sales representatives on payroll for months prior to publication of the first issue; fees to authors, writers, and photographers for editorial material sufficient to fill the first three issues; promotional expenses for national radio and television commercials, newspaper ads in numerous cities, billboards and countertop displays; sample copies by mail to certain households in desirable demographic areas. Also, the recent deaths of venerable magazines and precarious financial condition of some women's magazines made publishers wary.[39]

David Brown met with Richard Deems, president of Hearst Magazines, in January 1965. Deems liked the idea. He disliked the title. He also was wary of a startup, hardly surprising considering the corporation's tight budget set by Berlin and the persistently dismal performance of the surviving Hearst newspapers, which continued to drain cash from the magazines. Yet because his magazine career had involved selling ads, Deems recognized the market potential for a publication that targeted younger adult women who had jobs. At some point during a discussion with Brown about the concept, Deems seized on the idea that *Cosmopolitan* could be *Femme*.[40]

Deems and Frank Dupuy Jr., the *Cosmopolitan* executive responsible for budgets, marketing, and profitability, persuaded a reluctant Richard Berlin to let Gurley Brown try to save the magazine. Berlin agreed on the condition that Gurley Brown had to operate within the current editorial budget and that a promotional campaign to tout the new *Cosmopolitan* would be inexpensive. The plan was to capitalize on Gurley Brown's status as a celebrity and her notoriety as author of a "sex book."[41]

Deems and Dupuy were to supervise her and monitor her decisions. "Dick was my sponsor," Gurley Brown said. "Frank was my angel." Neither of the executives knew exactly what she might do with the magazine when it came to specific articles, illustrations, and photographs. She had assured them that *Cosmopolitan* would not be prurient or explicit. Still, they had hired a person with absolutely no magazine experience and no management background.[42]

Gurley Brown did not negotiate her own contract. Her literary agent and David Brown handled all the details. In mid-February 1965, Gurley Brown signed a two-year pact with Hearst Corporation. Her salary was $35,000 the first year (equivalent to $245,000 in 2010 dollars).[43]

Helen Gurley Brown had no doubt she would succeed. "I knew what I liked to read," she said. "That's what I wanted *Cosmopolitan* to be."[44]

8

Transformation

"Frisky"

Helen Gurley Brown first mentioned her idea for a nude male centerfold to executives at Hearst Magazines during autumn 1968. "I wanted someone fun, frisky," Gurley Brown said. Executives were not thrilled. *Cosmopolitan* already had endured ridicule and scorn from national magazines and network television programs for its seemingly obsessive preoccupation with sex since Gurley Brown had become editor three years earlier. However, all the negative attention was outweighed by simple economics. *Cosmopolitan* had increased its average monthly circulation from 782,000 copies to 1.05 million copies during the three-year span, and a consequent influx of advertisers had raised the monthly average from twenty-nine ad pages to sixty-four ad pages, amounting to additional actual revenue of approximately $157,000 each issue (equivalent to $942,000 in 2010 dollars). *Cosmopolitan* was making money again.[1]

On a practical note, though, a nude centerfold could cause problems with distributors and retailers who might fear angry reactions from customers at grocery stores, drugstores, and bookstores where the magazine was displayed at checkout counters. One concern was that a promotional cover blurb for a nude centerfold might attract minors who would open the magazine with or without parents present; another concern was that some vendors, especially in small towns and southern states, might put the magazine behind the checkout counter to avoid offending customers, which could reduce sales substantially. *Cosmopolitan* relied on single-copy buyers for almost its entire circulation. "The people at Hearst weren't too pleased with the idea," Gurley Brown said. "They thought we were going too far."[2]

Gurley Brown proceeded to search for the right man anyway. Executives at Hearst Magazines had disliked other ideas she had proposed regarding articles about sexual topics usually avoided by mainstream magazines—adultery, premarital sex, one-night stands. They almost always had agreed to publish eventually because the text itself never was explicit. "The Hearst people were putting up with me," Gurley Brown said. "They did that because of the sales. Early on, we were selling practically the entire print run every month. Ninety percent of what we placed at the newsstands. That was unheard of." True, the percentage of newsstand sales was remarkable for a magazine of the era, but the *Cosmopolitan* of Ray Long had sold equally well forty years earlier.

She focused her search for a centerfold on Hollywood actors. "Movies were so important then," Gurley Brown said. "Television was popular, but not important." A popular movie actor of the time, James Coburn, was chosen to pose. *Cosmopolitan* had published a profile article on Coburn during summer 1967, and Gurley Brown thought him boyish, charming, handsome, and suave. Coburn posed on the condition that he retain authority to select photographs for publication; with his wife's agreement he sent two photos from the session to Gurley Brown. She did not like them.[3]

Her memo to Hearst executives in December 1968 explained the problem: "Apparently he is in his mystical phase right now and they feel this fairly represents him whereas I'm thinking of something that's fun and all American and big smile and all that. I feel this feature must be absolutely right or not worth its investment." The investment would be approximately $42,000 for a four-color, three-page centerfold in a million copies of the magazine, which also would require a special folding process for insertion. Gurley Brown ended the memo to executives humorously, "If you ever see anybody famous and beautiful and male disrobing unexpectedly at a party, I hope you'll run for your camera!" The president of Hearst Magazines, Richard Deems, scrawled a reply to her, "How about Dick Nixon?!"[4]

Paul Newman was her next choice, but he refused to pose. So the idea was in limbo for a few years. There was no urgency. *Cosmopolitan* was selling well and ad pages were increasing, centerfold or not. Then an appearance on the *Tonight Show* in January 1972 provided inspiration. "I was a PR maven," Gurley Brown said. "If anyone asked me to speak or to appear as a panelist or to be on television, I would be there." Gurley Brown was a good conversationalist who could be counted on to talk about sexual topics without risking possible censure by the Federal Communications Commission if any viewers complained. Gurley Brown was a guest on the *Tonight Show* four times during 1971, her first year on the program.[5]

The *Tonight Show* on NBC was a late-night television institution by the early 1970s, and it attracted viewers from nine million households, or triple the number of any other late-night fare. The host, Johnny Carson, was the reason for its popularity. Carson was amiable, clever, folksy, witty, and a terrific interviewer who treated each guest politely. Gurley Brown appreciated it. On other television programs, she had encountered criticism either by a host or other guests, who berated her about *Cosmopolitan*'s emphasis on advising women to entrap, lure, or otherwise seduce men. These confrontations often had upset her, and sometimes she cried off-camera after a program ended.[6]

Besides offering a friendly setting to its guests, the *Tonight Show* format featured a comedy monologue, a comedy skit, and a series of five- to ten-minute interviews with four or five guests, at least one of whom was either a singer or a comedian who would also perform. Carson deftly guided his guests through discussions about topics familiar to them while also coaxing gossipy tidbits from them regarding the entertainment business. Carson, the host since 1962, had persuaded NBC to give him several weeks vacation annually and several Monday nights off whenever he wanted a day of rest from a weekend standup performance in Las Vegas. Guest hosts substituted for him. Sometime in January 1972 a scheduler for the *Tonight Show* telephoned Gurley Brown to ask if she would be available on Monday, the thirty-first. The scheduler told her a guest host would substitute for Carson, and wondered if it would be a problem for her. "A lot of people simply would not appear on the show if Johnny wasn't there," Gurley Brown said. "I'd go no matter who was host. It was wonderful for *Cosmopolitan*." She did not know who the guest host would be that night, not that it mattered.[7]

The day of the program Gurley Brown worked at the magazine's offices in the General Motors Building near Columbus Circle in Manhattan, then took a cab to the NBC studios at Rockefeller Center not quite a dozen blocks away. There she met the guest host, Burt Reynolds. Gurley Brown had found her centerfold. "He was handsome, humorous, wonderful body, frisky," she said. Reynolds, at age thirty-six, had acted in several movies and had starred in a weekly television series as a detective. Personable and possessed with a self-deprecating sense of humor, Reynolds had substituted for Carson previously. "During our conversation, I asked him if he would pose for us," Gurley Brown said. Reynolds agreed.[8]

They met the next day at *Cosmopolitan* to discuss details, including a guarantee by her that the magazine would only publish the nude photograph once. Gurley Brown contacted Francesco Scavullo, a fashion photographer who did almost every *Cosmopolitan* cover for her for thirty years. Scavullo scheduled an immediate photo session. Reynolds posed and selected his favorite photograph for publication. Gurley Brown loved it. "It was so wonderful!" She instructed the magazine's production manager to get the centerfold into the next possible issue.

"At the time, you know, men liked to look at women naked," Gurley Brown said. "Well, nobody talked about it, but women liked to look at men naked. I did." Men's magazines such as *Playboy*, famous for its nude female centerfold since its inception in 1953, and *Penthouse* sold millions of copies every month.[9]

Gurley Brown would be a guest on the *Tonight Show* another fifty-four times, but no appearance was more beneficial to *Cosmopolitan* than the night she met Burt Reynolds. The April 1972 *Cosmopolitan* cover displayed a diagonal banner announcing "At Last A Male Nude Centerfold—The Naked Truth About Guess Who!!" The photo featured a nude Reynolds lying on his back on a bear rug, a lit cigarillo in his mouth, his left hand placed over his genitals. Text preceding the centerfold justified its publication: "Some people (mostly men, past fifty!) thought our idea a perfect scandal. . . . The time for our photograph had not only come, it was long past due. We had the feeling that the reason naked women so abound in magazines, while there is such a dearth of nude men, is that, until recently, those in control of publications have been men, who thought only of pleasing their brother men, and neglected the visual appetites of us equally appreciative girls." The issue sold out completely across the nation, a total of 1.55 million copies.[10]

The day after *Cosmopolitan* was on the newsstands Reynolds walked out the door of his residence and had to thread his way through a mob of women standing around his car, each holding a copy of the magazine. For months, Reynolds would finish a theater performance of a play in different cities and happily sign autographs for women who had brought magazines to the play. His role in *Deliverance,* a movie released in July 1972, established Reynolds as a star actor. *Cosmopolitan* played a small part in his career, Gurley Brown said. "He had been a movie star; now he was a celebrity."[11]

A similar change in status affected *Cosmopolitan.* Before the centerfold issue, the magazine was known; after, it was notorious. Some stores in rural areas, mostly in the Midwest and South, removed the magazine from racks and placed copies behind the checkout counter for a while. *Cosmopolitan* did not make centerfolds a habit. Nearly two years passed until another centerfold was published, then more than three years until another.[12]

Cosmopolitan's centerfold issue was significant and symbolic. Significant because *Cosmopolitan* had crossed the threshold from mainstream magazine to sex magazine in the public mind, albeit for a quasi-feminist purpose and only on a rare basis. Symbolic because *Cosmopolitan* had completed its transformation to an entirely new category of women's magazine. Other publishers noticed: *New Woman,* a publication for working women with families, started in 1970; *Playgirl* magazine, which included a nude male centerfold, began in 1973; *Working Woman,* which focused on single and married careerists, appeared in 1976.[13]

In seven years, Gurley Brown had established an identity for *Cosmopolitan* as a magazine for young women whose personal circumstances, education, and training had taken them to careers as bank tellers, clerks, receptionists, secretaries, typists, and other "worker bee" jobs, and whose personal goal was to have a career, be independent, meet men, and marry one with a good income. *Cosmopolitan* provided these young working women with information about living alone, being fashionable on a budget, enjoying inexpensive vacations, attracting men, handling or initiating office romances, coping with office politics, and having sex on their own terms. To advertisers, *Cosmopolitan* pitched its demographic target as women in their twenties and thirties. But that was for business purposes. To Gurley Brown, young was attitude: "Dreams, hopes, fun! We inspired women to live."[14]

The summer after the centerfold issue *Cosmopolitan* attained a consistent circulation of 1.6 million copies each month. Gurley Brown earned $78,000 for 1972. (Equivalent to $390,000 in 2010 dollars.) Hearst Corporation reaped financial rewards, too, for its willingness to let her experiment with a dull, irrelevant publication rather than kill it. Not only had *Cosmopolitan* doubled its circulation, but advertisers bought a monthly average of 112 pages during summer 1972, which generated $434,000 actual revenue each month—compared with $57,000 actual revenue each month during summer 1965.[15]

The magazine's transformation proved its appeal and relevance to a readership composed mostly of women in their twenties and thirties, most of them married, some divorced, most without a college education, but most of them employed and earning above-median incomes, with most living in cities and suburbs. *Cosmopolitan* created its own niche within a very desirable demographic for advertisers. Its transformation also moved the magazine and its editor to the center of a furious debate about the meaning of feminism.[16]

The Formula

Cosmopolitan purposely became a niche magazine for a readership disdained or ignored by the Seven Sisters women's magazines. Those dominant, prosperous publications had missed an opportunity to build readership among younger married and unmarried women who worked outside the home. If editors from the early 1960s onward had allocated some pages to material directed at these women, while maintaining an emphasis on items for the core readership of married women with children, *Cosmopolitan* might have had a harder time establishing itself. As it was, Gurley Brown's format attracted them. *Cosmopolitan* aimed its eclectic format composed of articles about careers, dating, lifestyle, relationships, and sex at a target readership with tremendous potential. No other magazine had sought that particular demographic group by offering a complete editorial package. "It was common sense," Gurley Brown said, "but nobody had bothered to think about a magazine for young career women who had full lives." Her perceptiveness, accompanied by impressive determination, ultimately restored *Cosmopolitan* to its flagship status at the Hearst Corporation.[17]

The *Cosmopolitan* makeover had begun with the hiring of Helen Gurley Brown by Hearst Magazines in mid-March 1965. Richard Deems, the magazine division's president, and Frank Dupuy Jr., the magazine's publisher, promised her great latitude, but not complete autonomy, to implement her ideas. Gurley Brown planned to make *Cosmopolitan* an expression of her own outlook on life, and to rely on topics presented in *Sex and the Single Girl* for magazine material. Discussions among the three of them about the magazine's format pertained generally, but not specifically, to subjects the magazine would publish. Deems would review all editorial material, cover design, and cover blurbs for each issue; it was his prerogative to reject any material he considered inappropriate for whatever reason. Dupuy was responsible for the business side and would handle any problems, or potential trouble, with advertisers concerning *Cosmopolitan*'s editorial material. Deems, Dupuy, and Richard Berlin, the president of Hearst Corporation who had resisted hiring Gurley Brown, fully realized that *Cosmopolitan*'s risqué material might alienate the public and advertisers.[18]

Hearst Corporation by the mid-1960s was a risk-averse publisher. Except for *Harper's Bazaar*, an avant-garde fashion publication that often provoked a mixture of delight and outrage with its modernistic photo layouts, the corporation's other magazines earned healthy profits delivering reliable, useful material: *Good Housekeeping* for middle-class family women; *House Beautiful* to affluent homeowners; *Popular Mechanics* to tinkerers and do-it-themselves repairmen; *Town & Country* for wealthy residents of leafy suburban enclaves; *Motor, Motor-Boating*, and *Sports Afield* for specific niche categories; and *American Druggist*, a trade industry publication. Into this staid corporate culture walked Gurley Brown, hired in an act of desperation by executives who hoped to rescue a legacy magazine. In conversations, letters, and memos, Gurley Brown sought to assure Deems, Dupuy, and Berlin that *Cosmopolitan* would not cross the line to sleaziness.

"I don't think prurient or dirty stuff sells," Gurley Brown had stated in the formal concept for the magazine she submitted to Hearst Corporation early in 1965 prior to signing a contract. "But a pretty bosom, a discussion of a girl's love life, yes." She warned executives that converting *Cosmopolitan* to a publication for "reasonably sophisticated modern-minded" readers would require articles on topics that were "more visceral." The magazine must write about "exciting, emotional things."[19]

Cosmopolitan's alternately candid, casual, and jejune treatment of sexual relationships—sexual attraction in social settings and the workplace, premarital sex, extramarital sex—was new to the world of mainstream magazines during the mid-1960s. Those years were a transitional era for American media concerning the presentation of sexual topics. Editors, correspondents, columnists, and writers at magazines were fully aware of the various types of consensual sexual relationships that occurred between married and unmarried adults. Despite this awareness, editors and publishers of mainstream magazines were reticent to reveal this reality on their pages. The failure to present articles and commentary about the effects of sexual attraction, conduct, and tension on personal relationships and in the workplace distanced them from readers.[20]

Reality aversion among mainstream magazines was based on concerns that sexual topics would upset some readers for reasons of inappropriateness or impropriety, which might result in cancellations of subscriptions or a lower rate of subscription renewals. Also, some advertisers might pull their ads because they would not want to sponsor such material. Public opinion polls apparently verified these concerns of editors and publishers. A Gallup Poll conducted in 1969 reported that 68 percent of respondents agreed "it is wrong for a man and woman to have sex relations before marriage"; and it was not uncommon for employers to fire unmarried women employees who were pregnant. The polls revealed that younger respondents, ages twenty to twenty-nine, were less certain about premarital sex being wrong; half of respondents in that age group considered it wrong, while three-fourths of respondents older than forty-five did. On the matter of extramarital sex, a National Opinion Research Center poll conducted in 1973 reported that 84 percent of respondents considered it wrong.[21]

A certain hypocrisy existed, however. Many respondents told pollsters one thing about their attitudes on sexual behavior while actually behaving the opposite. On the matter of premarital sex, despite the overwhelming disapproval reported by the Gallup Poll, other researchers for various social science projects during the late 1960s to mid-1970s ascertained that 89 percent of men and 63 percent of women had engaged in premarital sex. The qualifier for those percentages, though, was that half of the women only had premarital sex with their fiancés. Also, social science researchers of the era determined that 31 percent of married men and 19 percent of married women had extramarital sex. Mainstream magazines wrote for the people supposedly represented by poll data, not for those whose conduct was known to the few in academe familiar with the research. Gurley Brown knew nothing about the research either; she just knew people.[22]

Beginning in mid-1965, *Cosmopolitan* violated mainstream standards— and got away with it. Its single-copy sales began to climb steadily and advertisers began to buy additional pages. Evidently, *Cosmopolitan* was closer to a realistic perspective about adult relationships than public opinion polls indicated. Gurley Brown was not alone—far from it—in recognizing the importance and relevance of sex to Americans. Society was confronting the topic of sex publicly during the 1960s, a decade of cultural and social conflict. *Human*

Sexual Response, an explicit report concerning sexual gratification and tech-niques, generated much controversy upon its release in 1966. Some movies were portraying sexual relationships, although not sex itself, and the effects of sexual tension on young adults and married couples; adverse public reaction compelled Hollywood studio executives in 1967 to create a rating system so parents would know whether a movie had an adult theme or steamy scenes. *Everything You Always Wanted to Know about Sex, but Were Afraid to Ask* was an adult self-education bestseller in 1969. Most mainstream media, however, pre-ferred to pretend that sex was not part of the public agenda.

Mainstream magazines did not admit their timidity. The Seven Sisters per-sistently avoided the topics of marital sexual dissatisfaction and the reality of workplace relationships among adults. Other magazines were contemptuous and scornful of Gurley Brown and *Cosmopolitan*. *Life*, a weekly pictorial maga-zine with a circulation of several million copies, summarized Gurley Brown's imprint on *Cosmopolitan* eight months into her reign: "The philosophy is sim-ple. Old-fashioned morality is out if it cuts down on the excitement and fun. Affairs and divorces are in, provided you can handle all of the problems." The article did recognize the variety of material *Cosmopolitan* published in addi-tion to sexual topics. "Page after page of the new *Cosmopolitan* is jammed with advice, heavy on the second person singular, about diets, exercises, yoga, hair styling, nose straightening," *Life* noted. The article also stated that the primary message of the magazine was for women "to be completely and responsively feminine." *Life* doubted the wisdom of an editorial strategy predominately fo-cused on women's relationships with men: "Some critics feel that *Cosmo* will have to broaden its perspectives beyond the simple question of catching a man, lest the readers become bored."[23]

Esquire also profiled the most well-known woman editor of the day. "If, at times, Helen Gurley Brown and her magazine are offensive, it is only because almost every popular success is offensive," the writer commented. "She is dem-onstrating, rather forcefully, that there are over 1,000,000 American women who are willing to spend sixty cents to read not about politics, not about the female-liberation movement, not about the war in Vietnam, but merely about how to get a man." Although directed at *Cosmopolitan*, a similar observation about a lack of substance also would have applied to the Seven Sisters maga-zines. Feminists and media critics alike commented on the insular world of women's magazines where momentous international, national, political, and social topics rarely intruded on pages.[24]

William F. Buckley Jr., a conservative political ideologue and editor-publisher of *National Review*, devoted a cover commentary in his magazine to *Cosmo-politan*. Buckley referred to the simplistic, sophomoric reasoning expressed by Gurley Brown in her monthly introductory column and to the overall theme of the magazine, which condoned adultery and premarital sex, and encouraged sexual encounters at a woman's behest. "You do understand? It's your duty, madam, not to go to bed with anybody, unless you want to," Buckley sarcastically commented. "Who says the Cosmopolitan Girl is without a sense of restraint?"[25]

Although the centerfold issue of April 1972 seemed to validate media judgment of *Cosmopolitan*—it was, after all, nothing but a sex magazine for women—an examination of every monthly issue Gurley Brown edited during her first seven years indicated the media characterization was somewhat skewed. Only a small percentage of articles and standard monthly columns actually dealt primarily with sexual topics. Certainly, *Cosmopolitan* articles routinely contained sexual innuendos and allusions to sex, but articles and columns specifically about relationships and sex were a mixture of risqué themes, suggestive anecdotes, and traditional moralistic advice. Text rarely was explicit, and descriptions of sexual situations were not erotic.

The decision to concentrate on separate phases of Gurley Brown's editorial era—the first from summer 1965 through 1972, the second from autumn 1972 to the magazine's centennial in March 1986—was based on the Reynolds centerfold being a clear marker. If readers, vendors, and advertisers had reacted negatively to the display of a nearly nude man in *Cosmopolitan,* the issues of autumn 1972 onward would have refrained from publishing overtly sexual material for fear of further public backlash or loss of advertising. Instead, *Cosmopolitan* became bolder, albeit incrementally.

An examination of eighty-seven monthly issues of *Cosmopolitan* published from July 1965—Gurley Brown's first actual issue—through summer 1972 sought to determine the nature of its nonfiction editorial material. Despite the derogatory comments made about it, the magazine was not all that daring. Of the 1,503 nonfiction articles presented in eighty-seven issues, sex was the topic in 78 (5.2 percent) and personal relationships were the focus of 161 (10.7 percent); other articles listed in the tables of contents were celebrity or newsmaker profiles (16.2 percent), décor/fashion (7.6 percent), career/financial (7.3 percent), movies/music/television (5.8 percent), health, excluding any regarding sexually transmitted diseases, which were categorized as sex topics (5.2 percent), political/social (3.6 percent), and travel (3.5 percent).

Because controversy and criticism pertaining to *Cosmopolitan* during the first phase of Gurley Brown's tenure as editor related to its articles on relationships and sex, an examination of editorial material in those categories permitted an evaluation of presentations on topics in those categories. Of the 161 articles on personal relationships, 16 dealt with extramarital sex, 9 with divorce or remarriage, 5 with premarital cohabitation, and the other 131 dealt with a range of topics relevant to unmarried women interested in romance with men or divorced women who were dating. Of the 78 items on sex, 11 dealt with sexual fantasies or fetishes, 4 with female masturbation, 4 with women initiating sexual activity, 2 with female orgasm, and the other 57 with a range of topics pertaining to sexual dissatisfaction, lack of interest in sex by a woman or her spouse, physical discomfort during sex, and so-called open marriages in which spouses agreed they could have sex with other people. (For purposes of categorization, this topic seemed sexual rather than relational.)

The text of articles concerning relationships and sex was not explicit. Specific sexual activity and methods of sexual pleasure were alluded to or suggested, not described. A few articles mentioned clitoris and vagina to explain arousal or physical response, but male genitalia was the preferred term rather than penis.

Photographs on inside pages also rarely were explicit. A limited study by scholars of photographs published in *Cosmopolitan* for 1965–1985 indicated that 2 percent showed fully exposed breasts, 3 percent showed partially exposed female buttocks, 4 percent showed partially exposed male buttocks, none showed either female or male genitals, and none showed female or male pubic hair.[26]

The examination of all eighty-seven monthly issues from summer 1965 through summer 1972 determined that in almost every other respect *Cosmopolitan* was an ordinary magazine for women. It published an abundance of editorial material devoted to beauty tips, celebrity profiles, decorating, popular culture features, and recipes helpful to women living alone. Its titles for these topics usually were catchy, provocative, sensationalistic, or titillating while the text itself usually was mundane.

Titles of articles were occasionally borderline risqué, but the majority would have fit in any mainstream women's magazine: Consider these sample titles for articles:

• "Careers: Four Right Jobs For Four Bright Girls"; "How To Be In Advertising"; "Nine To Five? Never!"

(*Cosmopolitan*'s career articles had encouraged women to consider owning a business and preparing for jobs usually associated with men. Articles profiled women who were either an airline pilot, architect, bank examiner, civil engineer, stock broker, or veterinarian. But the magazine also too often featured careers usually feasible for women who resided in big cities. An example was "It's Great To Be The Boss." The article focused on ten career women: two art gallery owners, a celebrity hair stylist, a photographers' agent, a documentary film producer, a clothes boutique owner, a personnel agency owner, a theatrical producer, an interior decorator, and a restaurant owner.)[27]

- Décor: "Mirrors Make Your Apartment Grow!"; "Bedrooms That Say 'Stay Here'!"
- Diets: "Working Girl's Hamburger Diet"; "Forbidden Fruit For Indulgent Dieters"; "Absolutely New—Diet Your Way Out Of Depression"; "Seductive Cookery"; "Six Immoral Chocolate Desserts!"
- Fashion: "Step Into My Closet"; "Swimsuits He'll Love You In This Summer"; "Dress To Be Undressed"
- Relationships: "What's Happened To Office Romances?"; "Diary Of An Unfaithful Wife"; "Hi-Fi Your Way Into His Heart"; "How Much Will He Earn?"; "Meeting His Mother"; "How To Buy Ties And Pipes"; "Night School Isn't All Education"; "Is There A Life After Marriage?"; "What Does Your Dog Think Of Your Boyfriend?"
- Travel: "A Girl's Fabulous Irish Vacation"; "Where The Men Are"; "Love Affair With The U.S. Virgins"; "What's New From London?!"
- Miscellaneous: "How To Give Your Cat A Pill"; "Girl's Guide To Churchgoing"; "Sangria And Other Winy Wonders"; "How To Fix An Electric Plug"; "What It Means To Be A Negro Girl"; "What It Means To Be A Protestant Girl"; "What It's Like To Be A Catholic Girl"; "Teeth-Capping Anyone?"; "20 Tips On Making Friends In the Big City"

Finally, columns such as The Analyst's Couch and The Five-Minute Gourmet Dinner dispensed advice on anxieties of the mind and clues to basic gastronomy. Columnists recommended budget vacation destinations, reviewed books and music, offered diet tips, and provided brief descriptions of new cosmetic, fragrance, and hair-care products. For the latter items, each was advertised in the magazine. *Cosmopolitan* was a complete package. It offered entertainment and information, of some worth if not absolutely credible.

All written material in *Cosmopolitan,* whether about ordinary topics or relationships and sex, provided evidence of Gurley Brown's standards and style. She edited everything. She specified sentences to be rewritten, often choosing phrases and terms. Sometimes she consulted with the writers, but mostly she told associate editors to tell writers what revisions were necessary and to make them whether or not a writer agreed. Gurley Brown insisted on lively descriptive writing, short declarative sentences, numerous quotes from people who were interviewed, an everyday vocabulary, and brevity; most articles consisted of four pages of text and some had only two pages. Liveliness to Gurley Brown meant plenty of italicized words and an abundance of exclamation points. *Time* mercilessly parodied the *Cosmopolitan* style in a sarcastic article replete with italics and exclamations, and other magazines poked fun, too, with a full-page *New Yorker* satire capturing the silliness.[28]

On a substantive note, *Cosmopolitan* was lax about customary standards for nonfiction articles practiced by most mainstream magazines. The *Cosmopolitan* trademark insisted on reliance on expert opinion from a single source rather than multiple sources, despite having weeks to complete an article; almost no data from reports or studies by government agencies or credible research-ers; frequent use of pseudonyms and first-name-only identifications of people depicted; photographs of models rather than actual people supposedly quoted; no disclosure of free airfare, hotel rooms, and meals to travel writers; lurid or risqué tabloid-style titles.

Perhaps readers of *Cosmopolitan* did not notice or miss the perspective tru-ly informative articles should provide. Perhaps readers did not care whether a person whose experiences were described in articles was an individual or a composite of two or more people. Perhaps it did not matter either whether real names or pseudonyms were used for identification. Perhaps credibility was not essential. Perhaps readers did not know why standards were important.

An example of why standards meant something appeared in the July 1968 *Cosmopolitan*. It was brazen deceit. Liz Smith, a *Cosmopolitan* associate editor who later became a syndicated gossip columnist for newspapers, wrote "The Park Avenue Call Girl," a profile of a prostitute who had sex with wealthy cli-ents. It would be fair to assume that readers realized the photograph accom-panying the article was a model, not the call girl herself, and it would be fair to assume that readers did not expect the woman's real name to be published, that Nicky was a pseudonym. However, it also would be fair to assume that readers did not expect the article to be pure fiction.

According to Smith's autobiography published thirty years later, Gurley Brown assigned her to find a high-class prostitute to interview for an article about the life of a contemporary courtesan. Smith explained that Gurley Brown was im-pressed by the range of people Smith knew and assumed that if anyone could find a call girl for wealthy men in the city Smith could. Smith tried mightily, but none of her acquaintances would admit to knowing a prostitute.

Discouraged but not defeated, Smith discussed her dilemma with a friend, who reminded her about a faux socialite they had met who might be helpful. The socialite was not a call girl, but Smith and the friend believed she somehow could help imagine it. A purely speculative endeavor from the start, Smith took a bottle of wine along to smooth the interview with the woman. On the basis of wine and mutual fantasy, the socialite and Smith concocted a story. Smith wrote the article. *Cosmopolitan* published it as fact.[29]

"Let's call her Nicky," the article by Smith informed readers. "She is a call girl who just happens to live on Park Avenue. She is twenty-eight years old. She sleeps with men she knows and men she doesn't know—for money. And she has been doing it since she was nineteen. Last year she made over $40,000." Nicky charged clients $200 an hour. None of this was real.[30]

Also fake were descriptive details about furniture and décor in the fictitious Park Avenue apartment rented by fictitious Nicky, her arrangements to sched-ule male clients, and the statement that Nicky "rattled off a litany of prominent names" of society women who formerly were prostitutes and had met their wealthy husbands on the job. To unsuspecting readers who had no reason to think *Cosmopolitan* was deceiving them, Smith reported that Nicky "included names on the Best-Dressed List and some now in the Social Register." The article amplified this aspect: "The women, now canonized by the sacred Mrs. before their names, had all known how to please."[31]

It was a slur, perfect fodder for gossip. The false statement undoubtedly cast suspicion, or led to speculation, on many women married to wealthy men in New York City. It was not libelous, of course, because no individual woman was identified nor was the potential group of wealthy women in the city small enough for a lawsuit on grounds of probable identification.

Smith did not confess the deception to anyone until several years had passed, and only because a situation arose that could have elevated her fakery to outright fraud. Sometime during the early 1970s, Smith had lunch with movie director Alan Pakula. Smith and Pakula met because the director wanted to hire her as a consultant for *Klute,* a thriller movie about a call girl in New York City. Pakula sought authenticity, and believed that Smith could provide it because of the magazine article about Nicky, which a production assistant had clipped and filed for future reference. Pakula offered Smith a fee to advise actress Jane Fonda for the movie. Smith, belatedly stricken with conscience, revealed the fabrication to Pakula. They laughed.[32] (*Klute* was a box office hit, and Jane Fonda received an Academy Award for best actress in 1972, without any advice from Smith.)

Gurley Brown was a storyteller, too, but not to the extent of concocting fact from fiction. (Her explanation to readers in April 1972 about the Reynolds centerfold had stated as fact, "About a year ago, *Cosmo* decided to find a handsome, huggable man, and then to run an enticing nude centerfold of our choice." Her memo to magazine executives referring to the Coburn photographs was written in December 1968, and it mentioned that the search had started months earlier.) The editor instructed associate editors to make vignettes "authentic" by omitting details that contradicted an article's premise. This insistence on style to the detriment of factual substance prevented *Cosmopolitan* from attaining stature among its magazine peers for credibility and substance. It also contributed to the disdain with which it was held within mainstream media. It certainly did not impede commercial success. "*Cosmo* had to fascinate people," Gurley Brown said.[33]

Upon starting work in mid-March 1965, Gurley Brown concentrated on two things: learning how to be a magazine editor and figuring out how quickly she could change the magazine. "We published nearly three months in advance," she said. "I walked into my office in March and we already were at work on July."

The time lag was her first lesson. Other lessons pertained to operating within a budget for written material and photographs, assessing strengths and weaknesses of associate editors, supervising the flow of text and editorial art (illustrations and photos) for production deadlines, choosing columnists and reviewers, developing ideas for articles, and imposing her will on the editorial staff. "I just got here that first week and was overwhelmed with what I had to learn to do."

When she walked through the *Cosmopolitan* offices her first day on the job, Gurley Brown was amazed by the stacks of manuscripts atop desks. Many articles were months old, never published because the size of the magazine continued to shrink as advertisers quit buying space. Other manuscripts arrived unsolicited by mail or from agents representing writers whose work had appeared in other low- to mid-tier magazines. Aware that a gem of an article might be hidden in a stack, Gurley Brown could not risk relying on the judgment of associate editors who were not familiar with her editorial vision for *Cosmopolitan*. Reading manuscripts became her life. "I read them all," Gurley Brown said. "I read them there. I read them at home. I took them to bed."

Disappointment was the predominant reaction. "Few were very interesting. Writers were writing to impress other writers; they were a very literary style, very self-conscious," she said. "The problem was using fancy words instead of everyday words. You must converse with your reader. Write the way you would talk. A person shouldn't have to have a dictionary in their lap when reading a magazine! I could not let that go on."

From the start, Gurley Brown shaped *Cosmopolitan* to conform to her intuitive sense of what a modern magazine for a modern woman should be. There were no focus groups to respond to ideas for articles, no marketing research surveys to set parameters for editorial material. *Cosmopolitan* would succeed or fail on the basis of her own personal preferences. "I had not gone to college and studied literature or the great philosophers or history," she said. "I had gone to high school, went to business school. I learned typing, shorthand. I was not an ignorant person. I read newspapers and magazines. I knew people, what they were like and what interested them."

Although her ultimate goal was a dramatic transformation of the magazine, Gurley Brown confronted a reality every new editor must cope with: filling the pages of the next issue. For the first two or three months, she had to work with editorial material already in the pipeline. Because the previous editor had commissioned the articles, Gurley Brown's only choices were either to discard an article entirely, yet pay a kill-fee to the writer, or to salvage an article by rewriting it. Hearst Magazines had not given her a bigger budget for *Cosmopolitan*, and would not approve additional money until the magazine showed evidence of popularity. Therefore, discarding all the manuscripts atop the desks was not an option.

"I decided I could use the most interesting manuscripts, but they had to be extensively revised," she said. An associate editor would contact the writer to discuss a rewrite. Writers had not encountered such treatment by *Cosmopolitan.* "Very few were happy about that," Gurley Brown said. "I gave each of them the option of rewriting it themselves or letting us do it."

She told associate editors to recruit new writers. "We needed new names, new approaches," she said. "I explained what must be done. *Cosmopolitan* must change." Change came, but it was incremental, not radical. A few years passed before the magazine truly established itself as reliably racy. "We really didn't do outrageous material," Gurley Brown said. "Everything was written in good taste."[34]

Harriet La Barre, a *Cosmopolitan* associate editor for several years prior to Gurley Brown's arrival and a person who survived the transition, remembered the reaction among colleagues. "We didn't know what to think when she arrived," La Barre said. "No one knew about her. She had written a best-selling book, and suddenly she was our editor. The other editors at *Cosmopolitan* had worked there or at other magazines. They had experience. Helen did not."[35]

A few editors quit or were told to find jobs at other Hearst magazines or anywhere else if they resisted the makeover. "You can imagine their horror that I was editor," Gurley Brown said. "She wrote a sex book! How can she be editor?" One who quit was the managing editor, a woman. The managing editor was the second most important person at *Cosmopolitan*—responsible for scheduling assignments, coordinating the process of rewriting and final editing, arranging for illustrations and photographs, enforcing deadlines, and planning editorial material for future issues. Gurley Brown quickly promoted an associate editor, a man, to managing editor. "I did not have time to discuss our new direction," Gurley Brown said. "*Cosmo* was dying."[36]

Reaction ranged from bemusement to embarrassment among executives at Hearst Corporation and editors at other magazines within the Hearst Building, a block east of *Cosmopolitan*'s offices. "All the men who worked at Hearst laughed at her at first," La Barre said, "at this sex-crazed person and her magazine."

In nearby magazine offices in midtown Manhattan, editors regarded Gurley Brown with derision. "They were sneering at her," La Barre said. "What is *Cosmopolitan* doing hiring that kind of person?" Gurley Brown not only was an outsider, having worked at an ad agency in Hollywood, but she lacked a family pedigree and had not attended an elite college, unlike many women employed as associate editors or editorial assistants at national magazines. A disproportionate number of graduates of private women's colleges—Mount Holyoke, Radcliffe, Smith, Vassar, Wellesley—and women graduates of top-tier, highly selective public universities worked at publishing houses and magazine offices in New York City. They had low-paying positions, but wealthy families often subsidized their daughters so they could enjoy the social swirl that accompanied working in the media center of the nation.[37]

Gurley Brown also was one of only two women editors actually in control of a women's magazine, another factor that made her an outsider. At the Seven Sisters magazines in 1965, *Woman's Day* had a woman editor-in-chief and *Ladies' Home Journal* had a woman managing editor, the number-two position. Fifteen men held the top editorial positions at the Seven Sisters. Five years later, only two women held the positions of editor, executive editor, and managing editor—Gurley Brown and the *Ladies' Home Journal* person—while nineteen men did. Women at the mid-level editor positions of art, copy chief, departmental, fiction, and nonfiction did outnumber men; thirty-eight to twenty in 1965 and thirty-two to twelve in 1970.[38]

La Barre and other associate editors at *Cosmopolitan* soon realized that Gurley Brown was serious about reforming the magazine. "She sat you down and counseled you," La Barre said. "Her message was polite and direct. You understood if you did not edit to her standards you would be fired. Most began looking for other jobs. Some of us stayed. It was exciting. People always talked about us when we came out. You simply could not ignore *Cosmopolitan*."[39]

Gurley Brown began to understand the role of a magazine editor, which involved thinking months ahead and constantly coming up with fresh ideas for articles and features. She realized one person could not do it all. "My procedure was to have all the editors turn in article ideas once a week," she said. "They wrote them up, and they suggested writers for the article ideas. We discussed them. I took them home, thought about them, and decided which ones we were going to do."[40]

The pressure to produce usable material took its toll. "Helen demanded much of us," La Barre said. "You had to come up with ideas or you were out. Not every week, but if you didn't have good ones for a while you were out. A couple of people had nervous collapses from the stress."[41]

Gurley Brown introduced herself to readers in the July 1965 *Cosmopolitan*. Step Into My Parlor, a column that ran every month during her tenure of thirty-two years, was her platform to summarize each issue's contents, offer brief biographies of writers and editors, and talk about herself. The initial column demonstrated her writing style: "Hello! I'm *Cosmopolitan*'s new editor . . . I'll get to visit with you every month through the pages of *Cosmopolitan*. The stories and articles in this issue were picked for one reason only. I thought they'd interest you, knowing that you're a grown-up girl, interested in whatever can give you a richer, more exciting, fun-filled, friend-filled, man-loved kind of life! You also want to be inspired, entertained and sometimes whisked away into somebody else's world."[42]

Gurley Brown decided to call the column Step Into My Parlor to foster a conversational tone. "I guess I thought I was inviting the reader to visit with me in a room of my house," she explained. "I think I felt that if someone were visiting with me in my home, that it would be intimate and everybody could be personal." The column included an inset photo of her, which was slightly or completely different almost every month: sometimes standing in her office or at an associate editor's desk or in a hallway; sometimes sitting at her desk or in the guest's chair on the *Tonight Show* or some other television program; sometimes standing at the doorway to an airliner or at a landmark in London or Paris; always wearing various fashionable clothing and hairstyles; frequently shown with associate editors of the magazine or with celebrities or with friends, also occasionally with husband David Brown, a movie producer. Step Into My Parlor regularly mentioned David Brown's travels to locales where his movies were in production and her visits with him to Hollywood parties or weekends at a celebrity's home.[43]

The July 1965 inaugural issue was only 124 pages, quite thin because Gurley Brown had inherited a magazine with relatively few advertisements. Only four articles were published, along with three short stories, a nonfiction book excerpt, a mystery novella, and twenty departments. The top article, "Oh What A Lovely Pill!," excitedly predicted that birth control pills would provide women with more than sexual freedom by benefiting them in other ways, such as smoother skin, lustrous hair, and postponement of menopause—all because of estrogen. "It was the only important story I had time to get," Gurley Brown said.[44]

But it was a narrowly focused article without relevant perspective. "Oh What A Lovely Pill!" did not discuss the legal barriers that prevented unmarried women from obtaining prescriptions for birth control pills. Some states had banned contraceptives altogether until the U.S. Supreme Court decided in 1965 that married women had a right to them, including prescriptions for birth control pills. Unmarried women were denied a similar right until the early 1970s, and some physicians continued to refuse to prescribe birth control pills to unmarried women, thus forcing those women to find a different physician. These political and social factors were not on the *Cosmopolitan* agenda.

Gurley Brown proclaimed a personal agenda, not a political one. "We're not writing about wars and things that are going on in other countries," she said. "We're writing about people, women in this country. We're not concerned with the grand issues of the day. You can find out about those other things from newspapers and television." The low percentage of articles pertaining to political and social topics attested to that.[45]

With the July issue done, several weeks passed while Gurley Brown selected material for rewrites for the August issue and contacted writers for new

(Top left) Helen Gurley Brown (right) saved *Cosmopolitan* from certain death upon becoming editor early in 1965. Her daring editorial format again made the magazine the centerpiece of the Hearst Corporation publications. Photograph by Walter Daran, *Life* magazine, 1965, Getty Images.

(Bottom right) Harriet La Barre was an associate editor at *Cosmopolitan* for twenty years beginning in the early 1950s. Shown working at her desk in the magazine's office in 1968, La Barre experienced its near death and its resurgence when Helen Gurley Brown became editor during 1965. Photograph courtesy of Harriet La Barre.

material for September. "My truly first *Cosmopolitan* was September," Gurley Brown said. The top article was "The Affair Vs. Marriage," along with a profile of actress Jane Fonda, a feature on businesses that arranged social events at which unmarried men and women met, and an article about compulsive gamblers. Also, she had cut the number of departments to nine, thereby opening more pages to articles. Each department typically was one page, often sharing space with an advertisement.

"The Affair Vs. Marriage" article was divided into components alternately written by an anonymous man and an anonymous woman, each comparing advantages and disadvantages of the "affair"—the magazine's term for an unwed couple living together, otherwise known as cohabitation—and of marriage. "Living together appears to get the worst of both worlds," the male writer stated. "Unless it is merely a prelude to marriage and recognized sooner or later as such, it inevitably contains within it the seeds of agony and crack-up." The judgment of the female writer sided with cohabitation. "Living in sin, if it lasts, develops a code of its own," she asserted. "The very lack of respectability breeds a particular kind of obligation. They don't own one another." The most candid sentence in the entire article was, "The couple become sexually adjusted and because they are in love it seems better than ever, because it is regular and spontaneous."[46]

Essentially, the article reviewed the practicality of cohabitation, which allowed either partner to end the relationship without any legal action, and the commitment of marriage, which conferred social status on the woman and some financial security. If the article was noteworthy at all, and perhaps a tad unusual for a mainstream magazine, it was because cohabitation by unwed couples then constituted a mere one of every ninety households during the late 1960s. Several years passed, by which time a multitude of baby boomers were well along into adulthood, and the cohabitation ratio increased to one of every thirty households by the late 1970s and one of every twenty-five households by the mid-1980s.[47]

Gurley Brown regarded cohabitation as one indicator of social transition at the time. "Our moral codes have changed slightly," she had explained to Hearst executives. She wanted to prepare them for the inevitable controversy and criticism *Cosmopolitan*'s presentations on sexual topics would provoke. People undoubtedly would react strongly to these heretofore taboo topics, but society once had tolerated injustice and oppression much more immoral. "What we have now is a lot better than the days of stricter moral codes when there was child labor, no equality for women, no federal aid for destitute people, plenty of robber barons and lynching."[48]

Obviously, even a magazine devoted to a wide range of topics relevant to careers, dating, health, relationships, and sexual relationships repeated material every so often. The examination of *Cosmopolitan* during its first seven years under

Gurley Brown's guidance indicated a two- to three-year cycle for most topics. Cohabitation, for example, was written about in September 1965 ("The Affair Vs. Marriage"), August 1967 ("Is Marriage Dying?"), April 1969 ("The Living-Together Handbook"), and February 1972 ("The Living-Together Thing"). Readers probably didn't mind, because it was unlikely many of them remembered previous articles on the same topic months earlier.

Sometimes, even Gurley Brown and associate editors at the magazine could not remember previous articles. Nora Ephron, a writer for various magazines during the late 1960s and early 1970s before becoming a movie screenwriter and director, described receiving an assignment from an associate editor for an article on how to start a conversation with a stranger. Upon reading a memo specifying the details the article must include, Ephron realized she already had written a similar article for *Cosmopolitan*. She told the associate editor, who decided it was all right to write it again. Obviously, Gurley Brown had not remembered the previous article, either.[49]

The themes of almost every *Cosmopolitan* article and feature concerning relationships pertained to women needing men, men needing women, and women taking responsibility for initiating and sustaining the process. Articles on cohabitation began the effort to shift *Cosmopolitan* toward topics relevant to younger women. Subsequent articles dispensed advice to women predicated on their situation: a single woman of any age, or single past a certain age; a divorced woman, or divorced with children; a single or divorced man; a married man. "Our area was sex and the man-woman relationship," Gurley Brown said. "We would not be doing babies or raising children. We'd leave that up to *Good Housekeeping*."[50]

A tabloid-style title in December 1965, "Uncensored: How Girls Really Get Husbands," enticed readers into text for a mundane article on simple, sensible behavior that presumably would lead to love and marriage. Essentially, the advice was to be a good listener, be kind (take soup to a man when ill and vacuum the apartment, too), be nice to a man's mother, write letters frequently if the man lives in another city or is in the military, be aware that most men prefer dependence to independence, and be patient but persistent to obtain a commitment to marry. "Once the American girl finds herself flung into the postgraduate mating race, our heroine, twenty-three contemplating thirty, finds herself increasingly cast in the role of aggressor," the article declared. The reference to postgraduate was curious, considering Gurley Brown's intent to target the magazine at ordinary women employed at what later would be termed "pink-collar" jobs. A college degree was not the norm for men or women during the 1960s; only one of eight men and one of fourteen women had graduated college. More likely, it referred to a woman with a high school diploma who at age twenty-three was ready for marriage. Approximately five of nine women had received a high school diploma by the mid-1960s compared to four of nine men, although the graduation rate for high school students enrolled during the late 1960s neared seven of ten women and six of ten men.[51]

The article exhibited a *Cosmopolitan* trademark for identification, or lack of it. Women whose stories were examples of how to get husbands were referred to only by their first names—Erica, Maria, Lillian, Carole—or anonymously. Their dominant message was that marriage provided companionship and financial security, and that there were fewer eligible men available than there were women. Census data for the era supported the message about the number of unmarried women outnumbering unmarried men by a ratio of seven to six. Therefore, competition was intense for men who had good jobs with good incomes. "When love doesn't come flying at you out of the blue, you find yourself pursuing it," the article concluded. "What these stories suggest is that the woman who 'gets' and the man who is 'gotten' are as likely as anyone else to wind up with a happy marriage." At no point did the article suggest that sexual allure was a primary attraction for men.[52]

Other articles in *Cosmopolitan* amplified the message to women that men with white-collar jobs were more desirable for marriage than men who were laborers, factory workers, or had jobs with lower incomes. The magazine affirmed popular sentiment presented in mainstream media that financial security in marriage was crucial, and not just for working-class women. *Newsweek* reported in a June 1966 cover story about women college students that marriage and material comfort were priorities. The newsmagazine article, though, also described fewer cases of "senior panic" among women who were not yet engaged to be married—because many of them eagerly anticipated beginning a career and attaining financial independence.[53]

"How To Get Married If You're Over Thirty" aimed to aid *Cosmopolitan* readers who feared their "nubile twenty-two-year-old" competitors. "You must sincerely want a husband, and that doesn't mean just coveting the security and social status of being a Married Woman," the article stated. "You must actively want to live with a man." If not, "You might be temperamentally geared for a formidable career of exciting love affairs." The article offered an extended checklist for a thirty-plus woman: do not share an apartment with a roommate; always have "fresh flowers or bouquets of lemon leaves in your apartment"; place the stereo in the bedroom so it "can be played from bed"; apply "lots of blusher" to remove "that pinched, pale, pathetic look that sometimes comes from loneliness" and "sleep with blusher on, he'll like having given you a glow!"; upon awakening "put on a cuddly bathrobe to look fleecy and rather dear!"; throw away "white underwear" and "buy panties and bras in yummy shades you'd want someone to see"; move from the city to the suburbs because "competition is less stiff, and the pace of life encourages men to settle down";

enroll in a German, Japanese, or Russian language course because "business-men and scientists study these languages for their work" or enroll in "comput-ing, stock brokering, applied economics, law—any area that attracts more men than women." Other than recommendations for a bedroom stereo, overnight blusher, and morning cuddly bathrobe, nary a word about sex.[54]

Betty Friedan, the feminist writer, detested *Cosmopolitan*. Friedan told *Life* the editorial material chosen for publication by Gurley Brown was "quite ob-scene and quite horrible" and "an immature teenage-level sexual fantasy." *Es-quire* described *Cosmopolitan* as a magazine for a helpless and hopeless young woman: "She cannot meet men. She cannot think of what to say when she meets them. She doesn't know how to take off her clothes to get into bed with them."[55]

Divorce was not uncommon by the late 1960s. Among men, nearly one of five was divorced or remarried; among women, two of nine were divorced or remarried. Mainstream magazines discussed the effects on children, economic hardships on women who had been homemakers for years and lacked job skills, factors for the escalating divorce rate, and methods to save a marriage, such as counseling or temporary separation. *Cosmopolitan* articles focused on life after divorce. "When Is A Man Remarriageable?" gave readers the essentials: three of every four divorced men and half of all widowers typically married again with-in three to five years; the average age at remarriage was thirty-six; divorced men were more likely to remarry than longtime bachelors ever were to marry. The article advised a woman that a widower presented a special problem, "You'll be competing with a dead paragon instead of a human, fallible, on-the-spot ex-wife." A twelve-point checklist offered "an intelligent woman's guide to getting a man to the altar—again." Some items on the checklist: be a tranquil person ("He doesn't want to take on a baby, a shrew or a hypochondriac"), be sooth-ing and silent ("A man rarely divorces his wife because she has nothing to say"), be affectionate ("With this kind of man, you can make the overtures"), and be assertive if too much time has elapsed without a marriage proposal ("Tell him frankly that your aim is the altar with him—soon").[56]

The article on remarriage had more research than usual. The writer referred to three books on the subject, cited Census Bureau statistics, and interviewed three experts who were either counselors or psychologists. The writer also used quotes from seven anonymous or pseudonymous people.

Cosmo's "Six-Week Crash Recovery Plan For A New Divorcée" interviewed Carla, Jane, Marianne, and Rosemary whose experiences provided all the facts readers needed to know on the subject. Week One was devoted to notifying family and friends via appropriate greeting cards (blank, so a message could be written) and telephone calls, which would enable a divorcée to get another man as soon as possible. "Many people are reluctant to introduce a woman who is separated to a new man, particularly if the people are friends of both you and your husband," the article stated. "Once you're divorced, that hurdle is eliminated." Divorcées were cautioned about generational differences, "Mothers, especially, give moral support on the surface but underneath there's the hint that you should have stuck it out and that you may not find a replacement." The writer included advice about a future relationship with a man: "Remember that sooner or later you will be meeting new men, which doesn't necessarily mean having an affair with them (again, unless you feel like it)." Also, the writer mentioned that loneliness was to be expected: "Needing company and admitting it doesn't make you any weaker than the divorcée who prefers to live by herself until her next husband comes along."[57]

"The Interim Man" quoted several anonymous and pseudonymous divorced men. Their message basically was they needed companionship more than sex, they disliked eating alone in restaurants, and they needed help with laundry. "Dating Rules For Women With Children" advised women to consider their motives for dating, whether it was to find another husband or simply to get out of the house. A first-person account, the writer argued that she was "not at all in favor of this business of going out with men to dinner, out with men to the theater, out with men just to get out." Common-sense suggestions comprised the core of the article. "It goes without saying that before you introduce a man to your children you ought to make sure he's sane, decent and not a burglar or the northeastern regional director of a Maoist cell," the writer recommended. Then a list of activities filled a column of the page: you, your children, and your date at a museum; at an airport "to watch the planes land and take off"; at a picnic; watching television programs together; eating at a Chinese restaurant because "they always seem very hospitable to children."[58]

"Second Wife" was a thorough exploration of the effects of remarriage on children, personal finances, emotional stress, and guilt for the turmoil wrought by divorce. The article was anecdotal and lacked perspective, of course, yet it did include interviews with several women fully identified by surnames—and most of them lived outside of New York: Chicago, Dallas, Los Angeles, St. Louis. The situations cited were plausible. Husbands who were responsible for alimony and child support relied on second wives for income from work, which eliminated any consideration of pregnancy until wife number one remarried. Blending of families often created friction among children, who then exploited any rift between a stepfather or stepmother. The most difficult problem mentioned was tension between a second wife and a stepchild or stepchildren, which invariably affected her role as a parent because of inevitable comparisons to the birth mother: "Why should the existence of your husband's ex-wife haunt you so? After all, he's left her—legally, officially, finally." The article did not attempt an answer.[59]

Advice from *Cosmopolitan* was heavy on platitudes and simplistic schemes. This made the magazine easy to ridicule. *Newsweek* derisively described a formula reliant upon "lots of sex, a dash of hope" and "single-minded advice." Gurley Brown was "the working girl's Simone de Beauvoir," *Newsweek* commented. *Time* wrote, "Cope and conquer as she might, the *Cosmo* girl is still treated like an idiot who can survive only if everything is spelled out for her and then underlined."[60]

Marital infidelity was the next rung on the *Cosmopolitan* ladder of relationships. It was an equal opportunity endeavor for women in the pages of the magazine. "The recognition of female sexuality and The Pill have freed many women to explore the depths of their sexual being," *Cosmopolitan* declared. Articles on the subject of extramarital relationships in *Cosmopolitan* created dramatically different scenarios for women than those seen in articles regarding divorce and remarriage. Married women with lovers were affluent and did not work outside the home. Their infidelity stemmed from boredom or inattentive husbands whose corporate careers had priority over marriage.[61]

"The Other Man (Men) In A Married Woman's Life" asserted that some men tacitly condoned adulterous wives while most men simply were unaware of infidelity. "The more successful the man, the more leisure and money his wife is left to spend alone," the article stated. "Someone must be delegated to perform the functions for which he has no time—and often no inclination." Anecdotes from women in this situation described their arrangements, but no specific details about trysts. Husbands who had no clue usually were to blame because they lacked interest in their wives. "They would much prefer that a wife wear down her elbows on the bridge table, so long as she is with women," the article asserted. "Whatever wonders the extra man performs on his wife's disposition, a husband does lose something. It is not easy to restage an intimacy."[62]

"Low-Fidelity Wives" in January 1969 explored the motivations of Kiki, Natalie, Louisa, and Jeannine. They represented a new woman, one liberated by the birth control pill. "There is another kind of woman, however, one whose sexual exploration continues—or only begins—with marriage," according to the article. Kiki, a wife who liked casual encounters with men, somehow lacked contentment despite her marriage to a handsome, rich man. "She has been independent and sexually emancipated for so many years, that extra sexual experience is simply a natural life style for her," the article stated. Natalie, a wife whose husband was "sexually bland," needed satisfaction from others. "She thrives on being the wife of a powerful man," the article asserted. "Money is no small part of this dedication, but there is also genuine affection and respect for her husband as well as strong feelings about the importance of family stability for their three young children." Why take the risk? "An extramarital affair makes her life fuller," the article explained. Louisa, a wife whose husband was under too much pressure from his career, which financed a nanny for their child, believed her lovers had made the marriage better. "Infidelity provably saved this marriage," she told the writer. Finally, Jeannine, a wife who sought more passion after eight years of marriage, "feels confident a onetime sexual adventure is not about to become a pattern of promiscuity for her."[63]

Infidelity definitely was a controversial topic, especially when delivered in explanatory, nonjudgmental articles. Scholars in women's studies have posited that *Cosmopolitan* objectively informed its readers about unfaithful wives whose behavior matched the more common pattern of unfaithful husbands, and therefore was an expression of gender equality. A critical analysis in 1967 of the *Playboy* format matched elements found in some *Cosmopolitan* articles on adultery. "*Playboy* seems to supply its readers a goal to achieve, a model of behavior to emulate, and an identity to assume," the analysis declared. "The psychological punishment of guilt is alleviated by the demonstration that nonmarital sexual activity is in most cases moral, and that it is the traditional morality which is wrong." American women did not violate their marriage vows despite the tolerance espoused by *Cosmopolitan* and *Playboy*: one of every eight married women during the 1960s told social researchers they had adulterous relationships; one of every five married women said the same during the 1970s; but the ratio declined to one of every seven married women by the 1980s. Also, researchers who surveyed married men and women during the mid-1980s learned that extramarital affairs were not condoned by an overwhelming majority.[64]

Cosmopolitan concocted a fantasy for unmarried women who were participants in extramarital sex, too. The magazine suggested it was a beneficial relationship. "Girls And Their Married Men" reviewed the steps by which a woman "moves quietly, undramatically from the boy-meets-girl world" to Married Man Syndrome. "In the beginning, the problem of his having a wife is not much more irritating than that of dating a boy who lives at home with mama," the article suggested. "It even adds a little spice." The only reference to sex was "the bed thing," and the article made clear it was not a requirement on the woman's part if she had qualms about sex with a married man.[65]

Also, becoming a mistress was an option to enhance a young woman's material comfort. *Cosmopolitan* wrote about advantages for a part-time mistress in "The Slightly Kept Girl." The woman had a day job, but "her income is supplemented (and not from home)," the article explained. "She has learned to accept favors, vacations, rent money, stock shares, plane tickets, and pure cash from her lover." According to the article, a modern mistress was not stigmatized socially because a "receptive climate" existed. "There are simply more helped-out girls than ever before," readers were told. "For most girls, being semikept is just a convenient situation prefacing a perfectly ordinary life being married to someone else." Naturally, all of the kept women named in the article were identified on a first-name only basis—Pam, Diane, Chantal—and lived in New York City or Paris or Palm Beach, Florida. They wore Cardin clothes and much jewelry; one mistress never took the subway or bus because she rode in a Rolls Royce.[66]

For a mistress of a married man who wanted permanency, *Cosmopolitan* listed "telltale signs" that her fling would not result in marriage. "Don't Be A Statistic, Baby" was a rare admission by *Cosmopolitan* that a woman actually might not control every aspect of a relationship. The article referred to the "always neatly wrapped, never cheap" gifts a mistress should expect to receive, but all were given at times convenient to the man, which meant daytime lunches and not nighttime dinners, weekday afternoons and not weekends—family, of course, had priority. "The fact is that x million single girls are having affairs with x million married men doesn't mean a thing," the article sarcastically commented. "Yours is not just an affair." The article's list of telltale signs proved a mistress was "one of those single-girl-married-man statistics" destined to never to be a Mrs.[67]

Articles about mistresses were abundant. During a six-month span beginning in late 1967, the magazine ran "The Young Mistresses," "The Mistress My Husband Can't Give Up," and "How To Be A Lady While Dating A Married Man." A two-year gap with no mistress articles ensued, then "Would You Rather Be The Wife Or The Mistress?" This attention to adultery and advice to mistresses was too much for *Time*. According to the newsmagazine, *Cosmopolitan* instructed readers on "how to get married, how to get divorced, how to be a successful mistress, how to make the most of 'brief encounters.'" Advice was directed to "single women, 18 to 34, who are not knockouts, who are unsure of themselves, who are searching for a man." *Cosmopolitan* ignored children, *Time* noted, because "they interfere with the free, untrammeled sex life."[68]

Cosmopolitan rarely referred to children because they never were a factor in the life of its editor. Gurley Brown had worked for twenty years either as a secretary or advertising copywriter, had married at age thirty-seven to a man five years older, and had embarked on a new career in publishing. "I didn't know anything about children," Gurley Brown said. "Therefore, we weren't going to write about them." Still, it was difficult to publish articles on divorce and remarriage without discussing children; when relevant the presence of children was alluded to, although children themselves rarely were quoted.[69]

Articles on sexual conduct appeared only when Gurley Brown had established a record of success by early 1967. Circulation was up, ad pages were up. She could be more daring. Nymphomania was the subject. "Compulsive promiscuity is the hallmark of the true nymphomaniac, yet the highly sexed woman, and the promiscuous woman who is not compulsive, are often wildly included in this sad category," the article informed *Cosmopolitan* readers. Nymphomania relied on generalizations from two books written by psychiatrists and anecdotes from pseudonymous women. The article blamed religion for deeming "sex as profligate, wrong and sordid and not for pleasure." This belief condemned women who sought sexual pleasure. "Men are allowed to get away with it because—well, they are men," the article asserted. "But there's no equality in the attitude when it comes to women. Her spontaneous desires are too often viewed with the darkest suspicion and considered unpleasantly unfeminine; all right for the dolls but not for ladies." It offered no details about sexual encounters involving the women.[70]

Cosmopolitan for December 1967 defended the one-night stand for women. "Live For The Moment . . . Or At Least The Night" relied entirely on an explanation by the writer—a woman—about her preference for sex with men that did not require a commitment. "By advocating the brief encounter," she wrote, "I am thinking of something very special and joyous. It can't happen often. It doesn't happen often. Its rarity is what consolidates its sweetness." It was independence for a woman. "She has the capacity to live for the moment," the writer declared. "She does not ask for gifts, meals, dates, real estate, or a till-death-do-us-part guarantee."[71]

Another article, "The Girl Don Juan," complimented women who could act like "an all-out supertease" and walk away. "Now any female worth her chromosomes loves to flirt," the article stated. "And let any girl who hasn't been involved with a married man in some way cast the first stone. These things happen, and all girls get a thrill out of wielding a certain amount of power over a man."[72]

Despite its apparent approval of women initiating a sexual encounter, *Cosmopolitan* reminded readers that some measure of restraint was essential. "The concept of sexual giving is totally absent from the growing acceptance that any casual date must inevitably end in bed—his or hers, it scarcely matters which," observed an article, "How Sexually Generous Should A Girl Be?" "Far too many girls have abdicated an active role in the sexual relationship and find themselves drifting aimlessly, almost listlessly, from bed to bed out of resignation, routine, habit, passive nonresistance. And all this joyless bedding about is accomplished under the guise of sensuality and free love."[73]

Hearst Corporation executives perhaps had winced at some articles in *Cosmopolitan*, but they had given Gurley Brown remarkable latitude to choose topics. Curiously, one article that encountered resistance from the Hearst Building and almost was spiked only implied adventurous sexual behavior. The topic was the romantic life of airline stewardesses, now known as flight attendants. "Oh, it was a fun story," Gurley Brown said. "You know, those beautiful young women flying everywhere, on their own in magnificent cities around the world. Well, they met very wealthy men on those flights. And they were friendly with the pilots. Things happened." The article was written, but Deems told the editor some changes must be made. Make it clear, he ordered, that most stewardesses kept to themselves on their days off in distant cities, that few of them became sexual partners of fellow travelers. Why the changes? "Some high-up person had married a stewardess," Gurley Brown said. "He was very touchy about the reputation stewardesses had."[74]

Another problem arose. Deems disapproved of the cover blurb for the article. "Those Flying Man-Hunters" was removed and a blurb for a different article substituted for it. Finally, "The Private World Of Airline Stewardesses" made it into print.[75]

Gurley Brown was not averse to confrontation. Her cordial demeanor masked a steely resolve. She and Deems regularly debated the content of articles and their propriety. She almost always won. Deems then would explain to Berlin why the editor's rationale had prevailed, sometimes when he had acted on behalf of Berlin. Gurley Brown credited her victories to always having a draft of an article on a potentially troublesome subject available for Deems or Berlin to read. This back-and-forth continued for a while. At last, Berlin backed off. "There can be only one Editor," he wrote to her a year after her first issue. "Publishers cannot successfully edit over the Editor's shoulder." Berlin ended the memo with, "I read Cosmo and I like it."[76]

Gurley Brown avoided controversy her first several years on substantive subjects, such as racism and sexual harassment. *Cosmopolitan,* for example, rarely ran articles on abortion. This was a significant evasion of responsibility for a magazine that advocated sexual assertiveness of women. Pregnancy was a risk for unmarried women, and for married women who wanted to delay having a family or who did not want another child. Prior to the 1970s, a pregnant woman who wished to have an abortion could not have the procedure performed legally in any state, other than for reasons of a life-threatening condition arising from pregnancy or a pregnancy from rape.

Only once did *Cosmopolitan* address the subject of abortion candidly and emotionally. Although written by an anonymous woman, an article in mid-summer 1967 explained the dilemma facing an unmarried woman whose male partner was not the man she wanted to marry; she did not confer with him about her pregnancy and her decision for an abortion. "I Didn't Have The Baby, I Had The Abortion" provided details about a woman's difficult task to find a physician who would agree to perform the procedure. "It was the crueler uncertainty of not knowing who would do the abortion, and where, and when, and how to set it up, and just what it would be like," she wrote. "Throughout this time there was the deepest loneliness."

The reality was, according to *Cosmopolitan,* that many women had abortions despite the illegality of the procedure. "Almost everyone I knew (at twenty-three) had had an abortion or knew someone who had," the writer stated.

Although the article did not cite statistics, a *Cosmopolitan* trademark, the National Association for Reform of Abortion Laws subsequently estimated that one abortion was performed for every four live births during the late 1960s.

The article described a secret meeting with a physician at a decrepit hotel in Manhattan. In the small room a "portable operating table set up in one corner" had "something at the foot of it that looked like an inner tube," beneath which were two plastic buckets. The writer described the procedure: "Then came the sensation of being pumped up, the dilation part, and the terrible cramps; and then the scraping, which I remember not as a feeling but as a wet, wet sound and a metallic smell, metal on metal; then the pumping up, then the scraping." It was over in several minutes. "Then I gave him the money, which he counted with an apologetic money-counting look, put on my coat, shook his hand again, went down the back stairs, out the back door."

A friend drove her to her apartment. She wrote: "That night I was the loneliest girl in the world. I wanted the baby so much then. More than I had ever wanted anything. I just wanted that baby."[77]

It was a dramatic article. Its focus on one woman's experience was effective. However, the magazine missed an opportunity to analyze the political and social factors that affected efforts to legalize abortion. Several years passed until the U.S. Supreme Court decided *Roe v. Wade* in 1973, which allowed a woman the right to an abortion during the first trimester of pregnancy.

An article in February 1968 amounted to a women's manifesto for sexual equality. Written by a British woman whom *Cosmopolitan* had published a few times previously, "The Sexual Drive In Women" denounced the double standard that permitted a man to have sex with a woman for physical pleasure without emotional attachment while denying the same to a woman. "A man's sexual drive is generally seen as virile, manly, and attractive," the writer noted. "A woman's sexual drive too often implies she is in pursuit, aggressive, and probably predatory. If a woman has to wait romantically for the right emotional and loving partner before she is 'permitted' to enjoy sex, then many would sexually starve to death."

The writer mentioned birth control pills as "the greatest liberator of the sexual drive in women," but predicted "the double sexual standard . . . will be around for a long while." Women need not forsake emotional attachment for sex, yet the idea that love was mandatory for self-respect made no sense. "Of course, sex without love or friendship is a graceless experience for anyone," the writer acknowledged. "Nevertheless, it can still be satisfying, releasing—and fun." The writer was a favorite of Gurley Brown because she advocated a modern viewpoint about women's sexual conduct. The writer herself, however, disagreed with Gurley Brown's relentless emphasis on women pursuing men for marriage, personal security, and status.[78]

Sexual satisfaction was the topic of "The Ostentatious Orgasm" in the January 1969 issue. Stimulation was mentioned, but techniques were not described. The idea was that women must lose their inhibitions. "The orgasm may seem ostentatious only because, for the first time in history, it can be discussed openly," the article asserted. "The ability and right for women as well as men to enjoy sexual expression and satisfaction is as important and relevant a subject today as any other physical ability or civil right."[79]

The December 1970 magazine published "Masturbation: A Doctor's Report," an explanation of its benefits to women without any explicit advice on practicing it. "Through masturbation we learn to banish the fear of 'loss of self' through climax and learn to deal with the disappointment of occasionally mild or even nonexistent responses," the article advised. "Sex is certainly more familiar and less frightening to a woman when she has learned to stimulate herself to climax."[80]

Articles that advocated women's independence in sexual matters and achievement of sexual satisfaction generated criticism. *Time* again expressed its disapproval of *Cosmopolitan*. "The One-Night Affair is accepted, even defended, as nothing shameful," the newsmagazine reported. *Ramparts,* a leftist magazine of the era, mentioned an article on self-detection by women of venereal diseases, judging it useful information "the *Cosmopolitan* reader will very possibly need if she follows the advice found in the rest of the magazine."[81]

One tidbit of advice that never saw print was "how men should treat women's breasts in love-making." For reasons known only to Deems and Berlin, they ordered Gurley Brown not to continue with an article on the topic. Considering that the magazine had presented information on masturbation and orgasms, their decision to draw the line on this is puzzling.

Evidently, the editor had anticipated a problem. In her memo to "girl staff members" early in 1969 asking for information, Gurley Brown had written, "It will either help us sell another hundred thousand copies or stop publication of *Cosmopolitan* altogether!" The girls were asked to let her know what "pleases you in terms of having your breasts caressed," what "men do that is wrong," and whether "girls are too self-conscious about size of their bosom." She promised all contributors anonymity. "If we do this tastefully and with real insight," she wrote, the article would "help a lot of men make a lot of girls more happy."[82]

A *Cosmopolitan* girl, identity unknown, slipped a copy of the memo to *Women's Wear Daily,* the fashion industry newspaper distributed to a highly influential sector in Manhattan. Deems and Berlin reacted immediately to the publicity. They were embarrassed personally, and they believed *Cosmopolitan* would embarrass Hearst Corporation. They spiked the article.[83]

Gurley Brown was an editor on a mission, and all sexual topics involving consenting adults were appropriate to her. "We should take cognizance of the fact that our nation is undergoing a cultural as well as a social revolution," she advised Hearst executives. Her assessment of a momentous shift in the way Americans thought was a generalization. Many factors affected the supposed cultural and social revolution of the sixties—age, education, income, ethnicity and race, social status; and its revolutionary effects hardly were acceptable to all men and women. Gurley Brown sensibly narrowed her focus on changes in man-woman relationships and lifestyle choices for young women.[84]

Years later, some feminist scholars issued positive judgments of *Cosmopolitan*'s editorial material on women and sex during the 1960s and 1970s. The magazine confronted the range of choices available to women, from a celibate life to a sexually active life. Articles discussed the hypocrisy of the sexual double standard, and presented examples—most of them real, some not—of women who had good jobs and good sex. Women chose their options.

Other scholars suggested that the role of women's magazines was to cue readers to acceptable behavior. Many women were misinformed or uninformed about sex. *Cosmopolitan* possibly was an influence on young women who were uncertain about the dynamics of sexual relationships. This did not mean that readers modeled their behavior on the women portrayed in articles, but they might have better understood how to anticipate or react to certain situations because of the information provided.[85]

Inevitably, too, *Cosmopolitan* was likened to *Playboy* by contemporary critics. Some thematic similarities existed. *Cosmopolitan* rarely published nude centerfold photographs, of course, but it and *Playboy* published articles on sex and also enlivened otherwise mundane material about fashion, personal fitness, and travel with opportunistic references to sexual attraction and sexual opportunities. "*Cosmopolitan* is frequently criticized for portraying as unreal a sex-charged world as *Playboy,* if a somewhat less affluent one," *Time* reported in February 1968. Four years later, *Time* asked, "Can *Playboy*'s guy liberate *Cosmo*'s girl, or vice versa." The answer: "Puritan swingers struggling dutifully for their orgasms as if doing homework for a self-improvement course, they do seem a couple with much in common."[86]

Some critics proposed that both magazines treated women as "sex objects" rather than humans. Hugh Hefner, the *Playboy* publisher, had used the magazine to build a nationwide network of membership clubs in which women hostesses and waitresses dressed in tight black corsets and fishnet stockings and wore pink rabbit ears on their heads—each woman a *Playboy* bunny for the male *Playboy* rabbit. "*Playboy*'s pornography consists in its transformation of women—i.e. female human beings—into Playmates and bunnies, i.e. into erotic art objects designed to titillate the sexual sense," a critic declared. "The *Cosmopolitan* 'moral' is just the other side of the *Playboy* coin—every girl/woman can be rich, alluring, sexually satisfying and satisfied, and, if she wishes, happily married."[87]

Gurley Brown had modeled *Cosmopolitan* after *Playboy* to an extent. Her revised prospectus that became the framework for *Cosmopolitan* had cited *Playboy* for its editorial focus. "Cosmo will now be a woman's magazine—not a general magazine—edited for a specific woman," she explained to Hearst executives. "I think *Playboy* Magazine comes closest to being edited this way of any magazine I know. Other magazines are also specific but I think of Hefner's book as an outstanding example of specific-hood." In effect, *Cosmopolitan* would never accept material another magazine might publish simply because *Cosmopolitan* would have its own distinctive style and tone, just like *Playboy* did.[88]

Cosmopolitan ran a profile of Hefner in May 1966, a way to acknowledge themes similar to both magazines. The profile opened with a brief biographical sketch of the publisher, then filled three pages of text with question-and-answer responses mostly pertaining to Hefner's opinions on relationships, sexual freedom, and the social "turmoil" wrought by new attitudes of men and women toward sex. Hefner chided the guardians of traditional morality and advocated polygamous relationships.[89]

The most interesting component of the Hefner presentation was not the profile but the follow-up article that began immediately afterward. "Hugh Hefner: That Dear, Dangerous Old-Fashioned Boy," written by Joanna Pettet, an actress "beautiful enough to be a Bunny and bright enough to debate with Mr. Hefner," rejected the *Playboy* message that women were primarily for sexual pleasure. "The women of his world are playthings, toys, amusements, pleasure units," Pettet argued. "He does it in order to give the adolescent American male (and some of them stay adolescents forever) some frail sense of superiority, no matter how tenuous." The article included an affirmation of the importance of marriage. Hefner's "personal preferences are his own concern, but his deprecation of marriage permeates his whole magazine," Pettet declared. "Marriage is the best means we've got for bearing and raising children. It's just plain socially useful for men as well as women."[90]

Years later, some feminist scholars credited *Cosmopolitan* for its portrayals of women who acted independently in their careers and personal lives, including sex. According to these feminists, Gurley Brown's basic message was that a woman should attain autonomy through a career, then seek a man for marriage. The message got garbled, however. Static from critics who were disgusted or dismayed by *Cosmopolitan* articles that focused on mistresses of married men and adulterous wives had drowned out whatever Gurley Brown meant to convey. Also, feminists objected to the materialistic messages delivered by *Cosmopolitan* almost every month, which urged women to accept gifts from men. Materialism mattered very much to Gurley Brown, to whom financial security and accumulation of material objects was an aspect of self-fulfillment. She espoused materialism on the pages of *Cosmopolitan* and in her book *Sex and the Single Girl*—whether it was receiving jewelry, artwork, airplane tickets, and clothes from a man or seeking marriage to a man with a good income. The combination of materialism and man-hunting bothered feminists of the era.[91]

Activists had founded the National Organization for Women in 1966 and the National Women's Political Caucus several years later. Two writers, Betty Friedan and Gloria Steinem, were among the prominent activists. Gurley Brown was not.

Early in 1970, a delegation from Media Women, an activist organization aligned with what news media called the Women's Liberation Movement, met with Gurley Brown in her *Cosmopolitan* office to request more substantive articles on items of interest to feminists. The women wanted *Cosmopolitan* to publish material regarding women's pay inequity, limits on career advancement for women, and the dearth of women in executive and managerial positions. Gurley Brown certainly was an example of the latter, but she was not sympathetic. *Cosmopolitan* was all about helping women individually, not about changing the system. "My beliefs were not necessarily different from theirs," Gurley Brown said. "They wanted to change everything. I wanted girls to have confidence in themselves, make money, be someone themselves, do something on their own." It was not a confrontational session. Gurley Brown told the delegation she would publish articles concerning feminist topics.[92]

Cosmopolitan did publish some feminist articles. "The Women's Liberation Movement!" reiterated grievances already reported in newspapers and newsmagazines about unequal pay, inadequate opportunities for career advancement, strength requirements that made women ineligible for jobs as ambulance attendants, firefighters, and police officers, and state laws conferring sole ownership of marital property to husbands. "It is what's behind the laws that is so terrible," the article stated. "Not the letter of the law but the spirit determining it, not the explicit but the implicit in the law, not the apparent but the actual condition of women. These things are terrible."[93]

The civility extended to Gurley Brown in January was not present several weeks later when several dozen feminists, including representatives from Media Women, staged a sit-in for eleven hours at the offices of *Ladies' Home Journal*. They protested the editorial format of "one of the most demeaning magazines toward women" and gave the *Ladies' Home Journal* editor, a man, a list of articles the magazine should publish. *Ladies' Home Journal* inserted an eight-page supplement written by feminists for its August issue.[94]

Cosmopolitan also was the target of a public demonstration by feminists on Equality Day in August 1970. A coalition of feminist organizations picketed several media entities and advertising agencies to protest portrayals of women in advertisements, commercials, magazines, newspapers, and television programs. *Cosmopolitan*—along with the makers of Silva Thins, a cigarette for women; Ivory Liquid, a detergent by Procter & Gamble; Pristeen, a women's hygiene deodorant by Warner-Lambert—was accused of stereotyping women in secondary career roles, subordinate status to men, and as sexual objects. Gurley Brown did not meet with protesters, despite being in the same demonstration march with a delegation of women editors from magazines and newspapers. She was quoted in newspapers that it was "wonderful that a woman is sexually desirable" and "it would be wrong to suggest that that's her only attraction."[95]

The demonstration against *Cosmopolitan* in summer 1970 led to publication in the November 1970 issue of a lengthy excerpt from *Sexual Politics* by feminist author Kate Millett. The excerpt analyzed Freudian concepts concerning femininity. Millett criticized conclusions that femininity was biological. Instead, she argued, femininity was an environmental determination imposed on women by men. Ironically, a statement by Millett explaining Freud's "notion of penis envy" probably was the first time *Cosmopolitan* had published the word penis since Gurley Brown became editor. It would not be the last.[96]

Feminists soon started their own magazine. *Ms.*, which took its title from the new word that would replace miss and Mrs. to identify a woman without specifying her marital status, published its prototype issue in December 1971. *Ms.* sold so well at newsstands that investors hurriedly financed a monthly schedule initiated during summer 1972. Its demographics were starkly different from *Cosmopolitan* in the categories of women with college degrees, jobs, and higher incomes. Never a direct competitor with *Cosmopolitan*, *Ms.* definitely was the thinking woman's alternative.

Gurley Brown's *Cosmopolitan* embodied differences in attitude and outlook between most women and elitist feminist activists. Gurley Brown aimed her magazine at ordinary women whose jobs provided income, not fulfillment, and whose aspirations usually involved personal happiness, not equality with men in the workplace. Her emphasis on physical attractiveness, material rewards, and just plain fun was at odds with the serious agenda of cultural, economic, and political reform put forth by feminists of the era. To feminists, *Cosmopolitan* needed to educate mainstream women about the sexism that limited their lives. *Cosmopolitan* was insufficiently political and Gurley Brown inexcusably tolerant of gender inequality. The magazine embarrassed feminists.[97]

Gurley Brown would not concede anything to feminists. An article titled "Liberation Now!" belittled activists by listing a page of trite recommendations for treatment of men by women: "Ask him to wash out your pantyhouse"; "Next time he takes you to dinner, you select the wine"; "Explain the stock market and capital gains tax to him"; "Insist on carrying his suitcase"; "Bury your nose in work when you get home tonight, make numerous business phone calls"; "Walk into the house tonight after work and say, 'What's for dinner'?"; "Ask him to let you take out the garbage once in a while"; "Stop faking orgasms."[98]

Gurley Brown was asked by editors of other women's magazines to publicize the effort to ratify the Equal Rights Amendment, a proposal to ban gender discrimination and create opportunity regardless of gender. She agreed, and urged the male editor of *Good Housekeeping* to join the editorial campaign. "What was decided was that each woman's magazine in its own way would run something on the ERA amendment in our June issues," Gurley Brown informed her colleague. "Whatever is run would not necessarily be in support of the bill, but just give information."[99]

Cosmopolitan published "ERA & You," a two-page summary of the amendment. "What it says, in effect, is that we are all free to be equal," the article stated. It explained that women encountered stricter standards to obtain a bank loan and credit card, had fewer opportunities for academic scholarships, and typically earned less money than men for comparable jobs. "Men and women will have equal rights or they will have unequal ones, as they do today," the article concluded.[100]

The magazine also presented a six-page primer on laws affecting women in the areas of marital property, divorce settlements, rape prosecutions (admissibility or inadmissibility of previous sexual behavior by the victim), and wage disparity.[101]

A presentation by Gurley Brown to *Cosmopolitan* advertisers declared, "Cosmo feels it was in the forefront of the Women's Liberation Movement and supports that movement totally." Imagery of women in advertisements displayed in *Cosmopolitan* and other national magazines depicted them as more free-spirited and independent—hiking and camping alone, traveling to Europe alone, shopping for cars alone.[102]

However, a commentary in *Cosmopolitan* defended femininity from assault by feminists. "Flirting, for both men and women, enables us to make feints and false starts, each testing out the other until the desired response has been won from the desired partner, at which point we can move on with confidence to the next level of human exchange," the commentary asserted. "True, as Women's Lib points out, we could vastly reduce the differences between the sexes if we really worked at it. There would be less and less need for male-female flirting, less consciousness among women and men that they were responding to a different gender. Once again, the question must be asked: Do we really want to do this, to chip away at this wonderful and mysterious sexuality with which the world is imbued?"[103]

An Offer

Seven consecutive years of fantastic success—tens of thousands of new readers every year, dozens of additional ad pages every month—had pleased Gurley Brown tremendously, although it had not rewarded her greatly. Her annual salary during the early 1970s surpassed $60,000 and her contract stipulated a dime bonus for each magazine copy sold above the prior year's circulation total, to a maximum of $25,000. She negotiated for a circulation bonus with no limit and also wanted a bonus equal to one-tenth the cover price for each additional single-copy sold. Had she gotten the circulation bonus and cover-price percentage in her contract for 1971, as an example, Gurley Brown would have received $38,000 and $13,000 respectively in bonuses, bringing total compensation to at least $110,000 (equivalent to $550,000 in 2010 dollars).

The president of magazines, Richard Deems, rejected her bonus proposals. He answered to Berlin, whose forty-year career with the corporation had concentrated on controlling costs. Berlin had won his first round of corporate infighting in 1931 when he persuaded William Randolph Hearst to fire Ray Long, the longtime and well-compensated *Cosmopolitan* editor. From that point onward, Berlin operated on the principle that anyone who asked for too much money was expendable.[104]

In mid-February 1972, corporate miserliness and her own sense of worth persuaded Gurley Brown to accept an invitation to meet with David Mahoney, chief executive officer of Norton Simon. Based in California, Norton Simon was an unconventional corporation for the era, a conglomerate that acquired businesses in unrelated sectors. Norton Simon owned Avis rental car, Max Factor cosmetics, Halston apparel—and *McCall's* magazine. Although still the largest women's magazine, *McCall's* was on a downhill slide. It had experimented unsuccessfully with a new editorial format, and had gone through three editors in four years. Mahoney quite naturally hoped to revive *McCall's* by hiring Gurley Brown.

What resulted was a farcical situation. Mahoney was in Manhattan to confer with Deems. The men were to discuss the possible sale of the faltering *McCall's* to Hearst Corporation. Mahoney decided he might as well meet with Gurley Brown to see if he could hire her in the event *McCall's* could not be sold at a good price. They agreed to meet on a Wednesday night. That night, after leaving work, Deems was walking near the Waldorf Hotel when he saw his *Cosmopolitan* editor entering the lobby. Deems knew that Mahoney was staying at the Waldorf. This made him nervous. Thursday afternoon, Deems was on the telephone to set a specific time for his appointment with Mahoney the next day when Gurley Brown walked into his office unannounced. Standing at the door, she overheard Deems refer to the Waldorf Hotel. Deems hung up the phone. Gurley Brown sat down, then told him she had met with Mahoney.

Deems now was near panic. His editor whose magazine contributed one-fourth of the magazine division's profits, second only to the one-third contributed by *Good Housekeeping*, was too valuable to lose. Deems quickly alerted Berlin to the situation. Despite his miserliness, Berlin realized that millions of dollars in revenue and profits were at stake. Deems soon informed Gurley Brown that she would receive a higher salary and a more generous bonus provision when her contract was renewed the next month. "Perhaps I should say at this point, Helen, that Mahoney's offer to you had no influence in my own decision to agree to your request for contract changes," Deems stated. "I decided that it was in the best interests of the Company to grant your wishes because, as I said to you, your enthusiasm and your devotion to the magazine are worth so very much."[105]

(Hearst Corporation did not purchase *McCall's*. Norton Simon sold *McCall's* to private investors the next year. It continued its slide. *McCall's* ceased publication in 2001.)

Deems and Berlin truly had no choice except to meet whatever feasible salary and bonus stipulations their editor wanted. Gurley Brown had saved *Cosmopolitan* by transforming it. She had enriched the Hearst Corporation. Because of her sense of what young women wanted to read, Gurley Brown had more than doubled the magazine's circulation during seven years—from 782,000 copies monthly to 1.68 million copies. Also, actual revenue from advertising had risen spectacularly from an estimated $57,000 each month to $434,000. *Cosmopolitan* was a money-loser when Gurley Brown walked through the door to become editor. Seven years later, *Cosmopolitan* made an estimated $4.1 million profit.

Stature

Other women's magazines lost circulation throughout the late 1970s to mid-1980s. Readership losses for *Ladies' Home Journal*, *McCall's*, and *Redbook*, which Hearst Corporation purchased in 1982, ranged from 6 percent to 11 percent. *McCall's* and *Redbook*, until its ownership by Hearst, emphasized fiction.[106]

Gurley Brown did not reserve much room for fiction. Gurley Brown decided at the start that *Cosmopolitan* had too many pages of fiction. She correctly concluded that television dramas and inexpensive paperback books met the fiction needs of most mainstream Americans. Within a year of becoming editor, she reduced the number of fiction stories from an average of four or five each month to two or three. Although she continued the tradition of running an abridged novel, usually a mystery, at the back of the magazine, she occasionally replaced it with an excerpt from a nonfiction book or a novel by a relatively unknown author. "Everybody loves a good mystery," Gurley Brown said, "but we didn't have a good one to publish every month."

The old *Cosmopolitan* had published novellas and book-length novels. The new *Cosmopolitan* carried lengthy excerpts from nonfiction books, mostly those that pertained to relationships, sexual topics, and emotional problems. "I liked the idea of publishing pieces of a book," Gurley Brown said. "Who had the money to buy a book you thought might be interesting but wasn't, you see? They could read an excerpt and decide if they would buy the book." Agents swarmed *Cosmopolitan*'s offices. "They were waving manuscripts at me," she said. "What better way to sell a book!"[107]

The magazine typically gave readers the equivalent of thirty-four to forty-two pages of fiction throughout most of the 1970s and into the early 1980s. On a proportional basis, the allocation for fiction pages was half its former share and amounted to approximately one-fourth of all editorial space. Gurley Brown enjoyed fiction, not necessarily literature. "I looked for interesting characters and strong stories," she said, describing herself as a reader of popular contemporary books rather than classics.[108]

Cosmopolitan never regained its reputation of the Ray Long era as a showcase both for the best and most popular authors. Although the most popular authors of the 1960s through mid-1980s appeared in the magazine, rarely were the best in its pages. It evidently did not matter to readers, who bought the magazine as it was, but Gurley Brown yielded to pleas and pressure from associate editors embarrassed by their association with a women's sex magazine. It was a rare demonstration of a concern by her for stature. Despite ridicule and scorn, she resolutely had refused to deviate from her editorial formula emphasizing nonfiction articles on relationships and sex, yet she wanted literary prestige for *Cosmopolitan*.

Despite her own lack of enthusiasm for literature, Gurley Brown embarked on a quest to publish the favorites of the literati. *Cosmopolitan* offered generous fees to authors whose work literary critics adored. Most of the era's esteemed authors did not respond, a list that included Truman Capote, John Cheever, Norman Mailer, William Styron, and John Updike. Memoranda to Hearst Corporation executives from Gurley Brown regarding the campaign to lure authors of literary reputation to *Cosmopolitan* reflected her frustration. "Once in a while they will write for Playboy and Esquire because the former is well-paid and masculine, the latter prestigious, not only in the public's mind but in the eyes of the writer's agents and peers," Gurley Brown wrote. "Even though we offer the same money as Playboy and more money than Esquire, they're not sure we're the right showcase for them."

She had anticipated rejection by those she courted. and defensively preempted their snubs by dismissing some authors for "dull, dull" writing whose themes were "obscure, male-oriented." Asking an author of literary repute to write something, anything, for *Cosmopolitan* was risky because it might be "totally out of line for the Cosmo girl reader." Still, she hoped these authors would allow *Cosmopolitan* to publish their fiction, even if it meant a story already published by another magazine of elite readership and much smaller circulation. "It's easier to get our hands on," Gurley Brown explained to executives, "and we can also tell whether it's right for Cosmo."[109]

Of significance was the willingness of Hearst executives to break the budget for *Cosmopolitan* in pursuit of literature. Executives had refused to give their editor additional money for travel, but they approved extraordinary fees for authors whose presence in the magazine would polish its image. The magazine operated on a monthly editorial budget of $30,000 until the early 1970s. The budget allocation financed a variety of editorial material: sixteen to twenty-two articles and nonfiction book excerpts at fees of $400 to $1,500 apiece; payments from $600 to $1,500 each for two to three stories; a typical fee of $2,500 for an excerpt from a novel; fees for four to six columnists at $350 each; a cover photograph for $1,500 by Francesco Scavullo; approximately $2,000 for nonfiction photography; and $1,000 for illustrations for regular departments and fiction.[110]

A special plea from Gurley Brown unlocked the corporate treasury at the start of the 1970s to pay $2,500 for stories by Bruce Jay Friedman and Louis Auchincloss, and an impressive $8,500 for an abridgment of *The French Lieutenant's Woman* by John Fowles. Gurley Brown did not find the Fowles excerpt "personally yummy" and published it only because her managing editor "made me" buy it, according to a memo to executives. Gurley Brown assumed *Cosmopolitan* ultimately would benefit from the pricey purchase of the Fowles novel because "agents and publishers then take you more seriously and will send you new important books." It did not happen.[111]

When it became obvious that authors of literary reputation did not want to be in *Cosmopolitan* no matter how much they might be paid, Gurley Brown stopped trying. She instead made certain the magazine ran stories and excerpts of novels from authors whose names appeared regularly on the era's bestseller lists: Frank Conroy, Dominick Dunne, Ken Follett, Frederick Forsyth, Gail Godwin, Graham Greene, Thomas Harris, Evan Hunter, Fletcher Knebel, Judith Krantz, John D. MacDonald, Ross MacDonald, Joyce Carol Oates, Edna O'Brien, Francoise Sagan, Irwin Shaw, Sidney Sheldon, Jacqueline Susann, Anne Tyler, and Irving Wallace.

One author of a certain literary reputation did agree to let *Cosmopolitan* publish his controversial novel, *Myra Breckinridge*. The sexual and social satire by Gore Vidal appeared in the August 1968 issue, soon after its book release. The title character was a transsexual whose explicit adventures in Hollywood made the book too risqué even to be reviewed by some mainstream newspapers and magazines, and got it banned in Australia. *Myra Breckinridge* was bizarre and outrageous—and perfectly suitable for publication by *Cosmopolitan*. It did little to lift the magazine's literary stature, however.[112]

And it was with some irony that *Cosmopolitan* published the fiction of William F. Buckley Jr., the public intellectual and political conservative whose September 1970 commentary in his magazine *National Review* criticized the licentiousness of the Cosmo Girl. The October 1976 *Cosmopolitan* ran an excerpt from a Buckley novel, *Saving the Queen*.[113]

Authors whose fiction *Cosmopolitan* published did not worry whether their subsequent new books would receive good reviews. In fact, no author need worry about a bad review. One book reviewer for the magazine remembered a note from the editor upon publication of a new Jacqueline Susann novel that emphasized Gurley Brown's friendship with Susann and, according to the reviewer, required a good review—the reviewer quit.[114]

But authors who were not friends of the *Cosmopolitan* editor received kind treatment, too. Gurley Brown instructed her reviewers to write only positive critiques of all books—and all movies and music albums. A Step Into My Parlor column explained her philosophy: "Why doesn't Cosmo do critical (putdown) book, movie, and record reviews? Well, I think Cosmo ought to help you choose what will bring the most pleasure." The column was a facile rationalization that differed slightly from the philosophy expressed in her concept for *Cosmopolitan* submitted to Hearst executives prior to being hired. "For the most part, anything that is reviewed must be a recommendation from the magazine," Gurley Brown had written. "If a book, record or movie is of major importance and the reviewer thinks it's a clinker, the subject can be brought up but written off quickly."[115]

A preference for positive reviews was an editor's prerogative, and the explanation to readers informed them of editorial policy so they knew what to expect. Readers were not informed, though, about a personal connection of the editor to the July 1974 publication in *Cosmopolitan* of an excerpt from *Jaws,* a bestseller about a shark that terrorized an ocean resort community. The movie rights to the book were owned by producers Richard Zanuck and David Brown, the editor's husband. Zanuck and David Brown had bought the movie rights to *Jaws* in May 1973. David Brown was a Hollywood producer who for twenty years had earned his living making movies from books and stories. His friendship with numerous Hollywood actors, directors, and producers were items in Step Into My Parlor quite regularly because Gurley Brown delighted in telling her readers about weekend visits to California and excursions to Europe where she mingled with celebrities. *Cosmopolitan* readers were not told about the connection between David Brown and *Jaws* until months after the novel's publication in the magazine when Gurley Brown began to promote the movie in her Step Into My Parlor column. Her column referred to *Jaws* on five separate occasions during its production and prior to its formal release to theaters, each time mentioning her husband's role as producer.[116]

Leading the Way

Continual success and a change in leadership at Hearst Corporation gave Helen Gurley Brown the confidence to push *Cosmopolitan* toward the boundary of acceptable material for a mainstream magazine by the mid-1970s. It was a boundary without definition, one that advertisers and readers would establish by their responses. Gurley Brown remained cautious about prurient material, but she was aware that readers were remarkably tolerant of the magazine's choices of topics and its language; advertisers, too, accepted her judgment.

Cosmopolitan's popularity with readers and advertisers placed her in a virtually unassailable position within the Hearst corporate hierarchy. Also, the retirement of Richard Berlin in 1973 removed the one person whose occasional opposition to certain topics had forced Gurley Brown to cancel articles. Berlin had insisted that executives with the magazine division, namely the president and publisher, monitor the *Cosmopolitan* editor to minimize embarrassment to the corporation. Upon his retirement, executives let Gurley Brown run the magazine without supervision, although they sometimes reacted negatively to articles after publication. Gurley Brown soon regarded *Cosmopolitan* as hers.

The editor worked long hours because she did everything. Hers was a management style that was inefficient because practically every manuscript was edited and revised three times: first by a copy editor, next by the copy chief, and then by Gurley Brown. Her involvement in cover design, selection of photographs, reviewing captions, and all other editorial aspects meant she spent seventy to eighty hours in the *Cosmopolitan* office and another dozen hours working at home on weekends. She enjoyed it. "It was my magazine," she said. "Each one."[117]

Cosmopolitan's associate editors worked hard, too, but not to that extent. "We would leave at six, have dinner, walk by Cosmo, look up, and see the light on in Helen's office," La Barre said. "You could imagine her up there, eating her yogurt at her desk, typing and writing notes."[118]

Gurley Brown closely edited all nonfiction articles and wrote lengthy, extremely detailed memos to writers who complained about editing of their manuscripts. "You are a famous writer and best-selling author—how can we dare take such liberties," she acknowledged, perhaps sarcastically, to one complainer. "It is entirely possible we shouldn't have, but we have such strange little stringent rules at Cosmo."[119]

Articles and nonfiction book excerpts became more explicit by the mid-1970s. References to penis were more prevalent, exceeding references to the previously preferred term male genitalia. References to specific sexual acts—cunnilingus, fellatio—prevailed over the general term oral sex. *Cosmopolitan* was not a how-to sexual manual, but its newfound frankness on sex differed appreciably from the earlier transformative phase when Gurley Brown allowed sensational titles and tabloid-style cover blurbs to insinuate that the magazine was explicit when it was not. From the mid-1970s onward, the titles more often accurately represented the content of articles.

"Confessions Of A Massage Parlor Girl" was a tabloid-style title that delivered on its promise. Based on an interview with a first-name-only woman whose skill as a masseuse was irrelevant, the article described sexual services purchased by male clients—prostitution. "About a fourth of the sessions involve a hand job," Angela informed readers, "another fourth straight intercourse, and the other half is taken up with blow jobs, or Frenches, or fellatio, or however you would like to most elegantly describe it." She earned $3,000 to $4,000 a month. Angela then discussed a lesbian relationship that included sex with her husband. "I would say that prostitution does lead to an understanding and acceptance of some fairly 'bizarre' sexual preferences: masochism, transvestism, fetishism, and so on, and a little bisexual fun on the side starts to seem rather ordinary by comparison."[120]

Deems, president of Hearst Magazines, disapproved of the explicit language in "Confessions Of A Massage Parlor Girl" and its lengthy digression concerning other sexual activity. Gurley Brown acknowledged "we had our slip-up." A few months later she made sure to alert Deems that an article titled "Fetishes" was ready for publication, and she sent a manuscript copy to him. He disliked it. Gurley Brown quickly decided to sell "Fetishes" and another potentially problematic article, "Sex Shops," to other magazines—*Playgirl* and *Viva*—known for their explicit material. A memo to her managing editor explained the reason for discarding the manuscripts and the need to salvage some of the cost: "We paid $500 for each article."[121]

Apparently, the repetitiveness of editorial material and the forgetfulness of Gurley Brown permitted a slightly less risqué article on the same topic to appear in *Cosmopolitan* two years later. "Massage Parlor Girls" did not spark any memos from Deems.[122]

The *Cosmopolitan* editorial formula recycled certain topics concerning relationships and sex: extramarital sex ("Can Adultery Save Your Marriage," "Beyond Monogamy," "Playing Around: The Long-Term Affair," "Creative Infidelity," "The Bisexual Lover," "Playing The Mistress Game: An Intimate Look At Adultery"); marital ("The Beginning Of The End Of Sex: The First Baby," "Marriage Yes! Children No!"); sexual dysfunction and practices ("The Bugaboo Of Male Impotence," "Why Girls Can't Have Orgasms," "Report On Fellatio"); and women's sexuality ("Nymphomania," "The Sexually Aggressive Woman," "Bisexuality: The Newest Sex Style," "Put A Little Sleaze In Your Life," "Lesbian Life Styles").

Cosmopolitan's attitude toward relationships and sexual behavior seemed to be at variance with society's attitude. A Gallup Poll in 1982 indicated that a majority of adult Americans were uneasy about so-called sexual freedom; 25 percent of all respondents stated they welcomed sexual freedom while 67 percent did not welcome it. However, attitudes varied widely by age; among adults eighteen to twenty-nine years old a plurality of 46 percent welcomed sexual freedom while 44 percent did not. *Cosmopolitan* apparently was attuned to younger attitudes.[123]

A survey by *Cosmopolitan* of its readership concerning attitudes toward relationships and sex generated such an incredible response that it became a book, *The Cosmo Report*. The January 1980 magazine offered readers a questionnaire to complete regarding sexual activity—and 106,000 people mailed their responses. It was an interesting look at self-reported frequency of sex, frequency of orgasms, specific sexual acts, and attitudes toward sex-related topics such as premarital and extramarital relationships. The survey suggested an unease similar to younger Gallup Poll respondents concerning sexual freedom; almost half of *Cosmopolitan* respondents felt pressure to have sex at times when they preferred not to.[124]

While offering its risqué material, *Cosmopolitan* continued to publish the basics: careers ("How To Get A Man's Pay," "How To Ask For A Raise," "When You Want—Or Have—To Make A Career Switch"); décor ("Paint Your Apartment Pretty," "Quilt A Sensuous Quilt," "Crafty Kitchens"); and general subjects ("Buying A Used Car," "To Insure Or Not To Insure," "What To Do With Your Old Falsies," "The Crisis At 30!," "How To Paper-Train A Puppy," "Women And Credit," "How To Answer Those Personal Ads"). Also, every month readers had regular columns available: Dieter's Notebook, Travel Bug, Analyst's Couch, Your Body.

The editorial formula that had evolved initially during the seven-year transformative phase of *Cosmopolitan* changed somewhat during the final thirteen years to the centennial. An examination of 129 monthly issues from autumn 1972 to the March 1986 centennial, certified that *Cosmopolitan* did write about sex and personal relationships more often, while devoting most of its pages to ordinary topics. Of the 2,706 nonfiction articles presented, sex was the topic in 189 (7 percent) and personal relationships were the focus of 354 (13.1 percent); other articles listed in the tables of contents were celebrity or newsmaker profiles (11.1 percent), health, excluding any regarding sexually transmitted diseases, which were categorized as sex topics (10.1 percent), movies/music/

television (7.8 percent), career/financial (7.4 percent), décor/fashion (6.4 percent), political/social (5.1 percent), and travel (4.4 percent). On a proportional basis, *Cosmopolitan* paid much more attention to profiles, health, and career/financial topics than during the first seven years Gurley Brown was editor.[125]

Although impossible to speculate about the impact *Cosmopolitan* had on society and its readers regarding gender relationships and sexual standards, the magazine's phenomenal commercial success assuredly influenced other magazines. The Seven Sisters attempted to modernize editorial material during the 1980s, new publications specifically appealed to younger working women, and heretofore taboo topics—sexual dysfunction, marital sexual unhappiness, premarital sex—were acceptable. Helen Gurley Brown and her magazine led the way.[126]

9

Celebration

March 2007

The visitor walked into the Hearst Tower in midtown Manhattan and stood for a moment in the lobby to admire the gentle cascade of water from far above that shimmered in sunlight. At the reception desk the visitor received a coded electronic card and directions to *Cosmopolitan.* An escalator passed between twin streams of the waterfall to carry the visitor to a vast plaza atrium on the third floor. From there, an elevator delivered him to the thirty-eighth floor.

The elevator opened and the visitor exited. To the left nearby, a glass door stenciled with Cosmopolitan; to the right, the same. The visitor went left, the wrong way. A helpful office worker only had taken a few steps to escort the visitor the right way when she stopped and pointed toward the other door, "There she is."

Across the corridor stood a tiny, elderly woman. She wore an amazingly bright reddish-pink, off-shoulder sweater and a knee-length cream skirt. She waved gently to the visitor.

Helen Gurley Brown.

She grasped her visitor's hands and spoke the first apology. "I am so dreadfully sorry," she said. "I should have greeted you. I was distracted by a message, and there you were. All by yourself! I am very sorry."

She led the way to her corner office on the northwest side, apologizing once or twice more on the way and again upon arrival. It was a roomy place, airy—at the far end a view of an adjacent taller building, on the side a vista of the Hudson River southward. Beneath a gold-frame mirror on a pale pink wall, a sofa upholstered with a floral fabric of fuchsia, green, pink, and yellow fit against an interior wall. A standard executive desk sat perpendicular to the diagonal frame of a side window. Two stacks of magazines filled much of the desktop, and notepads and a few books took up the remainder, except for a small clear space directly opposite a swivel chair. It was a business office first and foremost, but the sofa, artwork on the wall, a leopard-print rug, and a low table upon which were a small bowl of candy and vases of flowers lent a casual, comfy feel.

Gurley Brown was in no hurry to begin the interview. She asked questions about the visitor, listened attentively, and talked excitedly when Colorado was mentioned. "My mother and I took the train to Denver," she said. "I was a girl. We went to visit my sister. She was dating a man who had a car and we drove into the mountains." From a reference to her age at the time of the trip, she went there during the early 1930s. Her childhood home was a small town in Arkansas.

The interview began. Forty years had passed since she started at *Cosmopolitan*. The magazine's office was in the General Motors Building then, a block from the Hearst Magazine Building on Eighth Avenue near Columbus Circle. Now, the six-story shell of the original building formed the base for the forty floors of Hearst Tower above it.

She answered two different sets of questions. One set pertained to her ideas for *Cosmopolitan* from her first days on the job through the mid-1980s, also her methods of management, her dealings with corporate executives, and her memories of shaping the magazine into what she wanted and guiding it to stay on track. The second set concerned specific controversies and criticisms of *Cosmopolitan* during her early years as editor. Questions were preceded by reminders about facts relevant to specific incidents or situations, names of writers, subjects of articles, and categories of topics at various times from the mid-1960s to mid-1980s. These details were to aid her recall.

Her memory usually was clear about writers, former editors, past Hearst executives, and articles of which she was proud. She sometimes paused before answering and occasionally stopped while speaking, briefly falling silent to remember a person or an episode involving the magazine. She would resume, talking several minutes about accomplishments, controversies, and criticisms. She was proud of the magazine, often referred by name to associate editors whose ideas for articles deserved recognition, and was remarkably free of anger or resentment toward critics.

Any mention by the visitor about her role and *Cosmopolitan*'s part in making Hearst Corporation a very profitable business brought a similar reply: "The Hearst people have been good to me. They treated me well." She referred to a twenty-fifth anniversary dinner party Hearst Corporation gave in her honor in 1990: "They had invited everyone! Business people, theater people, writers, advertising people, fashion. On that night they gave me a Two-Twenty Mercedes Benz in appreciation of what *Cosmopolitan* had been doing for them." She paused. "Of course I don't drive. Which they knew! So when they gave me the keys they also gave me a chauffeur."

Her thirty-two-year tenure as *Cosmopolitan* editor officially ended in 1997, although she had shared editor's duties with her replacement for eighteen months. "But I had been good for them for so long and had brought in so much money, and they knew if I didn't have a job I would jump out a window or throw myself under a train to kill myself. They gave me the job as editor of *Cosmopolitan* international editions."

She picked up a magazine from one of the stacks on her desk. "We have fifty-nine editions! Every month I see all these *Cosmopolitans*! I review each one." She showed the magazine to the visitor. "This is from Latvia. Now I can't read Latvian and I can't read Chinese, but I go through them. I can tell by looking whether they have all the parts they should have. Sometimes there are too many blurbs—cover clutter. Are the girls on the cover beautiful? Do they show some of their boobs? Do they have articles on work and career? Do they feature women in their country who can serve as role models, be inspirational?"

She placed the magazine back on the stack, "These magazines make money."

The visitor told her how impressive, how magnificent Hearst Tower was, and asked her to compare the old days with the new. She smiled.

"There are people who say this building was able to be built because of *Cosmopolitan*," Helen Gurley Brown said. "But that may be going a bit far."

The Money Flow

Gurley Brown had inherited a magazine that was losing readers and advertisers. Her first issue of *Cosmopolitan* in July 1965 contained 124 pages, only 31 of which were ads. This editorial-to-advertising ratio of 3:1 was far higher than the industry standard of 5:4 for the era. The corporation should have reduced the page count for *Cosmopolitan* to achieve the 5:4 ratio, but that would have cut the magazine to a skimpy 72 pages and risked further circulation loss because readers might have considered the magazine too thin and not worth its price.[1]

Gurley Brown quickly attracted hundreds of thousands of new readers, of course. The tremendous growth in *Cosmopolitan* circulation during its transformative phase from mid-1965 to autumn 1972 continued at a dramatic pace through the mid-1970s, then slowed into the early 1980s, and stagnated just below three million copies until the centennial year. The number of copies circulated was impressive enough to attract advertisers, but the loyalty and quality of *Cosmopolitan* readers also helped sell pages. The magazine was unique. Ninety-two to 96 percent of its circulation derived from single-copy sales, which consistently averaged approximately 90 percent of copies distributed for sale—a percentage double the industry standard.[2]

Advertising fattened *Cosmopolitan* year after year, with only an odd down year caused by economic conditions that affected all media. Four years after Gurley Brown became editor the magazine sold 71 pages a month, five years after that it was 126 pages, and eleven years later—the last full year before the centennial—it was 205 pages. Actual revenue from advertisers grew exponentially for the same years, from $601,000 in 1964 to $3.1 million in 1969 to $9.1 million in 1974 and to $47.7 million in 1985. For each dollar spent by advertisers at the start of the era, eighty dollars were spent by the end. It was astonishing.

To appreciate the volume of advertising, consider that from the mid-1970s onward *Cosmopolitan* carried twice the number of ad pages published in *Ladies' Home Journal, McCall's,* or *Redbook,* half again as many ad pages seen in *Mademoiselle,* and one-fourth more than *Glamour.* Among the major magazines for women, only *Vogue* surpassed *Cosmopolitan* with approximately one-fifth more pages. Ad rates for magazines varied widely, of course, depending on total circulation and demographics, but *Cosmopolitan*'s cost-per-thousand-readers rate, a measure of its efficiency for advertisers, generally was 10 percent costlier than traditional women's magazines—a premium advertisers paid to reach the coveted *Cosmopolitan* readership.[3]

The late 1960s onward were not kind to older, general magazines such as *Life, Look, Saturday Evening Post.* Those venerable magazines died because advertisers found they could reach a similar but more sizable general audience through commercials on network television programs. Many women's magazines and specialty magazines for niche readership categories added advertisers from the late 1960s to early 1980s, despite two economic crises linked to dramatic increases in petroleum prices, one beginning in autumn 1973 and the other in summer 1979. They prospered because their publishers created or redirected their magazines to appeal to very specific kinds of readers, which advertisers then targeted. Among the successful new titles of the era were *People Weekly, Self, Us Weekly,* and the American edition of *Elle.* Women's magazines that delivered younger, affluent readers to advertisers prospered while those that served a predominately middle-aged readership lost some ad pages.[4]

Advertisers usually spent extra money because American consumer society blossomed during these years. Average household income by the mid-1970s was $14,000 and by the mid-1980s was almost $27,000. Most households spent approximately half of income on discretionary purchases, such as dining and entertainment, vacations, stereos, and similar nonessential items.[5]

Buying by consumers became remarkably easier with the introduction of credit cards usable nationwide rather than locally or for specific products. Until the issuance in 1966 of the MasterCharge credit card, later renamed Master-Card, and in 1970 of the Visa credit card, originally named BankAmerica Card, most consumers used credit cards from various local or national retailers, oil companies (for example, Standard Oil, Shell, Mobil) and credit card issuers such as American Express that required full payment of charges each month. The new nationwide credit cards gradually were accepted at most retailers, hotels and motels, gas stations, and airlines. Also, with an option to pay only some of the bill each month, although at a high interest rate, consumers started spending disposable income at a rate not previously seen. Only one of every eleven households had a MasterCard or Visa account in 1966; six years later seven of nine households did. At the start of the 1970s, the average credit card debt for an American household was $800—equal to approximately three weeks' average household income. The household savings rate decreased by the mid-1970s from 7 percent of income to 4 percent.

Prosperity and profligate spending by consumers did not guarantee profitability for all magazines because advertisers increasingly allocated a greater proportion of their annual expenditures to television. ABC, CBS, NBC, and independent stations in the twenty-five largest metropolitan areas received 29 percent of all national advertising revenue during the mid-1970s and 37 percent during the mid-1980s. Magazines received 11 percent of all national ad revenue during the mid-1970s and 9 percent during the mid-1980s. Proportionately, advertisers had reduced their allocation to magazines by nearly one-fifth.

Intense competition among magazines and with television produced distortion. Magazines at the top of their respective niches did well, while those with lower circulation struggled. *Cosmopolitan* was at the top of its niche, which included *New Woman, Playgirl,* and *Working Woman.* None of those magazines ever were serious competitors.[6]

Cosmopolitan definitely delivered the demographics certain advertisers wanted: millions of women readers mostly in their twenties and thirties; individual and household incomes above the national median. They were prime buyers of clothes, cosmetics, hair coloring, perfume, and shoes. They were keen on appearance and image. They were loyal to the magazine. Although advertisers could not measure precisely the effectiveness of their pages in *Cosmopolitan* because they also advertised in other magazines and bought television commercials, they were assured of reaching readers likely to buy their products. What also attracted some advertisers to *Cosmopolitan* was its status as a hot magazine. It had name recognition. People talked about it, whether they actually had read it or merely had heard about it. *Cosmopolitan* was the place to be for advertisers developing new products for younger women, a rather imprecise description that typically included women from their late teens to late thirties. Not that these women were not youthful, but few women at age twenty-three had much in common with women fifteen years older regarding careers, clothing, family, and lifestyle. Advertisers apparently did not care about these differences because most products served the entire age range.[7]

Cosmopolitan carried few ad pages for high-priced items, such as automobiles, crystal ware, fine china, pricey hotels, and resorts, or for providers of high-end services such as stockbrokers. Occasional ads appeared for airlines, insurance companies, and stereo systems. *Cosmopolitan*'s November and December issues regularly featured ads for expensive liqueurs, jewelry, and fine apparel. Every issue was filled with pages of ads for the most popular women's products of the era. Clairol was a major buyer of multiple pages in every *Cosmopolitan* for its cosmetics, several shampoos, and many hair-coloring products. Ads from Chanel, Coty, Esteé Lauder, Helena Rubinstein, Lanvin, Maybelline, Merle Norman, Revlon, and Yves St. Laurent appeared almost every month. Ads for feminine products by Kotex and Tampax also were in every issue. The magazine carried numerous ads for apparel, especially workplace clothes and casual wear, on a seasonal basis from Catalina and Sears. Basic undergarments from Bali and Maidenform advertised in the front pages while erotic garments from Frederick's of Hollywood were a back-pages staple. Several ad pages in the back section each issue promoted add-inches-to-your-bust exercise plans, album- and book-of-the-month clubs, diet regimens, early pregnancy tests, and secretarial schools.[8]

The magazine clustered color advertisements in the front, scattered some color ad pages in the middle, and loaded the back with black-and-white ads. Most ads in the back were one-third to one-half page and were adjacent to continuation text for articles and book excerpts.

An examination of advertisements in *Cosmopolitan* for the span noted no significant shift in product categories at the start, middle, or end of the era. The remarkably stable categories of products were cosmetics/fragrances (26 percent), hair products (13 percent), apparel/accessories (11 percent), soaps/lotions (9 percent), alcoholic beverages (6 percent), cigarettes (4 percent), and jewelry (4 percent). The solid presence of ads for apparel, accessories, and jewelry testified to the belief by advertisers that the magazine was a good buy despite the fact it had fewer pages devoted to fashion than its competitors. "We didn't let fashion get out of hand," Gurley Brown said. "It was confined to what was affordable for younger women, women who worked. That was the thing, you see, fashion for work and for fun."[9]

A fascinating aspect of advertisements in *Cosmopolitan* throughout these twenty-one years was an absence of imagery depicting children or families. People might have assumed its readership was primarily single women, but readership surveys indicated this was not the case. Early in the Gurley Brown era nearly two of every three women readers were married and late in the era the proportion was four of every nine; never-married women comprised one of every five readers early and three of every eight later. Married women were a sizable segment of readership. Advertisers were aware of this, but just as editorial material usually ignored children and family themes so did advertising. The magazine and its advertisers cultivated an identity for the readers at odds with reality.

Cosmopolitan welcomed advertisers, more so than most magazines. Gurley Brown and several associate editors assisted the ad sales staff by arranging photo shoots for new products to appear in monthly columns and departments. Ad sales staff guaranteed placement for certain products and services near or with columns and departments that complemented the advertisements: health and nutrition items near Dieter's Notebook; cosmetics and clothing items near beauty and fashion departments. Gurley Brown discussed special promotional campaigns for new products with advertisers and ad agency representatives. She met with them in her nearby office when they toured Hearst Magazine Building as guests of the ad sales staff, and courted them by accompanying ad sales staff on visits to ad agencies and makers of products. She dined with them on a weekly basis as hostess of a special luncheon at 21 Club. She pledged that products and services of advertisers would get some ink in monthly columns devoted to beauty, décor, and fashion. She monitored photographs to ensure display of advertised items on pages for special holiday sections. Also, Gurley Brown bartered with airlines for free travel by promising to refer to an airline in her own column, Step Into My Parlor, in exchange for tickets—a practice she believed necessary because Hearst Corporation strictly limited her travel expenses.

Some aspects of her involvement with the advertising end of the business were not unusual for an editor of a women's magazine. However, standards at women's magazines differed from those at newsmagazines and quality journals of opinion—among them *Newsweek, Time, U.S. News & World Report, Atlantic Monthly, Harper's, New Republic, New Yorker.* Editors there were not required to assist ad sales staff in any manner. Occasionally, a corporate executive from a new advertiser might be introduced to an editor during a tour or at a luncheon, but this was merely a courtesy. Editors liked to boast that an invisible wall separated them from the ad sales department.

Conversely, editors of women's magazines routinely met with advertisers and potential advertisers. They discussed upcoming promotional campaigns for new products and services. This was a courtesy without any assurance by editors of preferential treatment in articles or mention in monthly columns and holiday sections. Yet it was understood by editors that holiday sections and monthly columns devoted to beauty, fashion, and health would routinely mention or feature products and services from advertisers—and might even mention items from nonadvertisers, too, if space was available or if editors wished to be inclusive for the benefit of readers. As a courtesy to advertisers and supposedly to help readers, some women's magazines, particularly fashion publications, listed every item of accessories, clothing, and cosmetics worn by the month's cover model. *Cosmopolitan* also cooperated. Each month from the early 1970s onward the photo caption at the top of the table of contents listed the brands of lipstick, hair coloring, nail polish, jewelry, and clothes worn by the model.[10]

The tricky part for most editors of women's magazines was the frequency with which to mention items that were advertised in the same issue. It might become obvious to readers that the magazine was acting as a tout, which could harm its credibility. Another factor affecting editors was that publishers might expect them to provide free publicity for advertised products whenever possible. The ability of an editor to resist an insistent publisher usually depended on whether the magazine was gaining, holding, or losing readers.

Gurley Brown did everything other editors of women's magazines did, but she exceeded the involvement of most peers. A memo from her to the *Cosmopolitan* publisher to request a personal bonus for any additional ad revenue received by the magazine indicated her attitude. "Since I work about as hard hustling advertising as I do editing, I feel this is not unwarranted," she wrote. Her policy at the magazine accommodated advertisers. Gurley Brown knew the importance of pleasing advertisers from her own experience with an ad agency as a copywriter. She was a realist. "Advertising is what made money," Gurley Brown said. "Whenever we could, we were attentive to them."[11]

She spent a few days in Los Angeles almost every year during early spring to make the rounds of prominent advertisers with *Cosmopolitan*'s ad sales director for the West Coast. They had lunch or dinner with various advertising agency representatives handling name clients (Carnation Food, Munsingwear, Pendleton), presidents of beauty products manufacturers (Max Factor, Merle Norman, Neutrogena), and executives of other major entities (Nissan, California Avocado Advisory Board). While some editors of women's magazines might be professionally courteous but not enthusiastic, Gurley Brown enjoyed talking about new products and ad campaigns. A letter from the ad sales director praised her for being "most helpful" and referred to her receiving a gift of "a big package of the line" from Neutrogena. On one visit, Gurley Brown also contacted an ad agency that represented a fashion company to obtain information about a "New York retailer or show room at which we could pick merchandise in the future" to display on photo pages for special fashion sections. Some items also would be mentioned in the *Cosmopolitan* fashion column.

A memo from the *Cosmopolitan* ad sales director to the publisher after the session with the California Avocado Advisory Board formally noted that Gurley Brown was supposed to discuss "any detail on the possibility of the use of an avocado article in the magazine." She did. *Cosmopolitan* subsequently published "Avocados Can Peel Off Pounds" and "Lunch For Two: Avocado Surprise," the first as a feature article and the second as a food column.[12]

Another result of the annual California visit to major advertisers was the editor's involvement with creating a new ad for Nissan Motors, which manufactured Datsun automobiles. (Datsun was dropped as the brand name in favor of Nissan during the early 1980s.) Nissan had sent page proofs of two Datsun advertisements it planned to run in *Cosmopolitan* and had asked the magazine's ad sales director to forward them to Gurley Brown for comment. She disliked both ads. "They're totally wrong for a Cosmopolitan Girl or any girl," she responded. "Although the colors are pretty, they are basically masculine advertising with very little appeal in graphics or text for a warm-blooded, upward-striving, beauty and success oriented woman!" Nissan revised the ads. When published in *Cosmopolitan,* each ad just posed a casually dressed young woman next to a car while ads in newsmagazines posed a casually dressed young man. The idea that an editor helped an advertiser design an ad would have appalled most editors of the era.[13]

Gurley Brown also was hostess each Thursday for advertisers and ad agency representatives at a 21 Club luncheon paid for by Hearst Corporation. "A fancy place," Gurley Brown said, "but you wouldn't want to take these advertisers to any other place." Each week, a president of a company that advertised— Clairol, for example—and a vice president responsible for a particular category of products—cosmetics or shampoo, for example—would attend the luncheon accompanied by executives from the advertising agency handling the account. Gurley Brown would invite a few associate editors, and a lucky lowly editorial assistant would attend on a rotating basis. "They would have about twenty people for lunch," she said. "It was pretty expensive."

It was not a typical meet-and-greet event where a magazine editor mingled and chatted with all the guests. Gurley Brown kept her focus: "I would put the head guy next to me. While we ate I would go through that month's Cosmo page by page with him. I would explain the photography and the articles to him. I would tell him why his wife, his girlfriend, the women who worked for him read our magazine. Some advertisers didn't like what we were doing—too racy, too controversial. They needed to hear from me our purpose, why those articles were essential to the people who read us, why they liked us. Our sales were excellent! Women read our magazine. By the time we left Twenty-One, they knew their advertisement needed to be in Cosmo!"[14]

Cosmopolitan publisher Frank Dupuy appreciated the enthusiastic participation of Gurley Brown and her associate editors at these weekly luncheons. "Many thanks for your usual sterling performance," Dupuy wrote in a memo to her immediately after a 21 Club session with executives from Lanvin, a cosmetics manufacturer and major advertiser. Dupuy especially was impressed that a *Cosmopolitan* associate editor familiar with the cosmetics industry had agreed to meet separately with the new president of Lanvin, who had held a corporate position with a national retailer. The Lanvin president wanted to "pick her brains about the cosmetics business," a request that Dupuy realized was "most significant that he would want further help from us."[15] (Not only was this an editorial ethical breach at many publications, but it raised an interesting conflict-of-interest dilemma because a *Cosmopolitan* editor was assisting one cosmetics company to compete more effectively against other cosmetics companies, which also advertised in the magazine.)

Richard Deems, the magazine division president, received a copy of the memo regarding Lanvin. He seconded Dupuy's comments in a handwritten note to Gurley Brown, and also praised her for a recent reference to major advertisers in a Step Into My Parlor column. Gurley Brown had let readers know about her trip to London to launch a British edition of *Cosmopolitan*. She wrote in the column that her visit had included "calling on British advertisers—old friends like Max Factor, Revlon, Estée Lauder, Elizabeth Arlen, Coty, Yardley, etc." Deems appreciated the voluntary mention of "your ad calls in London" because of its presumed benefit to the advertisers cited, especially her calling them friends.[16]

A demonstration of the lengths to which *Cosmopolitan* would go to placate or please advertisers occurred during autumn 1972. A writer for another magazine had visited *Cosmopolitan* for an article on the complex process of introducing a new beauty product, in this case a deep-cleanser soap made by Estée Lauder. The article apparently described the cooperation of the *Cosmopolitan* editorial staff to arrange photo scenes for displays of the soap in the What's New, What It Does For You column, and the writer noted the friendly atmosphere that prevailed between magazine editors and Lauder ad agency representatives. Sometime later, a *Cosmopolitan* associate editor saw a prepublication version of the article and it contained nothing negative. Then the associate editor received a final draft in which the writer called the new soap harsh and irritating to skin. (Documents did not reveal why the *Cosmopolitan* associate editor had access to prepublication versions of an article for another magazine.)

Nervous that this critical judgment of the new soap somehow would reflect poorly on *Cosmopolitan,* the associate editor promptly warned Gurley Brown about the situation. "I could almost swear that nasty remark about the soap wasn't in the first version I did see," the associate editor stated in a memo. "It sort of snuck in after the fact." The associate editor told Gurley Brown she "wrote a cute letter, purportedly from a man reader, to go in letters column saying how terrific the soap was." The plan was for *Cosmopolitan* to publish the fake letter to atone for the other magazine's criticism of the Lauder soap. The associate editor sent a copy of the fake letter to Lauder executives, who disapproved the plan. The associate's memo to Gurley Brown also reminded her that *Cos-*

mopolitan often had publicized Lauder shampoos, skin creams, and makeup in the monthly beauty column, feature articles, photo displays of gift ideas, and a "cover credit in February" that listed lipstick. "We have also been generous with Clinique credits," the memo stated about another Lauder product. "August issue cover plus 2 What's New mentions so far this year." To further favor Lauder, the associate editor promised additional publicity: "We went over the credits in the horoscope book for the Jan. issue and changed a lot of non-advertiser mentions to ones that might do us more good: Estée Lauder has two."[17]

Gurley Brown was sufficiently concerned about the incident that she notified Deems. She attached a letter to her memo and asked Deems if it should be mailed to Estée Lauder herself. The letter referred to "some other things we have been thinking about on behalf of Estée Lauder," an allusion to details in the memo about product publicity in the January horoscope section and February cover. "We deeply value the advertising pages that you've placed with us," Gurley Brown assured Lauder in the draft letter. "It just isn't ever our intention to do something foolish in print." Deems replied to his editor, "I would not send." He also advised her, "Let's forget the past & treat them nicely in the future."[18]

The result of this anxiety was prominent placement in the December 1972 issue of *Cosmopolitan* of a Lauder perfume in a photo display promoting a small selection of Christmas gift ideas and an adjacent photo caption that mentioned the perfume first, although its position was in the middle. For unknown reasons, the article that had generated all the worry never appeared in print.[19]

An incident involving another major advertiser, Redken, resulted in a temporary suspension of its advertising contract. *Cosmopolitan* had run a article on a woman's disastrous experience with a hairdresser; although the article had not referred to any salon products, Redken executives disliked the gist of the story, namely that a woman might be unhappy with a stylist, and the company pulled its ads. *Cosmopolitan* sought to rectify the problem by running a corrective article several months later that focused on complaints by stylists about the unreasonable demands of some women customers. Redken refused to reconsider. Gurley Brown explained the problem to the magazine's West Coast ad director. "At this point I have nothing further in mind and really don't want to hear one more word about the subject," she wrote. "I feel they are total assholes . . . I really am disgusted with them at this point and would like not to discuss it any further."[20]

The behavior of Gurley Brown and *Cosmopolitan*'s editorial partnership with advertisers contrasted sharply to *Ms.,* the one women's magazine of the era that tried to maintain editorial independence from advertisers. Founded in 1972, *Ms.* attained a peak circulation of nearly 500,000 within several years, but struggled to attract advertisers. Gloria Steinem, a founder of the magazine and its first editor, refused to publish promotional material that would mention advertised products. Advertisers disliked the *Ms.* attitude, and because they had the cooperation of other women's magazines they could ignore it. *Ms.* suffered various financial crises during the 1980s.[21]

Hearst Corporation undoubtedly appreciated what Gurley Brown had done for its bottom line. It had hurriedly raised her salary and bonus when she seemed tempted by an offer from *McCall's* early in 1972. Yet corporate culture retained its penny-pinching methods. Deems and Dupuy simply refused to budget money for travel that Gurley Brown considered relevant to her job as editor. "I would like it understood that I may take one trip to Europe and two to California which are paid for by the company, first-class accommodations," she notified Deems. Her request was denied.[22]

Gurley Brown decided to barter with airlines. In exchange for free tickets, she would mention an airline in her Step Into My Parlor column. She was not happy with this and complained to Deems. "To get to Europe last year with TWA I had to give away so much I don't have much to give away the next time," her memo stated. "A story about their trips to Las Vegas, pictures of me with TWA in my column. I'm not sure it's dignified for an editor to be out selling pieces of herself this way!"[23]

Although publicity for any airline in a feature article was rare, an exception being "A Weekend In Las Vegas" to repay TWA by publicizing its flight schedule while describing an active two days of casino gambling and sunbathing, the monthly Step Into My Parlor column offered easy opportunities to settle her debts. Gurley Brown frequently told readers about her getaway weekends to Hollywood and Palm Springs in California and weeklong trips to London, Paris, and the Riviera. These chatty missives allowed her to drop in a sentence or two to fulfill her obligation to airlines. Gurley Brown did not disclose her free-travel-for-publicity arrangements to readers.[24]

"David (my husband) and I left New York for London on TWA's Flight 700," she told readers. "It leaves every night at 8:00 p.m. and is simply a floating pleasure palace! If they're not filet-mignoning you, they're white- and red-wining you, and there's the movie and the stereo." An inset photo showed Gurley Brown standing on an airliner's entry steps with the TWA logo over her left shoulder. A trip to France a year later produced this column item, which opened with a reference to a photo of her: "That's me in my TWA blanket. This darling airline let me borrow it off flight No. 800 because I was freezing when we got to Paris. There's always something you forget to take . . . like a coat! I returned the blanket to flight No. 801 (Paris to New York), and TWA said they'd got it back on the right aircraft." A few years later after a weekend in Los Angeles, she was "Back to New York on TWA's super-satisfying Flight 900."[25]

She bartered with Pan American Airways, too. A lengthy journey to Japan was repaid: "I packed up my Puccis, David packed a few things, and one crispy morning we took off. Pan Am's daily flight 801 cradled us from New York to Tokyo in thirteen and a half tiny hours with one stop in Fairbanks, Alaska. That is indeed a lot of flying and keeping it together without lie-down sleep at one stretch, but I find those overseas flights so posh, the food so divine, and the stewardesses such angels—at least they were on Pan Am's 801—a girl who works herself to frazzles at the office may be just better off on an airplane!" Pan Am received mention three more times in Step Into My Parlor the next few years after two other trips to Tokyo and an excursion to London. The final repayment to Pan Am included an enthusiastic, "I love that airline."[26]

On the other hand, Gurley Brown did not identify to readers an airline that had ruined a trip. "My luggage had been lost by a very naughty airline," she told readers of her column. "I was wearing the same little shift I'd been in for three days." Whether the naughty airline was a barter deal or an actual paid flight could not be determined.[27]

Exchanging publicity for free travel was not usual policy at most magazines. Two-thirds of editors at consumer magazines surveyed on ethics during the mid-1980s admitted they allowed staffers to accept free travel but did not promise publicity in return. One-sixth of editors did not accept free travel at all. One-sixth did accept and promised publicity in return. Certainly, the editor of *Cosmopolitan* should have disclosed to readers the fact she traveled for free in return for mentioning an airline. Disclosure would have allowed readers to better judge her fulsome praise of TWA and Pan Am.[28]

Cosmopolitan also should have informed readers that it occasionally accepted free travel and expenses from celebrities it profiled. Liz Smith, the writer who had faked the Park Avenue prostitute article, spent a week traveling with Sonny and Cher, a married singing duo whose prime-time television show was very popular during the early 1970s. Smith struggled to find a focus for the article because Cher would not speak to her and because Smith sensed that tension affected the couple's relationship. Smith and Gurley Brown agreed to forget the article and offered to reimburse the duo's publicist for airline expenses, food costs, and hotel bills. The publicist, irate that the magazine was not upholding its end of the bargain, refused the offer.[29] (Had the magazine published the Sonny and Cher profile, readers would not have known that the entertainers had paid all expenses for *Cosmopolitan*'s writer.)

Because of her cooperative relationship with the magazine's ad sales staff, Gurley Brown occasionally was able to deny requests for free publicity for advertisers. During summer 1975, the West Coast ad director was trying to put together a package of fashion ads for a Christmas section and had decided to use a motorcycle theme. Models wearing clothes suitable for riding would pose astride motorcycles. The ad director proposed a four-page photo spread. Gurley Brown firmly and politely rejected the idea. She explained that most of the twenty color pages allotted for the December issue already were scheduled for various departments, leaving only two pages unoccupied. "Now, there is almost no way you could do anything major on motorcycle accessories when that's the space we've got," she wrote. "Not enough ladies own motorcycles or probably ever will. As you know, we did a two page 4-color feature in September 1974 Cosmo on cycles." She closed by promising to consider placing fashions for motorcycling in a separate column.[30]

Cosmopolitan's monthly columns and departments sprinkled names of products, hotels, and resorts in the text. What's New, What It Does For You showcased new items to coincide with introductory marketing campaigns. Cosmetics, deodorants, fingernail polish, hair coloring, cleansers, and whatever else was advertised in *Cosmopolitan* also warranted routine promotional blurbs in What's New, What It Does For You. The décor column informed readers about retailers that sold the furniture and household accessories depicted in photos. Travel features cited specific resorts and hotels, and sometimes referred to an airline that flew to a vacation destination.

Perhaps the magazine's readers were sophisticated enough or jaded enough to recognize bartering and free publicity when they saw it. Yet the casual way in which these paybacks and favors were presented might have influenced some readers to buy an airline ticket with TWA or Pan American, or book a room at a favorably mentioned hotel, or stay at a resort because *Cosmopolitan* wrote such nice things about it. That, of course, was the intent.

Advertising expanded the magazine to a volume of pages unimaginable to Hearst Corporation executives at the start of the Gurley Brown era. Slender issues of 176 to 192 pages during the late 1960s swelled to a count of 224 to 256 pages by the early 1970s, and to a total of 328 to 352 pages by the mid-1980s. Some holiday issues and special issues exceeded 400 pages. At one point so many advertisers clamored to buy pages in *Cosmopolitan* Hearst executives set a limit of 200 ad pages to constrain costs for paper and printing. The editorial-to-advertising ratio of *Cosmopolitan* changed from 3:1 in 1965 to 3:2 at the end of the 1960s, then to 1:1 by the end of the 1970s and to 4:5 by the mid-1980s; on a percentage basis, a magazine that once was 25 percent ad pages had become a magazine of 55 percent ad pages. The preponderance of ads did not bother readers, who continued to buy an extremely high percentage of copies placed on store shelves and at checkout counters.

Gurley Brown never received a bonus for ad revenue. She did receive a generous salary. By the mid-1980s, the *Cosmopolitan* editor reportedly earned $500,000 a year.[31]

Hard Sell

The trick to sustaining magazine circulation almost completely dependent upon sales at newsstands and vendors, which could fluctuate by tens of thousands of copies from month to month and result in a terrible waste of money for printing and distribution, was to persuade potential buyers to look at inside pages, particularly the table of contents. The magazine cover was the key.

Cosmopolitan covers were special: every month a beautiful woman, alluring and confident, dressed in fashionable clothes and sparkling jewelry, staring confidently and directly at a prospective buyer. Inside pages might rarely be erotic or prurient, but its covers were provocative. Beautiful women models gradually showed greater amounts of skin as the magazine became more popular and profitable. "I like cleaveage if shown in good taste," Gurley Brown enthused, and misspelled, in her plan for *Cosmopolitan*. "I see no reason ever to have anything but a pretty girl or at least a sexy girl on each cover." This was a dramatic departure from the customary covers of women's magazines that pictured celebrities, wives of political leaders, and famous artists and writers. *Cosmopolitan* stopped using celebrity covers altogether by the late 1960s, except for two with Elizabeth Taylor and two with Jacqueline Kennedy; after those rare occurrences, the covers were models exclusively—some of whom became actresses afterward.[32]

Cover blurbs also were crucial to vendor sales. Bracketing the cover model were blurbs, each enticing an onlooker to peek inside. Examples were "Choose The Perfect Father And The Sex Of Your Baby"; "The Astonishingly Frank Diary Of An Unfaithful Wife"; "Makeup To Wear To Bed"; "Poor Girl's Guide To America's Rich Young Men"; "How To Make A Small Bosom Amount To Something"; "How To Love Like A Real Woman"; "How To Get Married If You're Over 30"; "All About Exercise—Who's Doing What?—And What's Good And Bad For You"; "A Survey Of Coeds Who Seduce Their Professors"; "When You Want More Love Than Your Husband Can Give"; "Dating By Computer, Actual Experiences Of Four Career Girls"; "Things I'll Never Do With A Man Again"; "What Kind Of Man Makes The Best Lover?"

A cover was a team effort involving Gurley Brown, associate editors, photographers, page-design editors, and David Brown. Gurley Brown's husband wrote every cover blurb the entire time she was editor. "David and I would sit at our dining table, and I would read bits of stories to him or he would look at the proofs," Gurley Brown said. "He would scribble something, read it to me aloud, change words, keep at it until it was absolutely perfect."[33]

Each cover had at least six blurbs, usually eight, and sometimes nine. The April 1970 cover was the first with a blurb to use orgasm ("Plain And Fancy Facts About Orgasm") and the June 1971 cover had the first blurb to mention "lesbian" ("Finally, An Honest Report On The Lesbian Experience"). Although explicit at the time, further blurbs referring to orgasm were infrequent—not more than once or twice a year—and no blurbs contained vulgarity.

Memoranda from Gurley Brown relentlessly prodded her associate editors and art director to create a masterpiece cover each and every month. "I had no formal training," she said. "I knew what worked, what did not work. *Cosmo* lived and died depending on a person deciding to pay for it or not when they saw it—talk about an impulse buy! Well, that put extreme importance on our covers." She critiqued the production proof of each cover, checking logo color, background color, hair color of the model, hairstyle of the model, lipstick color of the model, jewelry worn by the model, clothes worn by the model, the smile of the model, angle of eye contact by the model, position of cover blurbs—every imaginable facet of the cover. The editor told her subordinates to get tough with photographers. "I know you can only go so far with a photographer before he gets angry but someplace in this world must be the photographer who will take the color-on-color picture I want," she wrote.[34]

Frustration and disappointment were inevitable. Some photographers were temperamental, and the editor's judgment of design elements that distinguished a good cover from a mediocre one was subjective. Gurley Brown nitpicked. One weekend in autumn 1967 she decided to create a definitive list of standards for the cover. Gurley Brown distributed Rules For Covers For Cosmopolitan, a nine-item set of directives, a few of which were so fundamental it was surprising she had to say them:

- "The cover we are shooting for (the month) should look different from the month before. That means THE COLOR OF THE DRESS should be different—totally, if possible—and the color of the background should be different. The model's hair ought not to be in the same style as the style of the month before. What is wanted on the newsstand is impact. WOW, THE NEW COSMOPOLITAN IS OUT!"
- "We should keep our eye out for hot-colored dresses to use on the covers of Cosmo regardless of whether we're lining up a shooting at that moment. When we have only four or five days to track down such dresses, no wonder we can't find them. We couldn't care less whether the cover dress is available in stores to the reader of Cosmo; we have virtually no fashion advertising and as long as we are in this position, we are quite free to use dresses from somebody's closet, from a department store, or from a boutique."
- "About one cover in three should have bosom showing. Décolletage dresses are not in fashion so I know it's a challenge."
- "We should try for interesting effects with jewelry other than earrings; another good way to use color; necklaces, bracelets, arm-band bracelets."
- "Be careful about having wide, long scarves cover up the garment."
- "We'll use models on the covers. This picture is too important to take chances with!"
- "Male models are definitely heterosexual looking; avoid anything faggish."[35]

Cosmopolitan covers displayed a mostly modest exposure of breast cleavage, sometimes a bare midriff, sometimes a lot of leg. A memo from Gurley Brown to editors specified, with misspelling, "Show cleaveage at least every three months." The July 1965 issue, which technically was Gurley Brown's debut magazine, displayed a modest amount of cleavage of a woman model. Subsequent covers the next two years were a mix of similar displays of minimal cleavage, occasional deep cleavage, a bikini-clad woman, and modestly dressed models with no cleavage exposed. Covers after summer 1967 presented women models wearing much makeup and less concealment.[36]

Phenomenal

Cosmopolitan circulated 2.515 million copies monthly by late 1976, an average annual gain of 209,000 copies after the Burt Reynolds centerfold had brought it notoriety. Its circulation continued to grow at an average rate of 100,000 copies each year the remainder of the decade to attain 2.8 million copies at the start of the 1980s. A temporary three-month decline early in 1981 was reversed by year's end, and circulation then inched upward by an annual average of 36,000 copies to 2.98 million by the centennial month of March 1986. Gurley Brown's editorial formula was no fluke. "There's always the basics, the things that never change," she said. "Office politics, men and women in love and wrong relationships, ambition, personal fulfillment, health."[37]

Throughout the first seven years Gurley Brown was editor, *Cosmopolitan* consistently sold 90 percent of the copies placed with vendors. The rate stunned the magazine industry and amazed Hearst Corporation executives. Gurley Brown was surprised, too. Not being a veteran of magazines, she had no idea how extraordinary the single-copy sales percentage was. "The Hearst people were very excited about it all," she said. Memoranda to Gurley Brown from corporate executives were positively giddy. "Dear Helen," wrote Richard Deems, president of magazines, "you are great! great! great! Appreciate you." Richard Berlin, Hearst Corporation president, cited a monthly report on single-copy sales as "a remarkable achievement. My congratulations to you; you deserve a 'deep, deep bow.'"[38]

How did this happen? One reason was name recognition of *Cosmopolitan's* editor. Helen Gurley Brown was the author of a bestselling book about the Modern Woman, had been profiled in several national magazines, had written a syndicated newspaper column, and had appeared on national television talk shows. With the exception of Henry Luce, publisher of Time-Life, Inc., almost no other mainstream magazine executive was so well known during the mid-1960s. (Luce died in 1967.) It would be hard to argue that anything other than hiring her as editor of *Cosmopolitan* accounted for the immediate leap in circulation of almost

51,000 copies during summer 1965 and a temporary surge of another 180,000 by November—lifting the magazine to above a million copies for the first time in twelve years. Although newsstand sales would fluctuate moderately for several months, the trend definitely was up.

The results were spectacular. A series of memoranda from early 1968 to mid-1972 reported single-copy sales that ranged from 89 percent to 94 percent of the million-plus copies distributed. A memo from Deems to Gurley Brown one month declared, "This must be the best June report in the entire industry." Equally important financially was the impressive reduction in the monthly number of unsold copies by an average of 31,000 copies. The reduction in unsold copies saved $280,000 during 1972 alone.[39]

The incredible sales percentages did not take a dip for sixteen years despite periodic price increases. The cover price was raised to fifty cents in February 1966, to sixty cents in January 1969, and to seventy-five cents in February 1970. Hearst Corporation received roughly 55 percent of the cover price for each copy sold; 20 percent went to a distributor for delivering copies to vendors and another 5 percent as commission for each sale; 20 percent went to a vendor for each sale. Revenue for each copy sold had risen from twenty-seven cents to forty cents, which brought Hearst Corporation an additional $2 million annually by the mid-1970s.[40]

Despite the amazing sales percentage and the practically unbroken string of higher circulation every month, Gurley Brown encountered the same corporate second-guessing that plagued editors everywhere. Deems disliked the April 1968 cover; he told her the blue background color was tepid and the promotional blurbs dull. Deems did not dare tell the editor how to improve the cover. Gurley Brown did not change anything. She liked the cover. Several weeks later the circulation manager sent the usual monthly memo concerning vendor sales; the April issue sold 894,600 copies, a 90 percent rate. Gurley Brown forwarded the memo to Deems with a handwritten note: "Dear Dick, This is the blue Cosmo cover you were a little apprehensive about." Deems scribbled a reply: "I bow my head in shame and respect to your editorial perspicacity, Dick." He never again questioned her cover designs.[41]

Single-copy sales were so strong that Hearst executives actually made subscribers pay a premium of 25 percent—$15 for a year's subscription versus a single-copy price of $1, or $12 for the year. (This unusual pricing policy was the corporation's response to rapidly rising postal rates mandated by the federal government, which gradually enabled the U.S. Postal Service to wean itself from taxpayer subsidy.) The economics of readership circulation for most women's magazines revolved around subscriptions. Renewal rates varied widely from 40 percent to 70 or 80 percent; for a magazine with several million subscriptions this could mean replacing a half-million to a million or more subscribers each year simply to maintain a circulation guarantee to advertisers. Publishers financed advertising campaigns in newspapers and on radio, sent millions of direct-mail solicitations, and contracted with door-to-door solicitors who kept a commission of one-third to one-half of the initial subscription payment. Magazines restored circulation by a variety of methods, including discounts, short-term subscriptions of three to six months, and premiums in the form of packets of coupons for household products. *Cosmopolitan* avoided similar subscription churn and expense because it was practically all single-copy sales.[42]

Not all magazines enjoyed similar success attracting new readers, either from single-copy sales at vendors or from subscriptions. Despite the rapid growth of women in the workforce, their newfound financial independence, and the formation of millions of households during the era, women's magazines experienced widely different circulation patterns. *Good Housekeeping* and *Ladies' Home Journal* recorded insignificant circulation gains into the 1970s and *McCall's* lost one-eighth of its readership.

Despite the year-to-year circulation gains from 1965 through the mid-1980s, success by *Cosmopolitan* was not a smooth process. A brief panic ensued early in 1981 when single-copy sales plunged for the only time since Gurley Brown had become editor. The February issue declined 153,000 copies from the prior year, which took the sales percentage down to 87 percent. The March issue did worse, dropping by 276,000 copies from the prior year, or down to 84 percent. Gurley Brown's memo to executives demonstrated her concern: "I want to do something other than worry!"

The memo listed five items, three of which would determine what was wrong so a long-term corrective could be devised and two of which would attempt a short-term fix to reverse the trend quickly. Gurley Brown's plan recommended: (1) an interdepartmental group from within *Cosmopolitan* to refocus the magazine's editorial formula; (2) a readership study to determine the popularity of specific categories of articles and features, monthly columns, and the editorial format generally; (3) an analysis of methods to create better displays at checkout counters in grocery stores to boost sales of the magazine; (4) a test in certain cities to assess the results of reducing the price from $1.75 to $1.50; and (5) employment of a full-time promotional specialist to design ads for a marketing campaign for the magazine.[43]

The shock of a slump in single-copy sales was evident. Gurley Brown had never doubted her decisions previously. For her to ask for a readership study and to suggest a price reduction were extraordinary measures. She already had considered a redesign of the *Cosmopolitan* cover in 1979 by cutting the number of blurbs from eight or nine to only five and enlarging the typeface for dramatic effect. She canceled the redesign because it was too difficult to choose only five items for blurbs. "Alas, no articles usually stand out enough to justify their carrying the cover by themselves," Gurley Brown wrote to executives. "If we should have an issue containing three or four really outstanding articles or books, it still seems to me we might try layouts along the lines of the ones we did this time."[44]

Hearst Corporation approved a thorough study of reader preferences and rejected any price cut. *Cosmopolitan* dropped only one monthly column—music reviews—and slightly shortened the length of its traditionally short articles and features. Beginning in 1982, few occupied more than the equivalent of three full pages of text, or about 2,500 words (nine standard typewritten pages), while nonfiction book excerpts seldom filled more than six full pages.

Single-copy sales eventually steadied and the magazine's circulation continued its climb to nearly three million copies by the centennial month of March 1986. What happened was a transition from absolute reliance on newsstand sales to a slightly higher percentage of subscriptions, a completely unanticipated shift by *Cosmopolitan* readers that began in 1981. Cathleen Black, president of Hearst Magazines when this book was written and formerly ad director for *Ms.,* described the surprise transition. "Newsstand sales dipped about 1% per year, but subscriptions grew rapidly at over 25% per annum," Black wrote. When the single-copy scare began, *Cosmopolitan* had 97,000 subscribers and by the centennial issue it had 302,000 subscribers; for the same span, newsstand sales decreased slightly from 2.715 million copies to 2.62 million copies, or 3 percent.[45]

Ordinarily, a circulation decline for a magazine compelled its publisher either to hold ad rates steady or to lower rates because the circulation guarantee to advertisers had shrunk. Hearst Corporation did not adjust its ad rates because *Cosmopolitan* had kept its circulation guarantee comfortably below actual circulation for fifteen years. Therefore, the temporary plunge in single-copy sales early in 1981 had no adverse financial consequences. Black explained the so-called bonus effect: "Cosmo's rate base was between 2.25 million and 2.5 million over the period, but delivered an enormous bonus. A bonus of half-a-million was about the size of a small magazine."[46]

Gurley Brown and *Cosmopolitan* succeeded precisely because many newly independent women were eager to learn about careers, health, relationships, and sex. The magazine's success truly was phenomenal.

Demographic Drift

Who were those *Cosmopolitan* readers?

The prospectus written by Gurley Brown for *Femme* and her subsequent concept of *Cosmopolitan* had listed characteristics of women who might appreciate a magazine devoted to careers, contemporary lifestyles, and man-woman relationships:

- "They are equals of men and citizens, but they must also pay their bills, constantly improve themselves, do an honest day's work, love men, and what have you."
- "May be married or single."
- "Interested in sex but not preoccupied with it."
- "Intelligent."
- "Emotional, naturally!"
- "Chic, has class, and money to spend on the products we advertise (either her own or her husband's money)."
- "Probably has a job."
- "Not primarily house and home-oriented."
- "May or may not have children."[47]

Mainstream media had their own characterizations of *Cosmopolitan* readers. A *New York Times* article described the Cosmo girl "out there in Peoria, she is on the front lines" eagerly reading the "working girl's chronicle of the sexual revolution." The radical leftist magazine *Ramparts* decided the Cosmo girl was a "shy or slow-witted" person who relied on advice about "what kinds of things to say in bed." *Time* remarked, "The Cosmo girl is still drawing a straight chalk line down her full-length mirror to check her posture." *Esquire* described Cosmo girls as "the secretaries, the nurses, the telephone company clerks who live out there somewhere, miles from psychiatrists, plastic surgeons and birth control clinics" where they were "coping with their first pair of false eyelashes and their first fling with vaginal foam and their first sit-down dinners and their first orgasms."[48]

Data from readership surveys conducted for Hearst Corporation in 1969 and 1983 indicated that *Cosmopolitan* attracted all sorts of women readers, not unexpectedly, although proportional representations were sometimes surprising. It was not a readership of poorly paid yokels.

The 1969 demographics showed these readership characteristics: two of every six women readers were younger than twenty-four and three of every six were ages twenty-five to forty-four; six of nine were married and two of nine had never or not yet married; one of eight was a manager or professional person and three of eight were "pink-collar" employees, while another three of eight did not work outside the home; one of eight earned a median income of $5,050 and five of eight earned above the median, which made them an affluent group; three of eight attended or graduated college; and two of three lived in cities or suburbs.[49]

The 1983 demographics showed these characteristics: three of every eight women readers were younger than twenty-four and four of nine were ages twenty-five to forty-four; four of nine were married and three of eight had never or not yet married; two of ten were managers or professional occupations and three of ten were pink-collar employees, while four of ten did not work outside the home; two of ten earned a median income of $12,200 and five of ten earned above the median, a more affluent group than the first; four of ten attended or graduated college; and seven of eight lived in cities or suburbs.[50]

An amazing aspect of Gurley Brown's tenure at *Cosmopolitan* was the fact that the median age of its readership actually was younger by the mid-1980s than during the late 1960s. The editor who had started with *Cosmopolitan* at age forty-three and was sixty-four on the magazine's hundredth anniversary somehow produced a magazine that defied aging. Much credit for this feat was owed to the efforts of predominantly young women who were editorial assistants throughout the years.

The editorial formula accomplished other noteworthy demographic differences between the two reports: a tremendous surge in the proportion of women readers who had never married, which made *Cosmopolitan* more than ever a magazine for single women; a rise in the proportion of readers who had managerial or professional occupations.

Readership surveys could not reveal personality or psychology, of course, but because *Cosmopolitan* readers were predominantly young and employed the magazine indeed may have helped young women of the 1960s and 1970s adjust to a lifestyle markedly different from their parents. Much the same way that Gilded Age magazines had helped readers from the new middle class several decades earlier, *Cosmopolitan* guided young women who entered the workforce from the mid-1960s onward. During the 1960s, the number of women employed outside the home increased by 45 percent, or approximately eleven million. Most women were first-generation office workers and first-generation collegians. Many possibly were insecure about themselves. Many possibly were unfamiliar with workplace etiquette and behavior. Many possibly were uncertain about social norms outside their peer group. Therefore, they were not unlike adults of the Gilded Age middle class who obtained useful information from magazines about customs, manners, and standards to adjust to their new social status.

Cosmopolitan perhaps assisted many young women to navigate a world their mothers had not known. Mothers may have worked in a factory during World War II, sold clothes at a department store, stocked shelves at a drugstore, or kept the books for a hardware store. Daughters, however, went to work for large businesses to file and process paperwork, type correspondence and documents, answer the telephone and take dictation, keypunch data cards for computers, or operate mimeograph machines and mailroom equipment. If daughters obtained college degrees but did not become teachers, which was the career for almost four of nine women with degrees during the 1960s, they worked as laboratory researchers, medical technicians, librarians, pharmacists, and social workers. Such jobs paid well enough but rarely led to managerial positions.

Women with college degrees were underrepresented in professional and technical careers. At the start of the 1960s, women were only 1 percent of engineers, 3 percent of architects, 3 percent of lawyers, 8 percent of scientists, and 16 percent of accountants. At the start of the 1970s, women were 2 percent of engineers, 4 percent of architects, 5 percent of lawyers, 13 percent of scientists, and 26 percent of accountants.

A fantastic increase in the number of young women in the workforce occurred during the 1960s. Total full-time employment for women ages twenty to thirty-four was 9.6 million at the end of the 1950s and 15.1 million by the early 1970s, a surge of 55 percent in a dozen years. Many young women, and men, attained unprecedented financial independence compared to previous generations. Median income for women in 1969 was $5,100 and $8,900 for men. Young adults could rent their own apartments, and the number of single-person households soared by 3.2 million during the decade, an 80 percent rise. Also, the number of married households increased by 6.1 million primarily because the early members of the baby-boom generation were marrying.[51]

Leadership

Being editor of a popular and profitable magazine required skills other than editorial judgment. Gurley Brown learned through trial-and-error how to become a manager.

The editorial staff expanded greatly during her tenure. The tremendous number of additional editorial pages that accompanied the growth in advertising pages required extra associate editors, copy editors, art directors, and various others to handle assignments, editing, illustrations, page design, photo selection and display, and setups for editorial material dealing with décor, fashion, and new products. Gurley Brown's original staff of nineteen people included five men who held four of the six senior positions. By the mid-1970s the editorial staff had grown to thirty-seven people, which included three men, two of whom held two of the nine senior positions. Gurley Brown managed an editorial staff of fifty-eight people by 1985, which still included three men, two of whom continued to hold two of the nine senior positions.

Cosmopolitan did not pay its junior staff well. Salaries during the mid-1970s ranged from $14,000 to $18,000 for editorial assistants and reached the high $20,000s by the mid-1980s. This might have been good money in some cities, but it was not lucrative pay for New York City. Turnover was constant among office staff and junior editors. Gurley Brown persistently asked for higher pay for these essential employees. "Out of a copy department of four people, two are new as of this week," a Gurley Brown memo informed a Hearst Corporation executive. "Within another 3 weeks a third one will be new because somebody is leaving to have a baby. We have been unable to find a decorating editor for two months now." Magazines based in New York City competed for talent. Hearst Corporation was slow to make salaries at its magazines competitive.[52]

Gurley Brown was a micro-manager. Her attention to every detail had served *Cosmopolitan* well during its transformative phase when she imposed her editorial philosophy, but her unwillingness to delegate responsibility diverted much of her energy to tasks that associate editors should have done. Hiring new editorial assistants, secretaries, and clerks required personal interviews and time to review employment applications—functions that a managing editor or another senior editor fulfilled, but which Gurley Brown also performed because of her reluctance, or inherent inability, to let responsible subordinates make key decisions. "I spend half my time calling up people I know and don't know to ask them if they know anybody who'd be interested in coming over here," she explained in a memo. "It's just the shortage of qualified people or the shortage of time to be able to ferret them out and lure and pursue them when you are also putting out a magazine."

Gurley Brown was involved personally in every hire for many years, and she made mistakes. A disastrous hire prompted a long memo to an executive: "Remember the huge raise you gave me last week to hire a decent text editor? Well I hired him and he's an alcoholic! (stop laughing) In five days in my office, he has only edited four short manuscripts. . . . I've just managed to hire that idiot who drinks."[53]

Senior editors, including a managing editor and several associate editors, tended to stay with the magazine for many years. Pay for some of the senior positions reached $80,000 by the early 1980s. Another factor for longevity of senior editors at *Cosmopolitan* was the work atmosphere. Gurley Brown demanded much of her editors, but she treated them well—remembering their birthdays, praising their work, making them part of the editorial decision-making process (even though she ultimately tweaked almost everything to her liking), and generally creating a collegial workplace.[54]

Besides adding magazine staff to process text, photographs, and illustrations for additional pages, *Cosmopolitan* also substantially raised payments to nonfiction writers. Revenue from advertising permitted the magazine to offer exceptional fees by the 1980s. The best writers were given their choice of ideas to develop and picked from a list of short assignments for a $3,000 fee or longer assignments for a $5,000 fee.[55]

Gurley Brown, however, did not behave any differently than she had at the start when lesser writers were submitting material. Despite having superb writers supplying articles and features, she continued to edit every item thoroughly after associate editors already had reviewed each piece. The result was much rewriting and revising, and longer hours in the office than necessary for Gurley Brown. Twenty years on the job still meant working a usual twelve-hour day and an occasional fourteen-hour day when husband David was out of town, plus working several hours on weekends in their luxury tower townhouse at the Beresford on Central Park West at 81st Street. The workload became wearisome. Despite her all-consuming desire to be *Cosmopolitan* editor, Gurley Brown publicly announced in May 1983 her intent to retire at age sixty-five, specifically March 1987.[56]

She did not retire then, and the announcement possibly was a ploy to spur Hearst executives to grant her wish for a bonus. Hearst Corporation agreed to give Gurley Brown an unspecified percentage of *Cosmopolitan* profit each year. She remained editor of *Cosmopolitan* until January 1996 when a designated successor became coeditor. Exactly a year later Helen Gurley Brown retired from *Cosmopolitan* at age seventy-four, and began a new career as editor of international editions of *Cosmopolitan,* a position she continued to hold a dozen years later while working in the Hearst Tower.[57]

Centennial

The November 1985 cover of *Cosmopolitan* proclaimed, "Help Us Celebrate . . . Giant Birthday Issue." This self-congratulatory publication contained 480 pages, slightly more than half of them occupied by ads. It included articles on feminism by Gloria Steinem, on the allure of women by John Updike, on women in politics by William F. Buckley Jr., fiction by James Michener, and a photo essay of famous women by Franceso Scavullo. It also had the usual fare: "The Sexual Addict," "Do You Still Fake Orgasm?," "The Perils Of Loving A Poor Man," "I Hired An Escort."

But the twentieth birthday of what? Helen Gurley Brown had started as editor in March 1965. Her first *Cosmopolitan* issue was July 1965. The first issue entirely hers was September 1965. She did not explain to readers why November and not July or September was the twentieth anniversary issue. "First we thought we wouldn't, then we thought we should celebrate the twentieth birthday of the Cosmo girl," Gurley Brown wrote in the issue's Step Into My Parlor column. "The new Cosmo—and the Cosmo girl—came into being in July of 1965." The editor had reasons to celebrate, of course. Beyond the apparent validation of the appeal that her personal philosophy had on attracting millions of loyal readers was the amazing profitability that had made the magazine the star of the Hearst Corporation empire. Gurley Brown herself lived the dream she encouraged her readers to strive for. Through determination and self-confidence, she had rescued

Cosmopolitan, had herself become famous and wealthy, and had influenced the editorial format of other women's magazines.

Gurley Brown mentioned in her November 1985 column that *Cosmopolitan* also would attain a milestone soon, "The magazine itself actually will be one hundred years old next year."[58] And so the centennial issue of March 1986 was a perfect moment to celebrate a historic accomplishment, to pay tribute to a magazine that had endured periods of financial crises, mismanagement, and neglect while also achieving periods of distinction and prosperity, to inform its contemporary readers about the magazine's former stature.

It did not happen.

The March 1986 cover of *Cosmopolitan* displayed the usual beautiful woman model and an assortment of blurbs touting articles and features on inside pages—not a line about the magazine's centennial issue.

The table of contents listed fifty-three items. None pertained to the March 1886 debut of *Cosmopolitan.*

Step Into My Parlor was its usual chatty self. Helen Gurley Brown described a novelist who "a hundred years ago" worked with her at an advertising agency. She devoted several sentences to an event honoring her the previous November: "Does it make you nervous to have people make a big fuss over you . . . Does me, but I did get un-nervous enough to say yes when my beloved friends, columnist Liz Smith and television's first lady, Barbara Walters, said they'd like to give a party to celebrate my twentieth birthday at Cosmo . . . throngs of friends climbed the stairs to the banquet room at [the] Russian Tea Room for blinis, red caviar, and champagne. I was touched to tears by the outpouring of affection. I'm a lucky girl."[59]

Not a word from the editor to commemorate a century of transformation and survival by *Cosmopolitan.*

10

Continuation

The Future and a Past

The first decade of the twenty-first century accelerated a revolution in communications begun in the last decade of the twentieth. The World Wide Web matured, making accessible to an individual with a computer all matter of information and entertainment at all times. The development of wireless mode freed computers to receive information and entertainment anywhere a signal was receivable. Then the evolution of handheld mobile telephones enabled a person to talk, text, and watch/listen to information and entertainment whenever the need or a whim arose. Finally, the availability of portable digital-reader devices allowed downloading of text and imagery.

Every revolution creates and destroys. The communications revolution of the new century destroyed many magazines or compelled their publishers to cease printing and transition to an online publication. Rarely was a magazine's death or metamorphosis caused by lack of readers; rather, it usually resulted from a loss of advertisers. Media diffusion created newer cost-effective avenues to deliver advertisements, whether to Web sites, cell phones, digital readers, or other personal communications technology.

The future of print magazines cannot be forecast. Simply transitioning from print to online or to digital-reader screens will not necessarily save a magazine, any more than transforming an editorial format will prevent its demise. Neither will mere marketing research offer salvation. Most people can't describe what they want from a magazine if they haven't already seen it someplace else.

Cosmopolitan seemed not to be in danger at the start of the twenty-first century's second decade. Its circulation was sliding year by year, a situation afflicting practically every magazine, but the number of copies being sold and the amount of advertising pages being bought indicated its continuation for a while. Yet the history of magazines has recorded a sudden shift in fortune for many apparently invincible publications.

Cosmopolitan's editorial format was older in 2010 than most of its readers. The format had lasted the longest of any in the magazine's history, although it was tweaked to include explicit prose and imagery. Still, the format was fundamentally the same one envisioned by Helen Gurley Brown decades ago.

If *Cosmopolitan* will have a certain future beyond the exceptional 125 years it already has endured, it must come from the imagination, intelligence, and self-confidence of a person who believes people will respond to ideas expressed by the magazine. The lessons of *Cosmopolitan*'s past verify this, and signify the importance of audacity, constancy, and sincerity.

The three men and one woman who transformed *Cosmopolitan* at crucial moments embodied all three characteristics: John Brisben Walker, who created a modern magazine for middle-class Americans to enlighten them about national and international events; William Randolph Hearst, who wished for political power to change society and subsequently desired to create the finest magazine for popular literature; Ray Long, who considered the magazine an arbiter of middle-class literary standards; Helen Gurley Brown, who wanted the magazine to candidly describe women's attitudes and behavior.

John Brisben Walker transformed *Cosmopolitan* from a nondescript literary publication to an intelligent and provocative general magazine starting in 1889. Conventional thought at the time was that a magazine must emphasize quality fiction and perhaps offer a modicum of nonfiction to succeed. Walker instead reversed the formula. Topics concerning horrid working conditions at factories and foundries, unsafe and hazardous workplaces for women, racial tension, and the proper place for the United States in world affairs were presented to a readership of men and women eager to learn.

Nothing in Walker's background suggested he was a political radical. His wealthy and well-connected father helped him throughout his teenage years and early adult life. Walker was an adventurer, however, and his willingness to take personal and financial risks extended to an embrace of radical political ideas, including Christian socialism. Walker espoused his various principles through commissioning articles from like-minded activists, experts in a variety of subjects, and writers whose viewpoints challenged mainstream ideals. It was risky, but Walker believed *Cosmopolitan* must provoke discussion and reaction.

His anger at the robber barons and mistreatment of laborers, his advocacy of a global role for the United States, his effort to modernize American colleges and universities, his promotion of aviation and automobiles, and his optimism about the benefit of scientific and technological progress brought *Cosmopolitan* respect and success. Starting from a small base of fewer than 20,000 subscribers and newsstand purchasers, *Cosmopolitan* grew impressively to a distribution of 350,000 copies and the top spot among quality general magazines.

In the interim, other magazines altered their editorial formats to compete with *Cosmopolitan,* and one new publication, *McClure's,* gradually surpassed it. Perhaps frustrated by the intense pricing war and the prospect of never regaining preeminence, Walker decided to try another venture, the manufacture of steamer cars. His financial and personal commitment to the steamers lessened his devotion to *Cosmopolitan,* and the magazine lost vitality.

William Randolph Hearst bought the magazine in 1905 and transferred his journalistic sensationalism from newspapers to *Cosmopolitan* in order to further his political ambitions and accomplish political reform. Hardly an altruist, Hearst realized that a reputable magazine might be influential. He hid his ownership of *Cosmopolitan* from readers while attacking politicians he disliked or those who had thwarted his quest to be governor of New York and president of the United States. For a half-dozen years, *Cosmopolitan* educated its readers about the economic and social consequences of political corruption and favoritism that afflicted local, state, and national governments. A series that documented financial relationships between several United States senators and some of the largest corporations and railroads contributed to public pressure that brought a constitutional amendment for the direct election of senators. Another series that dramatically depicted harsh conditions for children laboring in factories and mines helped enact federal legislation to protect youngsters.

With an awareness that his own political dreams were implausible and a sense that Americans had tired of exposé journalism, Hearst changed *Cosmopolitan*'s editorial format to mostly fiction by 1912. He authorized top-dollar fees to authors and illustrators. Circulation doubled within a few years, and soon thereafter passed a million copies. Of equal significance, advertisers flocked to buy space. *Cosmopolitan* earned big profits.

To guarantee that his personal favorite magazine, and the corporate flagship, continued to thrive, Hearst finally persuaded Ray Long, a brilliant fiction editor, to take control of *Cosmopolitan.* Persuasion came in the form of perhaps the highest salary paid to a magazine editor during the 1920s. Long, although subordinate to Hearst, guided the magazine to a position as the most popular magazine among upper-middle-class readers by signing some authors and illustrators to exclusive contracts while paying extremely generous fees to others.

Long was a powerful person in New York literary society, a status he enjoyed. He helped authors develop their writing careers by urging them to write novels and serials. By carefully reading dozens of fiction manuscripts each week, Long identified novellas, stories, and serials most likely to please readers whose preference for fiction did not include avant-garde style. For a decade he unerringly chose fiction that readers wanted. Long's leadership culminated in the creation of a magazine known to many Americans for its roster of famous authors and illustrators.

Long also recognized the economic benefits to the Hearst Corporation of making movies from novellas and stories that *Cosmopolitan* published. His public profile helped sell the magazine, too. *Cosmopolitan*'s stature and evident popularity enhanced its value to advertisers. It was the epitome of commercialism.

The firing of Long for valid reasons relating to lax management and fiscal irresponsibility induced years of mediocrity for *Cosmopolitan.* Corporate control and miserliness deadened the magazine. Upon the death of Hearst, corporate executives regarded *Cosmopolitan* as a liability rather than an asset. The lack of corporate support and an unusual business strategy that eliminated all money for promotional campaigns doomed the magazine.

Then a magazine prospectus from Helen Gurley Brown, the author of a bestselling book published in 1962 about single women and their relationships with men, prompted Hearst Corporation executives to allow her to attempt to save *Cosmopolitan.* Gurley Brown, whose career as a secretary and advertising account representative had not prepared her to be an editor, fervently believed she knew what modern women wanted to read in a magazine.

Defying the strictures affecting media presentation of subjects deemed unsuitable for a mainstream publication, Gurley Brown steadily pushed open the gateway to topics of relevance to a generation of women living in an era of tremendous cultural and social change. Had readers complained or advertisers protested, her experiment would have failed. She succeeded. Articles covered the full range of adult relationships. Presentations also advised women on careers, décor, health, and mundane, but pertinent, matters regarding everyday life. Gurley Brown accomplished the most extraordinary transformation in the history of *Cosmopolitan.* Her editorial formula inspired copycats and caused traditional women's magazines to broaden their material to include similar, if not so boldly presented, topics.

Upon its hundredth anniversary *Cosmopolitan* was not only unrecognizable compared to its inaugural issue but also bore no resemblance to any of its other successful iterations of the 1890s, early 1900s, and 1920s. An amazing journey.

Walker, Hearst, Long, Gurley Brown—each one daring, each one obstinate, each one vain, and each one proven right. *Cosmopolitan* survived because these strong-willed individuals established a unique identity for it that attracted and retained readers and advertisers. *Cosmopolitan* flourished when it angered, educated, entertained, informed, provoked, and shocked. The public decided its fate.

The lessons learned from *Cosmopolitan*'s past demonstrate the primacy of individuals who create something new, something worthwhile. Because of them, *Cosmopolitan* survived.

Notes

Chapter 1: Creation

1. "Dissatisfied Creditors," *Rochester* (New York) *Union and Advertiser,* May 22, 1888, 3. All descriptive anecdotes and quotes from the meeting throughout this chapter derive from this newspaper article unless otherwise specified. Details about Powers Hotel from I. J. Isaacs, *The Industrial Advance of Rochester* (Rochester, N.Y.: National Publishing Company, 1884), passim, and from images at www.vintageviews.org, keyword Powers Hotel. The amount of debt in 1888 would equal $6.9 million in 2010 dollars. For perspective, all dollar amounts in this chapter can be multiplied by a factor of twenty-three to determine the approximate equivalent value in 2010 dollars.

2. "Dissatisfied Creditors" and "Patents Issued," *Rochester Union and Advertiser,* August 12, 1886, 3.

3. *Jacob J. Bausch v. The Schlicht & Field Company,* Monroe County (New York) Supreme Court, 1888; information on birth date, birthplace, and nationality of Paul J. Schlicht from passport 6560, U.S. Department of State, 1886. www.ancestry.com.

4. *Cosmopolitan,* April 1886, 2; the publisher's note explained canvassing for subscribers.

5. "Dissatisfied Creditors"; *Rochester Directory* (Rochester, N.Y.: Drew, Allis and Company, 1875–1889), see various entries for Paul J. Schlicht and Schlicht & Field Company.

6. "Dissatisfied Creditors."

7. Articles of Incorporation, Cosmopolitan Magazine Company, January 21, 1888, New York Department of State, Corporations Office, Albany.

8. *Jacob J. Bausch and German American Bank of Rochester v. Paul J. Schlicht,* Monroe County (New York) Supreme Court, 1888; "Dissatisfied Creditors."

9. "Dissatisfied Creditors."

10. Frank Luther Mott, *A History of American Magazines: 1865–1885* (Cambridge, Mass.: Belknap Press, 1938), 5–8.

11. Public school enrollment, compulsory school attendance laws, and educational attainment from *Historical Statistics of the United States, Millennial Edition Online* (New York: Cambridge University Press, 2009); exposure to literature and general knowledge from Carl F. Kaestle, Helen Damon-Moore, Lawrence C. Stedman, Katherine Tinsley, and William Vance Trollinger Jr., *Literacy in the United States: Readers and Reading Since 1890* (New Haven, Conn.: Yale University Press, 1991), 276–79.

12. Mary Ellen Zuckerman, *A History of Popular Women's Magazines in the United States, 1792–1995* (Westport, Conn.: Greenwood Press, 1998), 3–4.

13. Richard Ohmann, *Selling Culture: Magazines, Markets, and Class at the Turn of the Century* (New York: Verso, 1996), 89–91.

14. Susan Harris Smith and Melanie Dawson, editors, *The American 1890s: A Cultural Reader* (Durham, N.C.: Duke University Press, 2000), 15–19.

15. Rebecca Edwards, *New Spirits: Americans in the Gilded Age, 1865–1905* (New York: Oxford University Press, 2006), 71–72; occupational data from *Historical Statistics of the United States.*

16. Harold G. Vatter, *The Drive to Industrial Maturity: The U.S. Economy, 1860–1914* (Westport, Conn.: Greenwood Press, 1975), 171–74; Eric E. Lampard, "Urbanization," in *Encyclopedia of American Economic History: Studies of the Principal Movements and Ideas,* ed. Glenn Porter (New York: Scribner, 1980), 1051–52.

17. Wage data from *Historical Statistics of the United States.* Other household income data and expenditures from Daniel Horowitz, *The Morality of Spending: Attitudes Toward the Consumer Society in America, 1875–1940* (Baltimore, Md.: Johns Hopkins University Press, 1985), 13–21; and Vatter, 232–33 and 300–304.

18. Historians, all relying on Mott, cite $4 as the annual price of a *Cosmopolitan* subscription for its first few years. Schlicht listed $2 for the 1886–1888 editions of *N. W. Ayer & Son's Annual Newspaper Directory.* However, *Cosmopolitan* listed $2.50 on its cover for an annual subscription until 1888 and $3 afterward for several years. Also, *Cosmopolitan* promotional statements in the magazine itself specified $2.50 during the startup phase.

19. Population clusters from Robert Higgs, *The Transformation of the American Economy, 1865–1914: An Essay in Interpretation* (New York: Wiley, 1971), passim; Stuart W. Bruchey, *Enterprise: The Dynamic Economy of a Free People* (Cambridge, Mass.: Harvard University Press, 1990), passim.

20. Alfred D. Chandler, *The Visible Hand: The Managerial Revolution in American Business* (Cambridge, Mass.: Harvard University Press, 1977), 223–29.

21. *Century, Cosmopolitan,* and *Scribner's,* various issues, 1884–1891.

22. Alan Trachtenberg, *The Incorporation of America: Culture and Society in the Gilded Age* (New York: Hill and Wang, 1982), 136.

23. Ohmann, 70–72; Mott, 22–25; Ellen Gruber Garvey, *The Adman in the Parlor: Magazines and the Gendering of Consumer Culture, 1880s to 1910s* (New York: Oxford University Press, 1996), 70–71.

24. Postal rate and reform information from Richard B. Kielbowicz, "Postal Subsidies for the Press and the Business of Mass Culture, 1880–1920," *Business History Review* 64:3 (Autumn 1990): 451–88.

25. Mott, *A History of American Magazines: 1885–1905* (Cambridge, Mass.: Belknap Press, 1957), 19.

26. Frank E. Comparato, *Chronicles of Genius and Folly: R. Hoe & Company and the Printing Press as a Service to Democracy* (Culver City, Calif.: Labyrinthos, 1979), 532–37.

27. Comparato, 532–37.

28. Elizabeth T. Pearson, "Modern Processes of Engraving," *Bulletin of the Pennsylvania Museum* 24:134 (April 1930): 33–35; Michael L. Carlebach, *The Origins of Photojournalism in America* (Washington, D.C.: Smithsonian Institution Press, 1992), 160–62.

29. *Cosmopolitan,* April 1886, 2.

30. U.S. Department of State, passport number 6560, Paul J. Schlicht, June 1886, www.ancestry.com; Schlicht & Field information from Isaacs, 170, and *Rochester Directory.*

31. "Patents Issued," *Rochester Union and Advertiser,* August 12, 1886, 3; Schlicht, passport 6560.

32. *Ayer,* 1887.

33. John Tebbel and Mary Ellen Zuckerman, *The Magazine in America, 1741–1990* (New York: Oxford University Press, 1991), 65–66.

34. John Milton Cooper Jr., *Walter Hines Page: The Southerner as American, 1855–1918* (Chapel Hill: University of North Carolina Press, 1977), 114–15; Matthew Schneirov, *The*

Dream of a New Social Order: Popular Magazines in America, 1893–1914 (New York: Columbia University Press, 1994), 40–41; Arthur John, *The Best Years of the* Century: *Richard Watson Gilder,* Scribner's Monthly *and the* Century *Magazine* (Urbana: University of Illinois Press, 1981), 108 and 233.

35. John, 13–14.

36. John, 14, 115–16, and 234–37; *Ayer,* 1884 and 1887.

37. Mott, *1885–1905,* 8–10 and 44; Alan Nourie and Barbara Nourie, editors, *American Mass-Market Magazines* (New York: Greenwood Press, 1990), 126–12 and 193–94.

38. Kaestle, 250–52.

39. Mott, *1865–1885,* 482–83.

40. Mary Ellen Waller-Zuckerman, "Old Homes in a City of Perpetual Change: Women's Magazines, 1890–1916," *Business History Review* 63:4 (Winter 1989): 729.

41. *Cosmopolitan,* March 1886, inside front cover.

42. Mary Ellen Waller, "Marketing the Women's Journals, 1873–1900," *Business and Economic History* 18 (1989): 103–6.

43. D. D. Cottrell, *Wholesale Price List of Newspapers & Periodicals* (North Cohocton, N.Y.: annual catalog, 1889–1895 editions).

44. Waller, 104; Zuckerman, 739.

45. Mott, *1865–1885,* 8; Roy Quinlan, "The Story of Magazine Distribution," *Magazine Week,* October 5, 1953, 4–5.

46. A full page of text in *Cosmopolitan* contained 750 to 800 words, equal to three double-space typewritten pages today; this word count applied to the magazine from its inception until the early 1900s. Pages with photographs or illustrations contained fewer words, obviously, but a majority of pages until the late 1890s consisted of text only. Illustrations and photographs often ran on a page adjacent to text.

47. *Cosmopolitan,* March 1886, inside front cover.

48. Paul J. Schlicht, "The Manner of Electing The President," *Cosmopolitan,* March 1886, 28–30.

49. Kaestle, 282.

50. Emil Bari, "Easter In Russia," *Cosmopolitan,* March 1886, 46–48.

51. Household, *Cosmopolitan,* March 1886, 54–57; the need to appeal to women readers, Kaestle, 247–49.

52. *Cosmopolitan,* March 1886, inside front cover.

53. Mott, *1865–1885,* 12–13; Michael Ayers Trotti, "Murder Made Real: The Visual Representation of the Halftone," *Virginia Magazine of History and Biography* 111:4 (2003): 379–410.

54. Mott, *1865–1885,* 481.

55. "Dissatisfied Creditors," *Rochester Union and Advertiser.*

56. "John Brisben Walker," *Journalist,* September 9, 1893, 2–3, refers to a range of seventeen cents to thirty cents per copy for an illustrated magazine, although the variance in cost depended on the number of pages and number of copies printed.

57. *Cosmopolitan,* April 1886, 2.

58. *Cosmopolitan,* August 1886, 2.

59. Quinlan, 4–5.

60. Ohmann, 112; Mott, *1885–1905,* 16.

61. Garvey, 4.

62. Mott, *1885–1905,* 484; *Cosmopolitan* promotional announcements in *Ayer's* specified a 25 percent discount for a year's ad contract.

63. "A Literary Event," *New York Times,* July 12, 1887, 8; Mott, *1865–1885,* 25–26; Kielbowicz, 471.

64. "A Literary Event," *New York Times;* "Edward Payson Roe," *Literary News,* September 1888, 260.

65. Paul R. Baker, *Stanny: The Gilded Life of Stanford White* (New York: Free Press, 1989), 238–39; Charles C. Baldwin, *Stanford White* (New York: Dodd, Mead & Company, 1931), 81.

66. "The Making Of An Illustrated Magazine," *Cosmopolitan*, January 1893, 291.

67. "Dissatisfied Creditors," *Rochester Union and Advertiser*.

68. "Dissatisfied Creditors."

69. Articles of Incorporation, Cosmopolitan Magazine Company, January 21, 1888, New York Department of State, Corporations Office, Albany; the Grant Jr. scandal did not reveal any wrongdoing on his part, "He Realized in Credits," *New York Times*, January 22, 1885, 8.

70. "A New Departure," *New York Times*, February 4, 1888, 3.

71. "Louisa May Alcott," *Cosmopolitan*, April 1888, 156–58; "A Congress Of Famous Women," *Cosmopolitan*, May 1888, 217–24; "The Ladies Of The American Court," *Cosmopolitan*, June 1888, 321–26.

72. "Superstitions Of The Negro," *Cosmopolitan*, March 1888, 47–49.

73. "The Chinese In New York," *Cosmopolitan*, June 1888, 297–304.

74. See prior citation.

75. *Cosmopolitan*, March 1888, 73.

76. "An Interesting Interview," *New York Times*, May 26, 1888, 3.

77. Garvey, 94–95; Kielbowicz, 482.

78. Historians, again relying on Mott, cite suspension of publication by *Cosmopolitan* in June and July 1888.

79. "Dissatisfied Creditors" and "Settlement with Creditors on the Basis of Thirty Cents on the Dollar," *Rochester Union and Advertiser*, May 23, 1888, 2.

80. Mott, *1885–1905*, 481; "A Successful Magazine," *Journalist*, April 30, 1892, 2–3.

81. *Cosmopolitan*, September to December 1888.

82. "A Successful Magazine," *Journalist*, April 30, 1892, 2–3; Mott, *1885–1905*, 9–11.

83. John Brisben Walker, grantor, numerous warranty deeds, 1887–1888, Arapahoe County, Colorado.

84. "Journalistic Notes," *Publisher's Weekly*, December 22, 1888, 973. Curiously, *Science* magazine also noted the magazine's purchase by Walker, whose interests included agronomy, aviation, military science, and political science. Walker belonged to the American Academy of Political Science. "Among the Publishers," *Science*, December 28, 1888, 308.

Chapter 2: Salvation

1. Please note that excerpts from documents, newspapers, and magazines are verbatim, and represent grammar, punctuation, and spelling standards of the era. Elizabeth Bisland, "A Flying Trip Around The World," *Cosmopolitan*, April 1890, 691.

2. Brooke Kroeger, *Nellie Bly: Daredevil, Reporter, Feminist* (New York: Times Books, 1994), 139–73. This superb biography provides complete details on Bly's around-the-world journey.

3. Bisland, 692–93.

4. In The Library, *Cosmopolitan*, January 1890, 360–61.

5. The loss would be equivalent to $1.15 million in 2010 dollars. For perspective, all dollar amounts in this chapter prior to 1894 can be multiplied by a factor of twenty-three to determine the approximate equivalent value in 2010 dollars. "John Brisben Walker," *Journalist*, September 9, 1893, 2–3; Kroeger, 149–54.

6. Karen Roggenkamp, "Dignified Sensationalism: *Cosmopolitan*, Elizabeth Bisland, and Trips Around the World," *American Periodicals* 17:1 (2007): 26–40; "Society Topics of the Week," *New York Times*, November 24, 1889, 11.

7. "All Around the World," *New York Times*, January 19, 1890, 1.

8. "A Flying Trip Around The World," *Cosmopolitan* for April, May, June, July, August, September, October 1890; each serial installment was designated as a "Stage"—e.g., First Stage, Second Stage, etc.; Kroeger, 185–87.

9. "Successful," *Journalist*, 2–3.

10. Equal to $14.9 million in 2010 dollars. For perspective, all dollar amounts in this chapter from 1894 onward can be multiplied by a factor of twenty-four to determine the approximate equivalent value in 2010 dollars. This may seem odd because the multiple was lower (twenty-three) for dollar value during the mid–1880s, and should become lower with each passing year, but the depression of 1893–1897 caused deflation; thus, a slightly higher multiple is applicable for equivalency. Warranty deeds filed with Arapahoe County, Colorado, from summer 1887 through autumn 1888 document the sale by Walker of dozens of parcels of property at various prices. Some land was along the South Platte River in what is now lower downtown Denver and some was farmland in what is now urban northwest Denver, adjacent to Federal Boulevard near the convergence of Interstate 70 and Interstate 76. Though the original property deeds listed Arapahoe County, the actual custodian of the deeds is Denver County, which separated from Arapahoe County in 1902.

11. Walker explained to readers the economics of magazine publishing in "The Making Of An Illustrated Magazine," *Cosmopolitan*, January 1893, 259–68.

12. *Cosmopolitan*, February 1889, 1–2.

13. Schneirov, 29–31, discusses the attitude of middle-class reformers.

14. Edwards, 60–67 and 76–77; Morton Keller, *Affairs of State: Public Life in Late Nineteenth Century America* (Cambridge, Mass.: Belknap Press of Harvard University Press, 1977), 402; From The Editor's Window, *Cosmopolitan*, April 1890, 767; workweek hours from *Historical Statistics of the United States*.

15. "The Making Of An Illustrated Magazine," *Cosmopolitan*, January 1893, 259.

16. Review Of Current Events, *Cosmopolitan*, July 1890, 376–77.

17. In The Library, *Cosmopolitan*, June 1889, 205–7.

18. John Brisben Walker, "Public Baths For The Poor," *Cosmopolitan*, August 1890, 418–22.

19. Social Problems, *Cosmopolitan*, February 1890, 506–7.

20. Keller, 402; Review Of Current Events, *Cosmopolitan*, November 1891, 118–19.

21. "Queens Of The Shop: The Workroom And The Tenement," *Cosmopolitan*, November 1890, 99–103.

22. David Montgomery, *The Fall of the House of Labor: The Workplace, the State, and American Labor Activism, 1865–1925* (New York: Cambridge University Press, 1987), 131–13; "Women Clerks In New York," *Cosmopolitan*, February 1891, 487–90.

23. Schneirov, 197–98.

24. Explanations about workplace conditions and labor violence by Keller, 394–400; Vatter, 294–95; Montgomery, 36–37 and 126–29; Philip Yale Nicholson, *Labor's Story in the United States* (Philadelphia: Temple University Press, 2004), 118–21; and Sean Dennis Cashman, *America in the Gilded Age: From the Death of Lincoln to the Rise of Theodore Roosevelt*, 2nd ed. (New York: New York University Press, 1988), 252–61, who also discusses the Homestead violence. John Brisben Walker, "The 'Homestead' Object Lesson," *Cosmopolitan*, September 1892, 573–78.

25. Walker, "Lesson," 573–78.

26. Walker, "Lesson," 573–78.

27. Walker, "Lesson," 573–78.

28. "Walker," *Journalist*, 2–3; D. M. Rein, "Howells and the *Cosmopolitan*," *American Literature* 21:1 (March 1949): 49–55; *Cosmopolitan* cover, June 1892.

29. "The Cosmopolitan: Making Of A Magazine," *Cosmopolitan*, September 1897, 466–83.

30. Review Of Current Events, *Cosmopolitan*, April 1890, 756–57.

31. Review Of Current Events, *Cosmopolitan,* February 1891, 500–501.

32. Review Of Current Events, *Cosmopolitan,* July 1890, 378–79.

33. Social Problems, *Cosmopolitan,* June 1890, 251–53.

34. Henry Watterson, "The South and Its Colored Citizen," *Cosmopolitan,* May 1890, 113–16.

35. Keller, 477; Margaret W. Rossiter, "'Women's Work' in Science," *Isis* 71:3 (September 1980): 381–98.

36. "What Society Offers Mary Grew," *Cosmopolitan,* June 1893, 223–27.

37. "Women Clerks In New York," *Cosmopolitan,* February 1891, 490–92.

38. *Historical Statistics of the United States,* education and labor categories.

39. "The Teachers College," *Cosmopolitan,* March 1894, 579–85.

40. "A Biological Laboratory For Women," *Cosmopolitan,* March 1899, 71–75.

41. Rossiter, 381–98.

42. "Student Life In The University Of Michigan," *Cosmopolitan,* June 1889, 109–17.

43. *Historical Statistics of the United States*—education, income, and labor categories.

44. "Women As College Presidents," *Cosmopolitan,* May 1902, 72–75.

45. Keller, 442.

46. "For Maids And Mothers: The Overtaught Woman," *Cosmopolitan,* December 1898, 330–36.

47. "For Maids And Mothers: The Woman of To–Day and of To-Morrow," *Cosmopolitan,* June 1899, 150–61.

48. "Woman's Economic Place," *Cosmopolitan,* July 1899, 309–13.

49. Catherine J. Golden and Joanna Schneider Zangrando, editors, *The Mixed Legacy of Charlotte Perkins Gilman* (Newark: University of Delaware Press, 2000), passim; "The Cosmopolitan," *Cosmopolitan,* September 1897, 466–83.

50. John Brisben Walker, "Motherhood As A Profession," *Cosmopolitan,* May 1898, 89–91.

51. "The Ideal And Practical Organization Of A Home," *Cosmopolitan,* April 1899, 659–65.

52. "The Ideal and Practical Organization Of A Home," *Cosmopolitan,* July 1899, 297–302.

53. "The Art Of Buying Food For A Family," *Cosmopolitan,* August 1899, 545–50.

54. Helen Damon-Moore, *Magazines for the Millions: Gender and Commerce in the La-*
dies' Home Journal *and the* Saturday Evening Post, *1880–1910* (New York: State University of New York, 1994), 82–84.

55. *Ayer,* 1893; "Successful," *Journalist,* 2–3; "The Making Of An Illustrated Magazine," *Cosmopolitan,* January 1893, 266–67.

56. Several sources offer conflicting information on John Brisben Walker. Generally agreed upon were his place of birth, his attendance at the U.S. Military Academy at West Point, New York, and his business ventures in Colorado. An obituary in the *Charleston Daily Mail* of West Virginia described birthplace, childhood locale, and activity as a developer in Charleston, also his political ambition there. *Rowell's American Newspaper Directory* (New York: George P. Rowell Company, 1877) provides his journalism career information, although its sequence is at odds with other sources. Finally, the Walker article in *Journalist,* September 8, 1893, relied on an interview with him; none of the details were verified—and that article became the basis for many of the biographical facts written by later historians and journalists. An archivist for Georgetown University in Washington, D.C., confirmed that Walker attended from 1864 to 1865; the archives do not contain any information about coursework. The statement about his father's wealth from *Journalist,* 2.

57. General Court Martial, Cadet John B. Walker, United States Military Academy, Orders 109, April 20, 1866; and General Court Martial, Cadet John B. Walker, United States Military Academy, Orders 12, March 2, 1868.

58. United States Department of State, *Foreign Relations of the United States,* 1868–1870 reports; J. Ross Brown was minister plenipotentiary to Peking, China, 1868–1869.

59. John Brisben Walker, "Alfalfa Farming," *Cosmopolitan*, November 1891, 83–89.

60. "Walker," *Journalist*, 2–3; John Brisben Walker, "A Modern City's Factory Of Growth," *Cosmopolitan*, May 1890, 64–68.

61. Ellery Sedgwick, *The Happy Profession* (Boston: Little, Brown and Company, 1946), also describes Walker as "six feet odd inches tall," 113; "The Man in the Street," *New York Times*, August 18, 1901, Society 1.

62. John Brisben Walker, grantor, warranty deeds, Arapahoe County, Colorado, 1887–1889. The portion of Arapahoe County within the city of Denver was consolidated with Denver County in 1902. Property records for Arapahoe County from 1861 to 1902 remain in the Denver courthouse.

63. Walker, grantor, warranty deeds, Arapahoe County, Colorado, 1887–1888; Robert Olson, "The Suburbanization Process of Eastern Jefferson County, 1889–1941," *Historically Jeffco* 7:1 (1994): 10–12.

64. Olson, 10–12.

65. Rein, 50–53, describes correspondence between Howells and Walker, also Howells's literary style; "Successful," *Journalist*, 2–3, profiled Howells upon his being named an editor at *Cosmopolitan*, though the article appeared just two weeks prior to Howells's departure.

66. *Cosmopolitan*, February 1892, frontispiece.

67. "Dined by the Aldine Club," *New York Times*, December 24, 1892, 3; "Augustin Daly Honored," *New York Times*, April 23, 1896, 4.

68. *Cosmopolitan*, February 1890, 513, displayed the magazine's new offices; Rein, 50–55; Schneirov, Appendix 6 and 70–71.

69. Rein, 49.

70. "Walker," *Journalist*, 2–3; Charles Hanson Towne, *Adventures in Editing* (New York: D. Appleton and Company, 1926), 25.

71. "Walker," *Journalist*, 2–3, mentions an amicable parting and payment to Howells for stories.

72. "A Traveller From Altruria," *Cosmopolitan*, November 1892 to April 1893, and "Letters From An Altrurian Traveller," May 1893 to March 1894.

73. Albert Bigelow Paine, editor, *Mark Twain's Letters, Volume 4* (New York: Harper & Brothers, 1917), 73–74, 80, and 142; Lewis Leary, *Mark Twain's Correspondence with Henry Huttleston Rogers, 1893–1909* (Berkeley and Los Angeles: University of California Press, 1969), 150–53.

74. Paine, 80 and 142.

75. "The Merit System In Government Appointments," *Cosmopolitan*, May 1892, 66–71.

76. Sister Mary Damascene Brocki, "A Study of *Cosmopolitan* Magazine, 1890–1900: Its Relation to the Literature of the Decade," dissertation, University of Notre Dame, August 1958, 17–18; "Notes," *Journalist*, July 13, 1889, 5; John, 148–49; Mott, *1885–1905*, 39. Payments to new authors remained $5 to $10 a page for many years.

77. Brocki, 16.

78. "Illustrated," *Cosmopolitan*, January 1893, 265–66, devoted considerable space to explaining the selection of manuscripts for publication; "The Cosmopolitan," *Cosmopolitan*, September 1897, 479–80, declared Walker's lack of personal favoritism.

79. Brocki, 96.

80. "Sally Ann's Experience," *Cosmopolitan*, July 1898, 283–88; "Why I Wrote Sally Ann's Experience," *Cosmopolitan*, July 1908, 163–67.

81. "The Awakening," *Cosmopolitan*, April to July 1899.

82. "Discontinuance Of Count Tolstoy's Novel," *Cosmopolitan*, August 1899, 447–49.

83. "The War Of The Worlds," *Cosmopolitan*, April 1897 to December 1897.

84. Norman MacKenzie and Jeanne MacKenzie, *H. G. Wells: A Biography* (New York: Simon and Schuster, 1973), 159 and 187.

85. "Walker," *Journalist,* 2.

86. "Walker," *Journalist,* 2–3; Mott, *1885–1905,* 484–85; "Illustrated," 267–68; Kielbowicz, 479–88.

87. *Cosmopolitan* advertisement, *Journalist,* January 2, 1892, 15, lists Civil War memoirs of generals as subscription premiums.

88. "Illustrated," 267, specifies circulation achievements; also, *Ayer* entry and *Cosmopolitan* promotional ads in *Ayer* for 1890, 1891, 1893, and 1895 state circulation guarantee.

89. "Illustrated," 265.

90. "Illustrated" explains all costs associated with preparing and printing the magazine, 260–62.

91. *Ayer,* 1890.

92. Ohmann, 84 and Table 5; Mott, 22–25.

93. "Illustrated," 266–67; *Ayer* promotional ads, 1890–1893.

94. "Walker," *Journalist,* 2–3.

95. "Walker," *Journalist,* 2–3.

96. "Illustrated," 272.

Chapter 3: Competition

1. A local history librarian at the Irvington Public Library provided current information, as of 2009, about the Trent Building, including its use as a commercial/retail site. Photographs at various Web sites show the contemporary condition of the building. Google Satellite has an aerial view. A property map filed with the Westchester County Register in 1920 specified dimensions of the building and site.

2. Deeds filed at Westchester County Clerk list property purchases by Walker in July 1894 and May 1895. "Randolph Walker Doing Well," *New York Times,* April 24, 1893, 12, reported the attack on Walker's son and medical condition.

3. Towne, 18–26, mentions that Walker rode the train into Manhattan almost every weekday to visit the magazine's office. "A Concert at Lindhurst," *New York Times,* July 21, 1895, 8, listed society people in attendance at a concert at the mansion of Jay Gould in Irvington, among them Walker and his wife. Several *New York Times* society articles noted attendance by the Walkers at concerts and dances at mansions in various Westchester County towns. "The Cosmopolitan," *Cosmopolitan,* September 1897, 468–71, informed readers about the "cottages with garden plots" resided in by pressmen and other magazine employees at Irvington.

4. "The Cosmopolitan," *Cosmopolitan,* 465–82, offered complete details about the new building; Leland M. Roth, *The Architecture of McKim, Mead & White, 1870–1920: A Building List* (New York: Garland Publishing, 1978), 52, cites the architect's fee, but without explanation why it was so cheap.

5. "The Cosmopolitan," *Cosmopolitan,* September 1897, 465–82, explained the electrical, mechanical, and technical equipment inside the building, also the presence of labor unions, descriptions of outdoor areas, and general information about employees; the railroad spur and shipment of magazines from the printing plant were cited.

6. Equal to $8.6 million in 2010 dollars for the property and building. For perspective, all dollar amounts in this chapter can be multiplied by a factor of twenty-four to determine the approximate equivalent value in 2010 dollars. "Old Cosmopolitan Plant Sold," *New York Times,* December 2, 1915, 20, referred to original construction cost; "The Cosmopolitan," *Cosmopolitan,* September 1897, 467–74, recorded the lower expenses in Irvington. Warranty deeds for Westchester County, New York, listed property purchases by John Brisben Walker.

7. *Ayer* for 1894 through 1898.

8. Mott, *1885–1905,* 592–96; S. S. McClure, *My Autobiography* (New York: Frederick A. Stokes Company, 1914), 206–16; Theodore Greene, *America's Heroes: The Changing Models of Success in American Magazines* (New York: Oxford University Press, 1970), 84–85.

9. Robert Stinson, "McClure's Road to *McClure's:* How Revolutionary Were 1890s Magazines?" *Journalism Quarterly* 47:2 (Summer 1970): 256–62.

10. Review of *McClure's* tables of contents, June 1893 to November 1895; Greene, 85; Mott, *1885–1905,* 5; Schneirov, 68–69.

11. Ellen F. Fitzpatrick, *Muckraking: Three Landmark Articles* (Boston: Bedford Books, 1994), 12–15; McClure, 221.

12. Please note that excerpts from documents, newspapers, and magazines are verbatim, and represent grammar, punctuation, and spelling standards of the era. *Cosmopolitan* price changes from amount seen on magazine covers, McClure, 215; Harold S. Wilson, *McClure's Magazine and the Muckrakers* (Princeton, N.J.: Princeton University Press, 1970), 64.

13. Lyman Horace Weeks, *A History of Paper-Manufacturing in the United States, 1690–1916* (New York: Lockwood Trade Journal Company, 1916), 236–38 and 297–99; "Walker," *Journalist,* 3.

14. "Walker," *Journalist,* 2–3; The Cosmopolitan, *Cosmopolitan,* September 1897, 469–72.

15. *Ayer,* 1894; Mott, *1885–1905,* 20–21; Greene, 62–63; John, 232–35.

16. Ohmann, 104–5; Richard S. Tedlow, "Advertising and Public Relations," in *Encyclopedia of American Economic History: Studies of the Principal Movements and Ideas,* ed. Glenn Porter (New York: Scribner, 1980), 680–84.

17. Susan Strasser, *Satisfaction Guaranteed: The Making of the American Mass Market* (New York: Pantheon, 1989), 93–94.

18. Jackson Lears, *Fables of Abundance: A Cultural History of Advertising in America* (New York: Basic Books, 1994), 156.

19. *Historical Statistics of the United States,* employment and occupational groups.

20. Schneirov, 202–4 and 219–22; Kaestle, 278–85.

21. Mott, *1885–1905,* 8–9 and 608–19; Peterson, 7–9.

22. *Ayer* for years listed.

23. Kaestle, 153–74.

24. *Ayer,* 1899.

25. John Brisben Walker, "A New University," *Cosmopolitan,* September 1897, 463–64.

26. Cashman, 355–56; Smith and Dawson, 329.

27. "Cornell University," *Cosmopolitan,* November 1889, 59–63; "Columbia College," *Cosmopolitan,* December 1889, 267–72.

28. "Princeton University," *Cosmopolitan,* April 1890, 733–36; "Georgetown University," *Cosmopolitan,* February 1890, 455–57. University archives do not explain why John Brisben Walker received the honorary degree. It is doubtful that his ownership of *Cosmopolitan* warranted recognition, considering that publication of his first issue was the prior month.

29. "The University Of Chicago," *Cosmopolitan,* April 1893, 665–71.

30. "Student Life In The University Of Michigan," *Cosmopolitan,* June 1889, 109–17.

31. John Brisben Walker, "Modern College Education: Does It Educate In The Broadest And Most Liberal Sense Of The Term?" *Cosmopolitan,* March 1897, 681–88.

32. "Modern Education," *Cosmopolitan,* May 1897, 33–37.

33. "Modern College Education," *Cosmopolitan,* August 1897, 443–47. (Note that the article title includes "College," which other titles do not.)

34. John Brisben Walker, "Modern College Education," *Cosmopolitan,* January 1900, 471–72.

35. Walker, *Cosmopolitan,* January 1900, 472.

36. "Announcement—A Cosmopolitan University," *Cosmopolitan,* August 1897, frontispiece; "University and Educational News," *Science,* August 6, 1897, 213–14.

37. "Cosmopolitan University," *Cosmopolitan*, August 1897, frontispiece.

38. "The Cosmopolitan University," *New York Times*, August 1, 1897, 14.

39. Keller, 571–75.

40. *New York Times* articles and editorials on the Bryan candidacy and political activity in New York often mentioned Walker: "Mr. Walker Hires a Hall," July 3, 1896, 2; "Mr. Bryan Will Try Again," August 15, 1896, 1; "Mr. Bryan in Seclusion," August 16, 1896, 1; "Mr. Bryan in Brooklyn," September 23, 1896, 6; "Meeting May Be Exciting," September 28, 1896, 2; "Pairs, and One of a Kind," October 15, 1896, 4.

41. "The New Andrews University," *New York Times*, August 17, 1897, 4.

42. "The Cosmopolitan University," *New York Times*, August 1, 1897, 14.

43. Susan E. Tifft and Alex Jones, *The Trust: The Private and Powerful Family Behind the New York Times* (New York: Little, Brown and Company, 1999), 48–49; "Brisben Walker's Scheme," *New York Times*, August 17, 1897, 1, listed Trask as an advisor; "Education on a Paying Basis," *New York Times*, September 12, 1897, 16.

44. "Dr. Andrews's Dilemma," *New York Times*, September 4, 1897, 7.

45. "The Cosmopolitan," *Cosmopolitan*, September 1897, 482; "Dr. Andrews's Dilemma," *New York Times*, September 4, 1897, 7; "The Cosmopolitan University," *Cosmopolitan*, January 1898, 333; "The Cosmopolitan University—Progress In Organization," *Cosmopolitan*, May 1898, 116; "In The World Of Art And Letters," *Cosmopolitan*, September 1898, 596; "The Cosmopolitan University," *Cosmopolitan*, December 1898, frontispiece.

46. *Cosmopolitan* articles on Cosmopolitan University previously cited; Susan Waugh McDonald, "From Kipling to Kitsch, Two Popular Editors of the Gilded Age: Mass Culture, Magazines and Correspondence Universities," *Journal of Popular Culture* 5:2 (Fall 1981): 50–61, provides social context to Cosmopolitan University and also explains many facets of the effort.

47. "The Cosmopolitan University," *Cosmopolitan*, January 1898, 333–34.

48. In The World Of Art And Letters, *Cosmopolitan*, September 1898, 596; "The Cosmopolitan University," *Cosmopolitan*, December 1898, frontispiece.

49. "The Cosmopolitan University," *Cosmopolitan*, December 1898, frontispiece.

50. "National Guard Camps Of Instruction And Their Faults," *Cosmopolitan*, August 1890, 402–9.

51. "Gun Explodes at a Test," *New York Times*, April 14, 1896, 1.

52. Jerome Thomases, "Mechanized Mobility Proposed in 1900," *Military Affairs* 5:4 (Winter 1941): 267–70.

53. "Some Notes About Venezuela," *Cosmopolitan*, January 1896, 415–18; untitled item, *The Bookman*, June 1896, 301.

54. "International Arbitration," *Cosmopolitan*, May 1896, 103–4.

55. "In Case Of War With England—What?" *Cosmopolitan*, June 1896, 149–51.

56. "Report Of The Cosmopolitan's Special Commissioner To India," *Cosmopolitan*, July 1897, 231; "India Starving," *Cosmopolitan*, August 1897, 369–76.

57. John Brisben Walker, "England's Responsibility For Loss Of Life By Famine," *Cosmopolitan*, August 1897, 459.

58. "The Cosmopolitan," *Cosmopolitan*, September 1897, 476.

59. "Peppered By Afghans," *Cosmopolitan*, February 1892, 434–37.

60. Kirk Porter and Donald Bruce Johnson, *National Party Platforms, 1840–1960* (Urbana: University of Illinois Press, 1961), section on political party platforms election of 1900.

61. Remarks by Sen. Orville H. Platt, February 6, 1895, *Congressional Record*, 3rd Session, 53rd Congress, 1829.

62. Frederick Jackson Turner, "The Significance of the Frontier in American History," *The Frontier in American History* (New York: Henry Holt and Company, 1920), 38.

63. David M. Pletcher, *The Awkward Years: American Foreign Relations Under Garfield*

and Arthur (Columbia: University of Missouri Press, 1962), 68, 147–49, and 173–74; Arthur Power Dudden, *The American Pacific: From the Old China Trade to the Present* (New York: Oxford University Press, 1992), 58; Frank Ninkovich, *The United States and Imperialism* (Malden, Mass.: Blackwell Publishers, 2001), 11–12; Walter LaFeber, *The New Empire: An Interpretation of American Expansion, 1860–1898* (Ithaca, N.Y.: Cornell University Press, 1980), 203–9.

64. President's Message to Congress, December 18, 1893, "Affairs in Hawaii," *Congressional Record, House Executive Documents,* 3rd Session, 53rd Congress, Appendix II, 454–56.

65. David Healy, *U.S. Expansionism: The Imperialist Urge in the 1890s* (Madison: University of Wisconsin Press, 1970), 24; LaFeber, 203; "The Rise And Decline Of The Hawaiian Monarchy," *Cosmopolitan,* June 1893, 161–72.

66. "Hawaiian Monarchy," 161–72.

67. Remarks by Sen. Henry Cabot Lodge, January 19, 1895, *Congressional Record,* 3rd Session, 53rd Congress, 1137; and January 22, 1895, *Congressional Record,* 3rd Session, 53rd Congress, 1210–11.

68. Remarks by Sen. David Turpie, January 24, 1895, *Congressional Record,* 3rd Session, 53rd Congress, 1283–84.

69. Frederick J. Turner, "The Problem of the West," *Atlantic Monthly,* September 1896, 296.

70. "The Nicaragua Canal," *Cosmopolitan,* April 1891, 675–78.

71. LaFeber, 252–77 and 362–63.

72. "Shall We Annex Leprosy?" *Cosmopolitan,* March 1898, 557–61.

73. "Our Duty To Cuba, The Republic," *Cosmopolitan,* August 1895, 470–71; "Concerning The Independence Of Cuba," *Cosmopolitan,* June 1896, 121.

74. Message No. 65, Richard Olney, U.S. secretary of state, to Dupuy de Lóme, ambassador of Spain, January 7, 1896, *Foreign Relations of the United States 1895,* 1220.

75. Message No. 100, Olney to de Lóme, March 13, 1896, *Foreign Relations of the United States 1896,* 676–77; Memorandum No. 4, John Sherman, secretary of state, to Stewart L. Woodford, ambassador to Spain, July 16, 1897, *Foreign Relations of the United States 1898,* 559–60.

76. Lewis L. Gould, *The Spanish-American War and President McKinley* (Lawrence: University Press of Kansas, 1982), 25; Joyce Milton, *The Yellow Kids: Foreign Correspondents in the Heyday of Yellow Journalism* (New York: Harper & Row, 1989), 66–73.

77. "War," *Cosmopolitan,* June 1896, 142–51.

78. "In Case Of War With England—What?" *Cosmopolitan,* June 1896, 149–51.

79. "A Brief History Of Our Late War With Spain" appeared in *Cosmopolitan:* November 1897, 53–66; December 1897, 183–99; January 1898, 297–309; and February 1898, 441–52.

80. "A Brief History Of Our Late War With Spain," *Cosmopolitan,* February 1898, 450.

81. James Landers, "Island Imperialism: Discourse on U.S. Imperialism in *Century, Cosmopolitan, McClure's*—1893–1900," *American Journalism: A Journal of Media History* 23:1 (Winter 2006): 95–123, examines articles and commentary in three popular magazines.

82. Teller Amendment from Senate Document, No. 105, April 19, 1898, *Congressional Record,* 2rd Session, 55th Congress, 254.

83. "The Commercial Promise of Cuba, Porto Rico, and the Philippines," *McClure's,* October 1898, 481.

84. "The Commercial Promise of Cuba, Porto Rico, and the Philippines," *McClure's,* October 1898, 482–84.

85. "Spanish Rule In The Philippines," *Cosmopolitan,* October 1897, 600.

86. "The Philippines—Shall They Be Annexed?" *Cosmopolitan,* January 1899, 351–52.

87. "Annexed?" *Cosmopolitan,* January 1899, 351–52.

88. "Thoughts on American Imperialism," *Century,* September 1898, 782–86.

89. *Ayer,* 1899.

90. Circulation data and subscription prices from *Ayer* for cited years.

Chapter 4: Distraction

1. "Bryan Won't Interfere," *New York Times,* June 13, 1897, 1. Please note that excerpts from documents, newspapers, and magazines are verbatim, and represent grammar, punctuation, and spelling standards of the era.

2. Towne, 25–27.

3. "Bryan Won't Interfere," *New York Times,* June 13, 1897, 1.

4. "Mr. Walker Hires a Hall," *New York Times,* July 3, 1896, 2, and "Mr. Bryan in Seclusion," *New York Times,* August 16, 1896, 1, described the visit of Bryan to the Walker mansion in Irvington and also named prominent Democrats who spent the day there, including Hearst; W. A. Swanberg, *Citizen Hearst: A Biography of William Randolph Hearst* (New York: Charles Scribner's Sons, 1961), 87, mentions Hearst at the event for Bryan in Irvington.

5. "New Uptown Club Opens," *New York Times,* May 29, 1895, 9; Tifft and Jones, 46–48.

6. Towne, 34–35 and 42.

7. John Brisben Walker, "The Coming Race," *Cosmopolitan,* July 1896, 275–78.

8. "The Problem Of Aerial Navigation," *Cosmopolitan,* December 1891, unnumbered page.

9. John Brisben Walker, "The Problem Of Aerial Navigation," *Cosmopolitan,* March 1892, 624–28.

10. "Mechanical Flight," *Cosmopolitan,* May 1892, 55–59.

11. "The Aeroplane," *Cosmopolitan,* June 1892, 204–8.

12. "Aerial Navigation," *Cosmopolitan,* November 1892, 89–94.

13. "Race," *Cosmopolitan,* July 1896, 276.

14. "Race," *Cosmopolitan,* July 1896, 278.

15. "Dinner to Prof. Langley," *New York Times,* January 20, 1904, 3.

16. "No Thoroughfare," *New York Times,* January 21, 1904, 8.

17. John Brisben Walker, "The Langley Aeroplane," *New York Times,* January 24, 1904, 22.

18. John Brisben Walker, "The Final Conquest of the Air," *Cosmopolitan,* March 1904, 501–6.

19. "The Cosmopolitan," *Cosmopolitan,* September 1897, 481.

20. "City Of The World's Fair," *Cosmopolitan,* November 1891, 48–63.

21. "The Columbian World's Fair," *Cosmopolitan,* March 1892, 606–10.

22. John Brisben Walker, "The World's College Of Democracy," *Cosmopolitan,* September 1893, 517–27.

23. "A Farewell To The White City," *Cosmopolitan,* December 1893, 179–91.

24. "Travelling With A Reformer," *Cosmopolitan,* December 1893, 206–17.

25. John Brisben Walker, "The City Of The Future—A Prophecy," *Cosmopolitan,* September 1901, 473–75.

26. Schneirov discusses magazines and urban life, 258–60.

27. "A Word In Conclusion," *Cosmopolitan,* September 1904, 626.

28. John Brisben Walker, "Preface—Why And How," *Cosmopolitan,* September 1904, frontispiece.

29. "The Education Of The World," *Cosmopolitan,* September 1904, 495–99.

30. "Transportation In 1904," *Cosmopolitan,* September 1904, 527–28.

31. "Conclusion," *Cosmopolitan,* September 1904, 626.

32. Promotional ad, *Cosmopolitan,* August 1904, 493.

33. For perspective, all dollar amounts prior to 1900 in this chapter can be multiplied by a factor of twenty-four to determine the approximate equivalent value in 2010 dollars. "Progress Toward The Age Of The Horseless Carriage," *Cosmopolitan,* January 1896, 417–18.

34. "Horseless Carriage Contest," *Cosmopolitan,* September 1896, 544–45.

35. "Contest," *Cosmopolitan,* September 1896, 545–46; "Progress," *Cosmopolitan,* January 1896, 417–18.

36. "The Horseless Carriage Has Arrived," *Cosmopolitan,* July 1897, 339–40; John Brisben Walker, "Some Speculations Regarding Rapid Transit," *Cosmopolitan,* November 1895, 26–33.

37. "Speculations," *Cosmopolitan,* November 1895, 30.

38. John Brisben Walker, "The Motor Vehicle of the Near Future," *New York Times,* February 4, 1900, 23.

39. L. J. Andrew Villalon and James M. Laux, "Steaming Through New England with Locomobile," *Journal of Transport History* 5:2 (1979): 65–82.

40. Lien on Cosmopolitan Building property deed, Westchester County, New York, November 1901; certificate of incorporation, Mobile Rapid Transit Company, March 1903, New York Department of State, Corporations Office; "Steaming," identifies the Mobile Company as the original entity subsequent to the Locomobile split-up.

41. Jared McDade, "General Motors—How It All Began," *Westchester Historian* (Fall 1999): 115–21, describes the construction of the factory and its early years before its demise, then eventual role as an automobile factor for ninety years; "John Brisben Walker's Feat," *New York Times,* September 10, 1900, 3.

42. Thomases, 267–70.

43. "Hack, Stage, or Omnibus," *New York Times,* August 10, 1901, 7.

44. "Licenses for Wagonettes," *New York Times,* August 11, 1901, 8.

45. "A National Highway Commission," *Cosmopolitan,* March 1900, 590; "National Highway Plans," *New York Times,* March 15, 1900, 9.

46. "Motor Vehicle Makers Organize," December 4, 1900, 2.

47. Towne, 34–35.

48. Equal to $2,300 and $9.2 million respectively in 2010 dollars. For perspective, all dollar amounts after 1900 in this chapter can be multiplied by a factor of twenty-three to determine the approximate equivalent value in 2010 dollars. "An Automobile Combine," *New York Times,* March 26, 1903, 5.

49. John Brisben Walker (grantor), deeds, Westchester County, New York, 1904.

50. John Brisben Walker, "Great Problems in Organization," *Cosmopolitan,* April 1899, 620–25.

51. John Brisben Walker, "The Story Of The World's Largest Corporation," *Cosmopolitan,* November 1903, 121.

52. "Largest," November 1903, 123.

53. John Brisben Walker, "The Story Of The World's Largest Corporation," *Cosmopolitan,* October 1903, 686.

54. "Largest," November 1903, 128.

55. Edwards, 152–53; Morton Keller, *Regulating a New Society: Public Policy and Social Change in America, 1900–1933* (Cambridge, Mass.: Harvard University Press, 1994), 2–3.

56. Greene, 90–91.

57. "A Pound Of Meat," *Cosmopolitan,* August 1903, 370–74.

58. John Brisben Walker, "Report: Condition of the Chicago Packing House and Stock Yard," 1906. No publisher listed.

59. "Captains Of Industry" series, *Cosmopolitan,* May 1902 to March 1904.

60. "William Randolph Hearst," *Cosmopolitan,* May 1902, 48–51.

61. "The Sphinx Club Dinner," *New York Times,* April 11, 1901, 9.

62. "Big Park in Denver," *Denver Post,* November 2, 1901, 4; "Generosity Run Riot," *Denver Post,* November 3, 1901, 4.

63. A promotional statement in *Cosmopolitan* after its sale to Hearst declared that "twice

as many men and women are reading it to-day as were reading it a year ago." Circulation was 450,000 copies the summer of 1906.

64. "Hearst Buys Cosmopolitan," *New York Times,* May 3, 1905, 11.

65. Mrs. Fremont Older, *William Randolph Hearst: American* (New York: D. Appleton-Century, 1936), 256–57; Cathy Dittman, "Hall of Fame, 1988 Award Winner: John Brisben Walker," *Historically Jeffco* 1:2 (1988): 8–10; Ellen Kessler, "Dream Catcher: A Brief History of the John Brisben Walker Legacy," *Historically Jeffco* 10:18 (1997): 27–33.

66. Travelers Insurance Company, lien clearance, Westchester County, February 1915.

67. Dittman, 8–10; Kessler, 27–33; "Mount Falcon Historical Park" publication, Jefferson County, Colorado.

68. "J. Brisben Walker Dies at Age of 83," *New York Times,* July 8, 1931, 23.

Chapter 5: Sensation

1. Swanberg, 276.

2. David Nasaw, *The Chief: The Life of William Randolph Hearst* (Boston: Houghton Mifflin Company, 2000), 190–92.

3. Ben Procter, *William Randolph Hearst: The Early Years, 1863–1910* (New York: Oxford University Press, 1998), 177–82, 183–84, and 205–11; Nasaw, 202–14 and 168–83.

4. Hearst communicated almost daily by memorandum and telegram with *Cosmopolitan* editors and executives from 1919 until the 1940s, and the files pertaining to *Cosmopolitan* at the William Randolph Hearst (WRH) Papers, University of California–Berkeley, indicate his favoritism for the magazine. John Tebbel, *The Life and Good Times of William Randolph Hearst* (New York: E. P. Dutton, 1952), 149–50, refers to Hearst's thorough editing of *Cosmopolitan* editorial material.

5. Nasaw, 96–113 and 152–54; Procter, *Early,* 45–58, 84–88, 143–49, and 154–56; Peterson, 200.

6. WRH letter to Ray Long, *Cosmopolitan* editor, May 30, 1928, WRH Papers, Carton 36, Folder 35.

7. Fitzpatrick comments on *McClure's* landmark January 1903 exposé issue and offers perspective on economic, political, and social factors of the era, while reprinting three famous exposé articles, passim; Walter M. Brasch, *Forerunners of Revolution: Muckrakers and the American Social Conscience* (Lanham, Md.: University Press of America, 1990), 55–61.

8. Louis Filler, *The Muckrakers* (University Park: Pennsylvania State University Press, 1976), 245–47; Lewis L. Gould, *Reform and Regulation: American Politics, 1900–1916* (New York: John Wiley & Sons, 1978), 121–25.

9. Fitzgerald, passim; Brasch, 108.

10. *Ayer,* 1905 and 1906.

11. Mott, *1885–1905,* 75–76; Brasch, 108–10; Harold S. Wilson, *McClure's Magazine and the Muckrakers* (Princeton, N.J.: Princeton University Press, 1970), 158–59.

12. Procter, *Early,* 136–49; Nasaw, 120–24.

13. Abe C. Ravitz, *David Graham Phillips* (New York: Twayne Publishers, 1966), 82–83; Isaac F. Marcosson, *David Graham Phillips and His Times* (New York: Dodd, Mead & Company, 1932), 235–38; Robert Miraldi, "The Journalism of David Graham Phillips," *Journalism Quarterly* 63:1 (Spring 1986): 83–88; Nasaw, 146 and 386–90; WRH Papers for *Cosmopolitan* reveal that the magazine did not have a formal budget until 1929.

14. "Treason Of The Senate: An Editorial Foreword," *Cosmopolitan,* February 1906, 477–78; "Wall Street And The House Of Dollars," *Cosmopolitan,* March 1906, 483–84.

15. "Treason Of The Senate," *Cosmopolitan,* April 1906, 628–38. Equivalent to $4.7 million in 2010 dollars. For perspective, all dollar amounts from 1905 to 1909 can be multiplied by a factor of twenty-three to determine the approximate equivalent value in 2010 dollars.

16. "Foreword," February, 477–78.

17. *Cosmopolitan* cover, March 1906; "The Treason Of The Senate," *Cosmopolitan,* March 1906, 487–502.

18. "Treason," March 1906, 490.

19. "Dodge and Smith Quit the Equitable," *New York Times,* June 27, 1905, 1.

20. Older, 257–58; Hearst's "Treason" insert consisted of a half-column of text on page 498, a full column on page 500, and photographs of letters on page 501 of the March installment.

21. "Treason Of The Senate: An Editorial Foreword," *Cosmopolitan,* February 1906, 477–80.

22. "Treason," March 1906, 495.

23. "Wall Street And The House Of Dollars," *Cosmopolitan,* March 1906, 483–84.

24. Elting E. Morison, editor, *The Letters of Theodore Roosevelt, Volume 5* (Cambridge, Mass.: Harvard University Press, 1952), 156–57.

25. "Treason Of The Senate," *Cosmopolitan,* April 1906, 628–38.

26. "The Lesson Of Platt," *Cosmopolitan,* April 1906, 639–45.

27. Gould, *Reform,* 61–64.

28. Mark Neuzil, "Hearst, Roosevelt, and the Muckrake Speech of 1906: A New Perspective," *Journalism & Mass Communication Quarterly* 73:1 (Spring 1996): 29–39; Filler, 97–98.

29. Ray Stannard Baker, *American Chronicle: The Autobiography of Ray Stannard Baker* (New York: Charles Scribner's Sons, 1945), 201.

30. Baker, *Chronicle,* 201–4.

31. William H. Harbaugh, editor, *The Writings of Theodore Roosevelt* (New York: Bobbs-Merrill, 1967), 293–302, reprints the entire speech by the president.

32. Baker, *Chronicle,* 203–4.

33. "The Man With The Hose," *Cosmopolitan,* July 1906, 341.

34. "The Message Of The Dome," *Cosmopolitan,* May 1906, frontispiece and 2.

35. "Treason Of The Senate," *Cosmopolitan,* May 1906, 3–12.

36. Thomas C. Leonard, *The Power of the Press: The Birth of American Political Reporting* (New York: Oxford University Press, 1996), 205–7; "Treason Of The Senate," *Cosmopolitan,* August 1906, 368–77.

37. Robert D. Reynolds Jr., "The 1906 Campaign to Sway Muckraking Periodicals," *Journalism Quarterly* 56 (Autumn 1979): 513–20 and 589.

38. Morison, 268.

39. Morison, 262–66 and 307.

40. Magazine Shop Talk, *Cosmopolitan,* May 1906, 115.

41. F. Hopkinson Smith, "The Muck-Rake as a Circulation Boomer," *Critic,* June 1906, 511–12.

42. Morison, 362.

43. Stanley K. Schultz, "The Morality of Politics: The Muckrakers' Vision of Democracy," *Journal of American History* 52:3 (December 1965): 527–47.

44. Procter, *Early,* 183–84 and 212.

45. Morison, 269; Brasch, 112–14; Filler, 57–59.

46. Brasch, 43–44.

47. Filler, 57–58.

48. "Child-Wrecking In The Glass Factories," *Cosmopolitan,* October 1906, 567–75.

49. "Child-Wrecking," *Cosmopolitan,* October, 572; "Little Slaves Of The Coal Mine," *Cosmopolitan,* November 1906, 20–28.

50. "The Child At The Loom," *Cosmopolitan,* September 1906, 480–87.

51. "Child-Wrecking," *Cosmopolitan,* October, 568.

52. "The Smoke Of Sacrifice," *Cosmopolitan,* February 1907, 391–99.

53. "The Sweat-Shop Inferno," *Cosmopolitan,* January 1907, 327–34.

54. "To Free The Child-Slaves," *Cosmopolitan,* October 1906, 670–71; "Child Labor," *Cosmopolitan,* November 1906, 109–12; "Child Labor Must Be Swept Away," *Cosmopolitan,* December 1906, 233–34.

55. Filler, 269–73.

56. John Major, *Prize Possession: The United States and the Panama Canal, 1903–1979* (New York: Cambridge University Press, 1993), 70–71 and 100–105.

57. "Panama—The Human Side," *Cosmopolitan,* September 1906, 455–62.

58. "Panama—The Human Side," *Cosmopolitan,* October 1906, 606–12.

59. "Panama—The Human Side," *Cosmopolitan,* November 1906, 53–60.

60. Magazine Shop-Talk, *Cosmopolitan,* February 1907, 466–67.

61. Morison, 363–64; Report of the Committee on Interoceanic Canals, U.S. Senate, *Congressional Record,* February 9, 1909.

62. David Mark Chalmers, *The Social and Political Ideas of the Muckrakers* (New York: Citadel Press, 1964), 34–37; "Owners Of America: Andrew Carnegie," *Cosmopolitan,* June 1908, 3–16.

63. "Owners Of America: Andrew Carnegie," *Cosmopolitan,* June 1908, 9–15.

64. "Owners Of America: Thomas F. Ryan," *Cosmopolitan,* July 1908, 141–48.

65. "Owners Of America: J. Pierpont Morgan," *Cosmopolitan,* August 1908, 250–62; Ron Chernow, *The House of Morgan: An American Banking Dynasty and the Rise of Modern Finance* (New York: Atlantic Monthly Press, 1990), 67–72 and 83–86.

66. "Owners Of America: Charles M. Schwab," October 1908, 478–88.

67. "Owners Of America: The Armours," *Cosmopolitan,* February 1909, 279–86.

68. "Owners Of America: The Astors," *Cosmopolitan,* September 1909, 334–41.

69. "The Viper On The Hearth," *Cosmopolitan,* March 1911, 439–50.

70. "The Trail Of The Viper," *Cosmopolitan,* April 1911, 693–702; Robert Mullen, *The Latter-Day Saints: The Mormons Yesterday and Today* (New York: Doubleday & Company, 1966), 200–201 and 216–17; Klaus J. Hansen, *Mormonism and the American Experience* (Chicago: University of Chicago Press, 1981), 144–45.

71. "The Viper's Trail Of Gold," *Cosmopolitan,* May 1911, 823–33.

72. Filler, 218; Keller, *Regulating,* 132–39.

73. Procter, *Early,* 30–35; Nasaw, 35–36; William Randolph Hearst Jr. and Jack Casserly, *The Hearsts: Father and Son* (Latham, Md.: Roberts Rinehart, 2001), 295–96.

74. "The Fight Against Alcohol," *Cosmopolitan,* May 1908, 549–54.

75. "Why I Am A Total Abstainer," *Cosmopolitan,* May 1908, 554–58.

76. "Temperance Or Prohibition," *Cosmopolitan,* May 1908, 558–60.

77. "The Fight Against Alcohol: Georgia Pioneers The Prohibition Crusade," *Cosmopolitan,* June 1908, 83–90.

78. "Error Through Strong Drink," *Cosmopolitan,* July 1908, 198–200.

79. Keller, *Regulating,* 134–35; "Booze, Boodle, And Bloodshed In The Middle West," *Cosmopolitan,* November 1910, 761–74.

80. Lloyd Morris, "What Are You Going to Do about It?" in *The Empire City: A Treasury of New York,* ed. Alexander Klein (New York: Rinehart & Company, 1955), 207–13, discusses the legendary encounter between Tweed and a newspaper reporter; "Is Public Spirit Alive or Dead?" *New York Times,* July 26, 1871, 4, editorial cites Tweed's "unconcerned and flippant air"; "What Can They Do About It?" *New York Times,* July 31, 1871, 2, letter-to-the-editor headline asks citizens to act against corruption; "The Duty of the Citizens," *New York Times,* August 2, 1871, 4, editorial refers to a Tweed aide saying a variation of the phrase.

81. "What Are You Going To Do About It?: Graft As An Expert Trade In Pittsburgh," *Cosmopolitan,* August 1910, 283–91.

82. "What Are You Going To Do About It?: The 'Jack-pot' In Illinois Legislation," *Cosmopolitan,* September 1910, 466–78.

83. "What Are You Going To Do About It?: Colorado—New Tricks In An Old Game," *Cosmopolitan,* December 1910, 45–56.

84. "What Are You Going To Do About It?: Senator Gore's Strange Bribe Story," *Cosmopolitan,* January 1911, 151–58.

85. "What Are You Going To Do About It?: The Shame Of Ohio," *Cosmopolitan,* October 1911, 599–610; "What Are You Going To Do About It?: The Carnival of Corruption In Mississippi," *Cosmopolitan,* November 1911, 725–33.

86. Filler, 349.

87. Nasaw, 146–47.

88. Political campaigns for city, state, and national offices are the focus of Nasaw—168–83, 195–214, 227–28, 328–32; Procter, *Early*—177–92, 205–11, 218–27.

89. Harbaugh, 298–99.

90. Nasaw, 211–12; Procter, *Early,* 224–26.

91. "Senator Platt's Reminiscences Of Famous Political Events," *Cosmopolitan,* April 1909, 512–25.

92. "Roosevelt Afraid in 1898, Says Platt," *New York Times,* March 2, 1909, 2.

93. "Senator Platt's Memoirs," *Cosmopolitan,* May 1910, 801–12.

94. "Hearst Lauds Taft; Rejects Roosevelt," *New York Times,* April 21, 1910, 2.

95. "Progress And Politics," *Cosmopolitan,* October 1912, 717–18.

96. *Ayer,* 1907, and various *Cosmopolitan* editor's statements.

97. *Ayer,* 1909 and 1910.

98. Brasch, 64–65 and 126; Mott, *1865–1885,* 512–15.

99. For perspective, all dollar amounts from 1910 onward in this chapter can be multiplied by a factor of twenty-two to determine the approximate equivalent value in 2010 dollars. Earle Labor, Robert C. Leitz III, and I. Milo Shepard, editors, *The Letters of Jack London, Volume Two: 1906–1912* (Stanford: Stanford University Press, 1988), 990–91, 1008–11, 1026–27, 1092–93, and 1182–83.

100. Mott, *1885–1905,* 496.

101. "Phillips Dies of His Wounds," *New York Times,* January 27, 1911, 1; Magazine Shop-Talk, *Cosmopolitan,* April 1911, 722.

102. Magazine Shop-Talk, *Cosmopolitan,* December 1905, 243–45; Magazine Shop-Talk, *Cosmopolitan,* October 1911, 720; *Ayer,* 1911 to 1916.

103. *Ayer* promotional ads for *Cosmopolitan,* 1909 and 1912–1914; lineage statements in ads allowed computation of total ad pages and revenue; profit statements from Richard Berlin, Hearst Magazines general manager, to WRH, January 22, 1929, WRH Papers, Carton 36, Folder 8.

104. "The Mysterious Octopus," *Hearst's Magazine,* February to April 1912.

105. Brasch, 58, and Procter, *Early,* 249–53, discuss the first disclosure by Hearst of Standard Oil Letters during 1908 presidential election campaign; "New Standard Oil Letters and Their Lessons," *Hearst's Magazine,* June 1912; "Standard Oil Letters Contain Some Startling Revelations Hitherto Unpublished," *Hearst's Magazine,* August 1912; "More Letters Related to Mr. Roosevelt and Republican Campaign Committees," *Hearst's Magazine,* November 1912; "Says Archibold Gave $125,000 to Elect T.R.," *New York Times,* August 22, 1912, 1; "Roosevelt Wanted Archbold to Call," *New York Times,* September 25, 1912, 6.

106. *Ayer,* 1911 and 1916.

107. Nasaw, 266.

Chapter 6: Consolidation

1. Letter, Richard Berlin, Hearst Magazines general manager, to WRH, December 27, 1932, WRH Papers, Carton 36, Folder 13.

2. Letter and report, Berlin to WRH with cost reduction specifications, December 27, 1932; equivalent to $3.2 million and $800,000 in 2010 dollars, a multiple of sixteen. For perspective, all dollar amounts from 1931 to 1935 can be multiplied by a factor of sixteen to determine the approximate equivalent value in 2010 dollars. A multiple of fifteen applies to 1929–1930. The early years of the Depression produced deflation.

3. National Magazine Division, *National Advertising Records* (New York: Denney Publishing, 1927, 1929, 1931, and 1933), yearly analysis sections.

4. *National Advertising Records,* Monthly Magazines sections, *Cosmopolitan* (1927, 1929, 1931, and 1933).

5. Report, International Magazine Company and Affiliates, December 14, 1932, WRH Papers, Carton 36, Folder 8.

6. Ben Procter, *William Randolph Hearst: The Later Years, 1911–1951* (New York: Oxford University Press, 2007), 213–17; Nasaw, 426–33; "Hearst Assailed in Senate Speech," *New York Times,* April 1, 1936, 11; "Publisher Spent Millions for Art," *New York Times,* August 15, 1951, 21; Victoria Kastner, *Hearst Castle: The Biography of a Country House* (New York: Harry N. Abrams, 2000), 206–7.

7. Report, Berlin to WRH, February 4, 1941, WRH Papers, Carton 36, Folder 21.

8. Letter, Berlin to WRH, October 6, 1942, WRH Papers, Carton 36, Folder 30; "Salaries of 18,000 Over $15,000 in 1934," *New York Times,* January 8, 1936, 13; Ferdinand Lundberg, *Imperial Hearst: A Social Biography* (New York: Modern Library, 1936), 325–26.

9. Nasaw, 606–7; Procter, *Later,* 213–26.

10. Stephen W. Potts, *The Price of Paradise: The Magazine Career of F. Scott Fitzgerald* (San Bernardino, Calif.: Borgo Press, 1993), 40–41; Theodore Peterson, *Magazines in the Twentieth Century* (Urbana: University of Illinois Press, 1964), 357; Matthew J. Bruccoli, editor, *F. Scott Fitzgerald's* The Great Gatsby: *A Literary Reference* (New York: Carroll & Graff, 2002), 75; Andrew Turnbull, editor, *The Letters of F. Scott Fitzgerald* (New York: Charles Scribner's Sons, 1963), 168 and 300–301.

11. Ray Long, *20 Best Short Stories in Ray Long's 20 Years as an Editor* (New York: Crown Publishers, 1932), xi.

12. *Historical Statistics of the United States,* education.

13. Long, x–xi; Edwin P. Hoyt, *A Gentleman of Broadway* (Boston: Little, Brown and Company, 1964), 161 and 215–16; "The *Cosmopolitan* of Ray Long," *Fortune,* March 1931, 49–55.

14. Long, vi.

15. *Fortune,* 49 and 54–55; John K. Winkler, *W. R. Hearst: An American Phenomenon* (New York: Simon and Schuster, 1928), 248–49; Mott, *1885–1905,* 497; a multiple of fourteen applies to 1919–1920 dollars for the 2010 equivalent.

16. Long, viii.

17. *Fortune,* 54–55.

18. Brooke Kroeger, *Fannie: The Talent for Success of Writer Fannie Hurst* (New York: Times Books, 1999), 55–57.

19. *Fortune,* 55.

20. Kroeger, *Fannie,* 60.

21. *Cosmopolitan,* August 1919, table of contents.

22. *Cosmopolitan,* March 1921, table of contents.

23. *Cosmopolitan,* April 1924, 66 and 70.

24. Letter, Ray Long to WRH, July 7, 1927, WRH Papers, Carton 36, Folder 34; a multiple of twelve applies for 1921–1928 dollars for the 2010 equivalent.

25. Kaestle, 192–93 and 204–5; *Historical Statistics of the United States,* income.

26. Peterson, 59 and Table 3.

27. Peterson, Table 1, 23 and 29.

28. Promotional text in *Cosmopolitan*, table of contents for August 1919 and January 1920, and full-page ad March 1920, 4.

29. Letter, J. Mitchel Thorsen, business manager, to WRH, June 20, 1921, WRH Papers, Carton 37, Folder 3.

30. Winkler, 248–49; cover price and subscription price from *Cosmopolitan* table of contents, August 1920.

31. *Ayer*, 1924.

32. Full-page promotional ad, *Cosmopolitan*, June 1923 and May 1924; table of contents, *Cosmopolitan*, June 1922.

33. *The Cosmopolitan Market: A Merchandising Atlas of the United States* (New York: International Magazine Company, 1928). This corporate publication gives an extremely detailed look at demographics and distribution of the magazine.

34. Report, International Magazine Company to WRH, January 22, 1929, WRH Papers, Carton 36, Folder 8.

35. *Fortune*, 51, presented a range of fees to authors and a budget table for the magazine; Peterson, 126; "Talk of the Town," *New Yorker*, May 16, 1925, 2, referred to fees paid to two of the most popular *Cosmopolitan* authors.

36. Letter, Ray Long to WRH, August 15, 1929, WRH Papers, Carton 36, Folder 36.

37. "Authors Criticize Hearst Magazines," *New York Times*, February 26, 1921, 11; "Authors Accept Hearst Challenge," *New York Times*, March 1, 1921, 7; "Authors Agree to Terms," *New York Times*, July 10, 1921, 16.

38. Nasaw, 280–83 and 346–47; Procter, *Later*, 81–82.

39. Winkler, 254.

40. *Cosmopolitan*, January 1923, 65; February 1923, 65; June 1923, 67; Procter, *Later*, 109, 121–23, and 138–39.

41. Western Union telegram, Long to Joseph A. Willicombe, March 22, 1927, WRH Papers, Carton 36, Folder 33; and telegram, WRH to Long, March 23, 1927, WRH Papers, Carton 36, Folder 33.

42. *Cosmopolitan* articles during 1924 by Lord Churchill included "My Escape From The Boers," January; "The Joke That Helped Settle The Irish Question," March; "The Battle Of Sidney Street," April; "Adventures In The Air," June; "Perils In The Air," July; "When I Risked Court Martial In Search Of War," October 1924; "A Hand-to-Hand Fight With Desert Fanatics," December; and "A Trapped Armored Train," January 1925.

43. Letter, WRH to K. M. Goode, December 4, 1921, WRH Papers, Carton 37, Folder 12.

44. Mott, *1885–1905*, 500–502.

45. Letter, K. M. Goode to WRH, January 15, 1921, WRH Papers, Carton 37, Folder 11.

46. Exchange of correspondence between Goode and WRH regarding editorial format for *Hearst's Magazine* and title change to *Hearst's International*: Goode to WRH, March 21, 1921; WRH to Goode, April 4, 1921; WRH to Goode, December 4, 1921; Goode to WRH, December 5, 1921—all from WRH Papers, Carton 37, Folder 12.

47. *Hearst's International*, "The Inside Story of Henry Ford's Jew Mania," June to November 1922; *Hearst's International*, "The New Threat of the KKK," February 1923; "Plans to Unite Magazines," *New York Times*, December 11, 1924, 17.

48. Nasaw, 345; "Plans to Unite Magazines," *New York Times*, December 11, 1924, 17.

49. "Conjugation," *Time*, December 22, 1924, 34; James L. Baughman, *Henry R. Luce and the Rise of the American News Media* (Boston: Twayne Publishers, 1987), 34–36, notes that the co-founders of *Time*, Henry Luce and Briton Hadden, graduated from Yale University.

50. *Ayer*, 1925; "Conjugation," *Time*, December 22, 1924, 34; "Plans to Unite Magazines," *New York Times*, December 11, 1924, 17.

51. "Talk of the Town," *New Yorker*, June 6, 1925, 1.

52. *Cosmopolitan*, February 1925, 182.

53. Letter, Long to WRH, May 17, 1926, WRH Papers, Carton 36, Folder 32.

54. Telegram, Long to WRH, September 8, 1926, WRH Papers, Carton 36, Folder 32; telegram, WRH to Long, September 8, 1926, WRH Papers, Carton 36, Folder 32.

55. "Woman," *Cosmopolitan,* August 1928, 38 and 146–48; "Man is Master, Says Duce," *New York Times,* July 11, 1928, 47; "I Tax Bachelors," *Cosmopolitan,* July 1929, 81–82.

56. "Miss Earhart on Magazine Staff," *New York Times,* August 29, 1928, 14; Doris L. Rich, *Amelia Earhart: A Biography* (Washington, D.C.: Smithsonian Institution Press, 1989), 77–78; Susan Butler, *East to the Dawn: The Life of Amelia Earhart* (Reading, Mass.: Addison-Wesley, 1997), 219–20.

57. Earhart articles published by *Cosmopolitan* in November 1928, January 1929, February 1929, March 1929, July 1929, July 1930, January 1931, August 1931, August 1932.

58. "Why Are Women Afraid To Fly?" *Cosmopolitan,* July 1929, 70–71.

59. Letter, Amelia Earhart to Mrs. Charles A. Lindbergh, January 30, 1930, George Palmer Putnam Collection, Purdue University Library; "Mrs. Lindbergh," *Cosmopolitan,* July 1930, 78–79.

60. "Powder Puffs For Men," *Cosmopolitan,* July 1930, 27.

61. Letter, WRH to Thomas J. White, Hearst Corporation general manager, March 21, 1929, WRH Papers, Carton 36, Folder 10.

62. Letter, T. J. Buttikofer, International Magazine Company circulation director, to Long, January 16, 1929; WRH Papers, Carton 36, Folder 36.

63. Letter, WRH to White, March 6, 1929, WRH Papers, Carton 36, Folder 10.

64. Letter, WRH to White, March 21, 1929, WRH Papers, Carton 36, Folder 10.

65. Letter, White to WRH, March 28, 1929, WRH Papers, Carton 36, Folder 10.

66. Letter and report, White to WRH, June 25, 1929, WRH Papers, Carton 36, Folder 11.

67. Telegram, Long to WRH, January 14, 1929, WRH Papers, Carton 36, Folder 36.

68. Telegram, Long to WRH, January 26, 1929, WRH Papers, Carton 36, Folder 36; Letter and report, White to WRH, February 28, 1929, WRH Papers, Carton 36, Folder 10.

69. "Mr. Coolidge's Own Story," *Cosmopolitan,* April 1929, 24–26.

70. Telegram, White to WRH, March 11, 1929, WRH Papers, Carton 36, Folder 10; "Coolidge Finishes Writing His Life Story," *New York Times,* April 30, 1929, 1.

71. Telegram, Long to WRH, March 9, 1929, WRH Papers, Carton 36, Folder 36.

72. Letter and report, White to WRH, June 25, 1929, WRH Papers, Carton 36, Folder 11.

73. Letter, WRH to White, January 1, 1929, WRH Papers, Carton 36, Folder 8.

74. *Fortune,* 54.

75. Report, International Magazine Company to WRH, January 22, 1929, WRH Papers, Carton 36, Folder 8.

76. "Ray Long Shoots Himself on Coast; Suicide Is Laid to Despondency," *New York Times,* July 10, 1935, 1.

77. *Fortune,* 48–55.

78. Report, International Magazine Company to WRH, March 28, 1929, WRH Papers, Carton 36, Folder 11.

79. Letter and report, White to WRH, June 25, 1929, WRH Papers, Carton 36, Folder 11.

80. Telegram, Long to WRH, November 14, 1929, WRH Papers, Carton 36, Folder 36; telegram, Long to WRH, June 27, 1929, WRH Papers, Carton 36, Folder 36.

81. Telegram, WRH to White, January 13, 1929, WRH Papers, Carton 36, Folder 8; telegram, WRH to White, January 21, 1929, WRH Papers, Carton 36, Folder 8; Letter, WRH to White, January 1, 1929, WRH Papers, Carton 36, Folder 8.

82. Telegram, Long to WRH, August 1, 1927, WRH Papers, Carton 36, Folder 34.

83. Telegram, WRH to White, January 13, 1929, WRH Papers, Carton 36, Folder 8; telegram, WRH to White, January 21, 1929, WRH Papers, Carton 36, Folder 8; Letter, WRH to White, January 1, 1929, WRH Papers, Carton 36, Folder 8.

84. Telegram, WRH to White, January 11, 1929, WRH Papers, Carton 36, Folder 8.

85. Report, White to WRH, February 28, 1929, WRH Papers, Carton 36, Folder 9.

86. Letter, Berlin to WRH, December 10, 1940, WRH Papers, Carton 36, Folder 20. This letter also was a reminder to Hearst about Long's methods.

87. Telegram, Long to WRH, July 29, 1929, WRH Papers, Carton 36, Folder 36; letter, Long to WRH, July 31, 1929, WRH Papers, Carton 36, Folder 36.

88. Letter, Berlin to WRH, September 3, 1942, WRH Papers, Carton 36, Folder 30.

89. Letter, Berlin to WRH, January 22, 1929, WRH Papers, Carton 36, Folder 8.

90. Letter, White to WRH, March 14, 1929, WRH Papers, Carton 36, Folder 10.

91. Telegram, WRH to White, March 12, 1929, WRH Papers, Carton 36, Folder 10.

92. Telegram, WRH to Long, August 23, 1929, WRH Papers, Carton 36, Folder 36; telegram, Long to WRH, August 24, 1929, WRH Papers, Carton 36, Folder 36; telegram, WRH to Long, August 24, 1929, WRH Papers, Carton 36, Folder 36.

93. Telegram, WRH to Long, September 24, 1929, WRH Papers, Carton 36, Folder 36.

94. Telegram, Long to WRH, September 25, 1929, WRH Papers, Carton 36, Folder 36.

95. Telegram, WRH to Long, September 25, 1929, WRH Papers, Carton 36, Folder 36.

96. Letter, Long to WRH, February 11, 1930, WRH Papers, Carton 36, Folder 37; letter, WRH to Long, February 14, 1930, WRH Papers, Carton 36, Folder 37.

97. *Ayer,* 1931; *National Advertising Records,* 1933—the annual report listed several previous years.

98. *Fortune,* 48–55.

99. "Ray Long to Quit Hearst Magazines," *New York Times,* July 21, 1931, 23.

100. "Cosmopolitan Policy Unchanged," *New York Times,* July 30, 1931, 22.

101. Mott, *1885–1905,* 502.

102. "Ray Long Shoots Himself on Coast; Suicide Is Laid to Despondency," *New York Times,* July 10, 1935, 1.

103. Various annual reports from Berlin to WRH, 1939 to 1942, listed profits for previous years; "Hearst Magazine Earnings," *Printer's Ink,* March 16, 1939, 16.

104. Kroeger, *Fannie,* 263–65.

105. Letter, Berlin to WRH, September 3, 1942, WRH Papers, Carton 36, Folder 30.

106. Letter, Berlin to WRH, April 3, 1933, WRH Papers, Carton 36, Folder 13; letter, WRH to Berlin, July 11, 1933, WRH Papers, Carton 36, Folder 13.

107. Peterson, 151, 159, and 231.

108. Various annual reports from Berlin to WRH, 1934 to 1942; *Printer's Ink,* March 16, 1939, 16.

109. Report, Berlin to WRH, February 4, 1941, WRH Papers, Carton 36, Folder 21.

110. Peterson, 167–68.

111. Letter, Berlin to Joseph Willicombe, Hearst personal secretary, January 2, 1941, WRH Papers, Carton 36, Folder 21; letter, Berlin to Willicombe, January 17, 1941, WRH Papers, Carton 36, Folder 21.

112. *Ayer,* 1931 and 1941.

113. Letter, WRH to Berlin, January 11, 1941, WRH Papers, Carton 36, Folder 21.

Chapter 7: Transition

1. Nasaw, 579–80; Letter, WRH to Berlin, September 18, 1945, WRH Papers, Carton 36, Folder 31.

2. Procter, *Later,* 211–18; Albert Bermel, "The Future of the Hearst Empire," *Harper's,* January 1962, 42–48; Letter, WRH to Berlin, January 21, 1941, WRH Papers, Carton 36, Folder 21.

3. Letter, WRH to Berlin, February 20, 1941, WRH Papers, Carton 36, Folder 21; letter,

WRH to Berlin September 18, 1945, Carton 36, Folder 31.

4. Bermel, 44 and 46; letter, Berlin to WRH, April 17, 1947, WRH Papers, Carton 36, Folder 31.

5. Telegram, WRH to Berlin, June 12, 1947, WRH Papers, Carton 36, Folder 31; telegram, Berlin to WRH, June 13, 1947, WRH Papers, Carton 36, Folder 31.

6. Procter, *Later,* 225; Hearst and Casserly, 221.

7. Letter, WRH to Berlin, September 18, 1945, WRH Papers, Carton 36, Folder 31; letter, WRH to Berlin, December 9, 1947, WRH Papers, Carton 36, Folder 31.

8. Hearst and Casserly, 225–26.

9. *Ayer,* 1948, 1950 and 1955; Peterson, 204.

10. Author interview with Harriet La Barre (HLB), June 25, 2008.

11. Chris Welles, "Soaring Success of the Iron Butterfly," *Life,* November 19, 1965, 65–72; author interview with Helen Gurley Brown (HGB), March 23, 2007; Gurley Brown stated that the editorial budget she started with in 1965 was the same amount in effect at *Cosmopolitan* "since the war," meaning World War II.

12. Peterson, 203.

13. Bermel, 48.

14. Bermel, 42; Welles, 65–66.

15. Association of National Advertisers, *Magazine Circulation and Rate Trends, 1940–1971* (New York: Association of National Advertisers, 1972), summary of annual circulation, women's magazines; Laurence Soley and R. Krishan, "Does Advertising Subsidize Consumer Magazine Prices?" *Journal of Advertising* 16:2 (1987): 4–9.

16. *Magazine Circulation and Rate Trends,* advertising page rates, women's magazines; HLB interview, June 25, 2008.

17. HLB interview, June 25, 2008.

18. David Abrahamson, *Magazine-Made America: The Cultural Transformation of the Postwar Periodical* (Cresskill, N.J.: Hampton Press, 1996), 19–31, explains the impact of television on magazines and the success of specialty magazines.

19. *Historical Statistics of the United States,* media and advertising.

20. Peterson, 128–76, devotes a chapter to the demise of venerable magazines during the 1950s; Abrahamson, 20–21.

21. Kaestle, 162–63 and 188–89.

22. HLB interview, July 12, 2008.

23. Betty Friedan, "The Feminine Mystique," in *The Suburb Reader,* ed. Becky M. Nicoleaides and Andrew Weise (New York: Routledge, 2006), 300–303; Nancy A. Walker, *Shaping Our Mothers' World: American Women's Magazines* (Jackson: University Press of Mississippi, 2000), 9–11.

24. James Playsted Wood, *Magazines in the United States,* 3rd ed. (New York: Ronald Press, 1971), 125–26; Mott, *1885–1905,* 142–43.

25. "Advertising Notes," *New York Times,* March 28, 1957, 51.

26. HLB interview, July 12, 2008; a multiple of seven can be applied to dollar amounts from the mid–1950s to 1965 for a 2010 equivalent.

27. HLB interview, June 25, 2008.

28. HLB interview, July 12, 2008.

29. A. J. Van Zuilen, *The Life Cycle of Magazines: A Historical Study of the Decline and Fall of the General Interest Mass Audience Magazine in the United States During the Period 1946–1972* (Uithoorn, The Netherlands: Graduate Press, 1977), 29–34; Peterson, 75–76.

30. Welles, 66.

31. Hearst and Casserly, 309.

32. HLB interview, June 25, 2008.

33. HGB interview.

34. HGB interview.

35. HGB interview.

36. *Femme* prospectus, undated, HGB Papers, Box 37, Folder 1, Sophia Smith Collection, Smith College, Northampton, Massachusetts (Sophia Smith Collection at Smith College is the sole repository for Helen Gurley Brown archives).

37. Walker, 11–12.

38. "The Who, Why and What of *Femme*," prospectus, pages 6–8, HGB Papers, Box 37, Folder 1.

39. HGB interview; Robert Root and Christine W. Root, "Magazines in the United States: Dying or Thriving?" *Journalism Quarterly* 41:1 (Spring 1964): 15–22.

40. "Hearst Deficit," *Time*, April 20, 1962, 82; Bermel, 45–46; HGB interview.

41. HGB interview.

42. HGB interview.

43. Letter, HGB to Richard Deems, Hearst Magazines president, February 11, 1965, HGB Papers, Box 39, Folder 7.

44. HGB interview.

Chapter 8: Transformation

1. Memo, "Cosmopolitan Nude Man," Helen Gurley Brown to Richard Deems, December 4. 1968, refers to previous conversation with Deems and another executive about the idea for a nude male centerfold, HGB Papers, Box 39, Folder 7, Sophia Smith Collection, Smith College (for brevity, future citations for HGB Papers will omit references to Sophia Smith Collection at Smith College because it is the sole repository); Helen Gurley Brown interview with author, March 23, 2007; *Magazine Circulation and Rate Trends* and *Cosmopolitan* circulation reports, December 1968 to May 1972, HGB Papers, Box 39, Folder 7 and Box 42, Folder 8. For perspective, dollar amounts in this chapter for 1965 to 1969 can be multiplied by a factor of six to determine the equivalent value in 2010 dollars. The term "actual revenue" replaces the more common business term "net revenue" in the interest of clarity. Actual revenue means the amount of money remaining after the cost of printing ad pages and deductions for various standard commissions and discounts.

2. HGB interview. Unless otherwise specified, all quotes attributed to Gurley Brown are from the interview or letters to author; a citation for a series of paragraphs containing quotes will be noted when other sources are cited and when specification seems necessary.

3. HGB interview; memo, HGB to Deems, December 4, 1968, HGB Papers, Box 39, Folder 7.

4. Memo, HGB to Deems, December 4, 1968, HGB Papers, Box 39, Folder 7.

5. HGB interview; number of HGB appearances from list available on www.johnnycarson.com.

6. Nora Ephron, "Helen Gurley Brown Only Wants to Help," *Esquire*, February 1974, 74–75 and 117–18.

7. HGB interview.

8. HGB interview. Several attempts by the author to interview Burt Reynolds to verify Gurley Brown's version were unsuccessful.

9. HGB interview.

10. www.johnnycarson.com; *Cosmopolitan*, April 1972, cover and centerfold section; *Cosmopolitan* circulation report, HGB Papers, Box 39, Folder 7.

11. "Playmate of the Month," *Newsweek*, April 10, 1972, 57; "Frog Prince," *Time*, August 21, 1972, 43; HGB interview.

12. HGB interview.

13. Peter Michelson, "The Pleasures of Commodity, or How to Make the World Safe for Pornography," *Antioch Review* 29:1 (Spring 1969): 77–90; Kathleen L. Endres and Therese L. Lueck, editors, *Women's Periodicals in the United States: Consumer Magazines* (Westport, Conn.: Greenwood Press, 1995); Roland E. Wolseley, *Understanding Magazines* (Ames: Iowa State University, 1972), 298–99.

14. Presentation to advertisers, "Facts about Cosmo," April 23, 1970, HGB Papers, Box 41, Folder 6; HGB interview.

15. *Magazine Circulation and Rate Trends,* 1972 data; letter, HGB to Deems, April 29, 1969, HGB Papers, Box 39, Folder 7, discussed salary and bonus provisions for contract extension; basis for salary and bonus mentioned in letter, HGB to Deems, March 2, 1967, HGB Papers, Box 39, Folder 3; for perspective, dollar amounts in this chapter for 1970 to 1972 can be multiplied by a factor of five to determine the equivalent value in 2010 dollars.

16. Daniel Starch, *Starch Primary Magazine Audience Report* (New York: Starch/INRA/Hooper, 1974); Simmons Market Research Bureau, *Publications: Total Audiences* (New York: SMRB, 1973); Simmons Market Research Bureau, *Publications: Total Audiences* (New York: SMRB, 1979). Each market study provides demographic details about *Cosmopolitan* readers. Specific details will be reported when relevant.

17. HGB interview.

18. HGB interview.

19. *Femme* prospectus, undated, HGB Papers, Box 37, Folder 1.

20. Helen Woodward, *The Lady Persuaders* (New York: Ivan Obolensky, 1960), 170–74; Gigi Durham, "The Taming of the Shrew: Women's Magazines and the Regulation of Desire," *Journal of Communication Inquiry* 20:1 (Spring 1996): 18–31.

21. George Gallup, *The Gallup Poll: Public Opinion, 1935–1971* (New York: Random House, 1972). Gallup Poll, September 1969; Kristin Luker, *Dubious Conceptions: The Politics of Teenage Pregnancy* (Cambridge, Mass.: Harvard University Press, 1997), 96–99.

22. Tom W. Smith, "American Sexual Behavior: Trends, Socio-Demographic Differences, and Risk Behavior," *General Social Survey,* GSS Topical Report Number 25, March 2006.

23. Nancy A. Walker, *Shaping Our Mothers' World: American Women's Magazines* (Jackson: University Press of Mississippi, 2000), 163–71; Welles, 65–72.

24. Ephron, 117.

25. William F. Buckley Jr., "You Are the More Cupcakeable for Being a Cosmopolitan Girl," *National Review,* September 22, 1970, 999–1000.

26. Nicole R. Krassas, Joan M. Blauwkamp, and Peggy Wesselink, "Boxing Helena and Corseting Eunice: Sexual Rhetoric in *Cosmopolitan* and *Playboy* Magazines," *Sex Roles* 44:11–12 (June 2001): 751–62.

27. "16 Men's Jobs You Can Do Now (Most Of Which You Couldn't Do Before)," *Cosmopolitan,* May 1970, 75–88; "It's Great To Be The Boss," *Cosmopolitan,* July 1969.

28. "Cupcake v. Sweet Tooth," *Time,* March 20, 1972, 53–54; Robin Reisig, "Feminine Plastique," *Ramparts,* March 1973, 25–29 and 53–55; "That *Cosmopolitan* Girl," *New Yorker,* July 16, 1973, 26–27.

29. Liz Smith, *Natural Blonde: A Memoir* (New York: Hyperion, 2000), 204–6.

30. "The Park Avenue Call Girl," *Cosmopolitan,* July 1968, 70–72 and continuation.

31. "Call Girl," 70–72 and continuation.

32. Smith, 206.

33. Step Into My Parlor, *Cosmopolitan,* April 1972, 4; Robin Reisig, "Feminine Plastique," *Ramparts,* March 1973, 25–29 and 53–55; HGB interview.

34. HGB interview.

35. HLB interview.

36. HGB interview.

37. HLB interview; Mary T. Oates and Susan Williamson, "Women's Colleges and Women

Achievers," *Signs* 3:4 (Summer 1978): 795–806; Myrna E. Frank and Clyde V. Kiser, "Changes in the Social and Demographic Attributes of Women in *Who's Who,*" *Milbank Memorial Fund Quarterly* 43:1 (January 1965): 55–75.

38. Lee Joliffe and Terri Catlett, "Women Editors at the 'Seven Sisters' Magazines, 1965–1985: Did They Make a Difference?" *Journalism Quarterly* 71:4 (Winter 1994): 800–808.

39. HLB interview.

40. HGB interview.

41. HLB interview.

42. Step Into My Parlor, *Cosmopolitan,* July 1965, 8.

43. Letter, HGB to author, January 30, 2009.

44. "Oh What A Lovely Pill!" Cosmopolitan, July 1965, 33–37; HGB interview.

45. HGB interview.

46. "The Affair Vs. Marriage," *Cosmopolitan,* September 1965, 38–41.

47. "American Sexual Behavior: Trends, Socio-Demographic Differences, and Risk Behavior," National Opinion Research Center, General Social Survey Report 25, March 2006.

48. "A Proposal for Cosmopolitan Magazine," HGB, on Bernard Geis Associates letterhead, to unknown recipient, undated with "[1965]" notation, HGB Papers, Box 37, Folder 3. Geis published *Sex and the Single Girl.*

49. Ephron, 117–18.

50. HGB interview.

51. "How Girls Really Get Husbands," *Cosmopolitan,* December 1965, 49–51; *Historical Statistics of the United States,* education.

52. "How Girls Really Get Husbands," 49–51.

53. "What Educated Women Want," *Newsweek,* June 13, 1966, 68–75.

54. "How To Get Married If You're Over Thirty," *Cosmopolitan,* May 1970, 56–59.

55. Welles, 65–72; Ephron, 74–75.

56. "When Is A Man ReMarriageable?" *Cosmopolitan,* February 1966, 48–51.

57. "Cosmo's Six-Week Crash Recovery Plan For A New Divorcée," *Cosmopolitan,* October 1969, 106–9.

58. "The Interim Man," *Cosmopolitan,* January 1970, 78–80; "Dating Rules For Women With Children," *Cosmopolitan,* October 1965, 38–39.

59. "Second Wife," *Cosmopolitan,* August 1967, 54+.

60. "Down with 'Pippypoo,'" *Newsweek,* July 18, 1966, 60; "Cupcake v. Sweet Tooth," *Time,* March 20, 1972, 53–54.

61. "Low-Fidelity Wives," *Cosmopolitan,* January 1969, 77.

62. "The Other Man (Men) In A Married Woman's Life," *Cosmopolitan,* May 1967, 110.

63. "Low-Fidelity Wives," 77–79.

64. Julie Berebitsky, "The Joy of Work: Helen Gurley Brown, Gender, and Sexuality in the White-Collar Office," *Journal of the History of Sexuality* 15:1 (January 2006): 89–124; Walter M. Gerson and Sandra H. Lund, "Playboy Magazine: Sophisticated Smut or Social Revolution?" *Journal of Popular Culture* 1:3 (1967): 218–27; General Social Survey, March 2006; Linda Rouse, *Marital and Sexual Lifestyles in the United States: Attitudes, Behaviors, and Relationships in Social Context* (New York: Haworth Press, 2002), 122–24.

65. "Girls And Their Married Men," *Cosmopolitan,* July 1969, 54–56.

66. "The Slightly Kept Girl," *Cosmopolitan,* October 1970, 154–56.

67. "Don't Be A Statistic Baby," *Cosmopolitan,* February 1972, 62–63.

68. "Cupcake v. Sweet Tooth," *Time,* March 20, 1972, 53–54.

69. HGB interview.

70. "Nymphomania," *Cosmopolitan,* March 1967, 60–62.

71. "Live For The Moment . . . Or At Least For The Night," *Cosmopolitan,* December 1967, 68–70.

72. "The Girl Don Juan," *Cosmopolitan,* September 1969, 134–37.

73. "How Sexually Generous Should A Girl Be?" *Cosmopolitan,* May 1968, 139–40.

74. HGB interview; the article was "The Private World Of Airline Stewardesses," *Cosmopolitan,* October 1965, 90+.

75. HGB interview.

76. HGB interview; memo, Berlin to HGB, July 28, 1966; HGB Papers, Box 39, Folder 3.

77. "I Didn't Have The Baby, I Had The Abortion," *Cosmopolitan,* July 1967, 50–54.

78. "The Sexual Drive In Women (Greater, Equal, Or Inferior to Men's)," *Cosmopolitan,* February 1968, 72–74; Linda Grant, *Sexing the Millennium: Women and the Sexual Revolution* (New York: Grove Press, 1994), 116–17.

79. "The Ostentatious Orgasm," *Cosmopolitan,* January 1969, 98–100.

80. "Masturbation: A Doctor's Report," *Cosmopolitan,* December 1970, 98–100.

81. "Cupcake v. Sweet Tooth," *Time.*

82. Memo, HGB to Girl Staff Members, undated with "[1969?]" notation, HGB Papers, Box 42, Folder 1.

83. Ephron, 118.

84. *Femme* prospectus, undated, HGB Papers, Box 37, Folder 1.

85. Laurie Ouellette, "Inventing the Cosmo Girl: Class Identity and Girl-Style American Dreams," *Media, Culture & Society* 21:3 (1999): 359–83; Michelson, 89; Beatrice Faust, *Women, Sex, and Pornography: A Controversial and Unique Study* (New York: Macmillan Publishing, 1980), 162–65; Grant, 117–18.

86. "Big Sister," *Time,* February 9, 1968, 60.

87. Michelson, 87–89.

88. "Cosmopolitan," HGB, HGB Papers, Box 37, Folder 1.

89. "Cosmopolitan Interviews Hugh M. Hefner, Playboy's Controversial Editor," *Cosmopolitan,* May 1966, 76–79.

90. "Hugh Hefner: That Dear, Dangerous Old-Fashioned Boy," *Cosmopolitan,* May 1966, 82–84.

91. Ouellette, 370–72.

92. Patricia Bradley, *Mass Media and the Shaping of American Feminism, 1963–1975* (Jackson: University Press of Mississippi, 2003), 88–89; HGB interview.

93. "The Women's Liberation Movement," *Cosmopolitan,* April 1970, 140–42.

94. "Feminists Demand 'Liberation' in Ladies' Home Journal Sit-In," *New York Times,* March 19, 1970, 57.

95. "Women Seeking Equality March on 5th Ave. Today," *New York Times,* August 26, 1970, 44.

96. "Sexual Politics," *Cosmopolitan,* November 1970, 84–98.

97. Jennifer Scanlon, *Bad Girls Go Everywhere: The Life of Helen Gurley Brown* (New York: Oxford University Press, 2009), 172–78.

98. "Liberation Now!" *Cosmopolitan,* October 1972, 162.

99. Memo, HGB to John Mack Carter, December 30, 1975, HGB Papers, Box 39, Folder 6.

100. "ERA And You," *Cosmopolitan,* July 1976, 120 and 124.

101. "Women's Legal Rights: 1975: A Report," *Cosmopolitan,* October 1975, 209–16.

102. "Facts about Cosmo," presentation to advertisers, HGB, April 23, 1980, HGB Papers, Box 41, Folder 6.

103. "Speakeasy," *Cosmopolitan,* February 1972, 39–40 and 48.

104. Letters and memos, HGB to Deems and other executives regarding her contract and renewals, May 5 and June 10, 1966, undated, and April 29, 1969, HGB Papers, Box 39, Folder 7; also, letter, HGB to Deems, March 2, 1967, HGB Papers, Box 39, Folder 3.

105. Letter, Deems to HGB, February 15, 1972, HGB Papers, Box 39, Folder 7.

106. Standard Rate and Data Service annual reports.

107. HGB interview.

108. HGB interview.

109. Memo, HGB to Deems, August 21, 1969, HGB Papers, Box 39, Folder 14.

110. HLB interview; "Proposal for Cosmopolitan," HGB Papers, Box 37, Folder 3; memo, HGB to Deems, August 21, 1969, Box 39, Folder 14.

111. Memo, HGB to Deems, August 21, 1969, Box 39, Folder 14; memo, HGB to Deems, July 8, 1970, HGB Papers, Box 39, Folder 7.

112. "Myra Breckinridge," *Cosmopolitan,* August 1968, 111+.

113. "Saving The Queen," *Cosmopolitan,* October 1976, 282+.

114. Reisig, 25–29.

115. Step Into My Parlor, *Cosmopolitan,* November 1969, 4; "Proposal for Cosmopolitan," HGB Papers, Box 37, Folder 3.

116. "Jaws," *Cosmopolitan,* July 1974, 168+; Step Into My Parlor, *Cosmopolitan,* July 1974, 4; Step Into My Parlor, *Cosmopolitan,* February 1979, 10.

117. HGB interview.

118. HLB interview.

119. Memo, "Dear Gwen," HGB, April 21, 1971, HGB Papers, Box 42, Folder 1.

120. "Confessions Of A Massage Parlor Girl," *Cosmopolitan,* September 1974, 168–74.

121. Memo, HGB to Deems, December 5, 1974, HGB Papers, Box 39, Folder 13; memo, HGB to Walter Meade, managing editor, January 22, 1975, HGB Papers, Box 39, Folder 13.

122. "Massage Parlor Girls," *Cosmopolitan,* October 1976, 118–20.

123. *Gallup Poll Monthly Index, 1965–1990* (Princeton, N.J.: Gallup Organization, 1990).

124. Linda Wolfe, *The Cosmo Report* (New York: Arbor House, 1981), passim.

125. Research involved reading many *Cosmopolitan* issues obtained through interlibrary loan; unfortunately, some copies were missing or mutilated to such an extent that it was not possible to review articles and columns.

126. Endres and Lueck, see specific titles; Ellen McCracken, *Decoding Women's Magazines: From Mademoiselle to Ms.* (New York: St. Martin's Press, 1993), 158–62 and 173–95.

Chapter 9: Celebration

1. Benjamin M. Compaine, *The Business of Consumer Magazines* (White Plains, N.Y.: Knowledge Industry Publications, 1982), 19–20.

2. *Magazine Circulation and Rate Trends* for relevant years; Standard Rate and Data Service annual circulation reports for *Cosmopolitan; also, Cosmopolitan* internal reports, previously cited, compared to annual circulation data, previously cited.

3. *Advertising Age* annual statistics.

4. *Advertising Age* annual statistics.

5. *Historical Statistics of the United States,* income.

6. Zuckerman, 225–37; Endres and Luecke, 282–83.

7. Compaine, 68–72; HGB interview included discussion of *Cosmopolitan's* allure to advertisers of women's products because the magazine generated controversy and, therefore, public recognition; Donald G. Hileman, "Changes in the Buying and Selection of Advertising Media," *Journalism Quarterly* 45:2 (1968): 279–85, explained the importance of specific demographic categories to media buyers for advertising agencies.

8. Not all *Cosmopolitan* issues were available or intact from lending libraries because of vandalism and theft. In some cases, magazines were found on the second request, but many issues were missing. It was rather sad to note that almost all the instances of vandalism and theft affected magazines from the 1960s to 1980s, while few issues from prior decades were damaged or stolen.

9. Endres and Lueck, 107–11 and 197–200; HGB interview.

10. "Rival Women's Magazines Near Hair-Pulling Stage," *Business Week*, October 1, 1960, 88–96, profiled Herbert Mayes, editor of *McCall's* and former coeditor of *Good Housekeeping* and *Cosmopolitan*. Mayes discussed the relationships between editors and advertisers; Zuckerman, 213; J. Howland, "Ad vs. Edit: The Pressure Mounts," *Folio*, December, 92–100.

11. Memo, HGB to Deems, May 25, 1966, HGB Papers, Box 39, Folder 7; HGB interview.

12. Letter, Stan Perkins, *Cosmopolitan* ad sales representative, to Frank Dupuy Jr., April 19, 1968, HGB Papers, Box 39, Folder 8; "Avocados Can Peel Off Pounds," *Cosmopolitan*, November 1972, 100+, and "Lunch For Two: Avocado Surprise," *Cosmopolitan*, August 1976, 102+.

13. Memo, HGB to Dupuy, March 7, 1975, HGB Papers, Box 39, Folder 8.

14. HGB interview.

15. Memo, "'21' Luncheon," Dupuy to HGB, October 29, 1971, HGB Papers, Box 39, Folder 8.

16. Step Into My Parlor, *Cosmopolitan*, December 1971, 6; memo notation, Deems to HGB, October 29, 1971, HGB Papers, Box 39, Folder 8.

17. Memo, Mallen DeSantis to HGB, September 28 (1972), HGB Papers, Box 39, Folder 7.

18. Memo with draft letter to Estée Lauder, HGB to Deems, October 19, 1972, HGB Papers, Box 39, Folder 7; memo, Deems to HGB, undated but responding to HGB memo, HGB Papers, Box 39, Folder 7.

19. Two-page Christmas gift photo display, *Cosmopolitan*, December 1972; a search for the article in *New Yorker*, including the "Talk of the Town" section from June to November 1972 did not identify any material possibly pertaining to Lauder or *Cosmopolitan*.

20. Letter, HGB to Perkins, April 14, 1981, HGB Papers, Box 39, Folder 16.

21. Damon-Moore, epilogue; Endres and Luecke, 236–39.

22. Memo, HGB to Deems, March 2, 1967, HGB Papers, Box 39, Folder 3.

23. Memo, HGB to Deems, March 2, 1967, HGB Papers, Box 39, Folder 3.

24. "A Weekend In Las Vegas," *Cosmopolitan*, December 1966, 108+.

25. Step Into My Parlor, *Cosmopolitan*, November 1967, 6, and December 1973, 8.

26. Step Into My Parlor, *Cosmopolitan*, December 1970, 6, and February 1979, 10.

27. Step Into My Parlor, *Cosmopolitan*, October 1967, 4.

28. Vicki Hesterman, "Consumer Magazines and Ethical Guidelines," *Journal of Mass Media Ethics* (Spring/Summer 1987): 93–101.

29. Smith, 207–8.

30. Letter, HGB to Perkins, July 8, 1975, HGB Papers, Box 39, Folder 16.

31. James Kelly, "Spurning a Father's Advice," *Time*, June 1, 1987, 62–63.

32. "Concept for Cosmopolitan," HGB, undated with "[1965?]" noted, HGB Papers, Box 37, Folder 3.

33. HGB interview.

34. HGB interview; memo, HGB to staff editors, undated but references to Raquel Welch cover, which was August 1967, indicated autumn 1967, HGB Papers, Box 41, Folder 8.

35. Memo, "Art Format, HGB to staff editors, undated but references to October 1971 cover indicated autumn 1971 or early 1972, HGB Papers, Box 41, Folder 8.

36. Welles, 65–72; "Concept," HGB, undated with "[1965?]" noted, HGB Papers, Box 37, Folder 3.

37. Standard Rate and Data Service annual reports; HGB interview.

38. HGB interview; memo, Deems to HGB, undated but attached to April 1970 circulation report, HGB Papers, Box 39, Folder 7; memo, Berlin to HGB, May 16, 1968, HGB Papers, Box 39, Folder 3.

39. Hearst Magazines circulation reports for months listed, HGB Papers, Box 39, Folder 7 and Box 42, Folder 8; newsstand price percentage and computation of *Cosmopolitan* printing cost based on Compaine, 33–35 and 142–49.

40. Cover price increase noted on circulation report, April 20, 1968, HGB Papers, Box 39, Folder 7;

41. Memo, HGB to Deems and his response, April 17, 1968, HGB Papers, Box 39, Folder 7.

42. Hearst Magazines circulation reports previously cited.

43. Memo, HGB to Gilbert Maurer, publisher, April 6, 1981, HGB Papers, Box 39, Folder 12.

44. Memo, HGB to Maurer, March 30, 1979, HGB Papers, Box 39, Folder 12.

45. Letter, Cathleen Black, president of Hearst Magazines, to author, June 9, 2008.

46. Letter, Black to author.

47. "Prospectus," HGB Papers, Box 37, Folder 1.

48. Stephanie Harrington, "Ms. versus Cosmo: Two Faces of the Same Eve," *New York Times Magazine*, August 11, 1974, 10–11 and 36–38; Reisig, 25–29 and 53–55; Ephron, 74–75 and 117–18.

49. *Starch Primary Magazine Audience Report*, 1969.

50. *Simmons Study of Media & Markets*, 1983.

51. *Historical Statistics of the United States*, employment.

52. HLB interview; memo, HGB to Hearst Corporation executive, August 9, 1968, HGB Papers, Box 39, Folder 14; memo, HGB to Maurer, March 1, 1982, HGB Papers, Box 39, Folder 12; memo, HGB to executive, August 9, 1968.

53. Memo, HGB to executive, August 9, 1968.

54. Harrington, 10–11 and 36+; Reisig, 25–29 and 53–55.

55. HLB interview.

56. Ruth Weil and Jack Macurdy, "For David and Helen Gurley Brown, Their Non-Ivory Tower in Manhattan Is for Joyful Living," *House Beautiful*, May 1977, 118–23; "Helen Gurley Brown's Mix: Sex and the Bottom Line," *New York Times*, May 8, 1973, F8.

57. HGB interview. She did not remember precise salaries or bonus arrangements, however.

58. Step Into My Parlor, *Cosmopolitan*, November 1985, 28.

59. *Cosmopolitan*, March 1986, passim; Step Into My Parlor, *Cosmopolitan*, March 1986, 22.

Abbreviations for citations

HGB   Helen Gurley Brown papers, also interview with author and letters to author
HLB   Harriet La Barre interviews with author
REB   Richard E. Berlin papers
WRH William Randolph Hearst papers

Archive Collections

Richard E. Berlin papers, Herbert Hoover Presidential Library, West Branch, Iowa.
Helen Gurley Brown papers, Sophia Smith Collection, Smith College, Northampton, Massachusetts.
William Randolph Hearst papers, University of California at Berkeley.

Interviews

Brown, Helen Gurley (personal interview). New York City, March 23, 2007.
La Barre, Harriet (telephone interviews). Sag Harbor, New York, June 25 and July 12, 2008.

Correspondence, emails

Conway, Lynn (Georgetown University archivist)—March 17, 2009.
Sadewhite, Elizabeth (Irvington Public Library, New York; local history librarian)—March 23, 2009.

Correspondence, letters

Black, Cathleen; president, Hearst Magazines, New York City—June 9, 2008.
Brown, Helen Gurley; editor, *Cosmopolitan* International, New York City—July
    19, 2007; January 30, 2009.

Cosmopolitan, March 1886–February 1925 and May 1952–March 1986;
also, *Hearst's International combined with Cosmopolitan* (March 1925–
April 1952): advertisements, commentary, editorial material, illustrations,
and photographs cited

1886—March, April, August; **1888**—March, April, May, June, December;
    1889—February, June, November, December; **1890**—January, Feb-
    ruary, April, May, June, July, August, September, October, Novem-
    ber; **1891**—February, April, November, December; **1892**—February,
    March, May, June, September, November; **1893**—January, Febru-
    ary, March, April, May, June, December; **1894**—January, February,
    March; **1895**—August, November; **1896**—January, May, June, July,
    September; **1897**—January, March, April, May, June, July, August,
    September, October, November, December; **1898**—January, Febru-
    ary, March, May, June, July, September, December; **1899**—January,
    March, April, June, July, August, November; **1900**—January, March;
    1901—September; **1902**—May, June, July, August, September, Octo-
    ber, November, December; **1903**—January, February, March, April,
    May, June, July, August, September, October, November, December;
    1904—January, February, March; **1906**—February, March, April,
    May, June, July, August, September, October, November, December;
    1907—January, February; **1908**—May, June, July, August, October;
    1909—February, March, April, September; **1910**—August, Septem-
    ber, November; **1911**—January, March, April, May, October, Novem-
    ber; **1919**—August; **1920**—January, August; **1921**—March, June;
    1922—June; **1923**—January, February, June; **1924**—January, Febru-
    ary, March, April, May, June, July, October, December; **1925**—Janu-
    ary, February; **1928**—August, November; **1929**—February, March,
    April, July; **1930**—July; **1931**—January, August; **1932**—August;
    1951—May, June; **1952**—March, April, May, June, September, Octo-
    ber; **1953**—February, May; **1956**—June; **1957**—January, April, May,
    June; **1958**—April, May; **1960**—January, February, March; **1962**—
    June, July, October; **1965**—July, September, October, December;
    1966—February, May, December; **1967**—May, July, August, Novem-

ber, December; **1968**—February, May, July, August; **1969**—January, July, September, November; **1970**—January, April, May, October, November, December; **1971**—December; **1972**—February, April, October, November, December; **1973**—December; **1974**—July, September; **1975**—October; **1976**—July, August, October; **1979**—December; **1985**—November; **1986**—March.

Documents (listed chronologically)

Walker, John B., cadet, United States Military Academy, General Court Martial, Orders Number 109, War Department, Adjutant General's Office, Washington, D.C., April 20, 1866 (source: U.S. Military Academy, West Point, N.Y.).

Walker, John B., cadet, United States Military Academy, General Court Martial, Orders Number 12, Headquarters of the Army, Adjutant General's Office, Washington, D.C., March 2, 1868 (source: U.S. Military Academy, West Point, N.Y.).

Schlicht, Paul J., passport number 6560, U.S. Department of State, 1886.

Letters, Edward Payson Roe Collection, University of Virginia, 1887–1888.

Walker, John Brisben (grantor) and grantees et al., warranty deeds, 1887–1889, Arapahoe County, Colo.

Articles of Incorporation, Cosmopolitan Magazine Company, January 21, 1888, New York Department of State, Corporations Office.

Bausch, Jacob J., and plaintiffs et al. v. Schlicht, Paul J., defendant, Monroe County Supreme Court, New York, June 1888 to April 1890; also, The Schlicht & Field Company, defendant.

Walker, John Brisben (grantee) and grantors et al., deeds, 1894–1898, Westchester County, N.Y.

Walker, John Brisben (grantor) and grantees et al., deeds, 1901–1915, Westchester County, N.Y.

Travelers Insurance Company, mortgage lien, John Brisben Walker property, November 1901, Westchester County, N.Y.

Certificate of Incorporation, Mobile Rapid Transit Company, March 5, 1903, New York Department of State, Corporations Office.

Walker, John Brisben. "Report: Condition of the Chicago Packing House and Stock Yard." (Presented to President Theodore Roosevelt, 1906.)

Travelers Insurance Company, plaintiff lien clearance by court referee, defendant John Brisben Walker et al., Westchester County, February 1915.

Earhart, Amelia. Letter to Anne Morrow Lindbergh, January 30, 1930, George Palmer Putnam Collection, Purdue University.

Books

Abrahamson, David. *Magazine-Made America: The Cultural Transformation of the Postwar Periodical.* Cresskill, N.J.: Hampton Press, 1996.

Association of National Advertisers. *Magazine Circulation and Rate Trends, 1940–1971.* New York: Association of National Advertisers, 1972.

———. *Magazine Circulation and Rate Trends, 1975 Supplement.* New York: Association of National Advertisers, 1976.

Baker, Paul R. *Stanny: The Gilded Life of Stanford White.* New York: Free Press, 1989.

Baker, Ray Stannard. *American Chronicle: The Autobiography of Ray Stannard Baker.* New York: Charles Scribner's Sons, 1945.

Baldwin, Charles C. *Stanford White.* New York: Dodd, Mead and Company, 1931.

Baughman, James L. *Henry R. Luce and the Rise of the American News Media.* Boston: Twayne Publishers, 1987.

Bradley, Patricia. *Mass Media and the Shaping of American Feminism, 1963–1975.* Jackson: University Press of Mississippi, 2003.

Brasch, Walter M. *Forerunners of Revolution: Muckrakers and the American Social Conscience.* Lanham, Md.: University Press of America, 1990.

Brown, Helen Gurley. *Sex and the Single Girl.* New York: Bernard Geis Associates, 1962.

Bruccoli, Matthew J., ed. *F. Scott Fitzgerald's* The Great Gatsby: *A Literary Reference.* New York: Carroll and Graff, 2002.

Bruchey, Stuart W. *Enterprise: The Dynamic Economy of a Free People.* Cambridge, Mass.: Harvard University Press, 1990.

Butler, Susan. *East to the Dawn: The Life of Amelia Earhart.* Reading, Mass.: Addison-Wesley, 1997.

Carlebach, Michael L. *The Origins of Photojournalism in America.* Washington, D.C.: Smithsonian Institution Press, 1992.

Cashman, Sean Dennis. *America in the Gilded Age: From the Death of Lincoln to the Rise of Theodore Roosevelt.* New York: New York University Press, 1988, 2nd ed.

Chalmers, David Mark. *The Social and Political Ideas of the Muckrakers.* New York: Citadel Press, 1964.

Chandler, Alfred D. *The Visible Hand: The Managerial Revolution in American Business.* Cambridge, Mass.: Harvard University Press, 1977.

Chaney, Lindsay, and Michael Cieply. *The Hearsts: Family and Empire—The Later Years.* New York: Simon and Schuster, 1981.

Chernow, Ron. *The House of Morgan: An American Banking Dynasty and the Rise of Modern Finance.* New York: Atlantic Monthly Press, 1990.

Compaine, Benjamin M. *The Business of Consumer Magazines.* White Plains, N.Y.: Knowledge Industry Publications, 1982.

Comparato, Frank. *Chronicles of Genius and Folly: R. Hoe and Company and the Printing Press as a Service to Democracy.* Culver City, Calif.: Labyrinthos, 1979.

Congressional Record. Editions cited: 1893, 1895, 1896, 1897, 1898, 1909; also, "Report of the Committee on Interoceanic Canals," U.S. Senate, February 9, 1909.

Cooper, John Milton, Jr. *Walter Hines Page: The Southerner as American, 1855–1918.* Chapel Hill: University of North Carolina Press, 1977.

Cottrell, D. D. *Wholesale Price List of Newspapers and Periodicals.* North Cohocton, N.Y.: annual catalog, 1889–1895.

Damon-Moore, Helen. *Magazines for the Millions: Gender and Commerce in the* Ladies' Home Journal *and the* Saturday Evening Post, *1880–1910.* New York: State University of New York, 1994.

Dudden, Arthur Power. *The American Pacific: From the Old China Trade to the Present.* New York: Oxford University Press, 1992.

Edwards, Rebecca. *New Spirits: Americans in the Gilded Age, 1865–1905.* New York: Oxford University Press, 2006.

Endres, Kathleen L., and Therese L. Lueck, eds. *Women's Periodicals in the United States: Consumer Magazines.* Westport, Conn.: Greenwood Press, 1995.

Faust, Beatrice. *Women, Sex, and Pornography: A Controversial and Unique Study.* New York: Macmillan Publishing, 1980.

Filler, Louis. *The Muckrakers.* University Park: Pennsylvania State University Press, 1976.

Fitzpatrick, Ellen F. *Muckraking: Three Landmark Articles.* Boston: Bedford Books, 1994.

Ford, James L. C. *Magazines for Millions: The Story of Specialized Publications.* Carbondale: Southern Illinois University Press, 1969.

Foreign Relations of the United States. Editions cited: 1869, 1870, 1893, 1895, 1896, 1897, 1898.

Forker, Eugene. *The Cosmopolitan Market: A Merchandising Atlas of the United States.* New York: Hearst's International combined with Cosmopolitan, 1928.

Friedan, Betty. "The Feminine Mystique." *The Suburb Reader.* Ed. Becky M. Nicoleaides and Andrew Weise. New York: Routledge, 2006.

Gale, Robert L. *An F. Scott Fitzgerald Encyclopedia.* Westport, Conn.: Greenwood Press, 1998.

Gallup, George. *The Gallup Poll: Public Opinion, 1935–1971.* New York: Random House, 1972.

————. *Gallup Poll Monthly Index, 1965–1990*. Princeton, N.J.: Gallup Organization, 1990.

Garvey, Ellen Gruber. *The Adman in the Parlor: Magazines and the Gendering of Consumer Culture, 1880s to 1910s*. New York: Oxford University Press, 1996.

Golden, Catherine J., and Joanna Schneider Zangrando. *The Mixed Legacy of Charlotte Perkins Gilman*. Newark: University of Delaware Press, 2000.

Gould, Lewis L. *Reform and Regulation: American Politics, 1900–1916*. New York: John Wiley and Sons, 1978.

————. *The Spanish-American War and President McKinley*. Lawrence: University Press of Kansas, 1982.

————. *Reform and Regulation: American Politics from Roosevelt to Wilson*. New York: Alfred A. Knopf, 1986.

Grant, Linda. *Sexing the Millennium: Women and the Sexual Revolution*. New York: Grove Press, 1994.

Greene, Theodore. *America's Heroes: The Changing Models of Success in American Magazines*. New York: Oxford University Press, 1970.

Hansen, Klaus J. *Mormonism and the American Experience*. Chicago: University of Chicago Press, 1981.

Harbaugh, William H., ed. *The Writings of Theodore Roosevelt*. New York: Bobbs-Merrill, 1967.

Hearst, William Randolph, Jr., and Jack Casserly. *The Hearsts: Father and Son*. Lanham, Md.: Roberts Rinehart, 2001.

Higgs, Robert. *The Transformation of the American Economy, 1865–1914: An Essay in Interpretation*. New York: Wiley, 1971.

Historical Statistics of the United States, Millennial Edition Online. New York: Cambridge University Press, 2009.

Horowitz, Daniel. *The Morality of Spending: Attitudes Toward the Consumer Society in America, 1875–1940*. Baltimore: Johns Hopkins University Press, 1985.

Hoyt, Edwin P. *A Gentleman of Broadway*. Boston: Little, Brown and Company, 1964.

Isaacs, I. J. *The Industrial Advance of Rochester*. Rochester, N.Y.: National Publishing Company, 1884.

John, Arthur. *The Best Years of the* Century: *Richard Watson Gilder,* Scribner's Monthly *and the* Century *Magazine*. Urbana: University of Illinois Press, 1981.

Kaestle, Carl F., Helen Damon-Moore, Lawrence C. Stedman, Katherine Tinsley, and William Vance Trollinger Jr. *Literacy in the United States: Readers and Reading Since 1890*. New Haven, Conn.: Yale University Press, 1991.

Kastner, Victoria. *Hearst Castle: The Biography of a Country House.* New York: Harry N. Abrams, 2000.

Keller, Morton. *Affairs of State: Public Life in Late Nineteenth Century America.* Cambridge, Mass.: Belknap Press of Harvard University Press, 1977.

———. *Regulating a New Society: Public Policy and Social Change in America, 1900–1933.* Cambridge, Mass.: Harvard University Press, 1994.

Klein, Alexander, ed. *The Empire City: A Treasury of New York.* New York: Rinehart and Company, 1955.

Kroeger, Brooke. *Nellie Bly: Daredevil, Reporter, Feminist.* New York: Times Books, 1994.

———. *Fannie: The Talent for Success of Writer Fannie Hurst.* New York: Times Books, 1999.

Labor, Earle, Robert C. Leitz, and I. Milo Shepard, eds. *The Letters of Jack London, Volume One: 1896–1905.* Stanford, Calif.: Stanford University Press, 1988.

———. *The Letters of Jack London, Volume Two: 1906–1912.* Stanford, Calif.: Stanford University Press, 1988.

———. *The Letters of Jack London, Volume Three: 1913–1916.* Stanford, Calif.: Stanford University Press, 1988.

LaFeber, Walter. *The New Empire: An Interpretation of American Expansion, 1860–1898.* Ithaca, N.Y.: Cornell University Press, 1980.

Lampard, Eric E. "Urbanization." *Encyclopedia of American Economic History: Studies of the Principal Movements and Ideas,* ed. Glenn Porter. New York: Scribner, 1980.

Lears, Jackson. *Fables of Abundance: A Cultural History of Advertising in America.* New York: Basic Books, 1994.

Leary, Lewis. *Mark Twain's Correspondence with Henry Huttleston Rogers, 1893–1909.* Berkeley and Los Angeles: University of California Press, 1969.

Leonard, Thomas C. *The Power of the Press: The Birth of American Political Reporting.* New York: Oxford University Press, 1986.

Lipartito, Kenneth, and David B. Sicilia, eds. *Constructing Corporate America: History, Politics, Culture.* New York: Oxford University Press, 2004.

Long, Ray, ed. *20 Best Short Stories in Ray Long's 20 Years as an Editor.* New York: Crown Publishers, 1932.

Love, Eric T. L. *Race Over Empire: Racism and U.S. Imperialism, 1865–1900.* Chapel Hill: University of North Carolina Press, 2004.

Luker, Kristin. *Dubious Conceptions: The Politics of Teenage Pregnancy.* Cambridge, Mass.: Harvard University Press, 1997.

Lundberg, Ferdinand. *Imperial Hearst: A Social Biography.* New York: Modern Library, 1936.

MacKenzie, Norman, and Jeanne MacKenzie. *H. G. Wells: A Biography.* New York: Simon and Schuster, 1973.

Major, John. *Prize Possession: The United States and the Panama Canal, 1903–1979.* New York: Cambridge University Press, 1993.

Marchand, Roland. *Advertising the American Dream: Making Way for Modernity, 1920–1940.* Berkeley and Los Angeles: University of California Press, 1985.

Marcosson, Isaac F. *David Graham Phillips and His Times.* New York: Dodd, Mead and Company, 1932.

McClure, S. S. *My Autobiography.* New York: Frederick A. Stokes Company, 1914.

McCracken, Ellen. *Decoding Women's Magazines: From* Mademoiselle *to* Ms. New York: St. Martin's Press, 1993.

Milton, Joyce. *The Yellow Kids: Foreign Correspondents in the Heyday of Yellow Journalism.* New York: Harper and Row, 1989.

Montgomery, David. *The Fall of the House of Labor: The Workplace, the State, and American Labor Activism, 1865–1925.* New York: Cambridge University Press, 1987.

Morison, Elting E., ed. *The Letters of Theodore Roosevelt, Volume 5.* Cambridge, Mass.: Harvard University Press, 1952.

Mott, Frank Luther. *A History of American Magazines: 1865–1885.* Cambridge, Mass.: Belknap Press, 1938.

———. *A History of American Magazines: 1885–1905.* Cambridge, Mass.: Belknap Press, 1957.

———. *A History of American Magazines: 1905–1930.* Cambridge, Mass.: Belknap Press, 1968.

Mullen, Robert. *The Latter-Day Saints: The Mormons Yesterday and Today.* New York: Doubleday and Company, 1966.

Nasaw, David. *The Chief: The Life of William Randolph Hearst.* Boston: Houghton Mifflin Company, 2000.

National Magazine Division. *National Advertising Records.* New York: Denney Publishing, 1927; and 1929, 1931, 1933 editions.

Nicholson, Philip Yale. *Labor's Story in the United States.* Philadelphia: Temple University Press, 2004.

Ninkovich, Frank. *The United States and Imperialism.* Malden, Mass.: Blackwell Publishers, 2001.

Nourie, Alan, and Barbara Nourie, eds. *American Mass-Market Magazines.* New York: Greenwood Press, 1990.

N. W. Ayer and Son's. *American Newspaper Annual.* Philadelphia: N. W. Ayer and Son (various editions cited from 1891–1950).

Ohmann, Richard. *Selling Culture: Magazines, Markets, and Class at the Turn of the Century.* New York: Verso, 1996.

Older, Mrs. Fremont. *William Randolph Hearst: American.* New York: D. Appleton-Century, 1936.

Paine, Albert Bigelow, ed. *Mark Twain's Letters, Volume 4.* New York: Harper and Brothers, 1917.

Peterson, Theodore. *Magazines in the Twentieth Century.* Urbana: University of Illinois Press, 1964.

Pletcher, David M. *The Awkward Years: American Foreign Relations under Garfield and Arthur.* Columbia: University of Missouri Press, 1962.

Pope, Daniel. *The Making of Modern Advertising.* New York: Basic Books, 1983.

Porter, Kirk, and Donald Bruce Johnson. *National Party Platforms, 1840–1960.* Urbana: University of Illinois Press, 1961.

Potts, Stephen W. *The Price of Paradise: The Magazine Career of F. Scott Fitzgerald.* San Bernardino, Calif.: Borgo Press, 1993.

Procter, Ben. *William Randolph Hearst: The Early Years, 1863–1910.* New York: Oxford University Press, 1998.

———. *William Randolph Hearst: The Later Years, 1911–1951.* New York: Oxford University Press, 2007.

Rainbird, George. *Complete Encyclopedia of Motorcars, 1885 to the Present.* New York: E. P. Dutton and Company, 1973.

Ravitz, Abe C. *David Graham Phillips.* New York: Twayne Publishers, 1966.

Rich, Doris L. *Amelia Earhart: A Biography.* Washington, D.C.: Smithsonian Institution Press, 1989.

Rochester Directory. Rochester, N.Y.: Drew, Allis and Company, 1875–1889.

Roth, Leland M. *The Architecture of McKim, Mead and White, 1870–1920: A Building List.* New York: Garland Publishing, 1978.

Rouse, Linda. *Marital and Sexual Lifestyles in the United States: Attitudes, Behaviors, and Relationships in Social Context.* New York: Haworth Press, 2002.

Rowell's American Newspaper Directory. George P. Rowell Company, New York, 1877.

Scanlon, Jennifer. *Bad Girls Go Everywhere: The Life of Helen Gurley Brown.* New York: Oxford University Press, 2009.

Schneirov, Matthew. *The Dream of a New Social Order: Popular Magazines in America, 1893–1914.* New York: Columbia University Press, 1994.

Schudson, Michael. *Advertising, the Uneasy Persuasion: Its Dubious Impact on American Society.* New York: Basic Books, 1984.

Sedgwick, Ellery. *The Happy Profession.* Boston: Little, Brown and Company, 1946.

Simmons Market Research Bureau. *Publications: Total Audiences.* New York: SMRB, 1973.

———. *Publications: Total Audiences.* New York: SMRB, 1979.

Smith, Liz. *Natural Blonde: A Memoir.* New York: Hyperion, 2000.

Smith, Susan Harris, and Melanie Dawson, eds. *The American 1890s: A Cultural Reader*. Durham, N.C.: Duke University Press, 2000.

Soley, Laurence, and R. Krishan. "Does Advertising Subsidize Consumer Magazine Prices?" *Journal of Advertising* 16:2 (1987): 4–9.

Starch Primary Magazine Audience Report. New York: Starch/INRA/Hooper, 1974.

Statistical Abstract of the United States. U.S. Government, various editions cited.

Strasser, Susan. *Satisfaction Guaranteed: The Making of the American Mass Market*. New York: Pantheon, 1989.

Swanberg, W. A. *Citizen Hearst: A Biography of William Randolph Hearst*. New York: Charles Scribner's Sons, 1961.

Tebbel, John. *The Life and Good Times of William Randolph Hearst*. New York: E. P. Dutton, 1952.

Tebbel, John, and Mary Ellen Zuckerman. *The Magazine in America, 1741–1990*. New York: Oxford University Press, 1991.

Tedlow, Richard S. "Advertising and Public Relations." *Encyclopedia of American Economic History: Studies of the Principal Movements and Ideas*, ed. Glenn Porter. New York: Scribner, 1980.

Thom, Mary. *Inside Ms.: 25 Years of the Magazine and the Feminist Movement*. New York: Henry Holt and Company, 1997.

Tifft, Susan E., and Ale Jones. *The Trust: The Private and Powerful Family behind the* New York Times. New York: Little, Brown and Company, 1999.

Towne, Charles Hanson. *Adventures in Editing*. New York: D. Appleton and Company, 1926.

Trachtenberg, Alan. *The Incorporation of America: Culture and Society in the Gilded Age*. New York: Hill and Wang, 1982.

Turnbull, Andrew, ed. *The Letters of F. Scott Fitzgerald*. New York: Charles Scribner's Sons, 1963.

United States Bureau of the Census (various data cited from reports, decennial census).

United States Department of State. *Foreign Relations of the United States, 1868–1870, 1895–1898*.

Vatter, Harold G. *The Drive to Industrial Maturity: The U.S. Economy, 1860–1914*. Westport, Conn.: Greenwood Press, 1975.

Walker, Nancy A. *Shaping Our Mothers' World: American Women's Magazines*. Jackson: University Press of Mississippi, 2000.

Weeks, Lyman Horace. *A History of Paper-Manufacturing in the United States, 1690–1916*. New York: Lockwood Trade Journal Company, 1916.

White, Lawrence Grant. *Sketches and Designs by Stanford White*. New York: Architectural Book Company, 1920.

Wilson, Christopher P. "The Rhetoric of Consumption: Mass-Market Magazines and the Demise of the Gentle Reader, 1880–1920." In *The Culture of Consumption: Critical Essays in American History, 1880–1980*, ed. Richard Wightman Fox and T. J. Jackson Lears. New York: Pantheon Books, 1983.

Wilson, Harold S. McClure's *Magazine and the Muckrakers*. Princeton, N.J.: Princeton University Press, 1970.

Winkler, John K. *W. R. Hearst: An American Phenomenon*. New York: Simon and Schuster, 1928.

Wolfe, Linda. *The Cosmo Report*. New York: Arbor House, 1981.

Wolseley, Roland E. *Understanding Magazines*. Ames: Iowa State University Press, 1972.

———. *The Changing Magazine: Trends in Readership and Management*. New York: Hastings House, 1973.

Wood, James Playsted. *Magazines in the United States*. 3rd ed. New York: Ronald Press, 1971.

Woodward, Helen. *The Lady Persuaders*. New York: Ivan Obolensky, 1960.

Zuckerman, Mary Ellen. *A History of Popular Women's Magazines in the United States, 1792–1995*. Westport, Conn.: Greenwood Press, 1998.

Zuilen, A. J. Van. *The Life Cycle of Magazines: A Historical Study of the Decline and Fall of the General Interest Mass Audience Magazine in the United States during the Period 1946–1972*. Uithoorn, The Netherlands: Graduate Press, 1977.

Dissertation, unpublished

Brocki, Sister Mary Damascene. "A Study of *Cosmopolitan* Magazine, 1890–1900: Its Relation to the Literature of the Decade." PhD diss., University of Notre Dame, August 1958.

Journal Articles

Berebitsky, Julie. "The Joy of Work: Helen Gurley Brown, Gender, and Sexuality in the White-Collar Office." *Journal of the History of Sexuality* 15:1 (January 2006): 89–124.

Durham, Gigi. "The Taming of the Shrew: Women's Magazines and the Regulation of Desire." *Journal of Communication Inquiry* 20:1 (Spring 1996): 18–31.

Frank, Myrna E., and Clyde V. Kiser. "Changes in the Social and Demographic Attributes of Women in *Who's Who*." *Milbank Memorial Fund Quarterly* 43:1 (January 1965): 55–75.

Gerson, Walter M., and Sandra H. Lund. "Playboy Magazine: Sophisticated Smut or Social Revolution?" *Journal of Popular Culture* 1:3 (1967): 218–27.

Healy, John S., and Harold H. Kassarjian. "Advertising Substantiation and Advertiser Response: A Content Analysis of Magazine Advertisements." *Journal of Marketing* 47:1 (Winter 1983): 107–17.

Hesterman, Vicki. "Consumer Magazines and Ethical Guidelines." *Journal of Mass Media Ethics* (Spring/Summer 1987): 93–101.

Hileman, Donald G. "Changes in the Buying and Selection of Advertising Media." *Journalism Quarterly* 45:2 (1968): 279–85.

Joliffe, Lee, and Terri Catlett. "Women Editors at the 'Seven Sisters' Magazines, 1965–1985: Did They Make a Difference?" *Journalism Quarterly* 71:4 (Winter 1994): 800–808.

Kaiser, Kathy. "The New Women's Magazines: It's the Same Old Story." *Frontiers: A Journal of Women Studies* 4:1 (Spring 1979): 14–17.

Kielbowicz, Richard B. "Postal Subsidies for the Press and the Business of Mass Culture, 1880–1920." *Business History Review* 64:3 (Autumn 1990): 451–88.

Krassas, Nicole R., Joan M. Blauwkamp, and Peggy Wesselink. "Boxing Helena and Corseting Eunice: Sexual Rhetoric in *Cosmopolitan* and *Playboy* Magazines." *Sex Roles* 44:11–12 (June 2001): 751–62.

Landers, James. "Island Imperialism: Discourse on U.S. Imperialism in *Century, Cosmopolitan, McClure's*—1893–1900." *American Journalism: A Journal of Media History* 23:1 (Winter 2006): 95–123.

Lockley, Lawrence C. "Notes on the History of Marketing Research." *Journal of Marketing* 14:5 (April 1950): 733–36.

McDonald, Susan Waugh. "From Kipling to Kitsch, Two Popular Editors of the Gilded Age: Mass Culture, Magazines and Correspondence Universities." *Journal of Popular Culture* 5:2 (Fall 1981): 50–61.

Michelson, Peter. "The Pleasures of Commodity, or How to Make the World Safe for Pornography." *Antioch Review* 29:1 (Spring 1969): 77–90.

Miller, Tice. "Alan Dale: The Hearst Critic." *Educational Theatre Journal* 26:1 (March 1974): 69–80.

Miraldi, Robert. "The Journalism of David Graham Phillips." *Journalism Quarterly* 63:1 (Spring 1986): 83–88.

———. "Charles Edward Russell: 'Chief of the Muckrakers.'" *Journalism and Mass Communication Monographs* 150 (April 1995): 1–18.

Neuzil, Mark. "Hearst, Roosevelt, and the Muckrake Speech of 1906: A New Perspective." *Journalism and Mass Communication Quarterly* 73:1 (Spring 1996): 29–39.

Oates, Mary T., and Susan Williamson. "Women's Colleges and Women Achievers." *Signs* 3:4 (Summer 1978): 795–806.

Ouellette, Laurie. "Inventing the Cosmo Girl: Class Identity and Girl-Style American Dreams." *Media, Culture and Society* 21:3 (1999): 359–83.

Pearson, Elizabeth T. "Modern Processes of Engraving." *Bulletin of the Pennsylvania Museum* 24:134 (April 1930): 33–35.

Rein, D. M. "Howells and the *Cosmopolitan.*" *American Literature* 21:1 (March 1949): 49–55.

Reynolds, Robert D., Jr. "The 1906 Campaign to Sway Muckraking Periodicals." *Journalism Quarterly* 56 (Autumn 1979): 513–20, 589.

Roggenkamp, Karen. "Dignified Sensationalism: *Cosmopolitan,* Elizabeth Bisland, and Trips Around the World." *American Periodicals* 17:1 (2007): 26–40.

Root, Robert, and Christine W. Root. "Magazines in the United States: Dying or Thriving?" *Journalism Quarterly* 41:1 (Spring 1964): 15–22.

Rossiter, Margaret W. "'Women's Work' in Science." *Isis* 71:3 (September 1980): 381–98.

Schultz, Stanley K. "The Morality of Politics: The Muckrakers' Vision of Democracy." *Journal of American History* 52:3 (December 1965): 527–47.

Smith, Tom W. "American Sexual Behavior: Trends, Socio-Demographic Differences, and Risk Behavior." *General Social Survey,* GSS Topical Report Number 25, March 2006.

Soley, Laurence, and R. Krishan. "Does Advertising Subsidize Consumer Magazine Prices?" *Journal of Advertising* 16:2 (1987): 4–9.

Stinson, Robert. "McClure's Road to *McClure's:* How Revolutionary Were 1890s Magazines?" *Journalism Quarterly* 47:2 (Summer 1970): 256–62.

Thomases, Jerome. "Mechanized Mobility Proposed in 1900." *Military Affairs* 5:4 (Winter 1941): 267–70.

Trotti, Michael Ayers. "Murder Made Real: The Visual Revolution of the Halftone." *The Virginia Magazine of History and Biography* 111:4 (2003): 379–410.

Villalon, L. J. Andrew, and James M. Lau. "Steaming Through New England with Locomobile." *Journal of Transport History* 5:2 (1979): 65–82.

Waller, Mary Ellen. "Marketing the Women's Journals, 1873–1900." *Business and Economic History* 18 (1989).

Waller-Zuckerman, Mary Ellen. "Old Homes in a City of Perpetual Change: Women's Magazines, 1890–1916." *Business History Review* 63:4 (Winter 1989): 715–56.

Magazine Articles (listed chronologically; author cited when known)

"Edward Payson Roe." *Literary News,* September 1888, 260.

"Journalistic Notes." *Publisher's Weekly,* December 22, 1888, 973.

"Among the Publishers." *Science,* December 28, 1888, 308.

"Notes." *Journalist,* July 13, 1889, 5.

"Notes." *Journalist,* November 16, 1889, 9.

"A Successful Magazine: And the Men Who Make It." *Journalist,* April 30, 1892, 2–3.

"John Brisben Walker." *Journalist,* September 9, 1893, 2–3.

Untitled. *The Bookman,* June 1896, 301.

"University and Educational News." *Science,* August 6, 1897, 213–14.

Smith, F. Hopkinson. "The Muck-Rake as a Circulation Boomer." *The Critic,* June 1906, 511–12.

"Conjugation." *Time,* December 22, 1924, 34.

"Talk of the Town." *New Yorker,* May 16, 1925, 2.

"Talk of the Town." *New Yorker,* June 6, 1925, 1.

"Man is Master, Says Duce." *Time,* July 11, 1928, 47.

"The *Cosmopolitan* of Ray Long." *Fortune,* March 1931, 49–55.

Quinlan, Roy. "The Story of Magazine Distribution." *Magazine Week,* October 5, 1953, 4–5.

"Hearst Magazine Earnings." *Printer's Ink,* March 16, 1939, 16.

"Rival Women's Magazines Near Hair-Pulling Stage." *Business Week,* October 1, 1960, 88–96.

Bermel, Albert. "The Future of the Hearst Empire." *Harper's,* January 1962, 42–48.

"Hearst Deficit." *Time,* April 20, 1962, 82.

Welles, Chris. "Soaring Success of the Iron Butterfly." *Life,* November 19, 1965, 65–72.

"What Educated Women Want." *Newsweek,* June 13, 1966, 68–75.

"Down with 'Pippypoo.'" *Newsweek,* July 18, 1966, 60.

"Big Sister." *Time,* February 9, 1968, 60.

Buckley, William F., Jr. "You Are the More Cupcakeable for Being a Cosmopolitan Girl." *National Review,* September 22, 1970, 999–1000.

"Cupcake v. Sweet Tooth." *Time,* March 20, 1972, 53–54.

"Playmate of the Month." *Newsweek,* April 10, 1972, 57.

"Frog Prince." *Time,* August 21, 1972, 43.

Reisig, Robin. "Feminine Plastique." *Ramparts,* March 1973, 25–29, 53–55.

"That Cosmopolitan Girl." *New Yorker,* July 16, 1973, 26–27.

Ephron, Nora. "Helen Gurley Brown Only Wants to Help." *Esquire,* February 1974, 74–75, 117–18.

Harrington, Stephanie. "Ms. versus Cosmo: Two Faces of the Same Eve." *New York Times Magazine,* August 11, 1974, 10–11, 36+.

Weil, Ruth, and Jack Macurdy. "For David and Helen Gurley Brown, Their Non-Ivory Tower in Manhattan Is for Joyful Living." *House Beautiful,* May 1977, 118–23.

Kelly, James. "In His Grandfather's Footsteps." *Time,* February 3, 1986, 75.

Kelly, James. "Spurning a Father's Advice." *Time,* June 1, 1987, 62–63.

Dittman, Cathy. "Hall of Fame, 1988 Award Winner: John Brisben Walker." *Historically Jeffco* 1:2 (1988): 8–10.

"Profit Profile." *Magazine Week,* August 31, 1988, 7.

Olson, Robert. "The Suburbanization Process of Eastern Jefferson County, 1889–1941." *Historically Jeffco* 7:1 (1994): 10–12.

Kessler, Ellen. "Dream Catcher: A Brief History of the John Brisben Walker Legacy." *Historically Jeffco* 10:18 (1997): 27–33.

McDade, Jared. "General Motors: How It All Began." *Westchester Historian* (Fall 1999): 115–21.

White, Sally L. "John Brisben Walker, the Man and Mt. Morrison." *Historically Jeffco* 18:26 (2005): 4–8.

Newspaper articles (listed chronologically by source)

Denver Post: "Big Park in Denver," November 2, 1901, 4; "Generosity Run Riot," November 3, 1901, 4.

New York Times: "Is Public Spirit Alive or Dead?" July 26, 1871, 4; "What Can They Do About It?" July 31, 1871, 2; "The Duty of the Citizens," August 2, 1871, 4; "He Realized in Credits," January 22, 1885, 8; "A Literary Event," July 12, 1887, 8; "A New Departure," February 4, 1888, 3; "An Interesting Interview," May 26, 1888, 3; "Society Topics of the Week," November 24, 1889, 11; "All Around the World," January 19, 1890, 1; "Travelers on the Ocean," May 18, 1890, 16; "New Publications," June 23, 1890, 3; "Dined by the Aldine Club," December 24, 1892, 3; "Randolph Walker Doing Well," April 24, 1893, 12; "New Uptown Club Opens," May 29, 1895, 9; "A Concert at Lindhurst," July 21, 1895, 8; "Gun Explodes at a Test," April 14, 1896, 1; "Augustin Daly Honored," April 23, 1896, 4; "Mr. Walker Hires a Hall," July 3, 1896, 2; "Mr. Bryan Will Try Again," August 15, 1896, 1; "Mr. Bryan in Seclusion," August 16, 1896, 1; "Mr. Bryan in Brooklyn," September 23, 1896, 6; "Meeting May Be Exciting," September 28, 1896, 2; "Pairs, and One of a Kind," October 15, 1896, 4; "Bryan Won't Interfere," June 13, 1897, 1; "The Cosmopolitan University," August 1, 1897, 14; "Brisben Walker's Scheme," August 17, 1897, 1; "The New Andrews University," August 17, 1897, 4; "Dr. Andrews's Dilemma," September 4, 1897, 7; John Brisben Walker, "The Motor Vehicle of the Near Future," February 4, 1900, 23; "National Highway Plans," March 15, 1900, 9; "John Brisben Walker's Feat," September 10, 1900, 3; "Motor Vehicle Makers Organize," December 4, 1900, 2; "The Sphinx Club Dinner," April 11, 1901, 9; "Hack, Stage, or Omnibus," August 10, 1901, 7; "Licenses for Wagonettes," August

11, 1901, 8; "The Man in the Street," August 18, 1901, Society, 1; John Brisben Walker, "Solution of the Tunnel Problem," January 11, 1902, 2; "Dinner to Prof. Langley," January 20, 1904, 3; "No Thoroughfare," January 21, 1904, 8; John Brisben Walker, "The Langley Aeroplane," January 24, 1904, 22; "Hearst Buys Cosmopolitan," May 3, 1905, 11; "Dodge and Smith Quit the Equitable," June 27, 1905, 1; "Roosevelt Afraid in 1898, Says Platt," March 2, 1909, 2; "Hearst Lauds Taft; Rejects Roosevelt," April 21, 1910, 2; "Phillips Dies of His Wounds," January 27, 1911, 1; "Says Archbold Gave $125,000 to Elect T.R.," August 22, 1912, 1; "Roosevelt Wanted Archbold to Call," September 25, 1912, 6; "Authors Criticize Hearst Magazines," February 26, 1921, 11; "Authors Accept Hearst Challenge," March 1, 1921, 7; "Authors Agree to Terms," July 10, 1921, 16; "Plans to Unite Magazines," December 11, 1924, 17; "Miss Earhart on Magazine Staff," August 29, 1928, 14; "Coolidge Finishes Writing His Life Story," April 30, 1929, 1; "J. Brisben Walker Dies at Age of 83," July 8, 1931, 23; "Ray Long to Quit Hearst Magazines," July 21, 1931, 23; "Cosmopolitan Policy Unchanged," July 30, 1931, 22; "Ray Long Shoots Himself on Coast; Suicide Is Laid to Despondency," July 10, 1935, 1; "Salaries of 18,000 Over $15,000 in 1934," January 8, 1936, 13; "Hearst Assailed in Senate Speech," April 1, 1936, 11; "Hearst Built Corporate Empires in Newspapers, Magazines," August 15, 1951, 1; "Publisher Spent Millions for Art," August 15, 1951, 21; "Advertising Notes," March 28, 1957, 51; "Hearst Rents Offices," July 1, 1964, 56; "Feminists Demand 'Liberation' in Ladies' Home Journal Sit-In," March 19, 1970, 57; "Ladies Journal Has 'Lib' Section," July 28, 1970, 13; "Women Seeking Equality March on 5th Ave. Today," August 26, 1970, 44; "Helen Gurley Brown's Mix: Sex and the Bottom Line," May 8, 1973, F8.

Rochester (New York) Union and Advertiser: "Dissatisfied Creditors," May 22, 1888, 3; "Settlement with Creditors on the Basis of Thirty Cents on the Dollar," May 23, 1888, 2.

Index